PRAXIS I®:
POWER PRACTICE

PRAXIS I®:
POWER PRACTICE

LEARNINGEXPRESS®

NEW YORK

Library of Congress Cataloging-in-Publication Data:

Praxis I®: power practice.—1st ed.

     p.   cm.

  ISBN-13: 978-1-57685-892-9 (pbk. : alk. paper)

  ISBN-10: 1-57685-892-8 (pbk. : alk. paper)

  1. Pre-Professional Skills Tests—Study guides.   I. LearningExpress

(Organization)

  LB2367.75.P686   2012

  370.76—dc23   2011039212

Printed in the United States of America

9 8 7 6 5 4 3 2 1

First Edition

ISBN-10: 1-57685-892-8

ISBN-13: 978-1-57685-892-9

For more information or to place an order, contact LearningExpress at:

    2 Rector Street

    26th Floor

    New York, NY 10006

Or visit us at:

    www.learnatest.com

Editor: Marco A. Annunziata

Production Editor: Eric Titner

Assistant Editor: Nicole Murray

ABOUT THE CONTRIBUTORS ▶

Russell Kahn is a developer, writer, and editor of educational publishing products. He has developed scores of test prep guides and authored products for both children and adults. He is currently working toward dual master's degrees in education from Montclair State University. He lives in Montclair, NJ with his wife and two children.

Kim Stafford studied mathematics and secondary education in upstate New York, at Colgate University. From there, she went on to teach in both indoor and outdoor classrooms in Japan, Virginia, Oregon, and California. Kimberly currently lives in Los Angeles where she enjoys running Growing Minds, her private tutoring business, as well as A Stone's Throw, her own jewelry line.

Cindy Lassonde, PhD, is Associate Professor in the Elementary Education and Reading Department at the State University of New York College at Oneonta. She moved to the college level after teaching for more than 20 years at the elementary level. Currently, she teaches undergraduate and graduate courses in literacy, special education, and early childhood education. She is the 2010 recipient of the SUNY Chancellor's Award for Excellence in Teaching, and is also the author of several books and numerous journal articles.

Judith Hicks was a classroom teacher in Compton, California and has been a teacher-educator in the United States and abroad for nine years. She holds a Reading Specialist credential and has contributed to a variety of textbook and curriculum projects. She is currently pursuing a PhD in Education at Stanford University.

CONTENTS

ABOUT *PRAXIS I:* POWER PRACTICE

LearningExpress understands the importance of achieving top scores on your Praxis I Pre-Professional Skills Tests (PPST), and we strive to publish the most authentic and comprehensive Praxis I test preparation materials available today. Practice does indeed make perfect, and that's why we've created this book composed of five full-length Praxis I PPST practice exams complete with detailed answer explanations—it offers you all the extra practice you need to get a great score. Whether used on its own or as a powerful companion to other Praxis preparation titles, *Praxis I: Power Practice* is the key to a top score and a brighter future!

PRAXIS I®:
POWER PRACTICE

1 ▶ ABOUT THE PRAXIS I

CHAPTER SUMMARY
This chapter will familiarize you with the Praxis I test, which is administered by the Educational Testing Service (ETS). (Go to www.ets.org/praxis.) This chapter also discusses all of the pertinent information about the Praxis I, including contact information, the registration process, examination fees, and test formats and content. Additionally, you will learn about scoring, what the scores are used for, and how they are reported.

All of the exams in the Praxis Series of tests are designed to measure the scholastic and pedagogical capability of teachers at different stages of their careers. The first exam in the Praxis Series, the Praxis I Pre-Professional Skills Test (PPST), may be taken early in a student's college career to qualify for entry into a teaching credential program. It is also taken by prospective teachers to be considered for a license in states not requiring education degrees. The Praxis I PPST is comprised of individual tests that measure basic skills in reading, mathematics, and writing.

The Praxis I test is administered in both a paper- and computer-based format. This chapter will discuss both in detail. Although both forms of the test cover the same content, the procedures for registering and taking the tests are very different; therefore, these steps will be discussed separately in this chapter.

PURPOSES OF THE PRAXIS I TEST

The **Praxis I** is generally taken to gain entry into a teaching credential program and for state licensing. Some educational organizations require that you achieve passing PPST scores to gain membership. These organizations include the American Speech-Language-Hearing Association (ASHA), the Department of Defense Education Activity (DODEA), and the National Association of School Psychologists (NASP).

States Using the Praxis Series of Tests

Each state sets its own requirement for which tests to take and what score will be accepted as passing. Information regarding specific state or organization requirements may change from time to time. For accurate, up-to-date information, refer to the official Praxis website at www.ets.org/praxis/ and your state's Education Department.

Note: Although some information for the requirements of California is included on the Praxis website, those interested in meeting them should contact the California Commission on Teacher Credentialing (CTC) online at www.ctc.ca.gov.

IMPORTANT CONTACT INFORMATION

ETS—*The Praxis Series*
P.O. Box 6051
Princeton, NJ 08541-6051
Phone: 609-771-7395, M–F 8 A.M. to 7:45 P.M. (EST) (except for holidays)
Phone for the Hearing Impaired: 609-771-7714
Fax: 609-530-0581 or 609-771-7906
Website: www.ets.org/praxis/

What Is the Praxis I Like?

The Praxis I PPST is designed to see if you have the academic skills to be an effective teacher. How are your basic skills in:

- Reading?
- Math?
- Writing?

All of the questions on the Praxis I, with the exception of the essay portion of the PPST Writing test, are in multiple-choice format. Each multiple-choice question has five answer choices. Because test scoring is based only on the number of items answered correctly, you are not penalized for incorrect answers on the PPSTs—so be sure to fill in all of the answer blanks rather than leaving difficult questions unanswered. Even a guess is better than leaving an answer blank!

Let's look at each test.

Reading

The PPST Reading test measures your ability to comprehend, analyze, and evaluate written information. You will be asked to read a number of passages (which may vary in length from 100 to 200 words) and then answer questions that test your ability to comprehend what you have read. The genre and reading levels of the passages will vary. You will be tested only on your ability to understand and analyze the selection; you will not be required to have specific knowledge about the topics discussed in the passages. The following are general types of questions that you may be asked:

Literal Comprehension
- main idea questions
- supporting idea questions
- organization questions
- vocabulary questions

Critical and Inferential Comprehension
- argument evaluation questions
- inferential reasoning questions
- generalization questions

Mathematics

The PPST Mathematics test measures your proficiency in math. Generally speaking, the test requires a competency at the high school or first-year college level. Here are the four main math skills that will be tested:

Numbers and Operations
- order
- equivalence

- numeration and place value
- number properties
- operation properties
- computation
- estimation
- ratio, proportion, and percent
- numerical reasoning

Algebra
- equations and inequalities
- algorithmic thinking
- patterns
- algebraic representations
- algebraic reasoning

Geometry and Measurement
- geometric properties
- the *xy*-coordinate plane
- geometric reasoning
- systems of measurement

Data Analysis and Probability
- data interpretation
- data representation
- trends and inferences
- measures of center and spread
- probability

Writing

The PPST Writing test is divided into two sections: The first section consists of multiple-choice questions that require you to find and/or correct errors in standard English; the second part asks you to write a 30-minute essay on an assigned topic, which will represent 50% of your total writing test score.

The multiple-choice section of the writing test is designed to measure your ability to use standard

English correctly and effectively and is divided into two parts: usage and sentence correction.

Usage questions test your knowledge of:

- structural and grammatical relationships
- mechanics
- idiom or word choice

Usage questions also test your ability to identify error-free sentences.

Sentence correction questions test your ability to:

- select the best way to state a given phrase or sentence
- correct sentences with errors in grammar, mechanics, idioms, or word choice

You are not expected to know formal grammatical terminology.

The essay portion of the PPST Writing test is designed to evaluate your ability to express ideas clearly and effectively in standard written English. You will be presented with a topic and asked to state an opinion in essay form. The given topics present situations that are generally familiar to all educated people and do not require any specialized knowledge in a particular field. Although you will be posing an argument and drawing conclusions based on examples from personal experience or observation, you will not be graded on your opinion—you will be scored only on how effectively you are able to get your ideas across.

The following qualities will be taken into consideration when your essay is scored:

- *Appropriateness:* whether or not your essay was written appropriately for the task and intended audience
- *Organization:* your ability to organize and develop the essay logically and make clear connections between ideas
- *Unity and focus:* your ability to devise and sustain a clear thesis throughout the essay
- *Development:* the ability to develop your essay through examples and details that clearly and logically support the ideas presented in your essay
- *Mechanical conventions:* demonstration of a proficient use of the English language and ability to use proper syntax
- *Sentence structure:* the ability to effectively construct sentences, free from error, in standard written English

NONSCORABLE QUESTIONS

From time to time, the ETS needs to try out new questions to see if they are suitable to be used in future editions of the test. These questions will not be identified because the ETS is trying to determinine how examinees will respond under real testing conditions. The questions are unscored, meaning that they do not count toward or against your score. Not all tests include unscored questions.

What About Scores?

The ETS will mail your official score report about four weeks after your test date for the paper-based test and approximately two to three weeks after computer-based testing. If you take the computer-based test, you can (in most cases) view your reading and math scores at the end of your test session. Your score report will also be sent to the recipients (for example, schools) you designated on your registration form.

The report shows a separate test score for each PPST subject that you take. Reading and math test scores are based on the number of items answered correctly. There is no penalty for answering a question incorrectly. The writing test score is based on the number of multiple-choice questions answered correctly combined with the essay score, which is scored on a scale of 1 to 6.

Your score report will show your score, whether or not you passed, and the range of possible scores. If you took any test previously, it will also show your highest scores.

Can I Cancel My Scores?

For the paper-based test, you may cancel your scores for a particular test by submitting a Request for Score Cancellation form to the ETS within one week after the test date. If you take a computer-based test, you are given the option to cancel your scores at the end of your test session before viewing the scores (once you have viewed your computerized scores, you cannot cancel them). All score cancellations are permanent, and refunds are not given.

Passing Scores

Each state or institution determines its own passing score. The first thing you will want to do with your scores is to compare them to the passing scores set by your state. Along with your test scores, you will receive the *Understanding Your Praxis Scores* booklet that gives the passing scores for each state. The Praxis Series website (www.ets.org/praxis/) also has a complete state-by-state listing of required tests and passing scores.

Retaking the Tests

If you don't pass one or more of the PPST tests, you will be allowed to take them again. How many times or how often you may retake each PPST is determined by the policies of individual states or institutions. The ETS does not limit how many times you can take the paper-based tests. However, the ETS does mandate that you may take each of the computer-based tests only once per 30-day period, and no more than six times in one year. Individual states may have further restrictions.

Consult your scores from previous tests to see which areas require more study, so you will pass the tests the next time you take them.

What to Bring to the Test

If you are taking the paper-based test, you will need to bring valid photo identification, your admittance ticket (which is mailed to you following registration or printed after online registration), several #2 pencils, and (if you are taking the writing test) blue or black ink pens. You may also choose to bring a watch, as long as it does not have calculator or keyboard functions.

For the computer-based test, you will need your photo identification and your Social Security number. You may not bring calculators, cell phones, pagers, pencils or pens, books, bags, scratch paper, or other people into the test room with you. The test administrator will designate an area where you may keep your personal belongings during the test.

Time Allowed

Paper-Based Tests

For each paper-based test, you will have 60 minutes of actual testing time. The test administrator will begin timing after all test booklets and Scantron sheets have been handed out and the instructions have been given. You should allow about one and a half hours (90 minutes) for each individual test, or four and a half hours if you are taking all three tests on the same day.

Computer-Based Tests

You will be allowed two hours for each individual computer-based test or four and a half hours for the combined computer-based tests. This allows time for tutorials and the collection of background information. Please see "The Computer-Based Test at a Glance" box on page 10 for the time allotted for each individual test.

On test day, allow plenty of time in the morning to get to your test location, especially if you are unfamiliar with the area where the test is given. You should arrive at least 30 minutes before your test to sign in, present your identification, and get yourself settled.

The Paper-Based Test

The paper-based test is offered approximately four times during a testing year at testing centers around the country. Questions are presented in multiple-choice format in a test booklet, and answers are entered onto a Scantron form. The essay portion of the PPST Writing test must be handwritten in blue or black ink.

THE PAPER-BASED TEST AT A GLANCE

PPST	TEST CODE	NUMBER OF QUESTIONS	TIME ALLOWED
Reading	0710	40 multiple-choice	60 minutes
Mathematics	0730	40 multiple-choice (no calculators)	60 minutes
Writing	0720	38 multiple-choice	30 minutes
		1 essay	30 minutes

Breakdown of Paper-Based Tests

The following table provides the approximate number and percentage of each question type on the paper-based PPSTs:

QUESTION TYPE	NUMBER OF QUESTIONS	PERCENTAGE OF TEST
PPST Reading		
Literal Comprehension	18	45%
Critical and Inferential Comprehension	22	55%
PPST Math		
Numbers and Operations	13	32.5%
Algebra	8	20%
Geometry and Measurement	9	22.5%
Data Analysis and Probability	10	25%
PPST Writing		
Grammatical Relationships	13	17%
Structural Relationships	14	18.5%
Word Choice and Mechanics	11	14.5%
Essay	1	50%

PPST Reading:	$40
PPST Math:	$40
PPST Writing:	$40
Registration fee:	$50 (charged once per testing year, September to August)

Special Service Fees

Late registration:	$45
Test, test center, or test date change:	$45
Emergency registration:	$75
Telephone re-registration:	$35
File correction:	$40
Scores by phone:	$30 (per request)
Additional score reports:	$40 (per report)
Test surcharge (Nevada only):	$5

Payment Options

You may pay using a Visa, MasterCard, American Express, Discover, or JCB credit card. You can also use a debit card, bank check, or money order made payable to ETS—*Praxis*. Cash is never accepted. Fee waivers are available to applicants with financial need. Refund policies and a fee waiver application form may be found on the ETS website (www.ets.org/praxis).

How Do I Register?

Usually you will need to register at least four weeks prior to the test date. First-time applicants for the paper-based test **must** register by mail or online.

To register by mail, you must download and complete the Praxis Registration Form. Approximately one week before your test date, you will receive a testing admission ticket, which you will need to bring for entrance into the test.

You can also register online at www.ets.org/praxis/. Online registration is available Monday through Friday, 7 A.M. to 10 P.M. (EST), and Saturday 7 A.M. through Sunday 8 P.M. (EST). To register online, you will need a valid e-mail address, mailing address, and phone number. Order confirmations and test admission tickets will be e-mailed to your e-mail address—you will not be sent a paper admission ticket by postal mail when you register online. Online registration is available only to those not needing special accommodations such as considerations for disabilities or Monday testing.

If you have taken a Praxis Series test previously, you can register by phone with a credit card. There will be a nonrefundable $35 service fee for the transaction, in addition to the standard registration and test fees. To register by phone, call 800-853-6773, 8 A.M. to 7:45 P.M. (EST), Monday through Friday.

Special arrangements may be available for individuals with documented disabilities or for test takers whose primary language is not English (PLNE). Monday test dates are available to those who cannot test on a Saturday test date due to religious convictions or military orders. These accommodations may vary from state to state. You should contact the ETS long before the test date to make inquiries.

Emergency Registration

Those trying to register for a desired test date after the regular and late registration deadlines may still be able to take the test on that date by using the emergency registration service for an additional $75 fee. This service guarantees a seat at a test center. Emergency registration is not available for individuals needing special accommodations.

Changing Your Test, Test Center, or Test Date

You may add or change a test or change your test center or test date by submitting a completed *Test, Center and Date Change Request* form with the $45 fee to the ETS. Please see the website to download the form and to learn more about deadlines and restrictions associated with your specific request.

To change your test and/or test center, the request form must be received by the emergency registration deadline. To change your test date, you need to submit your request form within two weeks of your original test date. Also, you can change your test date only to a future test date in the same testing year.

To Cancel Your Test Date

You may cancel a test date if your written request is received by the ETS by the late registration deadline. To cancel a test date, you must download and complete the *Refund Request Form*, available online. Then, mail the form to:

Praxis, Registration Refund
P.O. Box 6051
Princeton, NJ 08541-6051

You will receive a refund of your test fees, but not any registration or service fees. Refunds will not be given for requests received after the late registration deadline or if you are absent on the test date. Registration deadlines are updated and posted on the website. Refunds are mailed approximately four to six weeks after receipt of your request. If you used a credit card to make a payment, the refund will be credited to your credit card account.

The Computer-Based Test

The Praxis I: Academic Skills Assessments are also available as computer-based tests in over 300 locations throughout the United States. In many ways, the computer-based test is more convenient than the paper-based version. It is given more frequently and provides faster score reporting. You don't have to know much about computers to take the computer-based version—each test begins with a tutorial on the use of the computer. You are encouraged to spend as much time as needed on the tutorial.

About the Computer-Based PPST (CPPST)

With the exception of the essay portion of the writing test, all questions are in multiple-choice format. The questions are presented on the computer screen, and you choose your answers by selecting one choice or highlighting a section. The computer-based tests now have a special "mark" function, which allows you to "mark" a question that you would like to temporarily skip and come back to at a later time during the same section on the test. Test takers will have a review screen to see if a question has been answered, not seen yet, or "marked." The computer-based test is designed to ensure fairness because each test taker receives:

- the same distribution of content
- the same amount of testing time
- the same test directions
- the same tutorials on computer use

THE COMPUTER-BASED TEST AT A GLANCE (CPPST)

CPPST	TEST CODE	NUMBER OF QUESTIONS	TIME ALLOWED
Reading	5710	46 multiple-choice	75 minutes
Mathematics	5730	46 multiple-choice (no calculators)	75 minutes
Writing	5720	44 multiple-choice	38 minutes
		1 essay	30 minutes

Breakdown of Computer-Based Tests

The following table provides the approximate number and percentage of each question type on the computer-based PPSTs:

QUESTION TYPE	NUMBER OF QUESTIONS	PERCENTAGE OF TEST
CPPST Reading		
Literal Comprehension	21	45%
Critical and Inferential Comprehension	25	55%
CPPST Math		
Numbers and Operations	15	32.5%
Algebra	9	20%
Geometry and Measurement	10	22.5%
Data Analysis and Probability	12	25%
CPPST Writing		
Grammatical Relationships	15	17%
Structural Relationships	16	18.5%
Word Choice and Mechanics	13	14.5%
Essay	1	50%

FEES FOR THE COMPUTER-BASED TEST

One test:	$80
Two tests:	$120
Three tests:	$160
Combined test:	$130

Special Service Fees

File correction:	$35
Scores by phone:	$30
Additional score reports:	$40 (per report)

How Do I Register?

To register for the CPPSTs, contact the test center where you would like to take the test, or call Prometric Candidate Services (800-853-6773). Hearing impaired registrants can call Prometric's TTY phone line (800-529-3590) to register. A list of computer-based testing centers and phone numbers is available at www.ets.org/praxis. For the computer-based tests, you do NOT register using the mail-in form included in the bulletin.

REMINDER

Again, you may take the computer-based test only once a month, and no more than six times over the course of a year. This even applies to situations where you may have canceled your scores. If you violate this rule, your retest scores will not be reported and your fees will not be refunded.

To Cancel a Computer-Based Test

You may cancel or reschedule an appointment by calling Prometric Candidate Services (800-853-6773) at least three business days prior to your first test date. You can receive a refund of $20 per test or $60 for the combined test as long as you have canceled the test at least three business days before the first scheduled test date. Refund requests must be made in writing and mailed to:

> The Praxis Series
> CBT Refund
> P.O. Box 6051
> Princeton, NJ 08541-6051

The ETS will mail your refund in the form of a check or refund your credit card account within eight weeks from the time the request was received.

NONSTANDARD TESTING ACCOMMODATIONS

If you have a documented disability, you may be able to receive nonstandard testing accommodations. Among a list of accommodations, you may qualify for

- extended test time
- a test reader
- a separate location
- a Braille test
- someone to record your answers

Online, you will find the Bulletin Supplement for Test Takers with Disabilities or Health-Related Needs, which contains contact information, registration procedures, and special registration forms. If you are requesting accommodations, you must register by mail. Send your completed requests for testing accommodations to:

ETS Disability Services
P.O. Box 6054
Princeton, NJ 08541-6054

Where Do I Begin?

You have already taken the first step by reading this chapter and familiarizing yourself with the Praxis I test. Perhaps you have even started researching to see when the test is offered and where you would like to take it. Now you should begin your study program: start with "The LearningExpress Test Preparation System" (Chapter 2). This exclusive system gives you valuable test-taking techniques and will help you devise a study schedule that works best for you. If you stick with your study plan and concentrate on improving the areas in which you need help, you are sure to succeed. Good luck!

2 ▶ THE LEARNINGEXPRESS TEST PREPARATION SYSTEM

CHAPTER SUMMARY

The Praxis I test can be challenging. A great deal of preparation is necessary for achieving top scores and advancing your career. The LearningExpress Test Preparation System, developed by leading experts exclusively for LearningExpress, offers strategies for developing the discipline and attitude required for success.

Fact: Taking the Praxis I test is not easy, and neither is getting ready for it. Your future career as a teacher depends on getting a passing score, but there is an assortment of pitfalls that can keep you from doing your best. Here are some of the obstacles that can stand in the way of success:

- being unfamiliar with the exam format
- being paralyzed by test anxiety
- leaving your preparation to the last minute
- not preparing at all!
- not knowing vital test-taking skills: how to pace yourself through the exams, how to use the process of elimination, and when to guess
- not being in tip-top mental and physical shape
- messing up on test day by arriving late at the test site, having to work on an empty stomach, or feeling uncomfortable during the exams because the room is too hot or cold

What's the common denominator in all these test-taking pitfalls? One thing: *control*. Who's in control: you or the exam?

Here's some good news: The LearningExpress Test Preparation System puts *you* in control. In nine easy-to-follow steps, you will learn everything you need to know to ensure that you are in charge of your preparation and your performance on the exams. Other test takers may let the test get the better of them; other test takers may be unprepared or out of shape, but not you. You will have taken all the steps you need to get a high score on the Praxis I test.

Here's how the LearningExpress Test Preparation System works: Nine easy steps lead you through everything you need to know and do to get ready to master your exams. Each of the following steps includes both reading about the step and one or more activities. It's important that you do the activities along with the reading, or you won't get the full benefits of the system. Each step tells you approximately how much time it will take you to complete.

Step 1. Get Information	50 minutes
Step 2. Conquer Test Anxiety	20 minutes
Step 3. Make a Plan	30 minutes
Step 4. Learn to Manage Your Time	10 minutes
Step 5. Learn to Use the Process of Elimination	20 minutes
Step 6. Know When to Guess	20 minutes
Step 7. Reach Your Peak Performance Zone	10 minutes
Step 8. Get Your Act Together	10 minutes
Step 9. Do It!	10 minutes
Total	**3 hours**

We estimate that working through the entire system will take you approximately three hours, though it's perfectly okay if you work faster or slower. If you take an afternoon or evening, you can work through the whole LearningExpress Test Preparation System in one sitting. Otherwise, you can break it up, and do just one or two steps a day for the next several days. It's up to you—remember, *you* are in control.

Step 1: Get Information

Time to complete: 50 minutes
Activities: Read Chapter 1, "About the Praxis I."

Knowledge is power. The first step in the LearningExpress Test Preparation System is finding out everything you can about the Praxis I test. Once you have your information, the next steps in the LearningExpress Test Preparation System will show you what to do about it.

Part A: Straight Talk about the Praxis I

Why do you have to take rigorous exams, anyway? It's simply an attempt to be sure you have the knowledge and skills necessary for a teacher.

It's important for you to remember that your score on the Praxis I test does not determine how smart you are or even whether you will make a good teacher. There are all kinds of things exams like these can't test, such as whether you have the drive, determination, and dedication to be a teacher. Those kinds of things are hard to evaluate, while a test is easy to evaluate.

This is not to say that the exam is not important! The knowledge tested on the exams is knowledge you will need to do your job. And your ability to enter the profession you've trained for depends on passing. And that's why you are here—using the LearningExpress Test Preparation System to achieve control over the exam.

Part B: What's on the Test

If you haven't already done so, stop here and read Chapter 1 of this book, which gives you an overview of the Praxis I test. Then, go to the Internet and read the most up-to-date information about your exam directly from the test developers at www.ets.org/praxis.

Step 2: Conquer Test Anxiety

Time to complete: 20 minutes
Activity: Take the Test Anxiety Test.

Having complete information about the exam is the first step in getting control of it. Next, you have to overcome one of the biggest obstacles to test success: test anxiety. Test anxiety not only impairs your performance on the exam, but also keeps you from preparing! In Step 2, you will learn stress management techniques that will help you succeed. Learn these strategies now, and practice them as you work through the exams in this book, so they will be second nature to you by exam day.

Combating Test Anxiety

The first thing you need to know is that a little test anxiety is a good thing. Everyone gets nervous before a big exam—and if that nervousness motivates you to prepare thoroughly, so much the better. It's said that Sir Laurence Olivier, one of the foremost British actors of the twentieth century, felt ill before every performance. His stage fright didn't impair his performance; in fact, it probably gave him a little extra edge—just the kind of edge you need to do well, whether on a stage or in an examination room.

Following is the Test Anxiety Test. Stop and answer the questions to find out whether your level of test anxiety is something you should worry about.

TEST ANXIETY TEST

You don't need to worry about test anxiety unless it is extreme enough to impair your performance. The following questionnaire will provide a diagnosis of your level of test anxiety. In the blank before each statement, write the number that most accurately describes your experience.

0 = Never	1 = Once or twice	2 = Sometimes	3 = Often

_____ I have gotten so nervous before an exam that I simply put down the books and didn't study for it.

_____ I have experienced disabling physical symptoms such as vomiting and severe headaches because I was nervous about an exam.

_____ I have simply not shown up for an exam because I was scared to take it.

_____ I have experienced dizziness and disorientation while taking an exam.

_____ I have had trouble filling in the little circles because my hands were shaking too hard.

_____ I have failed an exam because I was too nervous to complete it.

_____ **Total: Add up the numbers in the blanks above.**

Your Test Anxiety Score

Here are the steps you should take, depending on your score. If you scored:

- **Below 3,** your level of test anxiety is nothing to worry about; it's probably just enough to give you that little extra edge.
- **Between 3 and 6,** your test anxiety may be enough to impair your performance, and you should practice the stress-management techniques listed in this section to try to bring your test anxiety down to manageable levels.
- **Above 6,** your level of test anxiety is a serious concern. In addition to practicing the stress management techniques listed in this section, you may want to seek additional personal help by contacting your academic counselor. Tell the counselor that you have a level of test anxiety that sometimes keeps you from being able to take the exam. The counselor may be willing to help you or may suggest someone else you should talk to.

Stress Management Before the Test

If you feel your level of anxiety is getting the best of you in the weeks before a test, here is what you need to do to bring the level down again:

- **Get prepared.** There's nothing like knowing what to expect and being prepared for it to put you in control of test anxiety. That's why you are reading this book. Use it faithfully, and remind yourself that you're better prepared than most of the people taking the test.
- **Practice self-confidence.** A positive attitude is a great way to combat test anxiety. This is no time to be humble or shy. Stand in front of the mirror and say to your reflection, "I am prepared. I am full of self-confidence. I am going to ace this test. I know I can do it." Record it and play it back once a day. If you hear it often enough, you'll believe it.
- **Fight negative messages.** Every time someone starts telling you how hard the exam is or how it's almost impossible to get a high score, start telling them your self-confidence messages you learned about in the previous entry. Don't listen to negative messages. Turn on your recorder and listen to your self-confidence messages.
- **Visualize.** Imagine yourself reporting for duty on your first day as a teacher or in your teacher training program. Visualizing success can help make it happen—and it reminds you of why you are going to all this work in preparing for the exam.
- **Exercise.** Physical activity helps calm your body and focus your mind. Besides, being in good physical shape can actually help you do well on the exam. Go for a run, lift weights, go swimming—and do it regularly.

Stress Management on Test Day

There are several ways you can bring down your level of anxiety on test day. They will work best if you practice them in the weeks before the test, so you know which ones work best for you.

- **Practice deep breathing.** Take a deep breath while you count to five. Hold it for a count of one, then let it out for a count of five. Repeat several times.
- **Move your body.** Try rolling your head in a circle. Rotate your shoulders. Shake your hands from the wrist. Many people find these movements very relaxing.
- **Visualize again.** Think of the place where you are most relaxed: lying on the beach in the sun, walking through the park, or wherever. Now close your eyes and imagine you're actually there. If you practice in advance, you'll find that you need only a few seconds of this exercise to experience a significant increase in your sense of well-being.

When anxiety threatens to overwhelm you right there during the exam, there are still things you can do to manage the stress level.

- **Repeat your self-confidence messages.** You should have them memorized by now. Say them quietly to yourself, and believe them!
- **Visualize one more time.** This time, visualize yourself moving smoothly and quickly through the test, answering every question correctly and finishing just before time is up. Like most visualization techniques, this one works best if you've practiced it ahead of time.
- **Find an easy question.** Find an easy question, and answer it. Getting even one question finished gets you into the test-taking groove.

- **Take a mental break.** Everyone loses concentration once in a while during a long test. It's normal, so you shouldn't worry about it. Instead, accept what has happened. Say to yourself, "Hey, I lost it there for a minute. My brain is taking a break." Close your eyes and do some deep breathing for a few seconds. Then, you'll be ready to go back to work.

Try these techniques ahead of time and watch them work for you!

Step 3: Make a Plan

Time to complete: 30 minutes
Activity: Construct a study plan.

Maybe the most important thing you can do to get control of yourself and your exam is to make a study plan. Too many people fail to prepare simply because they fail to plan. Spending hours the day before the exam poring over sample test questions not only raises your level of test anxiety, but also is simply no substitute for careful preparation and practice over time.

Don't fall into the cram trap. Take control of your preparation time by mapping out a study schedule. On the following pages are two sample schedules based on the amount of time you have before you take the Praxis I. If you're the kind of person who needs deadlines and assignments to motivate you for a project, here they are. If you're the kind of person who doesn't like to follow other people's plans, you can use the following suggested schedules to construct your own.

Even more important than making a plan is making a commitment. You can't review everything you need to know for the Praxis I test in one night. You have to set aside some time every day for study and practice. Try for at least 20 minutes a day. Twenty minutes daily will do you much more good than two hours on Saturday.

Don't put off your studying until the day before the exam. Start now. A few minutes a day, with half an hour or more on weekends, can make a big difference in your score.

Schedule A: The 30-Day Plan for Praxis I

If you have at least a month before you take the Praxis I, you have plenty of time to prepare—as long as you don't waste it! If you have less than a month, turn to Schedule B.

TIME	PREPARATION
Day 1	Take the first practice exam in Chapter 3. Score it. Using the skills charts, identify two skill areas in each PPST that you will concentrate on before you take the second practice exam.
Days 2–4	Skim over any other study materials you may have. Concentrate on your identified weak skills.
Day 5	Take the second practice exam in Chapter 4.
Day 6	Score your second practice exam, noting any improvement in the skills you initially identified as weak points. Identify two other areas in each PPST that you will concentrate on before you take the third practice exam.
Days 7–14	Study all the areas you identified as weak points from the first two tests.
Day 15	Take the third practice exam in Chapter 5.
Day 16	Score the third practice exam. Identify one area in each PPST that you need to particularly concentrate on before you take the next practice exam.
Days 17–21	Study the areas you identified for review.
Day 22	Take the fourth practice exam in Chapter 6.
Day 23	Score the test. Note how much you have improved!
Days 24–27	Study any remaining topics you still need to review.
Day 28	As a final tune-up, take the final practice exam in Chapter 7. Score it.
Day 29	Take an overview of all your study materials, consolidating your strengths and improving on your weaknesses.
Day before the exam	Relax. Do something unrelated to the exam and go to bed at a reasonable hour.

Schedule B: The 10-Day Plan for Praxis I

If you have two weeks or less before you take the exam, use this 10-day schedule to help you make the most of your time.

TIME	PREPARATION
Day 1	Take the first practice exam in Chapter 3. Score it. Using the skills charts, identify two skill areas in each PPST that you will concentrate on before you take the second practice exam.
Days 2–4	Skim over any other study materials you may have. Concentrate on your identified weak skills.
Day 5	Take the second practice exam in Chapter 4. Score your second practice exam, noting any improvement in the skills you initially identified as weak points. Identify two other areas in each PPST that you will concentrate on before you take the third practice exam.
Day 6	Study all the areas you identified as weak points from the first two tests.
Day 7	Take the third practice exam in Chapter 5. Score it. Identify one area in each PPST that you need to particularly concentrate on before you take the next practice exam.
Day 8	Study the areas you identified for review.
Day 9	As a final tune-up, take the fourth or fifth practice exam in Chapter 6 or 7. Score the test. Note how much you have improved!
Day 10	Study any remaining topics you still need to review. Use the review chapters for help.
Day before the exam	Relax. Do something unrelated to the exam and go to bed at a reasonable hour.

Step 4: Learn to Manage Your Time

Time to complete: 10 minutes to read, many hours to practice!

Activities: Practice these strategies as you take the sample tests in this book.

Steps 4, 5, and 6 of the LearningExpress Test Preparation System put you in charge of your exams by showing you test-taking strategies that work. Practice these strategies as you take the sample tests in this book, and then you will be ready to use them on test day.

First, take control of your time on the exams. It's a terrible feeling to know there are only five minutes left when you are only three-quarters of the way through a test. Here are some tips to keep that from happening to you.

- **Follow directions.** You may choose to take the computer-based Praxis I exam. You should take your time taking the computer tutorial before the exam. Read the directions carefully and ask questions before the exam begins if there's anything you don't understand.

- **Pace yourself.** If there is a timer on the screen as you take the exam, keep an eye on it. This will help you pace yourself. For example, when one-quarter of the time has elapsed, you should be a quarter of the way through the test, and so on. If you are falling behind, pick up the pace a bit. If you do not take your exam on a computer, use your watch or the clock in the testing room to keep track of the time you have left.
- **Keep moving.** Don't waste time on one question. If you don't know the answer, skip the question and move on. You can always go back to it later.
- **Don't rush.** Though you should keep moving, rushing won't help. Try to keep calm and work methodically and quickly.

Step 5: Learn to Use the Process of Elimination

Time to complete: 20 minutes
Activity: Complete worksheet on Using the Process of Elimination.

After time management, the next most important tool for taking control of your exam is using the process of elimination wisely. It's standard test-taking wisdom that you should always read all the answer choices before choosing your answer. This helps you find the right answer by eliminating wrong answer choices. And, sure enough, that standard wisdom applies to your exam, too.

You should always use the process of elimination on tough questions, even if the right answer jumps out at you. Sometimes the answer that jumps out isn't right after all. You should always proceed through the answer choices in order. You can start with answer choice **a** and eliminate any choices that are clearly incorrect.

If you are taking the test on paper, like the practice exams in this book, it's good to have a system for marking good, bad, and maybe answers. We recommend this one:

   X = bad
   ✔ = good
   ? = maybe

If you don't like these marks, devise your own system. Just make sure you do it long before test day—while you're working through the practice exams in this book—so you won't have to worry about it just before the exam.

Even when you think you are absolutely clueless about a question, you can often use the process of elimination to get rid of one answer choice. If so, you are better prepared to make an educated guess, as you will see in Step 6. More often, the process of elimination allows you to get down to only two possibly right answers. Then you are in a strong position to guess. And sometimes, even though you don't know the right answer, you find it simply by getting rid of the wrong ones.

Try using your powers of elimination on the questions in the worksheet Using the Process of Elimination beginning on the next page. The questions aren't about teaching; they're just designed to show you how the process of elimination works. The answer explanations for this worksheet show one possible way you might use the process to arrive at the right answer.

The process of elimination is your tool for the next step, which is knowing when to guess.

Use the process of elimination to answer the following questions.

1. Ilsa is as old as Meghan will be in five years. The difference between Ed's age and Meghan's age is twice the difference between Ilsa's age and Meghan's age. Ed is 29. How old is Ilsa?
   a. 4
   b. 10
   c. 19
   d. 24

2. "All drivers of commercial vehicles must carry a valid commercial driver's license whenever operating a commercial vehicle." According to this sentence, which of the following people need NOT carry a commercial driver's license?
   a. a truck driver idling his engine while waiting to be directed to a loading dock
   b. a bus operator backing her bus out of the way of another bus in the bus lot
   c. a taxi driver driving his personal car to the grocery store
   d. a limousine driver taking the limousine to her home after dropping off her last passenger of the evening

3. Smoking tobacco has been linked to
   a. increased risk of stroke and heart attack.
   b. all forms of respiratory disease.
   c. increasing mortality rates over the past ten years.
   d. juvenile delinquency.

4. Which of the following words is spelled correctly?
   a. incorrigible
   b. outragous
   c. domestickated
   d. understandible

Answers

Here are the answers, as well as some suggestions on how you might have used the process of elimination to find them.

1. **d.** You should have eliminated answer **a** right off the bat. Ilsa can't be four years old if Meghan is going to be Ilsa's age in five years. The best way to eliminate other answer choices is to try plugging them into the information given in the problem. For instance, for answer **b**, if Ilsa is 10, then Meghan must be 5. The difference in their ages is 5. The difference between Ed's age, 29, and Meghan's age, 5, is 24. Is 24 two times 5? No. Then answer **b** is wrong. You could eliminate answer **c** in the same way and be left with answer **d**.

2. **c.** Note the word *not* in the question, and go through the answers one by one. Is the truck driver in choice **a** "operating a commercial vehicle"? Yes, idling counts as "operating," so he needs to have a commercial driver's license. Likewise, the bus operator in answer **b** is operating a commercial vehicle; the question doesn't say the operator must be on the street. The limo driver in **d** is operating a commercial vehicle, even if it doesn't have a passenger in it. However, the cabbie in answer **c** is *not* operating a commercial vehicle, but his own private car.

3. a. You could eliminate answer **b** simply because of the presence of *all*. Such absolutes hardly ever appear in correct answer choices. Choice **c** looks attractive until you think a little about what you know—aren't *fewer* people smoking these days, rather than more? So how could smoking be responsible for a higher mortality rate? (If you didn't know that *mortality rate* means the rate at which people die, you might keep this choice as a possibility, but you'd still be able to eliminate two answers and have only two to choose from.) And choice **d** is plain silly, so you could eliminate that one, too. And you're left with the correct choice, **a**.

4. a. How you used the process of elimination here depends on which words you recognized as being spelled incorrectly. If you knew that the correct spellings were *outrageous, domesticated, and understandable*, then you were home free. Surely you knew that at least one of those words was wrong!

Step 6: Know When to Guess

Time to complete: 20 minutes
Activity: Complete worksheet on Your Guessing Ability.

Armed with the process of elimination, you're ready to take control of one of the big questions in test taking: Should I guess? The first and main answer is *Yes*. Some exams have what's called a "guessing penalty," in which a fraction of your wrong answers is subtracted from your right answers—the Praxis I test does NOT work like that. The number of questions you answer correctly yields your raw score, so you have nothing to lose and everything to gain by guessing.

The following are ten really hard questions. You're not supposed to know the answers. Rather, this is an assessment of your ability to guess when you don't have a clue. Read each question carefully, just as if you did expect to answer it. If you have any knowledge at all of the subject of the question, use that knowledge to help you eliminate wrong answer choices. Use this answer grid to fill in your answers to the questions.

ANSWER GRID

	a	b	c	d
1.	ⓐ	ⓑ	ⓒ	ⓓ
2.	ⓐ	ⓑ	ⓒ	ⓓ
3.	ⓐ	ⓑ	ⓒ	ⓓ
4.	ⓐ	ⓑ	ⓒ	ⓓ

	a	b	c	d
5.	ⓐ	ⓑ	ⓒ	ⓓ
6.	ⓐ	ⓑ	ⓒ	ⓓ
7.	ⓐ	ⓑ	ⓒ	ⓓ
8.	ⓐ	ⓑ	ⓒ	ⓓ

	a	b	c	d
9.	ⓐ	ⓑ	ⓒ	ⓓ
10.	ⓐ	ⓑ	ⓒ	ⓓ

1. September 7 is Independence Day in
   a. India.
   b. Costa Rica.
   c. Brazil.
   d. Australia.

2. Which of the following is the formula for determining the momentum of an object?
   a. $p = mv$
   b. $F = ma$
   c. $P = IV$
   d. $E = mc^2$

3. Because of the expansion of the universe, the stars and other celestial bodies are all moving away from each other. This phenomenon is known as
   a. Newton's first law.
   b. the big bang.
   c. gravitational collapse.
   d. Hubble flow.

4. American author Gertrude Stein was born in
   a. 1713.
   b. 1830.
   c. 1874.
   d. 1901.

5. Which of the following is NOT one of the Five Classics attributed to Confucius?
   a. the *I Ching*
   b. the *Book of Holiness*
   c. the *Spring and Autumn Annals*
   d. the *Book of History*

6. The religious and philosophical doctrine that holds that the universe is constantly in a struggle between good and evil is known as
   a. Pelagianism.
   b. Manichaeanism.
   c. neo-Hegelianism.
   d. Epicureanism.

7. The third chief justice of the U.S. Supreme Court was
   a. John Blair.
   b. William Cushing.
   c. James Wilson.
   d. John Jay.

8. Which of the following is the poisonous portion of a daffodil?
   a. the bulb
   b. the leaves
   c. the stem
   d. the flowers

9. The winner of the Masters golf tournament in 1953 was
   a. Sam Snead.
   b. Cary Middlecoff.
   c. Arnold Palmer.
   d. Ben Hogan.

10. The state with the highest per capita personal income in 1980 was
   a. Alaska.
   b. Connecticut.
   c. New York.
   d. Texas.

Answers

Check your answers against the correct answers below.

1. c
2. a
3. d
4. c
5. b
6. b
7. b
8. a
9. d
10. a

How Did You Do?

You may have simply gotten lucky and actually known the answer to one or two questions. In addition, your guessing was more successful if you were able to use the process of elimination on any of the questions. Maybe you didn't know who the third chief justice was (question 7), but you knew that John Jay was the first. In that case, you would have eliminated answer **d** and therefore improved your odds of guessing right from one in four to one in three.

According to probability, you should get 2.5 answers correct, so getting either two or three right would be average. If you got four or more right, you may be a really terrific guesser. If you got one or none right, you may be a really bad guesser.

Keep in mind, though, that this is only a small sample. You should continue to keep track of your guessing ability as you work through the sample questions in this book. Circle the numbers of the questions you guess on as you make your guess; or, if you don't have time while you take the practice tests, go back afterward and try to remember on which questions you guessed. Remember, on an exam with four answer choices, your chances of getting a right answer is one in four. So keep a separate "guessing" score for each exam. How many questions did you guess on? How many did you get right? If the number you got right is at least one-fourth the number of questions you guessed on, you are at least an average guesser, maybe better—and you should always go ahead and guess on the real exam. If the number you got right is significantly lower than one-fourth of the number you guessed on, you would, frankly, be safe in guessing anyway, but maybe you would feel more comfortable if you guessed only selectively, when you can eliminate a wrong answer or at least have a good feeling about one of the answer choices.

Step 7: Reach Your Peak Performance Zone

Time to complete: 10 minutes to read; weeks to complete!

Activity: Complete the Physical Preparation Checklist.

To get ready for a challenge like a big exam, you have to take control of your physical as well as your mental state. Exercise, proper diet, and rest will ensure that your body works with, rather than against, your mind on test day, as well as during your preparation.

Exercise

If you don't already have a regular exercise program going, the time during which you're preparing for an exam is actually an excellent time to start one. And if you're already keeping fit—or trying to get that way—don't let the pressure of preparing for an exam fool you into quitting now. Exercise helps reduce stress by pumping wonderful good-feeling hormones called *endorphins* into your system. It also increases the oxygen supply throughout your body, including your brain, so you'll be at peak performance on test day.

A half hour of vigorous activity—enough to raise a sweat—every day should be your aim. If you're really pressed for time, every other day is okay. Choose an activity you like and get out there and do it. Jogging with a friend or exercising to music always makes the time go faster, or take a radio.

But don't overdo it. You don't want to exhaust yourself. Moderation is the key.

Diet

First of all, cut out the junk. Go easy on caffeine and nicotine, and eliminate alcohol and any other drugs from your system at least two weeks before the exam. Promise yourself a binge the night after the exam, if need be.

What your body needs for peak performance is simply a balanced diet. Eat plenty of fruits and vegetables, along with protein and carbohydrates. Foods high in lecithin (an amino acid), such as fish and beans, are especially good brain foods.

The night before the exam, you might carbo-load the way athletes do before a contest. Eat a big plate of spaghetti, rice and beans, or whatever your favorite carbohydrate is.

Rest

You probably know how much sleep you need every night to be at your best, even if you don't always get it. Make sure you do get that much sleep, though, for at least a week before the exam. Moderation is important here, too. Extra sleep will just make you groggy.

If you're not a morning person and your exam will be given in the morning, you should reset your internal clock so that your body doesn't think you're taking an exam at 3 A.M. You have to start this process well before the exam. The way it works is to get up half an hour earlier each morning, and then go to bed half an hour earlier that night. Don't try it the other way around; you'll just toss and turn if you go to bed early without having gotten up early. The next morning, get up another half an hour earlier, and so on. How long you will have to do this depends on how late you're used to getting up. Use the Physical Preparation Checklist on the next page to make sure you're in tip-top form.

PHYSICAL PREPARATION CHECKLIST

For the week before the test, write down what physical exercise you engaged in and for how long and what you ate for each meal. Remember, you're trying for at least half an hour of exercise every other day (preferably every day) and a balanced diet that's light on junk food.

Exam minus 7 days

Exercise: _____ for _____ minutes

Breakfast: _____

Lunch: _____

Dinner: _____

Snacks: _____

Exam minus 6 days

Exercise: _____ for _____ minutes

Breakfast: _____

Lunch: _____

Dinner: _____

Snacks: _____

Exam minus 5 days

Exercise: _____ for _____ minutes

Breakfast: _____

Lunch: _____

Dinner: _____

Snacks: _____

Exam minus 4 days

Exercise: _____ for _____ minutes

Breakfast: _____

Lunch: _____

Dinner: _____

Snacks: _____

Exam minus 3 days

Exercise: _____ for _____ minutes

Breakfast: _____

Lunch: _____

Dinner: _____

Snacks: _____

Exam minus 2 days

Exercise: _____ for _____ minutes

Breakfast: _____

Lunch: _____

Dinner: _____

Snacks: _____

Exam minus 1 day

Exercise: _____ for _____ minutes

Breakfast: _____

Lunch: _____

Dinner: _____

Snacks: _____

Step 8: Get Your Act Together

Time to complete: 10 minutes to read; time to complete will vary
Activity: Complete Final Preparations worksheet.

You're in control of your mind and body; you're in charge of test anxiety, your preparation, and your test-taking strategies. Now it's time to take charge of external factors, like the testing site and the materials you need to take the exam.

Find Out Where the Exam Is and Make a Trial Run

Do you know how to get to the testing site? Do you know how long it will take to get there? If not, make a trial run, preferably on the same day of the week at the same time of day. Make note on the Final Preparations worksheet on the next page of the amount of time it will take you to get to the exam site. Plan on arriving 30–45 minutes early so you can get the lay of the land, use the bathroom, and calm down. Then figure out how early you will have to get up that morning, and make sure you get up that early every day for a week before the exam.

Gather Your Materials

The night before the exam, lay out the clothes you will wear and the materials you have to bring with you to the exam. Plan on dressing in layers; you won't have any control over the temperature of the examination room. Have a sweater or jacket you can take off if it's warm. Use the checklist on the Final Preparations worksheet to help you pull together what you will need.

Don't Skip Breakfast

Even if you don't usually eat breakfast, do so on exam morning. A cup of coffee doesn't count. Don't eat doughnuts or other sweet foods, either. A sugar high will leave you with a sugar low in the middle of the exam. A mix of protein and carbohydrates is best: Cereal with milk and just a little sugar, or eggs with toast, will do your body a world of good.

Step 9: Do It!

Time to complete: 10 minutes, plus test-taking time
Activity: Ace the Praxis I!

Fast-forward to exam day. You're ready. You made a study plan and followed through. You practiced your test-taking strategies while working through this book. You're in control of your physical, mental, and emotional state. You know when and where to show up and what to bring with you. In other words, you're better prepared than most other people taking the exam. You're psyched.

Just one more thing. When you're done with the exam, you will have earned a reward. Plan a celebration. Call up your friends and plan a party, or have a nice dinner for two—whatever your heart desires. Give yourself something to look forward to.

And then do it. Go into the exam, full of confidence and armed with test-taking strategies you've practiced until they became second nature. You're in control of yourself, your environment, and your performance on the exam. You're ready to succeed. So do it. Go in there and ace the exam. And look forward to your future career as a teacher!

Getting to the Exam Site

Location of exam site: _____

Date: _____

Departure time: _____

Do I know how to get to the exam site?   Yes ___   No ___

If no, make a trial run.

Time it will take to get to the exam site: _____

Things to Lay Out the Night Before

Clothes I will wear   _____

Sweater/jacket   _____

Watch   _____

Photo ID   _____

Four #2 pencils and
blue or black ink pens
(if taking the paper-
based test)   _____

Other Things to Bring/Remember

_____

_____

_____

_____

_____

_____

_____

3

▶ PRAXIS I:
POWER PRACTICE
EXAM 1

CHAPTER SUMMARY
Here is a full-length test based on the three elements of
the Praxis I, the Pre-Professional Skills Tests (PPSTs) of
Reading, Mathematics, and Writing.

The exam that follows is made up of three tests: Reading (multiple-choice questions), Mathematics
(multiple-choice questions), and Writing (multiple-choice questions and one essay).

With this practice exam, you should simulate the actual test-taking experience as closely as you
can. Find a quiet place to work where you won't be disturbed. Use the answer sheet on the next page and write
your essay on a separate piece of paper. Allow yourself an hour for the Reading test, an hour for the Mathematics
test, 30 minutes for Section 1 of the Writing test, and 30 minutes for Section 2 of the Writing test (your essay).

Set a timer or stopwatch for each part of the exam, but do not worry too much if you go over the allotted
times on this practice exam. You can work more on timing when you take the Praxis I Practice Exam 2 in
Chapter 4.

After the exam, use the answer explanations to learn more about the questions you missed and use the
scoring guide in Chapter 8 to figure out how you did.

SKILLS TEST IN READING

1. (a) (b) (c) (d) (e)
2. (a) (b) (c) (d) (e)
3. (a) (b) (c) (d) (e)
4. (a) (b) (c) (d) (e)
5. (a) (b) (c) (d) (e)
6. (a) (b) (c) (d) (e)
7. (a) (b) (c) (d) (e)
8. (a) (b) (c) (d) (e)
9. (a) (b) (c) (d) (e)
10. (a) (b) (c) (d) (e)
11. (a) (b) (c) (d) (e)
12. (a) (b) (c) (d) (e)
13. (a) (b) (c) (d) (e)
14. (a) (b) (c) (d) (e)
15. (a) (b) (c) (d) (e)
16. (a) (b) (c) (d) (e)
17. (a) (b) (c) (d) (e)
18. (a) (b) (c) (d) (e)
19. (a) (b) (c) (d) (e)
20. (a) (b) (c) (d) (e)
21. (a) (b) (c) (d) (e)
22. (a) (b) (c) (d) (e)
23. (a) (b) (c) (d) (e)
24. (a) (b) (c) (d) (e)
25. (a) (b) (c) (d) (e)
26. (a) (b) (c) (d) (e)
27. (a) (b) (c) (d) (e)
28. (a) (b) (c) (d) (e)
29. (a) (b) (c) (d) (e)
30. (a) (b) (c) (d) (e)
31. (a) (b) (c) (d) (e)
32. (a) (b) (c) (d) (e)
33. (a) (b) (c) (d) (e)
34. (a) (b) (c) (d) (e)
35. (a) (b) (c) (d) (e)
36. (a) (b) (c) (d) (e)
37. (a) (b) (c) (d) (e)
38. (a) (b) (c) (d) (e)
39. (a) (b) (c) (d) (e)
40. (a) (b) (c) (d) (e)

SKILLS TEST IN MATHEMATICS

1. (a) (b) (c) (d) (e)
2. (a) (b) (c) (d) (e)
3. (a) (b) (c) (d) (e)
4. (a) (b) (c) (d) (e)
5. (a) (b) (c) (d) (e)
6. (a) (b) (c) (d) (e)
7. (a) (b) (c) (d) (e)
8. (a) (b) (c) (d) (e)
9. (a) (b) (c) (d) (e)
10. (a) (b) (c) (d) (e)
11. (a) (b) (c) (d) (e)
12. (a) (b) (c) (d) (e)
13. (a) (b) (c) (d) (e)
14. (a) (b) (c) (d) (e)
15. (a) (b) (c) (d) (e)
16. (a) (b) (c) (d) (e)
17. (a) (b) (c) (d) (e)
18. (a) (b) (c) (d) (e)
19. (a) (b) (c) (d) (e)
20. (a) (b) (c) (d) (e)
21. (a) (b) (c) (d) (e)
22. (a) (b) (c) (d) (e)
23. (a) (b) (c) (d) (e)
24. (a) (b) (c) (d) (e)
25. (a) (b) (c) (d) (e)
26. (a) (b) (c) (d) (e)
27. (a) (b) (c) (d) (e)
28. (a) (b) (c) (d) (e)
29. (a) (b) (c) (d) (e)
30. (a) (b) (c) (d) (e)
31. (a) (b) (c) (d) (e)
32. (a) (b) (c) (d) (e)
33. (a) (b) (c) (d) (e)
34. (a) (b) (c) (d) (e)
35. (a) (b) (c) (d) (e)
36. (a) (b) (c) (d) (e)
37. (a) (b) (c) (d) (e)
38. (a) (b) (c) (d) (e)
39. (a) (b) (c) (d) (e)
40. (a) (b) (c) (d) (e)

SKILLS TEST IN WRITING

1. (a) (b) (c) (d) (e)
2. (a) (b) (c) (d) (e)
3. (a) (b) (c) (d) (e)
4. (a) (b) (c) (d) (e)
5. (a) (b) (c) (d) (e)
6. (a) (b) (c) (d) (e)
7. (a) (b) (c) (d) (e)
8. (a) (b) (c) (d) (e)
9. (a) (b) (c) (d) (e)
10. (a) (b) (c) (d) (e)
11. (a) (b) (c) (d) (e)
12. (a) (b) (c) (d) (e)
13. (a) (b) (c) (d) (e)
14. (a) (b) (c) (d) (e)
15. (a) (b) (c) (d) (e)
16. (a) (b) (c) (d) (e)
17. (a) (b) (c) (d) (e)
18. (a) (b) (c) (d) (e)
19. (a) (b) (c) (d) (e)
20. (a) (b) (c) (d) (e)
21. (a) (b) (c) (d) (e)
22. (a) (b) (c) (d) (e)
23. (a) (b) (c) (d) (e)
24. (a) (b) (c) (d) (e)
25. (a) (b) (c) (d) (e)
26. (a) (b) (c) (d) (e)
27. (a) (b) (c) (d) (e)
28. (a) (b) (c) (d) (e)
29. (a) (b) (c) (d) (e)
30. (a) (b) (c) (d) (e)
31. (a) (b) (c) (d) (e)
32. (a) (b) (c) (d) (e)
33. (a) (b) (c) (d) (e)
34. (a) (b) (c) (d) (e)
35. (a) (b) (c) (d) (e)
36. (a) (b) (c) (d) (e)
37. (a) (b) (c) (d) (e)
38. (a) (b) (c) (d) (e)

Skills Test in Reading

Directions: Read the following passages and answer the questions that follow.

Use the following passage to answer questions 1–3.

It is generally allowed that Guiana and Brazil, to the north and south of the Pará district, form two distinct provinces, as regards their animal and vegetable inhabitants. This means that the two regions have a very large number of forms peculiar to themselves, and which are supposed not to have been derived from other quarters during modern geological times. Each may be considered as a center of distribution in the latest process of dissemination of species over the surface of tropical America. Pará lies midway between the two centers, each of which has a nucleus of elevated tableland, while the intermediate river valley forms a wide extent of low-lying country. It is, therefore, interesting to ascertain from which the latter received its population, or whether it contains so large a number of endemic species as would warrant the conclusion that it is itself an independent province. To assist in deciding such questions as these, we must compare closely the species found in the district with those of the other contiguous regions, and endeavor to ascertain whether they are identical, or only slightly modified, or whether they are highly peculiar.

1. Which sentence best summarizes the main point of the passage?
   a. The fauna and flora of Pará are distinct from both the flora and fauna of Guiana and the fauna and flora of Brazil.
   b. Pará supports a very large number of ecologically distinct habitats.
   c. Ecological considerations override all others with respect to Pará.
   d. It has not yet been determined whether Pará is an ecologically distinct district.
   e. The government of Pará has historically not been supportive of biological expeditions.

2. Each of the following conclusions can be made from the passage EXCEPT
   a. both Guiana and Brazil are ecologically distinct provinces in South America.
   b. both Guiana and Brazil are centers of distribution for the dissemination of species into Pará.
   c. Pará consists of a nucleus of elevated tableland and a low-lying river valley.
   d. the Pará district can be found to the north of Brazil.
   e. Guiana, Brazil, and the Pará district can all be considered part of tropical America.

3. It can be inferred from this passage that the main criterion for declaring any given area a distinct province in terms of its flora and fauna is
   a. the particulars of the district's geographical features, including its isolation or lack thereof.
   b. the number of peculiar species endemic to the district.
   c. the district's proximity to natural populations of endemic species.
   d. the number of identical species inhabiting contiguous regions.
   e. the diversity of species within geographical boundaries.

Use the following passage to answer questions 4 and 5.

1   Laughter is always the laughter of a group. It
2   may, perchance, have happened to you, when
3   seated in a railway carriage, to hear travelers
4   relating to one another's stories which must
5   have been comic to them, for they laughed
6   rapturously. Had you been one of their com-
7   pany, you would have laughed like them; but, as
8   you were not, you had no desire whatsoever to
9   do so. However spontaneous it seems, laughter
10   always implies a kind of complicity with other
11   laughers, real or imaginary. How often has it
12   been said that the fuller the theater, the more
13   uncontrolled the laughter of the audience! On
14   the other hand, how often has the remark been
15   made that many comic effects are incapable of
16   translation from one language to another,
17   because they refer to the customs and ideas of a
18   particular social group!

4. What role does the author's anecdote about the travelers in the railway carriage serve in the passage's central argument?
   a. It demonstrates through personal experience that laughter is an isolated phenomenon.
   b. It illustrates how the specific customs and ideas of his or her society dictate what is and what is not funny.
   c. It accentuates that an individual apart from an intended audience may lack a necessary connection to find humor in a situation.
   d. It shows the significant impact of proximity on a humorous situation.
   e. It demonstrates that laughter is an inexplicably spontaneous event.

5. In the context of the text, the word *rapturously* in line 6 could be replaced with which of the following words to have the LEAST impact on what the sentence means?
   a. sanguinely
   b. painfully
   c. morosely
   d. awkwardly
   e. hilariously

Use the following passage to answer question 6.

As album sales have dwindled dramatically over the past decade, likely at least in part to the proliferation of file-sharing sites for illegal song downloads, some record companies claim that fans are manipulating their favorite artists' creative abilities by limiting potential earnings. In lieu of selling 100,000 albums from record stores, one producer explains, the same band may now only be selling 20,000 albums—scantly earning enough royalties for musicians to pay for their instruments and food for their families.

6. Which statement, if it were true, would most significantly weaken the argument made by the record companies that fewer album sales are negatively impacting musicians' abilities to support themselves?

   a. Some users of illegal file-sharing sites have been sued by the record labels for theft of copyrighted property.

   b. In response to lackluster album sales, bands have frequently increased their touring schedules to play additional concerts.

   c. Many bands have recently set up their own websites where fans have purchased albums directly from the musicians, avoiding the cut of profits taken by record companies.

   d. Due to rising gas prices, the costs involved for shipping albums have increased at a time when album sales have decreased.

   e. Thanks to modern technology, a greater number of bands have been able to reach a wider audience without depending on record labels.

Use the following passage to answer questions 7 and 8.

1   Astronauts expose themselves to a wide range of
2   dangers and hardships as a result of their pro-
3   fession. Space travel is itself, of course, a risky
4   endeavor. But one of the most imperceptible
5   sources of distress for astronauts is the constant
6   exposure to microgravity, a gravitational force
7   in space that is one millionth as strong as the
8   force on Earth. In prolonged space flight, aside
9   from the obvious hazards of meteors, rocky
10   debris, and radiation, astronauts have to deal
11   with muscle atrophy brought on by weightless-
12   ness caused by this microgravity. To try to coun-
13   teract this deleterious effect, astronauts engage
14   in a daily exercise regimen while in space. Effec-
15   tive workouts while in space include riding a
16   stationary bike, treadmill running while har-
17   nessed, and working against a resistive force,
18   such as a bungee cord. When they return to
19   Earth, astronauts face a protracted period of
20   weight training to rebuild their strength.

7. Which sentence in the passage best presents readers with a major point rather than a minor point of the passage?

   a. "Astronauts expose . . . profession."

   b. "Space travel . . . endeavor."

   c. "But one . . . Earth."

   d. "To try . . . space."

   e. "Effective workouts . . . cord."

8. As it appears in the passage, the word *atrophy* (line 11) most closely means

   a. pain.

   b. deterioration.

   c. weakening.

   d. cramping.

   e. augmentation.

Use the following passage to answer question 9.

Part of the United States' Bill of Rights, the Fourth Amendment to the Constitution protects citizens against unreasonable search and seizure. The amendment states that no search of a person's home or personal effects may be conducted without a written search warrant issued on probable cause. This means that a neutral judge must approve the factual basis justifying a search before it can be conducted. This process can take several days, a frustrating wait for police anxious to conduct their search.

9. This paragraph best supports the statement that the police cannot search a person's home or private papers unless they have

   a. legal authorization.

   b. direct evidence of a crime.

   c. read the person his or her constitutional rights.

   d. a reasonable belief that a crime has occurred.

   e. requested that a judge be present.

Use the following passage to answer questions 10–13.

Necessity is the first lawgiver; all the wants that had to be met by this constitution were originally of a commercial nature. Thus, the whole constitution was founded on commerce, and the laws of the nation were adapted to its pursuits. The last clause, which excluded foreigners from all offices of trust, was a natural consequence of the preceding articles. So complicated and artificial a relation between the sovereign and his people, which in many provinces was further modified according to the peculiar wants of each, and frequently of some single city, required for its maintenance the liveliest zeal for the liberties of the country, combined with an intimate acquaintance with them. From a foreigner, neither could well be expected. This law, besides, was enforced reciprocally in each particular province; so that in Brabant no Fleming, and in Zealand no Hollander could hold office; and it continued in force even after all these provinces were united under one government.

Above all others, Brabant enjoyed the highest degree of freedom. Its privileges were esteemed so valuable that many mothers from the adjacent provinces removed thither about the time of their accouchement, in order to entitle their children to participate, by birth, in all the immunities of that favored country; just as, says Strada, one improves the plants of a rude climate by removing them to the soil of a milder.

10. The author of this passage would most likely agree with which of the following assumptions?
    a. Foreigners are generally not to be trusted.
    b. Crossing borders to give birth is morally suspect.
    c. Laws, as a rule, develop in response to a need for laws.
    d. Unification is a natural tendency for smaller provinces.
    e. No person should be immune to legal restrictions.

11. Which statement, if true, would most weaken the position that foreigners are not able to hold a position of trust?
    a. People are able to study the laws of other countries through comprehensive programs designed to immerse them in the intricacies of the laws.
    b. Even many years after living in a foreign land, politicians have generally shown favoritism toward their native land.
    c. Research shows that the age of a candidate holding an office of trust has a greater influence than his or her country of origin on his or her ability to succeed.
    d. The level of distrust a population feels for a foreign-born leader or politician can rarely be eradicated.
    e. Many successful nations, such as the United States, were built on a population that mostly originated from other locations.

12. This passage can best be summarized as a
    a. defense of a thesis that increased freedom leads to more vigorous commerce.
    b. reconciliation of opposing views of constitutional development.
    c. contrast and comparison of vagaries of preunification provincial law.
    d. review of similarities and contrasts among preunification provincial laws.
    e. polemic advocating the desirability of legal reciprocity among neighboring provinces.

13. Which justification does the text provide as support for the exclusion of foreigners from all offices of trust?

    a. The laws were extremely complex, necessitating extensive familiarity with their nuances.

    b. Stringent enforcement of the laws would be impossible.

    c. Mutual distrust prevailed at this time among the various provinces.

    d. The election of foreigners to offices of trust would necessitate an unnatural unification.

    e. Opening up positions to foreigners that were previously limited to citizens could take away local job opportunities.

Use the following passage to answer questions 14–17.

1   The night and the day are not generally equal.
2   There is, however, one occasion in spring, and
3   another in autumn about half a year later, on
4   which the day and the night are each twelve
5   hours at all places on Earth. When the night
6   and day are equal, the point which the Sun
7   occupies on the heavens is termed the equinox;
8   an equinox occurs in March and then again in
9   September. In any investigation of the celestial
10   movements, the positions of these two equi-
11   noxes on the heavens are of primary impor-
12   tance. The discovery of this remarkable celestial
13   movement known as the precession of the equi-
14   noxes is attributed to the mastermind Hippar-
15   chus. The inquiry that led to his discovery
16   involved a most profound investigation, espe-
17   cially when it is remembered that in the days of
18   Hipparchus, the means of observation of the
19   heavenly bodies were only of the crudest
20   description. We can but look with astonishment
21   on the genius of the man who, in spite of such
22   difficulties, was able to detect such a phenome-
23   non as the precession, and to exhibit its actual

24   magnitude. The ingenuity of Hipparchus
25   enabled him to determine the positions of each
26   of the two equinoxes relative to the stars that lie
27   in its immediate vicinity. After examination of
28   the celestial places of these points at different
29   periods, he was led to the conclusion that each
30   equinox was moving relatively to the stars,
31   though that movement was so slow that 25,000
32   years would necessarily elapse before a com-
33   plete circuit of the heavens was accomplished.
34   It can be said of his discovery that this was the
35   first instance in the history of science in which
36   we find that combination of accurate observa-
37   tion with skillful interpretation, of which, in
38   the subsequent development of astronomy, we
39   have so many splendid examples.

14. It can be inferred from the passage that the way in which Hipparchus contributed most importantly to science was which of the following?

    a. He was the first to observe the heavens.

    b. He was first to perceive the equinoxes.

    c. He was the first to combine observation with skillful interpretation.

    d. He worked primarily with crude instruments of observation.

    e. He was the first to realize that the Earth rotates with a tilted axis around the Sun.

15. According to the passage, which is NOT a true statement about the earth's equinoxes?

    a. Day and night are equivalent in length on the equinoxes.

    b. The equinoxes fall on the same day for both the northern and southern hemispheres.

    c. It takes 25,000 years for a complete precession to occur.

    d. The distance from the Earth to the Sun is the same on the equinoxes.

    e. One equinox follows about six months after another.

16. Which best describes the general organization of the passage?
   a. Two opposing scientific theories are introduced, and then those theories are dissected.
   b. The problem of balanced sunlight is presented, and then the solution is determined.
   c. An inequality is established, and then the causes of the inequality are investigated.
   d. A scientific breakthrough is portrayed, and then the resulting effects are illustrated.
   e. A natural phenomenon is described, and then its definition and discovery are detailed.

17. In the context of the text, the word *immediate* in line 27 could be replaced with which of the following words to have the LEAST impact on what the sentence means?
   a. swift
   b. neighboring
   c. firsthand
   d. current
   e. remote

Use the following passage to answer question 18.

1   It weighs less than three pounds and is hardly
2   more interesting to look at than an overly ripe
3   cauliflower. Nevertheless, the human brain may
4   very well be the most mysterious and complex
5   object on the planet. It has created poetry and
6   music, planned and executed horrific wars, and
7   devised intricate scientific theories. It thinks
8   and dreams, plots and schemes, and easily holds
9   more information than all the libraries on
10 Earth.

18. In the context of the passage, the word *executed* (line 6) means
   a. assassinated.
   b. participated in.
   c. destroyed.
   d. joined.
   e. initiated.

Use the following passage to answer questions 19–21.

1   Geometry sets out from certain conceptions
2   such as "plane," "point," and "straight line," with
3   which we are able to associate definite ideas,
4   and from certain simple propositions (axioms)
5   which, in virtue of these ideas, we are inclined
6   to accept as "true." Then, on the basis of a logi-
7   cal process, the justification of which we feel
8   ourselves compelled to admit, all remaining
9   propositions are shown to follow from those
10 axioms, i.e., they are proven. A proposition is
11 then correct ("true") when it has been derived
12 in the recognized manner from the axioms. The
13 question of "truth" of the individual geometri-
14 cal propositions is thus reduced to one of the
15 "truth" of the axioms. Now it has long been
16 known that the last question is not only unan-
17 swerable by the methods of geometry, but that
18 it is in itself entirely without meaning. We can-
19 not ask whether it is true that only one straight
20 line goes through two points. We can only say
21 that Euclidean geometry deals with things
22 called "straight lines," to each of which is
23 ascribed the property of being uniquely deter-
24 mined by two points situated on it.

19. The author's assertion in line 18 that *it is in itself entirely without meaning* refers to
   a. geometrical propositions.
   b. the nature of straight lines.
   c. the truth of the axioms of geometry.
   d. the methods of geometry.
   e. any question of the truth of geometry.

20. It can be inferred from the passage that the truth of a geometrical proposition depends on which of the following?
   a. the concept of straight lines
   b. the validity of Euclidean geometry
   c. the logical connection of the ideas of geometry
   d. our inclination to accept it as true
   e. the truth of the axioms

21. In this passage, the author is chiefly concerned with which of the following topics?
   a. a definition of geometric axioms
   b. the truth, or lack thereof, of geometrical propositions
   c. the logical process of defining straight lines
   d. the ability to use geometrical propositions to draw conclusions
   e. the precise conceptions of objects such as planes or points.

Use the following passage to answer questions 22 and 23.

Wolfgang Amadeus Mozart's remarkable musical talent was apparent even before the age most children are able to sing a simple nursery rhyme. His father Leopold recognized his unique gifts and devoted himself to Mozart's musical education. By age five, Wolfgang had composed his first original work. By age six, when Wolfgang was not only a virtuoso harpsichord player, but also a master violin player, Wolfgang gave his first public concert. The audience was stunned, and word of his genius traveled. Leopold was soon inundated with invitations for Wolfgang to play. Leopold seized the opportunity and booked as many concerts as possible at courts throughout Europe. **A concert could last up to three hours, and Wolfgang played at least two of these concerts per day.** Today, Leopold might be considered the worst kind of stage parent, but at the time, it

was not uncommon for prodigies to make extensive concert tours. Even so, it was an exhausting schedule for a child who was just past the age of needing an afternoon nap.

22. Each of the following statements about Wolfgang Mozart is directly supported by the passage EXCEPT
   a. Mozart's father Leopold was instrumental in shaping his career.
   b. Wolfgang had the ability to play multiple instruments at a professional level.
   c. Wolfgang's childhood was devoted to his musical career.
   d. he played only the harpsichord and the violin in his career.
   e. he traveled extensively across the European continent.

23. The portion of the text in **boldface** serves what primary purpose in the passage?
   a. It provides support for Wolfgang's immense musical talent.
   b. It provides proof for Wolfgang's heavy touring schedule.
   c. It demonstrates that Leopold was justified in booking Wolfgang's concerts.
   d. It provides support that Wolfgang was mistreated as a young musician.
   e. It showed that Wolfgang was physically unhealthy.

Use the following passage to answer questions 24–30.

1   For reasons scientists haven't yet under-
2   stood but that may be related to warming water
3   temperatures or overfishing, jellyfish popula-
4   tions are swelling across the planet's oceans. For
5   swimmers and recreational divers, this is bad
6   news, as jellyfish are not only a nuisance but
7   also a potential danger. Unfortunately, jellyfish
8   offer almost no nutritional value and serve little

9   function in the seas—meaning that their
10 unpleasant population growth may be difficult
11 to curtail. However, one animal that can help is
12 the ocean sunfish. One of the most unusual-
13 looking creatures found in the oceans, the
14 mammoth and oddly-shaped ocean sunfish is
15 the heaviest bony fish ever discovered. This
16 giant fish averages more than a ton in weight,
17 and its diet consists almost entirely of jellyfish.
18 Because jellyfish contain so few nutrients, the
19 sunfish must eat the jellyfish in large quantities.
20 Though sunfish are a delicacy in some coun-
21 tries, such as Japan, the world would be better
22 served to adopt the European Union's ban on
23 the sales of all sunfish.

24. Which animal is most similar to the sunfish, in
that its diet is beneficial to human beings?
   a. spiders, whose diet includes mosquitoes and
   other insects
   b. tuna, whose diet includes squid and shellfish
   c. rhinoceros, whose diet includes grass and
   fruits
   d. grizzly bears, whose diet includes fish
   e. ticks, whose diet includes mammalian blood

25. Which description of a sunfish best represents a
statement of opinion rather than a fact?
   a. It is the largest bony fish.
   b. It eats primarily jellyfish.
   c. It has an unusual appearance.
   d. Its sale is banned in Europe.
   e. It is eaten by people.

26. Which organization best describes how the passage is structured?
   a. Two ocean creatures are compared and
   contrasted.
   b. The main idea is presented, and then
   supporting ideas provide support.
   c. A fascinating sea creature is defined, and
   then its attributes are detailed.
   d. The dietary constraints of one creature is
   listed, and then a solution is given.
   e. A distressing trend is described, and then a
   potential solution is provided.

27. In the context of the passage, the word *curtail*
(line 11) most nearly means
   a. reverse.
   b. increase.
   c. withstand.
   d. curb.
   e. liberate.

28. Which key word from the passage helps transition the passage from the negative characteristics of jellyfish to the positive attributes of
ocean sunfish?
   a. unfortunately
   b. difficult
   c. however
   d. entirely
   e. though

29. Which statement best describes the author's
attitude toward the ocean sunfish?
   a. It is not necessarily the largest creature in
   the ocean.
   b. Its population change remains a mystery to
   scientists.
   c. It should expand its diet to other non-
   jellyfish creatures to better adapt.
   d. It should be protected to help limit the
   escalation of jellyfish populations.
   e. It does not serve a valuable or important
   purpose in the oceans.

30. Which supporting idea provides the best support for the statement in the last sentence of the passage?
   a. The ocean sunfish is the largest known bony fish in the world.
   b. The increase in jellyfish populations may be related to warming waters or overfishing, but scientists are not certain.
   c. Due to the limited nutritional value of jellyfish, ocean sunfish must eat a lot of them in their diet.
   d. The ocean sunfish is an unusual-looking creature and oddly shaped.
   e. Jellyfish do not serve an important role in the oceans.

Use the following passage to answer questions 31–36.

1   The first bicycle, a fragile wooden model called
2   a *draisienne*, was invented in Germany in 1818
3   by Baron Karl de Drais de Sauerbrun. Riders
4   moved it by pushing their feet against the
5   ground. In 1839, Kirkpatrick Macmillan, a
6   Scottish blacksmith, developed an improved
7   model with tires that had iron rims to keep
8   them from getting worn down. He also used
9   foot-operated cranks, similar to pedals, as an
10 instrument to faster riding. It didn't look much
11 like the modern bicycle, though, because its
12 back wheel was substantially larger than its
13 front wheel. Although Macmillan's bicycles
14 could be ridden easily, they were never pro
15 duced in large numbers. In 1861, Pierre and
16 Ernest Michaux invented a popular bicycle
17 called a *velocipede* ("fast foot") with an
18 improved crank mechanism that connected to
19 the front wheel. Ten years later, James Starley,
20 an English inventor, made several innovations
21 that revolutionized bicycle design. He made the
22 front wheel many times larger than the back
23 wheel, put a gear on the pedals to make the
24 bicycle more efficient, and lightened the wheels

25 with wire spokes. Although this bicycle was
26 much lighter and less tiring to ride, it was still
27 clumsy and top-heavy. It wasn't until 1874 that
28 the first truly modern bicycle appeared.
29 Invented by another Englishman, H.J. Lawson,
30 the safety bicycle had equal-sized wheels, which
31 made it much less prone to toppling over. Law
32 son also attached a chain to the pedals to drive
33 the rear wheel, and, by 1893, improved the
34 bicycle further with air-filled rubber tires, a
35 diamond-shaped frame, and easy braking.

31. It can be inferred from the passage that Kirkpatrick Macmillan affected the development of the bicycle by
   a. improving the overall energy efficiency of the design.
   b. increasing the durability of the bicycle.
   c. allowing the bicycle to be ridden by the masses.
   d. making it lighter and therefore easier to ride.
   e. adjusting the size of the wheels so that the front wheel was larger.

32. Based on the information from the passage, which series of improvements to the bicycle represents the sequence of changes in chronological order?
   a. iron rims, improved crank mechanism, wire spokes, rubber tires, equal-sized wheels
   b. iron rims, gears on pedals, improved crank mechanism, equal-sized wheels, diamond-shaped frame
   c. iron rims, improved crank mechanism, wire spokes, easy braking, chain to the pedals
   d. diamond-shaped frame, easy braking, equal-sized wheels, iron rims, wire spokes
   e. iron rims, improved crank mechanism, wire spokes, equal-sized wheels, diamond-shaped frame

33. The development of the bicycle was most similar to the development of the
   a. hot-air balloon, because it helped transport passengers great distances without an engine.
   b. radio, because it improved the methods and speed of communications.
   c. space station, because its components were constructed over a period of several years.
   d. atomic bomb, because an advancement in technology allowed for the development.
   e. automobile, because its design was improved upon by many different inventors over a long period of time.

34. In the context of the passage, *instrument* (line 10) most nearly means
   a. musical mechanism.
   b. monitoring device.
   c. formal document.
   d. impediment.
   e. mechanical contraption.

35. Based on the information in the passage, which prediction for the future of bicycle development is most likely?
   a. The development of the bicycle will cease as all potential improvements have been achieved.
   b. The design will regress to the conditions of the nineteenth-century bicycle, including unequal wheel sizes.
   c. Future modifications to the bicycle will further enhance the design and specifications.
   d. Added weight to the framework design will improve stability and control.
   e. The advent of jet propulsion and safety features will allow for potential air travel.

36. Which description of a bicycle design represents a statement of opinion rather than fact?
   a. Starley's bicycle design made the bicycle clumsy to ride.
   b. Lawson's chain on the pedals drove the rear wheel of the bicycle.
   c. The inclusion of wire spokes made the bicycle lighter.
   d. A gear for the pedals made the bicycle more efficient.
   e. Pierre and Ernest Michaux invented a popular bicycle in 1861.

Use the following passage to answer question 37.

The demotion of Pluto's status in our solar system from planet to dwarf planet in 2006 was an upsetting development for many fans. After all, Pluto is shaped like the other planets—and Pluto even has its own moon! However, the recent discovery of additional celestial bodies similar to Pluto's shape and size forced scientists to agree on the definition of a planet; planets must now be round, orbit the sun, and dominate the neighborhood along its orbit through its gravitational pull.

37. Which statement, if true, would best help to explain why Pluto lost its official designation as a planet?
   a. Its size was significantly smaller than any other designated planet.
   b. Its general orbit contains a greater amount of debris in its path than the other planets.
   c. Its moon was discovered to be merely an asteroid that was captured by Pluto's gravity.
   d. Its orbit around the sun had a greater elliptical shape than the orbits of the other planets.
   e. Its mass is responsible for hydrostatic equilibrium, creating a nearly round shape.

Use the following passage to answer questions 38–40.

Considered one of the great patriots of America's early history, Patrick Henry was an outspoken leader in every protest against British tyranny and in every movement for colonial rights, openly speaking against the unfair taxation and overly burdensome regulations imposed upon the American colonists by the British Parliament. In March 1775, Patrick Henry urged his fellow Virginians to arm themselves in self-defense. He spoke boldly in Richmond, Virginia, during the meeting of the state legislature. He closed that famous speech with the immortal words, "I know not what course others may take; but as for me, give me liberty or give me death." Patrick Henry later served as the first governor of the great state of Virginia, then again as its sixth governor five years later.

38. The author provides a Patrick Henry quote from the state legislature in order to
  a. illustrate the level of bravery of one of the country's founding fathers.
  b. describe the politician as a tempestuous and fiery leader.
  c. demonstrate the leader's commitment to the struggle against oppression.
  d. provide an example of the politician's unvarying pursuit of power.
  e. exhibit the leader's prowess as a poignant orator.

39. It can be inferred from the passage that Patrick Henry was involved in which of the historic colonial or early American events?
  a. authorship of the United States Constitution
  b. participation in the American Revolution
  c. maintenance of the Stamp Act
  d. appeal of the Bill of Rights
  e. secession of the Confederacy

40. Which statement best describes the primary purpose of the passage?
  a. to define the events leading up to the American Revolution
  b. to describe the role one man had in the formation of his country
  c. to compare Patrick Henry with the other great patriots of the time
  d. to illustrate the staying power and impact of a well-constructed quotation
  e. to examine the British injustices that led directly to the Revolution

Skills Test in Mathematics

1. In Mr. Cortez's swim class, $\frac{1}{5}$ of the students are age nine, and the remaining students are age eight. Once students can tread water for two minutes they are said to be "guppy" level; age is not a factor in this test. $\frac{1}{8}$ of all the students have reached this level. What is the best estimate of the fraction of students in this class that are eight-year-old "guppies"?
  a. $\frac{1}{40}$
  b. $\frac{2}{13}$
  c. $\frac{1}{10}$
  d. $\frac{5}{13}$
  e. $\frac{13}{40}$

2. Approximately 9.8 million people live in Los Angeles County, according to the U.S. Census Bureau. One source believes that there are approximately 1.8 cars per person in Los Angeles County. Given this information, what is the best estimate of the total number of cars in Los Angeles County?
  a. 17,640
  b. 176,400
  c. 1,764,000
  d. 17,640,000
  e. 176,400,000

Use the following table to answer questions 3–5.

CITY OF HULE 911 CALL FREQUENCY		
MONTH	911 CALLS	POLICE DISPATCHED
May	213	66
June	194	70
July	257	61
August	267	79
September	279	70
October	308	68

3. What was the average (arithmetic mean) of 911 calls in Hule for the six months listed in the table?
   a. 262
   b. 253
   c. 308
   d. 79
   e. 69

4. When a call comes in to the police, they decide whether they need to dispatch an officer. On average, what is the closest estimate of the percentage of incoming 911 calls for which the police were dispatched over the six-month period in the table?
   a. 10%
   b. 25%
   c. 50%
   d. 75%
   e. 90%

5. The data in the table supports which of the following conclusions?
   a. The city of Hule has a high crime rate.
   b. October is always a high crime month.
   c. 911 call frequency tended to increase over the period range shown.
   d. The number of 911 calls can be used to predict how many times police will be dispatched.
   e. The police usually dispatch an officer when a call comes in.

6. The first four terms of a series are given below. What will the seventh term of this series be?
   $-5x, -2x - 2, x - 4, 4x - 6 \ldots$
   a. $7x - 8$
   b. $10x - 10$
   c. $10x - 12$
   d. $13x + 10$
   e. $13x - 12$

Use the following table to answer question 7.

DISTANCE TRAVELED FROM CHICAGO WITH RESPECT TO TIME	
TIME (HOURS)	DISTANCE FROM CHICAGO (MILES)
1	60
2	120
3	180
4	240

7. A train moving at a constant speed leaves Chicago for Los Angeles at time $t = 0$. If Los Angeles is 2,000 miles from Chicago, which of the following equations describes the distance from Los Angeles at any time t?
   a. $D(t) = 60t - 2{,}000$
   b. $D(t) = 60t$
   c. $D(t) = 2{,}000 - 60t$
   d. $D(t) = 60 - 2{,}000t$
   e. $D(t) = 2{,}000t - 60t$

8. Parker spends eight hours a day in the office. If $\frac{5}{12}$ of her workday is spent answering e-mails, how much time does she spend doing other things?

   a. 4 hours and 40 minutes
   b. 5 hours and 20 minutes
   c. 3 hours and 20 minutes
   d. 4 hours and 20 minutes
   e. 5 hours and 40 minutes

9. A rug weaver is making a rope rug. He has 100 meters of rope. How many pieces will he have if he cuts the rope into 50-centimeter lengths?

   a. 2
   b. 20
   c. 200
   d. 2,000
   e. 5,000

10. Summit County Mortgage is offering a refinance rate of $4\frac{3}{4}\%$. What decimal equivalent of $4\frac{3}{4}\%$ would be used to figure out how much the interest would be on a loan from Summit County Mortgage?

    a. 4.34
    b. 0.434
    c. 0.0434
    d. 0.475
    e. 0.0475

11. There is an express train from Chicago that can travel 180 miles in just 150 minutes. What is the average speed of the train in miles per hour?

    a. 120 miles per hour
    b. 30 miles per hour
    c. 90 miles per hour
    d. 72 miles per hour
    e. 75 miles per hour

12. Maddie's soccer team used three different colors for their socks: maroon socks for tournaments, gold socks for away league games, and white socks for home league games. Maddie owns two pairs of tournament socks, three pairs for away league games, and four pairs for home league games, but she is terrible about matching or folding them and just stuffs them all into a drawer. If she grabs a sock at random from her sock drawer, what is the probability that it will NOT be white?

    a. $\frac{5}{9}$
    b. $\frac{4}{9}$
    c. $\frac{2}{3}$
    d. $\frac{7}{9}$
    e. $\frac{5}{18}$

13. In the United States, the yearly average is 15 births for every 1,000 people. Which of the following proportions can be used to determine x, the total number of births expected in one year if the population is 301,000,000?

    a. $\frac{15}{10} = \frac{x}{301,000,000}$
    b. $\frac{15}{1,000} = \frac{301,000,000}{x}$
    c. $\frac{1}{15} = \frac{x}{301,000,000}$
    d. $\frac{1}{15} = \frac{301,000,000}{x}$
    e. $\frac{15}{1,000} = \frac{x}{301,000,000}$

14. Which fraction has the largest value?

    a. $\frac{11}{100}$

    b. $\frac{6}{50}$

    c. $\frac{7}{25}$

    d. $\frac{23}{200}$

    e. $\frac{1}{10}$

15. For \$2, a person can throw 3 balls at a dunk-tank target in an attempt to dunk whoever is sitting on the platform. All proceeds from the dunk tank go to the police department. Of the 252 balls thrown at the target while Police Chief Hector Bailey was on the platform, only 12 resulted in a dunking. On average, how much money was spent for each dunking?

    a. \$21.00

    b. \$14.00

    c. \$16.80

    d. \$10.50

    e. \$7.00

16. If R is divisible by 4, S is divisible by 5, and B is divisible by 3, then any multiple of RBS must be divisible by all the following EXCEPT

    a. 6.

    b. 8.

    c. 10.

    d. 12.

    e. 15.

17. What is the area, in square units, of the following figure drawn on the coordinate grid?

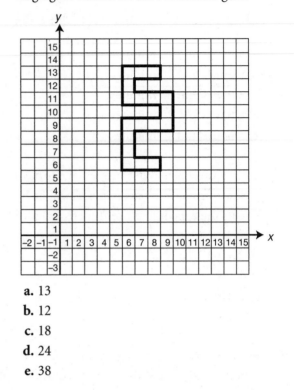

    a. 13

    b. 12

    c. 18

    d. 24

    e. 38

18. If $H = 2w$, and $G = 3w - 1$, then what will the value of $5H - 4G$ be in terms of w?

    a. $-2w + 4$

    b. $-2w - 4$

    c. $2w + 4$

    d. $2w$

    e. $-2w$

19. Vinyl records at Joe's music store cost between $7 and $20. The table below shows the number of records sold during a period of four days. Which inequality represents the sales, not including tax, of records at Joe's store during those four days?

DAY OF THE WEEK	NUMBER OF RECORDS SOLD
Monday	15
Tuesday	20
Wednesday	10
Thursday	15

a. $\$0 \leq s \leq \$60$
b. $\$7 \leq s \leq \$20$
c. $\$70 \leq s \leq \$400$
d. $\$70 \leq s \leq \$1,200$
e. $\$420 \leq s \leq \$1,200$

20. A rectangular yard is 30 feet wide. The length of the yard is $\frac{4}{3}$ the width. If Jeannie wants to hang a clothing line diagonally across the yard, how many feet of line will Jeannie need?
a. 35 feet
b. $\sqrt{70}$ feet
c. 50 feet
d. 70 feet
e. 40 feet

21. The following bar graph represents a shoe store's sneaker sales over a four-month period. What would be the correct frequency distribution table for the data illustrated?

a.

MONTH	FREQUENCY
March	7,000
April	17,000
May	32,000
June	42,000

b.

MONTH	FREQUENCY
March	7,000
April	10,000
May	15,000
June	10,000

c.

MONTH	FREQUENCY
March	$\frac{7}{42}$
April	$\frac{17}{42}$
May	$\frac{32}{42}$
June	$\frac{42}{42}$

d.

MONTH	FREQUENCY
March	7,000
April	10,000
May	15,000
June	25,000

e. None of the above frequency distribution tables is correct.

22. Given the following truth statement, which other statement below must be true? "If Sierra visits for the weekend, then Stan will be happy."

    a. If Sierra does not visit for the weekend, then Stan will not be happy.

    b. If Stan is not happy, then Sierra visited for the weekend.

    c. If Sierra can go away for the weekend, then she will be happy.

    d. If Sierra visits for a week, then Stan will be happier.

    e. If Stan is not happy, Sierra did not visit.

23. A pole which casts a 15-foot-long shadow stands near an 8-foot-high stop sign. If the shadow cast by the sign is 3 feet long, how high is the pole?

    a. $5\frac{5}{8}$ feet

    b. 28 feet

    c. 30 feet

    d. 40 feet

    e. 45 feet

24. Inside which of the following two-dimensional shapes does a point exist that is equidistant to all the points on the perimeter of the shape?

    a. equilateral triangle

    b. square

    c. regular pentagon

    d. circle

    e. no shape exists that contains a point that is equidistant to all the points on the perimeter of the shape

25. The main fish tank at the East Point Aquarium is shaped like a rectangular prism. The tank is 10 feet deep, 24 feet wide, and 40 feet long. If the tank contains 4,660 cubic feet of water, how many more cubic feet of water must be added to completely fill the tank?

    a. 9,600 ft.^{3}

    b. 14,260 ft.^{3}

    c. 4,660 ft.^{3}

    d. 5,000 ft.^{3}

    e. 4,940 ft.^{3}

26. What is the final answer when 0.08 is multiplied by 475, and then that product is divided by 6?

    a. $6\frac{1}{3}$

    b. 228

    c. 6.2

    d. $\frac{190}{3}$

    e. 38

27. The angles of a four-sided polygon are in the ratio 1:2:2:4. What is the measure, in degrees, of the largest angle?

    a. 40°

    b. 120°

    c. 80°

    d. 160°

    e. 360°

28. The Huntington Cottage Grove Inn charges $1.50 for the first minute of an outgoing call and 60¢ for every additional minute of the call. If Terry makes a call for m minutes, which of the following equations accurately represents the cost of the call in terms of c dollars?

    a. $c = 60(m) + 1.50$

    b. $c = 0.60(m) + 1.50$

    c. $c = 0.60(m - 1) + 1.50$

    d. $m = 0.60(c - 1) + 1.50$

    e. $c = 60(m - 1) + 1.50$

29. Twenty slips of paper, numbered 1 through 20, are placed in a bag. If one slip of paper is drawn at random from the bag, what is the probability that a multiple of three is written on the paper?

  a. $\frac{1}{3}$

  b. $\frac{3}{10}$

  c. $\frac{3}{20}$

  d. $\frac{1}{10}$

  e. $\frac{1}{20}$

30. The following graph shows a solution to a system of two equations. Use the graph to determine which point is a solution to the system of equations.

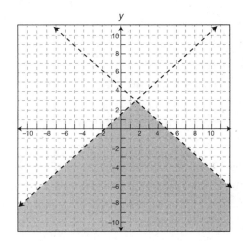

  a. (0,3)

  b. (−4,0)

  c. (−4,−3)

  d. (5,0)

  e. (0,2)

31. The following table shows the scores for four players on a high school golf team over a three-day period.

NAME	DAY 1	DAY 2	DAY 3
Randy	98	89	94
Monica	87	92	90
Erin	81	81	80
Maria	75	79	79

  a. The team shot approximately the same overall score each day.

  b. The team scores got lower over the three days.

  c. The team scores got higher over the three days.

  d. The team was inconsistent.

  e. Monica is the best golfer.

32. If Carmen biked a distance of 18,480 feet, how many miles did she travel? (There are 5,280 feet in a mile.)

  a. 3 miles

  b. $3\frac{1}{4}$ miles

  c. $3\frac{2}{3}$ miles

  d. 3.264 miles

  e. $3\frac{1}{2}$ miles

33. What is the estimated product when both 162 and 849 are rounded to the nearest hundred and then multiplied?

  a. 160,000

  b. 180,000

  c. 16,000

  d. 1,000

  e. 128,000

34. Let the operation "#" be defined as follows:

When $a \le 5$, a # b represents $a^2 - 3b$

When $a > 5$, a # b represents $2a + b$.

Find the value of (5 # 6) # 3.

  a. 7

  b. 17

  c. 16

  d. 35

  e. 90

35. Loretta bought a DVD player for $77. She bought the DVD player on sale for 30% off the original price. What was the original price of the DVD player?

  a. $47.00

  b. $107.00

  c. $110.00

  d. $100.10

  e. $256.00

36. In isosceles triangle *VIC*, $\angle V$ is the vertex. If $\angle V$ is three times as large as each of the base angles, then what is the sum of one of the base angles and the vertex?

  a. 142°

  b. 36°

  c. 72°

  d. 108°

  e. 60°

The following graph shows the amount of money in a savings account over four years. Use it to answer questions 37 and 38.

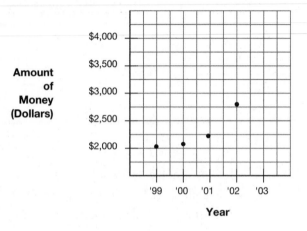

37. Between which two years was the growth in savings the largest?

  a. between 1998 and 1999

  b. between 1999 and 2000

  c. between 2000 and 2001

  d. between 2001 and 2002

  e. cannot be determined from this graph

38. Assuming that the growth trend shown in the graph will continue, what is a reasonable prediction for the amount of money in the account in 2003?

  a. $2,800

  b. $3,000

  c. $3,800

  d. $8,000

  e. $10,000

39. The following table shows several pairs of x and y values. Which equation represents the relationship shown in the table?

x	y
2	6
4	18
6	38
8	66
10	102

a. $y = x + 4$
b. $y = x^2 + 2$
c. $y = 2x + 2$
d. $y = 3x$
e. $y = 10x + 2$

40. On an exam, Bart is asked to choose two ways to determine $n\%$ of 40. He is given these four choices:

I. $n \div 100 \times 40$
II. $(n \times 0.01) \times 40$
III. $(n \times 100) \div 40$
IV. $(n \div 0.01) \times 40$

Which two ways are correct?

a. I and II
b. I and IV
c. II and III
d. II and IV
e. III and IV

Skills Test in Writing

Section 1, Part A

Directions: Choose the letter for the underlined portion that contains a grammatical error. If there is no error in the sentence, choose **e**.

1. <u>Following a honeymoon</u> in the <u>Pocono Mountains</u>, the <u>couple were</u> eager <u>to settle</u> into a new
        a   **b**   **c**   **d**
routine. <u>No error</u>
      e

2. The <u>student's</u> mind went <u>blank, he</u> could not think of anything appropriate to write about when <u>he got</u>
     a   **b**   **c**
to the essay part <u>of the test.</u> <u>No error</u>
         d   **e**

3. Startled by the <u>barking, the</u> chicken ran <u>quick</u> into <u>its</u> coop for shelter as the hopeful dog <u>plummeted</u>
            a   **b**   **c**   **d**
up the hill. <u>No error</u>
        e

4. Saturday was the <u>33rd running</u> of the <u>Freihofer's Run for Women</u> in <u>Albany, New York;</u> over 4,000
              a   **b**   **c**
<u>women ran</u> in the 5-kilometer race. <u>No error</u>
 d   **e**

5. <u>In my opinion</u>, Norman Rockwell, <u>who's</u> work chronicled the times, <u>was</u> an illustrator <u>of</u>
    a   **b**   **c**
<u>tremendous ingenuity and energy.</u> <u>No error</u>
            d   **e**

6. Several landscape <u>designers</u> submitted bids on the shopping mall <u>project, and</u> the property owner
              a   **b**
awarded the contract to the designer <u>whose</u> proposal was <u>less expensiver</u> than all the rest. <u>No error</u>
                         c   **d**   **e**

7. <u>Ruby, a robot</u> invented at <u>Melbourne's</u> Swinburne University, recently completed a <u>Rubik's</u> cube in
  a   **b**   **c**
<u>10.18 seconds.</u> <u>No error</u>
  d   **e**

8. The record time for solving a Rubik's cube <u>is</u> held by a <u>14-year-old</u> male named Feliks Zemdegs,
                                a   **b**
who <u>affectively</u> completed the puzzle in 6.77 seconds on <u>November 13, 2010.</u> <u>No error</u>
   c   **d**   **e**

9. There are many types of extreme sports, <u>such like</u> slacklining, a sport of <u>daredevil</u> proportions
a b

<u>in which</u> athletes walk and tumble across nylon webbing that has been stretched across <u>a cavern</u> and
c d

anchored on each end. <u>No error</u>
e

10. Either the <u>physicians or</u> the hospital administrator <u>are</u> going to have to make a decision to <u>ensure</u> the
a b c

<u>fair</u> treatment of patients. <u>No error</u>
d e

11. When the owner returned from a <u>week's</u> vacation to pick up his dog at the <u>kennel,</u> the terrier wagged
a b

<u>it's</u> tail to and fro with excitement <u>and licked</u> the owner's face from ear to ear. <u>No error</u>
c d e

12. There were three wedding gowns that she liked <u>more</u> <u>than</u> all the others she tried on, but the <u>more</u>
a b c

ornate gown with the inlaid pearls was the one she thought she liked <u>best.</u> <u>No error</u>
d e

13. Contestants in the Scripps <u>national spelling bee</u> watched <u>eighth-grader</u> Sukanya Roy from
a b

Pennsylvania win the spelling <u>bee's</u> coveted trophy and $40,000 in <u>college scholarship funds.</u> <u>No error</u>
c d e

14. The soil that composes the giant ant hills found in Zambia <u>is</u> often used to make <u>bricks;</u> the ants
a b

excavate the clay from below ground level and bring <u>them</u> to the top of the <u>earth.</u> <u>No error</u>
c d e

15. Growing up, Kate Middleton <u>was</u> an excellent student in school, <u>was</u> very athletic, and some day
a b

<u>becomes</u> <u>British</u> royalty. <u>No error</u>
c d e

16. I think I will do <u>good</u> on my final exam because I am <u>confident</u> that I am <u>well prepared,</u>
a b c

rested, and relaxed <u>going into</u> the classroom. <u>No error</u>
d e

17. The <u>new,</u> exhausted <u>parents</u> <u>have watched</u> television when the baby <u>began</u> to cry in the next
a b c d

room. <u>No error</u>
e

18. Violent <u>storms</u> pounded the <u>capital region</u> causing widespread damage to homes and trees,
             a   b

    <u>but yet</u> no human deaths were caused <u>by</u> the severe weather. <u>No error</u>
     c   d   e

19. The new MyPlate icon promoted by the <u>U.S. Department of Agriculture</u> has dismantled the
                                              a

    <u>Food Guide Pyramid</u> that once assisted <u>Americans</u> in their quest to eat a <u>well-balanced</u> diet. <u>No error</u>
        b   c   d   e

20. My father had an antique 1957 Studebaker <u>Transtar</u> pickup truck with a wide-mouthed <u>grille, and</u> I
                                  a   b

    remember riding in the cab with my <u>dad</u> as the old engine <u>noisily</u> sputtered. <u>No error</u>
                                c   d   e

21. Although e-readers have been on the market for only a few <u>years,</u> the managers of Amazon.com report
                                                   a

    <u>they</u> sell <u>more</u> e-books <u>then</u> all print books combined. <u>No error</u>
     b   c   d   e

Section 1, Part B

Directions: Choose the best replacement for the underlined portion of the sentence. If no revision is necessary, choose **a**, which always repeats the original phrasing.

22. My <u>father who is an avid gardener</u> is teaching me everything I need to know about raising deliciously tasty tomatoes.
    a. father who is an avid gardener
    b. father, who is an avid gardener
    c. father who is an avid gardener,
    d. father, who is an avid gardener,
    e. father, whom is an avid gardener,

23. The students <u>can't hardly</u> believe there are only 23 school days left before summer vacation.
    a. can't hardly
    b. cannot hardly
    c. can hardly
    d. who can't hardly
    e. whom can hardly

24. When elementary school-aged children were asked what health goals they would like an adult's help to achieve, they responded they would like adults to <u>help them learn how to cook, getting additional exercise, and eating healthy foods.</u>
    a. help them learn how to cook, getting additional exercise, and eating healthy foods.
    b. help them learn how to cook, help them get additional exercise, and help them eat healthy foods.
    c. helping them learn how to cook, getting additional exercise, and eating healthy foods.
    d. help them learn how to cook, get additional exercise, and eat healthy foods.
    e. help them learning how to cook, getting additional exercise, and eating healthy foods.

25. Would <u>he or me</u> be a better bowling partner?
    a. he or me
    b. him or me
    c. him or I
    d. he or I
    e. him or he

26. The committee threw <u>we retirees</u> a huge end-of-the-year party.
   a. we retirees
   b. us retirees
   c. them retirees
   d. those retirees
   e. retirees we

27. The promotional staff had <u>less innovative ideas</u> than the marketing staff.
   a. less innovative ideas
   b. less innovative idea
   c. fewer innovative ideas
   d. fewer innovative idea
   e. fewer innovation ideas

28. In the <u>past, Dawn hadn't liked the taste of coffee, so she passed</u> on the tiramisu dessert after dinner.
   a. past, Dawn hadn't liked the taste of coffee, so she passed
   b. passed Dawn hadn't liked the taste of coffee, so she passed
   c. passed Dawn hadn't liked the taste of coffee, so she past
   d. past Dawn hadn't liked the taste of coffee, so she past
   e. past Dawn hadn't liked the taste of coffee so she past

29. We were missing <u>a vital piece of information:</u> the timeline, the expense report, and the list of participants.
   a. a vital piece of information:
   b. a vital piece of information;
   c. vital pieces of information:
   d. vital pieces of information;
   e. vital piece of information:

30. The dates we are considering for our annual party are <u>Thursday, January 13; Friday, January 14; and January 15, Saturday.</u>
   a. Thursday, January 13; Friday, January 14; and January 15, Saturday.
   b. Thursday January 13, Friday January 14, and January 15 Saturday.
   c. Thursday January 13; Friday January 14; and January 15 Saturday.
   d. Thursday, January 13; January 15, Saturday; and January 14, Friday.
   e. Thursday, January 13; Friday, January 14; and Saturday, January 15.

31. <u>While cleaning up after dinner, the phone rang.</u>
   a. While cleaning up after dinner, the phone rang.
   b. While I was cleaning up after dinner, the phone rang.
   c. The phone rang while cleaning up after dinner.
   d. The phone cleaned up after dinner.
   e. While I was cleaning up, the phone rang after dinner.

32. The <u>number of hours</u> we have for this telethon has been reduced.
   a. number of hours
   b. numbers of hours
   c. numbers of hour
   d. amount of hours
   e. amount of hour

33. The warehouse <u>doesn't have no</u> surplus stock at this time.
   a. doesn't have no
   b. does have no
   c. doesn't have any
   d. does have any
   e. doesn't has any

34. The swimmer explained how to do the back-stroke in the subway.
  a. The swimmer explained how to do the backstroke in the subway.
  b. The swimmer explain how to do the backstroke in the subway.
  c. The swimmers explains how to do the backstroke in the subway.
  d. The swimmer in the subway explained how to do the backstroke.
  e. The swimmer in the subway explain how to do the backstroke.

35. The new keyboard looked strangely to me.
  a. looked strangely
  b. look strange
  c. looking strangely
  d. looking strange
  e. looked strange

36. During our brake, we noticed a break in the pipeline.
  a. brake, we noticed a break
  b. brakes, we noticed brakes
  c. breaks, we noticed brakes
  d. break, we noticed a break
  e. brake, we noticed a brake

37. Flooding several major cities along the banks of the Mississippi River.
  a. Flooding several major cities along the banks of the Mississippi River.
  b. Several major cities along the banks of the Mississippi River flooded.
  c. Floods several major cities along the banks of the Mississippi River.
  d. Along the banks of the Mississippi River, flooding several major cities.
  e. Several major cities caused flooding along the banks of the Mississippi River.

38. The massage therapist felt gently along the patient's spine.
  a. felt gently
  b. felt gentle
  c. feel gentle
  d. feel gently
  e. fell gently

Section 2, Essay Writing

Carefully read the essay topic that follows. Plan and write an essay that addresses all points in the topic. Make sure that your essay is well organized and that you support your central argument with concrete examples. Allow 30 minutes for your essay.

Should high school students be required to pass a standardized test to graduate? Some think the best way to make students and schools responsible is to create graduation-determining tests. They believe students will take their coursework more seriously. Others feel these tests will do nothing to improve education in America but will instead do much to worsen it as teachers "teach to the test" and schools' populations explode with seniors who do not pass the test. In your essay, take a position either supporting or condemning these graduation tests. Be sure to support your position with logical arguments and specific examples.

Answers

Skills Test in Reading

1. d. The author's main point in this passage is to set forth the need to investigate the ecological status of Pará and the means by which the investigation should proceed. The flora and fauna of Guiana are distinct from the flora and fauna of Brazil. However, the fauna and flora of Pará are not necessarily distinct; the passage even asks whether the species in the Pará district are identical, modified, or peculiar to the species of the other regions. Therefore, choice **a** is incorrect. The passage states that Guiana and Brazil support a very large number of ecologically distinct habitats, but it does not make this claim definitively about Pará, making choice **b** incorrect. The focus of the passage is not about the overriding importance of Pará's ecological considerations, and there is no support in the passage to make the claim that Pará's government has not been supportive of expeditions; therefore, choices **c** and **e** are incorrect.

2. c. The physical description in this answer choice is not correct for Para, though it is correct for both Guiana and Brazil. The first sentence of the passage describes both Guiana and Brazil as ecologically distinct provinces. Because this is a true statement, choice **a** cannot be correct. The passage says that both Guiana and Brazil are centers of distribution for the dissemination of species into Pará, so choice **b** is not correct. It can be concluded from the passage that Para lies in between Guiana and Brazil, with Brazil to the south. Therefore, choice **d** is not correct. Both Guiana and Brazil are listed as a center of distribution in the latest process of dissemination of species over the surface of tropical America. Pará lies in between them, so it would also belong to tropical America; this means choice **e** is incorrect as well.

3. b. The author suggests evaluating Pará to see if it "contains so large a number of endemic species as would warrant the conclusion that it is itself an independent province." The species in an area determines whether it is a distinct province, not the area's geographical features, so choice **a** is incorrect. The passage does not indicate that it is a district's proximity that determines whether it is distinct, so choice **c** is incorrect. It is not the number of *identical* species that determines if a province is distinct, so choice **d** is incorrect. The species that are endemic to the district determine whether the province is distinct, so choice **e** is incorrect.

4. c. The author shows support for the statement in choice **c** in the anecdote about the group of laughing travelers on the railway; because you were not part of the group and were apart from the intended audience, you lacked a connection and did not find the humor funny. The final sentence in the text ("many comic effects are incapable of translation from one language to another …") support the role listed in choice **b**, but the railway anecdote not does relate specifically to the customs and ideas of a society. The statement provided in choice **a** is contradicted throughout the passage and therefore could not be correct. Because the author is not using the anecdote to show that laughter is spontaneous or that proximity affects the humor, choices **d** and **e** are incorrect.

5. a. The adverb *rapturously* as it appears on line 6 describes how the travelers in the railway carriage are laughing. You need to examine the surrounding context to determine *how* they are laughing specifically. The word *for* can be replaced with the word *because*, meaning that the travelers laughed *rapturously* because of "stories which must have been comic to them." If the stories must have been comic, then it was truly funny. Laughing *sanguinely* means laughing joyfully. The travelers' laughter is true because the context of the sentence states that they were laughing at something comic. They would not be laughing *painfully*, so choice **b** is incorrect. Laughing *morosely* would mean laughing miserably, which would be a difficult situation in almost any context. There is no indication of any morose context in the sentence, so choice **c** is incorrect. The travelers are laughing at something comical in the train car. Nothing in the context of the sentence or surrounding sentences would suggest that they would be laughing *awkwardly*, so choice **d** is incorrect. To laugh *hilariously* would mean a funny way of laughing. The travelers may have been laughing because of something hilarious, but that does not mean the same thing as laughing hilariously, so choice **e** is incorrect.

6. c. The record companies claim that bands have sold fewer albums at record stores, cutting into the musicians' profits. But if this statement were true, then bands would be able to generate more income through paths other than record store sales. Furthermore, by selling their albums directly to the fans through a website, musicians can earn a greater amount per album sold instead of traditionally selling the albums at a record store. The fact that some users of illegal file-sharing sites may have been sued would not influence the musicians' earning potentials, so choice **a** is incorrect. While it may be true that additional touring results in additional revenue for the musicians, it is still true that musicians are earning significantly less money through their album sales. There is a better choice than choice **b**. If the statement in choice **d** were true, it would not significantly weaken the companies' argument. Perhaps the higher gas costs resulted in higher album prices, but that still would not affect the main argument that fewer album sales are negatively impacting musicians' abilities to support themselves. The fact that bands may be able to reach out to a wider audience does not necessarily mean that they are able to earn more money, so it does not damage the producer's argument. Illegal downloads may expose more people to a band, but the musicians in the band may still not be able to support themselves or their families. Therefore, choice **e** is not correct either.

7. c. The main point of the passage is the effect of microgravity on astronauts. This third sentence of the passage both introduces microgravity to the reader and describes it as an imperceptible source of distress for astronauts. The initial sentence of the passage, choice **a**, makes a general claim about the difficulties of life as an astronaut. However, the passage is not merely about these difficulties, but it is specifically about one particular danger: microgravity and its effects. The fact that space travel is a risky endeavor, choice **b**, is not the main point of the passage. This sentence serves to point out the obvious, but it is the following sentence— which serves to contrast this apparent fact— that better sums up the main point of the passage. The main point of the passage is not the astronauts' attempts to counteract the negative effects of microgravity or a list of astronauts' workouts, so choices **d** and **e** are incorrect.

8. b. Atrophy represents *deterioration*, frequently in response to underuse. When in space, muscles adapt to the lack of gravity and lose their strength through deterioration. There is no indication in the passage that atrophied muscles cause the astronauts any amount of *pain*, so choice **a** is incorrect. Although a muscle that atrophies may be *weakened*, the primary meaning of the phrase *to atrophy* is *to waste away* or *deteriorate*, making choice **c** incorrect. The passage does not suggest that astronauts' muscles *cramp* during space flight, so choice **d** is not correct. An *augmentation* means an increase or an expansion. This is the opposite effect that microgravity has on astronauts' muscles, so choice **e** is not correct either.

9. a. The second and third sentences combine to give support to choice **a**. None of the other choices provides ample reason for a search, according to the passage. Choice **b** is incorrect because the passage suggests that it is not enough for the police to have direct evidence of a crime; legal authorization is still required. Criminal suspects in police custody must be read their rights, but that is not the same as reading the constitutional rights before searching a home (choice **c**). The passage makes no mention of reading rights in order to conduct a search. It is not merely enough for the police to have direct evidence or a reasonable belief, so choice **d** is not correct. The statement in choice **e** is not mentioned in the passage, so it cannot be correct either.

10. c. The assertion that laws develop in response to a need for laws is contained in the first sentence of the passage and further supported in the second sentence. Choice **a** is incorrect; while the author explicitly argues that foreigners should not hold a position of offices of trust, the reason is not simply because they are "not to be trusted." The author provides the example of children being born in a different province "to entitle their children to participate," but he or she gives no clear indication as to whether such a practice is or is not morally suspect, so choice **b** is incorrect. The author gives no indication that unification is a natural tendency for smaller provinces, making choice **d** incorrect. The statement in choice **e** may seem like something the author might agree with, given that the author supports foreigners' exclusion from holding offices of trust. However, it is a leap to assume that he or she would necessarily agree that just because foreigners should not hold an office of trust, no person should be immune to legal restrictions. It is beyond the scope of the passage.

11. a. One reason the author provides as to why foreigners cannot hold offices of trust is because they cannot be as familiar with the laws as natural-born citizens. However, such a program described in this choice might eliminate this unfamiliarity, thus weakening the author's argument. Choices **b** and **d** are incorrect because either would *strengthen* the author's position; they would provide further evidence that foreigners should not hold offices of trust. The fact in choice **c** might weaken the author's argument slightly—by suggesting that age is an even greater factor in a person's ability to hold an office of trust—but it does not say that being born abroad is not still a factor. A better choice more significantly weakens the argument. The overly general statement in choice **e** does not address the specific issues that the author raises in regard to a foreigner's ability to hold an office of trust. While this point may help weaken the argument somewhat, there is a more specific statement that weakens the argument more significantly.

12. d. The author discusses the laws of pre-unified European provinces, specifically pointing out similarities and differences, such as that certain laws were enforced in each province but that other provinces were so free that mothers moved there before giving birth to earn the immunities of that land. The passage does not defend the argument that increased freedom leads to increased commerce, so choice **a** is incorrect. Choice **b** is incorrect: This passage discusses the origins of provincial law in pre-unified Europe, but the only mention of a constitution is to suggest that it was founded on commerce. Choice **c** is incorrect. To know that this choice is incorrect requires you to know the meaning of the word *vagaries,* which connotes capriciousness and does not apply to the author's discussion of legal development in the provinces. Choice **e** is incorrect; the reciprocity amounts in neighboring provinces is mentioned in this passage in regard to the rights of foreigners holding office. However, this specific attribute of the law—or the advocacy of its desirability—is *not* the main point of the passage.

13. a. The first three sentences set up and support the discussion of the exclusion of foreigners from office. In that section of the passage, it is mentioned that a foreigner could not be expected to be acquainted with these unnecessarily complicated laws, meaning that choice **a** is correct. The end of the first paragraph refers to the reciprocity of the laws across provinces, suggesting that the laws would need to be enforced. But that did not say that enforcement would be *impossible,* making choice **b** incorrect. Even though foreigners were excluded from holding office, the passage does not provide *distrust,* choice **c,** as a cause of the exclusion. Neither a necessary unification nor a potential job loss is given as support for the main idea, so choices **d** and **e** are both incorrect.

14. c. This passage discusses Hipparchus's discovery of the equinoxes. The final sentence in the passage sums up the importance in terms of the discovery's contribution to science, saying that it was the "first instance in the history of science" in which observation was combined with such skillful interpretation. Hipparchus observed the heavens as part of his investigation, but the passage does not suggest that he was the *first* to do this, making choice **a** incorrect. The statement in choice **b** is not supported by the passage; Hipparchus may have discovered the equinoxes and determined the magnitude of its precession, but he was not the first to perceive them. The passage states that Hipparchus used crude instruments, but this statement is not given to describe his most important contribution to the sciences, so choice **d** is incorrect. The statement in choice **e** is not a contribution made by Hipparchus, at least not as mentioned in the given passage. The Earth's tilt may cause the seasons, but that is not mentioned in the passage, nor is Hipparchus given the credit for the contribution.

15. d. The passage makes no statement about the distance from the Sun to the Earth on the equinoxes, so there is no support for the statement in choice **d**. The passage begins with the statement that day and night are not generally equal. However, it then states that the day and night *are* equal on the equinoxes, making choice **a** incorrect. By suggesting that this occurs "at all places on Earth," the passage indicates that the equinoxes fall on the same day for both hemispheres. While the spring equinox occurs in the northern hemisphere in March and the southern hemisphere in September, the two general equinoxes both share the same day on Earth. Therefore, choice **b** is also incorrect. Hipparchus discovered that the equinox was moving relatively to the stars, but that it would take 25,000 years to complete a precession, making choice **c** incorrect. Because the equinoxes are separated by "half a year" in the passage, choice **e** must be incorrect as well.

16. e. The passage begins with a description of the phenomenon of the equinoxes, then the passage goes on to define the term "equinox" and explain its discovery by Hipparchus. The passage does not begin with an introduction of opposing scientific theories or a problem, so choices **a** and **b** are incorrect. Likewise, the passage does not begin with a scientific breakthrough, so choice **d** cannot be correct. Choice **c** mentions an inequality, which could describe the unequal day and night, but it is not the inequality but the equality—the equivalent day and night on the equinoxes—that the passage focuses on, making choice **c** incorrect.

17. b. The word *immediate* in the sentence is being used to describe the nearby stars that are adjacent to the area of the equinoxes. The words in choices **a**, **c**, and **d** could each be used to replace the word *immediate* in different sentences, but they would impact the meaning of the sentence from this passage. Therefore, each is incorrect. *Remote*, choice **e**, nearly means the opposite of the word *immediate* as it appears in this passage, so it is not correct either.

18. e. The sentence in the passage is suggesting that the human brain is responsible for horrific wars. Therefore, the word *executed* most nearly means that it began, or *initiated*, those wars. The word *executed* often means *assassinated*, but it does not have this meaning in the context of this passage, so choice **a** is incorrect. Choice **b** is also incorrect; it may be true that people—and their brains—have *participated in* wars, but that is not the meaning of *executed* in the given sentence. Choices **c** and **d** are incorrect. The human brain is not responsible for *destroying* or *joining* horrific wars, at least not in terms of the context of the passage.

19. c. To answer this question, you have to find the antecedent of *it*. First, you discover that *it* refers to *the last question*. Then you must trace back to realize that *the last question* itself refers to *the "truth" of the axioms* in the previous sentence. By determining how the parts of the text relate to one another, you can determine the meaning of the assertion. Choice **a** is incorrect; the *it* in this line does not refer to geometrical propositions. While the question of the "truth" of the individual geometrical propositions is thus reduced to one of the "truth" of the axioms, it is therefore the *truths* that are being referred to as without meaning, not the propositions themselves. The passage does not delve into the nature of straight lines until after the line referred to in this question, so choice **b** is not correct. Choice **d** is incorrect; the passage states that *the last question is not only unanswerable by the methods of geometry*, meaning that the *it* is referring to the *last question* and not the subject of the prepositional phrase that follows: *by the methods of geometry*. Choice **e** is a bit tricky, but it can help to identify the subject. The *it* from this line refers to *the last question*, which can be traced back to mean *the "truth" of the axioms* in the previous sentence. It is not, therefore, the *questions* of the truth, but the truth itself.

20. e. Lines 12–15 contain the statement that argues that the truth of the propositions depends on the truth of the axioms, making choice **e** correct. The concept of straight lines is not addressed until late in the passage, and it is not introduced as the basis for the truth of geometrical propositions, so **a** is not correct. It is the truth of the axioms, not the validity of Euclidean geometry or a connection of geometric ideas, choices **b** and **c**, that plays the role of determining the truth of a geometrical proposition. Choice **d** is incorrect; there is no indication that suggests that it is merely our inclination to accept the truth that determines whether a geometrical proposition is indeed true.

21. b. The author repeatedly refers to *truth* in relation to geometrical propositions. See, for example, lines12–15. The author (Albert Einstein) is laying the groundwork for an argument that the principles of geometry are only *apparently* true. Choices **a** and **c** are incorrect. While the author presents a definition for axioms and straight lines, they are not the topic, which presents his chief concern. While geometrical propositions are a key aspect of the passage and the subject of the author's chief concern, it is not the ability to use them to draw conclusions, which is his primary focus, so choice **d** is incorrect. Choice **e** is also incorrect. The author introduces planes and points as a starting point to show how geometry is built upon certain conceptions. However, these conceptions are not the author's primary concern, so choice **e** is not the best answer choice.

22. d. The passage states that Mozart played both the harpsichord and the violin at a master level, but it does not state that these were the *only* instruments he ever played in his career. According to the passage, Leopold devoted himself to his son's musical education. Therefore, choice **a** cannot be the right answer. It is mentioned in the passage that by age six, Wolfgang Mozart could play both the violin and the harpsichord at a professional level. Therefore, choice **b** is not right. Given the amount of time that Mozart spent performing and playing music, it would be fair to suggest that Mozart's childhood was dedicated to his career. Therefore, choice **c** cannot be correct. The passage states that Mozart's father *booked as many concerts as possible at courts throughout Europe.* This means that Mozart traveled throughout the continent, making choice **e** incorrect.

23. b. As part of his early musical career, Wolfgang Amadeus Mozart toured extensively across Europe. As support for this fact, the author describes the length and number of shows he performed each day. The fact that Wolfgang played so many concerts does not necessarily relate to his talent level. One may assume that he must have been musically talented to play as many shows, but choice **a** is incorrect. Choice **c** is also incorrect; the number of hours that Mozart spent performing concerts does not justify the fact that his father booked him at such a young age. The following sentence may serve this purpose, suggesting that it was not uncommon at the time. The purpose of the sentence is not to suggest that Mozart was mistreated, making choice **d** incorrect. Choice **e** is also incorrect; Mozart must have had a strong stamina and decent physical health to perform as many concerts as he did.

24. a. The ocean sunfish eats jellyfish, which is beneficial to human beings. The spider's diet of mosquitoes is likewise beneficial to human beings, making **a** the correct choice. The diet of tuna or grizzly bears may be similar to that of sunfish because both eat sea creatures, but that's not what the question asked about; it asked about similar diets that are beneficial to human beings, so choices **b** and **d** cannot be correct. The diet of a rhinoceros or a tick is neither similar to the sunfish nor beneficial to human beings, so choices **c** and **e** cannot be correct.

25. c. A statement of opinion is a statement that cannot be proven with facts; it cannot be proven that a fish has an unusual appearance because *unusual* is not a clearly defined term. On the other hand, it *can* be proven that the sunfish is the largest bony fish, choice **a**. Its diet of jellyfish, choice **b**, can likewise be verified and is therefore not an opinion. The fact that the sunfish is banned in Europe and is eaten as a delicacy by some people is mentioned in the final sentence of the passage; both statements are facts and not opinions, so choices **d** and **e** are not correct.

26. e. The beginning of the passage mentions the rapidly expanding population of jellyfish and the problems that the jellyfish present. The second half of the passage describes a specific type of fish that eats jellyfish in large quantities, thus acting as a potential solution for overpopulation; this describes the statement in choice **e** perfectly. While two creatures are described in the passage, the passage is not entirely about the comparison and contrast of them, making choice **a** incorrect. The main idea does not actually appear in the passage until the final sentence, so **b** cannot be correct. The passage does not begin with the definition of a fascinating sea creature or its dietary constraints, so choices **c** and **d** are not correct.

27. d. The word *curtail* in the passage is describing the difficulty of limiting the population growth of jellyfish. Curtail, therefore, must have a similar meaning as "limit," such as *curb*, choice **d**. If a growth were curtailed, it may not reverse completely, so choice **a** is not the closest meaning of *curtail* in this context. Choice **c**, *withstand*, does not refer to the potential for the population growth to continue unabated, so it is not correct. Both *increase* and *liberate*, choices **b** and **e**, mean the opposite of *curtail*, so they are not correct.

28. c. The beginning of the passage includes a negative description of jellyfish. The key word *however* suggests a change in direction within the passage as the positive attributes of the sunfish are introduced. The words *unfortunately*, *difficult*, and *entirely* do not help provide a transition from one direction to an opposite direction within the passage, making choices **a**, **b**, and **d** incorrect. The word *though* in choice **e** does provide a transition at the end of the passage, but it does not help transition from content about jellyfish to that of sunfish.

29. d. The author makes the case throughout the passage that unpleasant jellyfish are increasing in numbers, but the sunfish may be able to curtail their population growth. Therefore, the author would most likely agree that sunfish should be protected, choice **d**. There is no evidence in the passage that suggests the author's attitude is that the sunfish is not the largest creature in the ocean, choice **a**, even if that were true. Similarly, there is no proof to support the statement in choice **c**. The statements in choices **b** and **e** are in regard to jellyfish and not the ocean sunfish, so those choices cannot be correct.

30. c. The final sentence of the passage serves as its main idea, suggesting that the ocean sunfish should be protected across the world like it is in the European Union. The best support for this declaration is given in choice **c**, which states that ocean sunfish eat a lot of jellyfish, which is beneficial to human beings. The statements in choices **a** and **d** do not better support the reason why ocean sunfish should be protected, so they are not correct. The statements in choices **b** and **e** do not relate to the ocean sunfish and therefore do not support the final sentence of the passage.

31. b. The passage states that the iron rims kept the tires *from getting worn down*. This is in contrast to the earlier fragile model from 1818. Therefore, Macmillan increased the durability of the bicycle, choice **b**. It may be tempting to suggest that Macmillan's improvements to the bicycle improved its efficiency, choice **a**, but there is no direct correlation in the passage from his improvements to energy efficiency. The passage states that Macmillan's bicycles were never produced in large numbers; therefore, there is no indication that he helped the bicycle to be ridden by the masses, choice **c**. Although the passage says that Macmillan's bicycles could be ridden easily, it does not indicate that the lighter weight, choice **d**, was the reason for this. One of the wheels in Macmillan's bicycle design was much larger than the other, but it was not the front wheel that was larger. Therefore, choice **e** cannot be correct either.

32. e. The list of the improvements in choice **e** correctly represents the chronology of events in the history of the bicycle from the passage. The list in each of the other answer choices is not in correct chronological order. The order of the changes are nearly in order in choice **a**, but the *diamond-shaped frame* as indicated in the final sentence represents a *further improvement* made after the inclusion of rubber tires. The inclusion of gears on pedals did not come until 10 years after Pierre and Ernest Michaux created the improved crank mechanism, so choice **b** is incorrect. According to the final sentence in the passage, the "*easy braking*" represents a *further improvement* that Lawson made only after attaching a chain to the pedals to drive the rear wheel, thus making **c** incorrect. The list of improvements to the bicycle's design in choice **d** is provided in alphabetical order instead of chronological order, so this answer is incorrect as well.

33. e. Like the automobile, the bicycle was developed over the course of a long time and through the contributions of many different inventors. The ability to transport passengers or improve communications, choices **a** and **b**, have nothing to do with the *development* of the bicycle. The space station, choice **c**, may have been constructed over several years, but the bicycle was not; it was improved upon, not built, over the long time period. There was no one specific technological advancement that led to the development of the bicycle, so choice **d** is not correct.

34. e. The instrument in this sentence refers to the foot-operated cranks that improved the riding experience. These cranks can be described as a mechanical contraption, choice **e**. The word *instrument* frequently refers to a musical mechanism, choice **a**, such as a guitar or a piano. But this passage does not relate to music in any way, so there is a different definition of *instrument* in this case. An *instrument* can also be a *monitoring device*, such as a medical instrument to record a heart rate, or a *formal document*. However, the *instrument* in this passage is a tool that improves the design of the bicycle; it does not record any information, nor is there any indication of a document used. Therefore, choices **b** and **c** are not correct. The *instrument* that this sentence refers to, the foot-operated cranks on the new design of the bicycle, allowed for faster riding. An *impediment*, choice **d**, is a blockage, which would have the opposite meaning of the facilitating instrument.

35. c. The passage details a series of modifications made to the design of the bicycle over the years that improved its usability. Therefore, it would be prudent to presume that additional modifications would be made to continue its development (choice **c**). Because additional changes will likely occur, choice **a** cannot be correct. Because there is no indication in the passage to predict that the design will regress to older conditions or that a bicycle will be able to fly, choices **b** and **e** can be eliminated. Similarly, the passage does not indicate that a bicycle will gain weight, making choice **d** incorrect.

36. a. The only statement in the answer choices that cannot be verified or proven to be true is given in choice **a**; the term *clumsy* is not something that can be proven, making that sentence a statement of opinion. The statements in choices **b**, **c**, and **e** can each be proven, making them statements of fact rather than opinion. It can also be proven that a gear does or does not make a bicycle more efficient, meaning that the statement in choice **d** is an opinion rather than a fact.

37. b. The final stipulation of a planet's attributes, according to the new definition of a planet, is that it must dominate the neighborhood along its orbit through its gravitational pull. The statement in choice **b**, referring to the debris in its path, suggests that Pluto does *not* dominate its neighborhood in the same way that the other planets do. It is true that Pluto is much smaller than the other planets, choice **a**, but the size of an object is not listed among the new criteria for a planet. Pluto had always been much smaller than any other planet. The passage mentions that Pluto has a moon as evidence for its status as a planet. However, the absence or presence of a moon is not cited as justification for the classification of a planet, making choice **c** incorrect. According to the new definition of a planet, a planet must orbit the sun. But the passage makes no mention about the specific orbit of the sun—or its shape—so the statement in choice **d** cannot be concluded as a possible explanation. The statement in choice **e** describes why Pluto is round, as are the eight planets in our solar system. This actually meets the first definition of a planet and would therefore *not* be a reason why Pluto lost its status as an official planet.

38. c. Patrick Henry, above all else, was a patriot; this aspect of his life is made clear in the opening sentence of the passage. The quote illustrates his patriotism perfectly by showing that he'd prefer to die rather than live under British tyranny. He was therefore *very* committed to the struggle against oppression, choice **c**. This quote *does* serve to show that Patrick Henry was brave, choice **a**; after all, he put his life on the line in the pursuit of freedom. But is the author's point in the article to show Henry's courage? The point of the passage is to label Henry as a patriot devoted to the cause of American liberty. There is a better choice that explains the author's likely purpose in including the quote. Certainly the quote sounds emotional, and it perhaps paints the picture of Patrick Henry as a fiery leader, choice **b**. However, the author's main idea is to paint Patrick Henry as a patriot—not as just an impassioned leader. Similarly, the quote does show Patrick Henry as a poignant orator, choice **e**. However, you need to determine whether that was the author's intention by including the quote. Is the passage about Henry's legendary speaking abilities? Because the passage is mostly about Henry's unbridled patriotism, the better choice will focus on how the quote accentuates that dedication. There is no indication that Henry was a power-hungry politician, choice **d**. He served as governor, but the quote does not portray him as being consumed by the power of elected office.

39. b. The passage states that Patrick Henry was a leader in every protest against British tyranny and in every movement for colonial rights. Therefore, it can be inferred that he was involved in any event that related to colonial rights, including the Revolution itself (choice **b**). While the authorship of the Constitution may seem like a reasonable event for Henry to have been involved with, it was not a direct movement for colonial rights, because the United States had already earned its independence by then; therefore, choice **a** is not the best choice. Likewise, choice **d** cannot be correct because the Bill of Rights was part of the Constitution. The Stamp Act was one of the most significant taxes imposed on colonial America by the British Parliament in that it helped trigger a movement for independence. Henry was involved in the opposition to this Act; he helped lead the movement for its appeal, making choice **c** incorrect. The secession of the Confederacy occurred during time of the Civil War, nearly 100 years after the time of Patrick Henry, so choice **e** cannot be correct.

40. b. The passage is primarily about Patrick Henry and his important role in helping the colonies establish their independence (choice **b**). It defines some of the events leading up to the Revolution and examines some of the British injustices, but only in context of Patrick Henry, so choices **a** and **e** are not correct. Patrick Henry is not being compared to or contrasted with any other patriots in the passage, so choice **c** cannot be correct. While Henry's famous quote did have a great impact and is well known more than 200 years later, choice **d**, this passage was not primarily about Patrick Henry's quotation, but about the man himself.

The following is a chart of the different skills assessed by the questions in this practice PPST; you can use it to identify your strengths and weaknesses in this subject to better focus your study.

READING SKILLS CHART FOR PRACTICE EXAM 1	
LITERAL COMPREHENSION SKILLS	**QUESTIONS**
Main Ideas	1, 7, 12, 40
Supporting Ideas	13, 30
Organization	16, 19, 23, 26, 28, 32
Vocabulary in Context	5, 8, 17, 18, 27, 34
CRITICAL AND INFERENTIAL COMPREHENSION SKILLS	
Evaluation	4, 6, 11, 25, 36, 37, 38
Inferential Reasoning	3, 9, 10,14, 15, 20, 21, 22, 29, 31, 39
Generalization	2, 24, 33, 35

Skills Test in Mathematics

1. c. Because the class is exclusively populated by eight- and nine-year-olds and nine-year-olds represent $\frac{1}{5}$ of the class, it can be determined that eight-year-olds represent $\frac{4}{5}$ of the class. To estimate the fraction of "guppies" that are eight-year-olds, you must multiply this $\frac{4}{5}$ fraction representing the eight-year-olds by the $\frac{1}{8}$ of the students who are "guppies." To multiply fractions, multiply numerator by numerator and denominator by denominator, and then reduce if necessary: $\frac{4}{5} \times \frac{1}{8} = \frac{4}{40}$, which reduces to $\frac{1}{10}$. Choice **a**, $\frac{1}{40}$, is the result when $\frac{1}{8}$ is multiplied by $\frac{1}{5}$. This gives an estimate of the *nine*-year-old "guppies." Choice **b**, $\frac{2}{13}$, is the result when $\frac{1}{5}$ is incorrectly added to $\frac{1}{8}$. The numerator and denominator were added straight across, which is incorrect (needs a common denominator); multiplication is the operation that must be used when a question asks to calculate a fraction *of* something. Choice **d**, $\frac{5}{13}$, is the result when $\frac{4}{5}$ is incorrectly added to $\frac{1}{8}$ (see explanation for choice **b**). Choice **e**, $\frac{13}{40}$, is the answer to $\frac{4}{5} + \frac{1}{8}$, but multiplication is what was necessary.

2. d. 9.8 million is 9,800,000. Multiply this by 1.8 cars per person and the answer is 17,640,000. Choice **a** is 1.8 times 9,800. Choice **b** is 1.8 times 98,000. Choice **c** is 1.8 times 980,000. Choice **e** is 1.8 times 98,000,000.

3. b. Add up the 911 calls for every month, and then divide by the number of months. The total number of calls was 213 + 194 + 257 + 267 + 279 + 308 = 1,518. Divide 1,518 by 6 months to get 253. Choice **a** is the median. Choice **c** is the maximum. Choice **d** is the maximum number of calls that were dispatched. Choice **e** is the mean of the calls for which the police were dispatched.

4. b. Add up the police dispatched calls for every month, and divide that sum by the number of months to see the average number of calls dispatched: 66 + 70 + 61 + 79 + 70 + 68 = 414; $\frac{414}{6}$ = 69. To estimate what percentage of calls for which police are dispatched on average, put the average number of police dispatched calls over the average number of 911 calls: $\frac{69}{253}$. Choice **a**, 10%, is not a good estimate because 10% of 253 is 25.3 (move the decimal in 253 once to the left), and 69 is much more than 25.3. An average of 50% could only exist if the average of police dispatched calls was around 126 (which is half of 253). Therefore, choices **c**, **d**, and **e** are all incorrect because they are 50% or higher. This leaves 25% as the best estimate.

5. c. The number of 911 calls per month in chronological order is 213, 196, 257, 267, 279, and 308. With the exception of the second month, the frequency of calls has increased with every month in question. Thus, the data supports the conclusion that the frequency of 911 calls tended to increase over the period range shown. Choice **a** does not work because the population of Hule is unknown, so it is impossible to know what the *rate* of crime is. Choice **b** is not supported by the table because we do not know if other Octobers have had high call rates. Choice **d** is not supported by the table since the police dispatched data was relatively stable over the six months while the 911 calls increased, so there does not exist a strong correlation between calls and dispatches. Choice **e** is incorrect because the average number of calls for which police were dispatched was around 25%, and that does not qualify as "usually."

6. e. In each term, the x value is *increasing* by $3x$, and the constant number value is *decreasing* by 2. Therefore, $3x - 2$ is being added to each term as you move along in the series. So to get the fifth term, add $3x - 2$ to the fourth term: $(4x - 6) + (3x - 2) = 7x - 8$. Repeat this to get the sixth term: $(7x - 8) + (3x - 2) = 10x - 10$. Repeat again to get the seventh term: $(10x - 10) + (3x - 2) = 13x - 12$. Choice **a**, $7x - 8$, is only the fifth term in the series. Choice **b**, $10x - 10$, is only the sixth term in the series. Choice **c**, $10x - 12$, has the correct constant term but the incorrect x-term. Choice **d**, $13x + 10$, has the correct x-term but the incorrect constant term.

7. c. The starting distance from Chicago to Los Angeles is 2,000 miles, so that comes first in the equation. Then, for every hour, the train gets 60 miles closer to Los Angeles, so subtract $60t$ from 2,000 to create the correct equation. Choice **a** could not be correct since the answer would be a negative number until t was above 33. In this case $60t$ and 2,000 are in the wrong order. Choice **b** ignores the information that Los Angeles is 2,000 miles from Chicago; the only thing being calculated here is the total distance traveled, not the distance to Los Angeles. Choice **d** is wrong because the speed, 60 mph, is not being multiplied by time, which is part of the *distance = rate × time* formula. Choice **e** is incorrect because t is being multiplied by both the rate and the total distance.

8. a. Since 60 minutes are in an hour, multiply the 8-hour workday by 60 to get a total of 480 minutes. To find $\frac{5}{12}$ of 480, multiply $\frac{5}{12} \times 480 = 200$. So Parker spends 200 minutes, or 3 hours and 20 minutes, answering e-mails. 3 hours and 20 minutes subtracted from 8 hours is 4 hours and 40 minutes. Choice **b** is incorrect because 3 hours was subtracted from 8 hours and the minutes weren't considered. Choice **c** is the amount of time Parker spends answering e-mails, *not* doing other things. Choice **d** correctly subtracts the 3 hours from 8 hours, but forgets to subtract the 20 minutes from 60 minutes. Choice **e** correctly subtracts the 20 minutes from 8 hours, but forgets to reduce the 8 hours to 7 hours before subtracting the full 3 hours.

9. c. Because there are 100 centimeters in a meter, 100 meters = 10,000 centimeters. $\frac{10,000}{50} = 200$. Choice **a** does not turn the 100 meters into centimeters before dividing by 50. Choice **b** only turns 100 meters into 1,000 centimeters before dividing by 50. Choice **d** turns 100 meters into 100,000 centimeters before dividing. Choice **e** divides 50 meters by 0.01 meters, which is incorrect.

10. e. The fraction $\frac{3}{4}$ is equivalent to 0.75 (you can do long division of 3 divided by 4 if you don't have this memorized). So $4\frac{3}{4}\%$ is the same as 4.75%. When working with percents, you put the percent *over 100*, which causes the decimal place to be shifted back to the left two times: $\frac{4.75}{100} = 0.0475$. Choice **a**, 4.34, incorrectly writes the fraction of $\frac{3}{4}$ as .34 and does not move the decimal at all. Choice **b** incorrectly writes the fraction of $\frac{3}{4}$ as .34 and only moves the decimal back once. Choice **c** incorrectly writes the fraction of $\frac{3}{4}$ as .34 but moves the decimal back correctly. Choice **d**, 0.475, correctly converts the fraction into decimal, but only moves the decimal point back one place.

11. d. Recall the formula: *distance = rate × time*. Time must be in hours because you are asked to find miles per *hour*. 150 minutes = 2.5 hours, so calculate 180 = rate × 2.5. To solve, divide both sides by 2.5 to get 72 miles per hour. Choice **a**, 120 mph, cannot be correct since 150 minutes is more than two hours, and if the train went 120 miles each hour, it would have traveled over 240 miles. Choice **b**, 30 mph, subtracts 150 from 180, but the relationship between distance and speed involves division. Choice **c**, 90 mph, assumes incorrectly that the train traveled 180 miles in two hours. Choice **e**, 75 mph, assumes incorrectly that the train traveled 150 miles in two hours.

12. a. Because Maddie has 9 pairs of socks in total, there are 18 socks in her drawer. Four pairs, or 8 socks, are white, which means that 10 socks are not white. The chance of her selecting a non-white sock at random is $\frac{10}{18}$, which reduces to $\frac{5}{9}$. Choice **b**, $\frac{4}{9}$, is the probability that the sock she selects *will* be white ($\frac{8}{18}$). Choice **c**, $\frac{2}{3}$, is the probability that the sock she selects will be white or maroon ($\frac{12}{18}$). Choice **d**, $\frac{7}{9}$, is the probability that the sock she selects will be white or gold. ($\frac{14}{18}$). Choice **e**, $\frac{5}{18}$, is the number of *pairs* of non-white socks divided by the total number of non-white socks.

13. e. To set up a proportion, put the number of births in the numerator and the corresponding total number of people in the denominator:

$$\frac{\text{births}}{\text{total \# of people}} = \frac{15}{1,000} = \frac{x}{301,000,000}$$

Choice **a** is almost correct, but the $\frac{15}{10}$ represents that there were 15 births for every 10 people, where it is actually 15 births for every *1,000* people. Choice **b** has the ratio on the left set up as births ÷ total # of people, but the ratio on the right is the reciprocal of that: total # of people ÷ births. This is incorrect because both ratios need to be set up the same. Choices **c** and **d** ignore that the 15 births come from 1,000 people, and these choices have 15 paired with one, which is incorrect.

14. c. In order to compare fractions, first look to see if they have a common denominator. In this case, all the denominators can go evenly into 200, so rewrite every fraction with a denominator of 200 and then compare their numerators: $\frac{11}{100} = \frac{22}{200}$; $\frac{6}{50} = \frac{24}{200}$; $\frac{23}{200} = \frac{23}{200}$; $\frac{7}{25} = \frac{56}{200}$; $\frac{1}{10} = \frac{20}{200}$. Because 56 is the largest numerator, $\frac{56}{200}$, or $\frac{7}{25}$, has the largest value.

15. b. $\frac{252}{3} = 84$ shows how many $2 packages were purchased. Because 84 chances were purchased at $2 each, $168 was earned. To find the average amount of money spent for each dunking, divide $168 by 12 to get $14. Choice **a** makes the mistake of dividing the 252 balls thrown by the 12 dunkings without investigating how much money was earned: $\frac{252}{12} = 21$. Choice **c** is $168 divided by 10 dunkings, but it should be divided by 12. Choice **e** was found by dividing the 84 packages purchased by the 12 dunkings, without first calculating the total amount the 84 packages cost.

16. b. Because R is divisible by 4, S is divisible by 5, and B is divisible by 3, then any multiple of RBS must be divisible by $4 \times 5 \times 3 = 60$. Any number that is divisible by 60 will also be divisible by 6, 10, 12, and 15, because these are all factors of 60. The only number listed that is not a factor of 60 is 8.

17. c. The area within the figure is the total number of unique boxes within the shape. Starting at the top and counting down to the bottom, there are 18 unique boxes. Choice **a**, 13, is the maximum height of the figure. Choice **b**, 12, does not count all the squares that are in the corners of the figure. Choice **d**, 24, counts all the corner squares twice, but each square within the figure must be unique in order to be counted. Choice **e**, 38, is the *perimeter* of the figure, not the area.

18. a. Replace $5H - 4G$ with the expressions given for H and G, then distribute while remembering to also distribute the minus sign: $5(2w) - 4(3w - 1) = 10w - 4(3w) - 4(-1)$ (Here the negative must stay with the 4 when it is distributed) $= 10w - 12w - (-4)$ $= -2w + 4$. Choice **b** forgets that the distributed 4 must stay negative, which will cancel out the negative sign that is in front of the 1. Choice **c** incorrectly does the subtraction between $10w - 12w$ and forgets that $2w$ should be negative. Choice **d** incorrectly combines $-2w + 4$, forgetting that two terms cannot be added or subtracted unless they have all the same variables. Choice **e** also incorrectly combines $-2w + 4$, forgetting that two terms cannot be added or subtracted unless they have all the same variables, *and* making a negative sign mistake of keeping the sign of the smaller number.

19. e. The total number of records sold is $15 + 20 + 10 + 15 = 60$. The lowest amount of sales would be $60(\$7) = \$420$, and the highest amount of sales would be $60(\$20) = \$1,200$. Choice **a** cannot be correct since the store sold 60 records, so making $0 is impossible. Choice **b** is the range of *individual prices* of the records, not total sales. Choices **c** and **d** use $7 times the least amount of records sold, which was 10, in order to get the least amount of sales, but since 60 records were sold this is incorrect.

20. c. Because the length is $\frac{4}{3}$ as long as the width, the length will be $\frac{4}{3} \times 30 = 40$ feet. A rectangular yard of 30 feet by 40 feet cut by a diagonal will give two congruent right triangles.

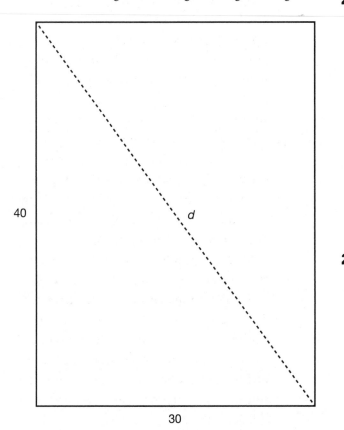

Because this is a right triangle, you can use the Pythagorean theorem, $a^2 + b^2 = c^2$, to solve for the diagonal, where a and b are legs and c is the hypotenuse, or diagonal. In this case, you can use d as your hypotenuse, and plug 30 in for a, and 40 in for b:

$a^2 + b^2 = d^2$

$30^2 + 40^2 = d^2$

$900 + 1{,}600 = d^2$

$2{,}500 = d^2$

$\sqrt{2{,}500} = \sqrt{d^2}$

$50 = d$, so the hypotenuse d equals 50 feet. Choice **a**, 35 feet, is the average of the 30 and 40, not the diagonal. Choice **b**, $\sqrt{70}$ feet, adds the 30 and 40 *without* squaring them, but it is necessary to square each of the legs first, *before* taking the square root. Choice **d**,

70 feet, is the sum of 30 and 40, not the square root of the sum of their squares. Choice **e**, 40 feet, is just the length of the garden, not the diagonal.

21. b. Looking at the bar graph, the height of each column indicates the frequency by using the scale on the left. March sales were a little less than halfway between $5,000 and $10,000, so $7,000 is a good reading. April and June both go up to the $10,000 mark, and May is at $15,000. Choice **a** is incorrect because April's sales were not above $10,000. Choice **c** is incorrect because fractions in a frequency table are not appropriate. Choice **d** is incorrect because the June sales were much lower than $25,000. Choice **e** does not apply since **b** has the correct table.

22. e. Every logic statement that is in the form "if *a* then *b*" has an equivalent statement, called the contrapositive, which is always true. The contrapositive of "if *a* then *b*" is "if not *b*, then not *a*." Therefore, by flipping the order of the statements and negating both statements you get, "If Stan is not happy, Sierra did not visit." Choice **b** is incorrect because it reverses the order and only negates the first statement. Choice **c** is not provable because the initial statement does not mention whether Sierra would or would not be happy to go away for the weekend. Choice **d** is not provable because the initial statement does not mention that a longer stay would make Stan happier.

23. d. This problem is modeled with two similar right triangles: the smaller one has a height of 8 and a shadow of 3. The larger one has a height of h and a shadow of 15. Setting up a proportion of height over shadow and then cross-multiplying gives:

$$\frac{height}{shadow} = \frac{8}{3} = \frac{h}{15}$$

$$3h = 120$$

$$h = 40 \text{ feet}$$

Choice **a**, $5\frac{5}{8}$, is the answer when the second fraction in the preceding proportion is accidentally inverted to be $\frac{15}{h}$. Choices **b**, **c**, and **e** are reasonable estimates that someone might make if not using a proportion to solve this.

24. d. By definition, a circle is a collection of points that are equidistant from a fixed center point. Although equilateral triangles, squares, and regular pentagons are all symmetrical shapes that can contain a center point, that center point will be farthest away from the vertexes in that shape, so choices **a**, **b**, and **c** are incorrect.

25. e. The total volume of the tank is depth × width × length = 10 × 24 × 40 = 9,600 cubic feet. Because there are already 4,660 cubic feet of water in the tank, subtract 4,660 from 9,600 to see how many cubic feet of water are needed to fill the tank: 9,600 − 4,660 = 4,940 ft³. Choice **a** is incorrect since 9,600 ft³ is the full volume of the tank. Choice **b** is incorrect since 14,260 ft³ is the *sum* of 9,600 and 4,660. Choice **d** is incorrect since it contains a subtraction error.

26. a. 475 multiplied by 0.08 gives 38 (multiply 475 by 8 and then move the decimal two places to the left). To simplify $\frac{38}{6}$, 6 goes into 38 six times, with a remainder of two, and that remainder gets put over 6, the divisor. The final answer is $6\frac{1}{3}$. Choice **b**, 228, is 0.08 × 475 × 6, not divided by 6. Choice **c**, 6.2, is incorrect because the remainder of 2 must not be used as the decimal, but must be put over the divisor. Choice **e** is the answer to only the first step of the problem.

27. d. The sum of the angles of a four-sided polygon is 360°. Since the angles of this quadrilateral are in the ratio 1:2:2:4, there are 1 + 2 + 2 + 4 = 9 parts to consider. Divide 360° by 9 to find that each part equals 40°. Using the ratio, the angles of the quadrilateral are 1(40°), 2(40°), 2(40°), and 4(40°). The largest of these is 4(40°), or 160°. Choice **a**, 40°, represents the measure of the smallest angle. Choice **b** represents the sum of the three smallest angles in the four-sided polygon. Choice **c** represents the measure of the two middle angles. Choice **e** represents the measure of all the interior angles of a polygon.

28. c. Because the first minute is charged only the $1.50 fee and not the 60¢ fee, when calculating the charges for the m minutes, m must be subtracted by one before multiplying it by the 60¢ per minute charge. It is also critical to write 60¢ in decimal terms, as 0.60. Therefore, $0.60(m - 1)$ represents what Terry will be charged for all his minutes *after* his first minute. Since his first minute costs $1.50, add this to $0.60(m - 1)$ to get the total price, c. Choices **a** and **b** do not take into consideration that the first minute is not billed the 60¢ per minute charge. Choice **d** is not solving for the cost in terms of c and has the variables in the wrong places. Choice **e** is almost correct, but the 60¢ was not correctly converted into a decimal.

29. b. 3, 6, 9, 12, 15, and 18 are the multiples of three between 1 and 20. Therefore, 6 out of the 20 numbers are multiples of three. $\frac{6}{20} = \frac{3}{10}$. Choice **a**, $\frac{1}{3}$, is impossible since there is not a probability fraction with a denominator of 20 that could be reduced to $\frac{1}{3}$. Choice **c**, $\frac{3}{20}$, put "3" from "multiple of 3" over 20, but there are six, and not three, multiples of three. Choice **d**, $\frac{1}{10}$, would only be true if there were only two multiples of three between 1 and 20, but there are six. Choice **e**, $\frac{1}{20}$, would only be true if there were one multiple of three between 1 and 20, but there are six.

30. c. To graph a coordinate pair of numbers, start at the center of the graph, where the x-axis and y-axis intersect at the origin. Move left or right according to a negative or positive first coordinate, and then, staying on that number, move up or down, according to a negative or positive second coordinate. Using this method, it is true that $(-4, -3)$ lies three spaces to the left of the origin and four units down. This is in the shaded region and is therefore a solution. Choice **a**, $(0,3)$, is on the y-axis at three, which is above the shaded area. Choice **b**, $(-4,0)$, is on the x-axis at negative four, which is to the left of the shaded area. Choice **d**, $(5,0)$, is on the x-axis at five, which is on the dotted line. When the lines are solid in graphs, then the points on them exist as a solution, but when the line is dotted, then the line's points are outside the solution set. Choice **e**, $(0,2)$, is on the y-axis at two, which is on the dotted line and, as explained for choice **d**, is not a solution.

31. a. The sum of all four golfer's scores was 341 on day one, 341 on day two, and 343 on day 3, so they shot approximately the same overall score each day. Choices **b** and **c** are incorrect since the team's score did not change at all on the second day. Choice **d** is incorrect since the team was consistent. Choice **e** is incorrect since Monica's score was not the lowest (or highest) score on any of the three days.

32. e. To begin solving this problem, divide the distance of 18,480 feet by 5,280 in order to see how many full miles were biked and what the remainder is. $18,480 \div 5,280 = 3$ with a remainder of 2,640 feet. Put 2,640 feet over 5,280 feet to see what fraction of a mile 2,640 feet is. $\frac{2,640}{5,280}$ is $\frac{1}{2}$, so Carmen biked $3\frac{1}{2}$ miles. Choice **a** is only the number of full miles that Carmen biked and ignores the remaining 2,640 feet. Choices **b** and **c** are estimates of how much of a mile the remaining 2,640 feet are, but they were not calculated correctly. Choice **d** took the remainder of 2,640 feet and tacked it onto 3 miles, which is incorrect.

33. a. Rounding 162 to the nearest hundred yields 200 (since the tens place is greater than 5), and rounding 849 to the nearest hundred yields 800 (since the tens place is less than 5). Multiplying 200 times 800 yields a product of 160,000, since $2 \times 8 = 16$, and then you have four zeros to tack onto 16. Choice **b**, 180,000, incorrectly rounds 849 up to 900. Choice **c**, 16,000, only adds three zeros instead of four. Choice **d**, 1,000, *adds* 200 and 800 instead of multiplying them. Choice **e**, 128,000, multiplies 160 and 800, but 160 should have been rounded to 200.

34. b. To compute $(5 \# 6) \# 3$, begin looking at $(5 \# 6)$. The a term here is 5, and the b term is 6. Because $5 \le 5$, use $a^2 - 3b$: $5^2 - 3(6) = 25 - 18 = 7$. Now compute $7 \# 3$ by using the rule for when $a > 5$: $2(7) + (3) = 14 + 3 = 17$. Choice **a**, 7, is the answer of only the first step, $(5 \# 6)$. Choice **c**, 16, is the answer reached when the rule for $a > 5$ is used and the second step is left out. Choice **d**, 35, is the answer reached when the rule for $a > 5$ is used and the second step is carried out. Choice **e**, 90, is $5 \times 6 \times 3 = 90$.

35. c. If Loretta bought the DVD player for 30% off, that means that she only paid 70% of the original price: (70%)(original price) = $77. Divide $77 by 0.70 to get $110.00 as the original price. Choice **a**, $47.00, is $77 *minus* 30% as an integer, and percents are never handled as integers. Choice **b**, $107.00, is $77 *plus* 30% as an integer; again, percents are never handled as integers. Choice **d**, $100.10, is $77 plus 30% of $77, but the 30% discount was off the original and not off the sale price. Choice **e**, $256.00, is $77 divided by 30%, but it should have been $77 $\div$ 70%.

36. a. The sum of the interior angles of a triangle is 180°. Because the vertex is 3 times as large as the base angles, let the measure of the vertex angle be $3b$ and each of the base angles measure b. Solve the equation $3b + b + b = 180°$; $5b = 180°$; $b = 36°$. Therefore, the base angles will each equal 36° and the vertex will be $3 \times 36° = 108°$. The sum of one base angle and the vertex is $36° + 108° = 142°$. Choice **b**, 36°, is the measure of one base angle. Choice **c**, 72°, is the sum of both base angles. Choice **d**, 108°, is the measure of the vertex. Choice **e**, 60°, is the measure of each angle in an equilateral triangle.

37. d. In 2001 the savings account had approximately $2,250 in it, and in 2002 it had grown to about $2,750, which was a $500 increase. Choice **a** is impossible to determine since we do not have any information about 1998. Choices **b** and **c** both showed less than $250 in growth. Choice **e** is wrong since this information can be determined from the graph.

38. c. The trend of this graph is that the growth was slow in the beginning, but as the years have increased, so has the rate of growth of the savings account. If the curve were to be naturally extended through 2003, the next point would be between $3,500 and $4,000. Choices **a**, $2,800, and **b**, $3,000, would not show enough growth for the trend to continue its arc. Choices **d**, $8,000, and **e**, $10,000, are too large, and the curve would be too dramatic to follow the trend shown.

39. b. Because x is increasing steadily by 2 and the increase of y is not steady, this relationship cannot be linear, so choices **a**, **c**, **d**, and **e** are ruled out. These are all linear equations because the x value does not have an exponent. This just leaves choice **b**, and testing a few of the values in $y = x^2 + 2$ shows that this is the correct equation: $38 = 6^2 + 2$ and $18 = 4^2 + 2$.

40. a. The quantity $n\%$ means "n parts out of 100." $n\%$ can be written as $\frac{n}{100}$ or equivalently as $n \times 0.01$. This equivalent of $n\%$ then gets multiplied by 40 in order to find $n\%$ of 40. This yields the equivalent expressions I and II. Selection IV is incorrect because when a percentage is divided by 0.01, it moves the decimal point two times to the right and the final answer would be larger than the number that is being taken a percentage of. Selection III is incorrect because multiplying the percentage by 100 will have the same result that dividing it by 0.01 would have, which was covered in the explanation of IV.

The following is a chart of the different skills assessed by the questions in this practice PPST; you can use it to identify your strengths and weaknesses in this subject to better focus your study.

MATH SKILLS STUDY CHART FOR PRACTICE EXAM 1	
NUMBER AND OPERATIONS SKILLS	**QUESTIONS**
Order	14
Equivalence	10
Numeration and Place Value	2
Number Properties	16
Operation Properties	18, 40
Computation	1, 11, 26
Estimation	4, 33
Percent, Proportion, and Ratio	13, 23, 35
Numerical Reasoning	
ALGEBRA SKILLS	
Equations and Inequalities	8
Algorithmic Thinking	7
Patterns	6, 39
Algebraic Representations	28, 34
Algebraic Reasoning	22

(continued)

MATH SKILLS STUDY CHART FOR PRACTICE EXAM 1 *(Continued)*	
GEOMETRY AND MEASUREMENT SKILLS	
Geometric Properties	20, 27, 36
The *xy*-Coordinate Plane	17, 30
Geometric Reasoning	24
Systems of Measurement	9, 32
Measurement	25
DATA ANALYSIS AND PROBABILITY SKILLS	
Data Interpretation	31, 37
Data Representation	19, 21
Trends and Inferences	5, 38
Measures of Center and Spread	3, 15
Probability	12, 29

Skills Test in Writing—Section 1, Part A

1. c. The word *couple* is a singular noun, which requires a singular verb. In this case, the sentence should read *the couple was eager.*

2. b. The comma is incorrect punctuation. Because this sentence contains two independent clauses, a semicolon (;) should be used instead of the comma.

3. b. The word *quick* is used as an adverb in this sentence, telling how the chicken ran. The adverbial form of *quick* is *quickly.*

4. e. Because there are no grammatical, idiomatic, logical, or structural errors in this sentence, choice **e** is the best answer.

5. b. This sentence contains an error in word choice. The word *who's*—meaning *who is*—must be replaced with *whose.*

6. d. When comparing expensiveness, the correct use of the term is *less expensive.* There is no such word as *expensiver.* This reflects an error in double comparison.

7. e. Because there are no grammatical, idiomatic, logical, or structural errors in this sentence, choice **e** is the best answer.

8. c. The correct word choice would be *effectively,* meaning "to cause a result." *Affective* refers to "the ability to influence or alter someone's mental state."

9. a. In this comparison, the word *as* should be used instead of *like.* The use of *as* completes the idiom *such as.*

10. b. When two subjects are connected with the conjunction *or,* the subject that is closer to the verb will determine whether the verb is singular or plural. The verb in this sentence should be *is* because *administrator*—the closer subject—is singular.

11. c. This is a grammatical error. The contraction *it's*—meaning *it is*—does not make sense in this sentence. *Its* should replace *it's.*

12. c. This sentence compares three gowns; therefore, the superlative *most* should be used. *More* is incorrect because it is the comparative form and should be used only when comparing two things. In choice **a**, *more* is correct because the comparison is between the three gowns and all the others (two collective groups).

13. a. Scripps National Spelling Bee is a proper noun. It is the specific name used to identify a contest, so it must be capitalized.

14. c. In this pronoun error, the pronoun *them* is plural. The noun the pronoun is replacing is *clay*, which is singular.

15. c. This is an error in parallelism. Because the other two phrases in the series begin with a verb in past tense and the topic is "growing up," *becomes* should be replaced with something Kate did growing up that relates to becoming British royalty. For example, the sentence could end with "and dreamed of someday becoming British royalty."

16. a. In this sentence, the word *good* is being used as an adverb telling how the student thinks he or she will do on the test. Therefore, *good* should be replaced with *well*. This is a word-choice error.

17. c. The verbs *have watched* and *began* contradict each other. The sentence is poorly constructed. It would make better sense if the parents *were watching* (the past progressive form of the verb to show the action that was going on at the time) television when the baby began to cry.

18. c. *But yet* is redundant and unnecessary. One word or the other should be deleted.

19. e. Because there are no grammatical, idiomatic, logical, or structural errors in this sentence, choice **e** is the best answer.

20. e. Because there are no grammatical, idiomatic, logical, or structural errors in this sentence, choice **e** is the best answer.

21. d. When comparing two things—in this case, selling e-books and selling print books—the word *than* is used instead of *then*. The word *then* refers to a time or the next thing in a series or sequence.

Skills Test in Writing—Section 1, Part B

22. d. The clause "who is an avid gardener" is a nonrestrictive (not essential) clause and should be set off by commas. Choices **a**, **b**, **c**, and **e** are all punctuated incorrectly. In addition, choice **e** uses the pronoun *whom*, which is the wrong case.

23. c. *Can't hardly* and *cannot hardly* are double negatives. Inserting *who* or *whom* ruins the structure and meaning of the sentence. Therefore, the sentence should just read *can hardly*.

24. d. The parts of the underlined series must be parallel with each other. Only choice **d** contains the appropriate parallel construction. Choices **a**, **c**, and **e** break the parallel flow of the sentence with the use of inconsistent forms of the verbs. Choice **b** is unnecessarily wordy and redundant.

25. d. Because the pronouns are being used as the subject in this sentence, nominative case pronouns (i.e., I, we, you, he, she, they, it) must be used. The only choice in which both pronouns are nominative case is choice **d**.

26. b. Sometimes a pronoun is immediately followed by a noun in a sentence. To make certain which pronoun to use, delete the noun from the pair to see which makes sense. Choices **c**, **d**, and **e** change the meaning of the sentence. They are incorrect.

27. c. Use the adjective *fewer* to modify plural nouns that can be counted. Use *less* for singular nouns that represent a quantity or a degree. Most nouns to which an –s can be added require the adjective *fewer*. Choices **b**, **d**, and **e** change the meaning of the sentence.

28. a. *Past* as a noun means history. *Passed* is the past-tense verb of pass, meaning *went by*. Choice **a** is the only choice that correctly uses both *past* and *passed* and is also punctuated correctly.

29. c. The list of information following the colon must correlate with the description preceding the colon. Choices **a** and **b** infer that just one piece of information is missing, when three items are listed as missing. Choice **d** has the wrong punctuation, and choice **e** is missing the article.

30. e. When dates or days are listed and there is a particular order to them, they should be listed in sequence. Choice **e** is the only one that lists the dates in sequence with the correct use of commas and semicolons for a series.

31. b. Choices **a**, **c**, and **d** imply that the phone was cleaning, not the person. Choice **e** changes the meaning of the sentence.

32. a. Use the noun *number* when referring to things that can be made plural or that can be counted. Use the noun *amount* when referring to singular nouns. *Hours* is a plural noun, so it requires the noun *number*. Choices **b** through **e** do not follow this rule.

33. c. Choice **a** introduces a double negative. Choice **c** corrects the double negative and makes sense. Choices **b** and **d** do not make sense. In choice **e**, the verb doesn't agree with the subject.

34. d. Choices **a** through **c** have misplaced modifiers that make the sentence unclear. You can't do the backstroke in the subway, but a swimmer who is in the subway can explain how to do the backstroke in a pool. In choices **b**, **c**, and **e** the subjects and verbs do not agree.

35. e. *Strange* describes the keyboard (a noun), not how it looked (a verb), so choice **e** is correct. Choice **a** is an adverb. Choices **b** through **d** change the meaning of the sentence.

36. d. *Break* as a verb means "separate, shatter, or adjourn." As a noun it means "separation, crack, pause, or opportunity." *Brake* as a verb means "slow or stop." As a noun it means "hindrance or drag." Choice **d** is the only choice in which *break* is used correctly in both instances.

37. b. Choice **a** is a subordinate clause and cannot stand alone as a complete sentence without a main clause. Choices **c** through **e** do not make sense.

38. a. Take special care to choose the correct word when using verbs that deal with the senses, such as *feel*. *Gently* describes how the therapist felt the spine, not how he or she felt personally. Choice **a** is correct because *gently* describes the verb; it is an adverb. In choice **b**, *gentle* is describing the therapist; it is an adjective. Choices **c** through **e** change the meaning of the sentence.

The following is a chart of the different skills assessed by the questions in this practice PPST; you can use it to identify your strengths and weaknesses in this subject to better focus your study.

WRITING SKILLS STUDY CHART FOR PRACTICE EXAM 1	
GRAMMATICAL RELATIONSHIP SKILLS	**QUESTIONS**
Identify Errors in Adjectives	27, 32, 35
Identify Errors in Adverbs	3, 16, 38
Identify Errors in Nouns	28, 36
Identify Errors in Pronouns	14, 25, 26
Identify Errors in Verbs	1, 10
STRUCTURAL RELATIONSHIP SKILLS	
Identify Errors in Comparison	6, 12, 21
Identify Errors in Coordination	34
Identify Errors in Correlation	17, 29, 31
Identify Errors in Negation	23, 33
Identify Errors in Parallelism	15, 24, 30
Identify Errors in Subordination	37
WORD CHOICE AND MECHANICS SKILLS	
Identify Errors in Word Choice	5, 8, 9, 18
Identify Errors in Mechanics	2, 11, 13, 22
Identify Sentences Free from Error	4, 7, 19, 20

Skills Test in Writing—Section 2, Essay Writing

Following are sample criteria for scoring a PPST essay.

A score "6" writer will:

- create an exceptional composition that appropriately addresses the audience and given task
- organize ideas effectively, include very strong supporting details, and use smooth transitions
- present a definitive, focused thesis and clearly support it throughout the composition
- include vivid details, clear examples, and strong supporting text to enhance the themes of the composition
- exhibit an exceptional level of skill in the usage of the English language and the capacity to employ an assortment of sentence structures
- build essentially error-free sentences that accurately convey intended meaning

A score "5" writer will:

- create a commendable composition that appropriately addresses the audience and the given task
- organize ideas, include supporting details, and use smooth transitions
- present a thesis and support it throughout the composition
- include details, examples, and supporting text to enhance the themes of the composition
- generally exhibit a high level of skill in the usage of the English language and the capacity to employ an assortment of sentence structures
- build mostly error-free sentences that accurately convey intended meaning

A score "4" writer will:

- create a composition that satisfactorily addresses the audience and given task

- display satisfactory organization of ideas, include adequate supporting details, and generally use smooth transitions
- present a thesis and mostly support it throughout the composition
- include some details, examples, and supporting text that typically enhance most themes of the composition
- exhibit a competent level of skill in the usage of the English language and the general capacity to employ an assortment of sentence structures
- build sentences with several minor errors that generally do not confuse the intended meaning

A score "3" writer will:

- create an adequate composition that basically addresses the audience and given task
- display some organization of ideas, include some supporting details, and use mostly logical transitions
- present a somewhat underdeveloped thesis but attempt to support it throughout the composition
- display limited organization of ideas, have some inconsistent supporting details, and use few transitions
- exhibit an adequate level of skill in the usage of the English language and a basic capacity to employ an assortment of sentence structures
- build sentences with some minor and major errors that may obscure the intended meaning

A score "2" writer will:

- create a composition that restrictedly addresses the audience and given task
- display little organization of ideas, have inconsistent supporting details, and use very few transitions
- present an unclear or confusing thesis with little support throughout the composition

- include very few details, examples, and supporting text
- exhibit a less-than-adequate level of skill in the usage of the English language and a limited capacity to employ a basic assortment of sentence structures
- build sentences with a few major errors that may confuse the intended meaning

A score "1" writer will:

- create a composition that has a limited sense of the audience and given task
- display illogical organization of ideas, include confusing or no supporting details, and lack the ability to effectively use transitions
- present a minimal or unclear thesis
- include confusing or irrelevant details and examples, and little or no supporting text
- exhibit a limited level of skill in the usage of the English language and little or no capacity to employ basic sentence structure
- build sentences with many major errors that obscure or confuse the intended meaning

Sample 6 Essay

Many state legislatures are considering adopting a new requirement for graduation from their public high schools: a passing score on a standardized test. Standardized testing is nothing new; in fact, since the No Child Left Behind Act was passed in 2001, a record number of such tests are given at many grade levels in order to hold schools accountable for levels of student performance. But do these tests deliver what they promise, and is a graduation testing requirement a good idea?

First, let's examine what standardized tests aim to achieve. Because they are based on a "standard," they purport to measure achievement based not on grading discrepancies, curriculum differences, and varying teaching styles, but based on one set of questions and answers. That's the theory. But how well does it hold up in practice? Studies show that standardized tests are biased—white, affluent, suburban students perform better than their non-white, underprivileged urban counterparts. In addition, some tests are poorly written, and grading procedures (including computer grading) have sometimes been found to be faulty. Should eligibility for high school graduation be based on these kinds of inequities?

But what if a test that was fairly written, administered, and graded could be used? There are still other problems with standardized testing. The high stakes involved with a high school graduation requirement test could cause a number of undesired results. Schools, wanting to maintain their reputations through high graduation rates, would redesign curricula to emphasize the material on the tests. Teachers would have to "teach to the test," leaving little or no time for lessons not directly included on the test. Students with special needs and those experiencing academic difficulties—who could be at greater risk for failure—could be encouraged to drop out of school.

The idea that standardized tests would help the education system by highlighting those schools in need of extra help is simply wishful thinking. Poor test results are used to punish schools in our current system, including reducing or cutting off funding, taking over control of schools from local school boards, and replacing administrators. The threat of these punitive measures increases pressures to perform some of the measures described in the previous paragraph, including teaching to the test and removing students who could perform poorly.

In summary, requiring high school seniors to pass a standardized test in order to graduate will do nothing to improve the educational standards of our country. In fact, it will produce a number of undesired results that will inevitably weaken the very system that testing was designed to improve.

Sample 4 Essay

High school students may soon be required to pass a standardized test in order to graduate. This test would be similar to the state tests students already take throughout their elementary, middle, and high school years. However, this test would be different in that it would carry a brick weight with it. That is, seniors would not be able to graduate from high school without first passing the test. This would lead to overpopulated schools and students dropping out without graduating.

Schools would be required to provide an education to students who did not pass the graduation test. Inner city schools, which are already overpopulated, would be busting at the seams with students who could not pass the test. We know from our experiences with the state tests students already take that they are easier for some cultures to pass than others. For example, we know that African Americans do not do as well on these tests as white Americans do.

Furthermore, students who fail the tests may choose to drop out, even at the end of their senior year, rather than return to school as a failure. I know some people who say they wouldn't return if this happened to them.

We have to be careful and think of all the possibilities before we adopt this and any other new graduation requirements.

Sample 1 Essay

I believe it is a good idea to make high school students pass a standardized test in order to graduate. Sure, we have grades and course requirements that help tell us how good a student is doing, but right now there is no way to figure out how our high school's do against each other. A standard test would do just that.

If students knew that they would have to pass this test in order to graduate, they would work real hard during there four years in high school. The test would be like a kind of carrot that's held in front of them. If they want it, they have to work for it. Schools would also work harder if they knew their kids had to pass the test. I mean, what would they do with a bunch of seniors who failed the test? The next year, they'd have to teach them again? I can just imagine how crowded some schools would get with al those seniors coming back every year! How old would you

have to be before a school said you were to old to come there?

So the schools that had a lot of students who didn't pass would obviously need some help. With the test they would stand out and help would be given to them. This would be another positive benefit of the test. I think the standardized test idea is a good one. It will help kids and help schools, and who could argue with that?

C H A P T E R

PRAXIS I:
POWER PRACTICE
EXAM 2

CHAPTER SUMMARY
This practice exam is also based on the three elements of the Praxis I, the Pre-Professional Skills Tests (PPSTs) of Reading, Mathematics, and Writing. This exam gives you another chance to master your test-taking skills and get ready for your exam.

The exam that follows is made up of three tests: a Reading test (multiple-choice questions), a Mathematics test (multiple-choice questions), and a Writing test (multiple-choice questions and an essay).

Once again, you should pretend you are taking a real exam. Work in a quiet place, away from interruptions. Use a timer or stopwatch and allow yourself an hour for the Reading test, an hour for the Mathematics test, 30 minutes for Section 1 of the Writing test, and 30 minutes for Section 2 of the Writing test (your essay).

After the exam, use the answer explanations to learn about why you missed certain questions. Then, use the scoring section in Chapter 8 to see how you did overall.

SKILLS TEST IN READING

1. (a) (b) (c) (d) (e)
2. (a) (b) (c) (d) (e)
3. (a) (b) (c) (d) (e)
4. (a) (b) (c) (d) (e)
5. (a) (b) (c) (d) (e)
6. (a) (b) (c) (d) (e)
7. (a) (b) (c) (d) (e)
8. (a) (b) (c) (d) (e)
9. (a) (b) (c) (d) (e)
10. (a) (b) (c) (d) (e)
11. (a) (b) (c) (d) (e)
12. (a) (b) (c) (d) (e)
13. (a) (b) (c) (d) (e)
14. (a) (b) (c) (d) (e)
15. (a) (b) (c) (d) (e)
16. (a) (b) (c) (d) (e)
17. (a) (b) (c) (d) (e)
18. (a) (b) (c) (d) (e)
19. (a) (b) (c) (d) (e)
20. (a) (b) (c) (d) (e)
21. (a) (b) (c) (d) (e)
22. (a) (b) (c) (d) (e)
23. (a) (b) (c) (d) (e)
24. (a) (b) (c) (d) (e)
25. (a) (b) (c) (d) (e)
26. (a) (b) (c) (d) (e)
27. (a) (b) (c) (d) (e)
28. (a) (b) (c) (d) (e)
29. (a) (b) (c) (d) (e)
30. (a) (b) (c) (d) (e)
31. (a) (b) (c) (d) (e)
32. (a) (b) (c) (d) (e)
33. (a) (b) (c) (d) (e)
34. (a) (b) (c) (d) (e)
35. (a) (b) (c) (d) (e)
36. (a) (b) (c) (d) (e)
37. (a) (b) (c) (d) (e)
38. (a) (b) (c) (d) (e)
39. (a) (b) (c) (d) (e)
40. (a) (b) (c) (d) (e)

SKILLS TEST IN MATHEMATICS

1. (a) (b) (c) (d) (e)
2. (a) (b) (c) (d) (e)
3. (a) (b) (c) (d) (e)
4. (a) (b) (c) (d) (e)
5. (a) (b) (c) (d) (e)
6. (a) (b) (c) (d) (e)
7. (a) (b) (c) (d) (e)
8. (a) (b) (c) (d) (e)
9. (a) (b) (c) (d) (e)
10. (a) (b) (c) (d) (e)
11. (a) (b) (c) (d) (e)
12. (a) (b) (c) (d) (e)
13. (a) (b) (c) (d) (e)
14. (a) (b) (c) (d) (e)
15. (a) (b) (c) (d) (e)
16. (a) (b) (c) (d) (e)
17. (a) (b) (c) (d) (e)
18. (a) (b) (c) (d) (e)
19. (a) (b) (c) (d) (e)
20. (a) (b) (c) (d) (e)
21. (a) (b) (c) (d) (e)
22. (a) (b) (c) (d) (e)
23. (a) (b) (c) (d) (e)
24. (a) (b) (c) (d) (e)
25. (a) (b) (c) (d) (e)
26. (a) (b) (c) (d) (e)
27. (a) (b) (c) (d) (e)
28. (a) (b) (c) (d) (e)
29. (a) (b) (c) (d) (e)
30. (a) (b) (c) (d) (e)
31. (a) (b) (c) (d) (e)
32. (a) (b) (c) (d) (e)
33. (a) (b) (c) (d) (e)
34. (a) (b) (c) (d) (e)
35. (a) (b) (c) (d) (e)
36. (a) (b) (c) (d) (e)
37. (a) (b) (c) (d) (e)
38. (a) (b) (c) (d) (e)
39. (a) (b) (c) (d) (e)
40. (a) (b) (c) (d) (e)

SKILLS TEST IN WRITING

1. (a) (b) (c) (d) (e)
2. (a) (b) (c) (d) (e)
3. (a) (b) (c) (d) (e)
4. (a) (b) (c) (d) (e)
5. (a) (b) (c) (d) (e)
6. (a) (b) (c) (d) (e)
7. (a) (b) (c) (d) (e)
8. (a) (b) (c) (d) (e)
9. (a) (b) (c) (d) (e)
10. (a) (b) (c) (d) (e)
11. (a) (b) (c) (d) (e)
12. (a) (b) (c) (d) (e)
13. (a) (b) (c) (d) (e)
14. (a) (b) (c) (d) (e)
15. (a) (b) (c) (d) (e)
16. (a) (b) (c) (d) (e)
17. (a) (b) (c) (d) (e)
18. (a) (b) (c) (d) (e)
19. (a) (b) (c) (d) (e)
20. (a) (b) (c) (d) (e)
21. (a) (b) (c) (d) (e)
22. (a) (b) (c) (d) (e)
23. (a) (b) (c) (d) (e)
24. (a) (b) (c) (d) (e)
25. (a) (b) (c) (d) (e)
26. (a) (b) (c) (d) (e)
27. (a) (b) (c) (d) (e)
28. (a) (b) (c) (d) (e)
29. (a) (b) (c) (d) (e)
30. (a) (b) (c) (d) (e)
31. (a) (b) (c) (d) (e)
32. (a) (b) (c) (d) (e)
33. (a) (b) (c) (d) (e)
34. (a) (b) (c) (d) (e)
35. (a) (b) (c) (d) (e)
36. (a) (b) (c) (d) (e)
37. (a) (b) (c) (d) (e)
38. (a) (b) (c) (d) (e)

Skills Test in Reading

Use the following passage to answer questions 1–5.

1 The atmosphere forms a gaseous, protective
2 envelope around Earth. It protects the planet
3 from the cold of space, from harmful ultravio-
4 let light, and from all but the largest meteors.
5 After traveling over 93 million miles, solar
6 energy strikes the atmosphere and Earth's sur-
7 face, warming the planet and creating the bio-
8 sphere, the region of Earth capable of
9 sustaining life. Solar radiation in combination
10 with the planet's rotation causes the atmo-
11 sphere to circulate. Atmospheric circulation is
12 one important reason that life on Earth can
13 exist at higher latitudes, because equatorial heat
14 is transported poleward, moderating the
15 climate.
16   The equatorial region is the warmest part
17 of Earth because it receives the most direct and,
18 therefore, strongest solar radiation. The plane
19 in which Earth revolves around the sun is called
20 the ecliptic. Earth's axis is inclined $23\frac{1}{3}$ degrees
21 with respect to the ecliptic. This inclined axis is
22 responsible for the seasons because, as seen
23 from Earth, the sun oscillates across the equator
24 in an annual cycle. On or about June 21 each
25 year, the sun reaches the Tropic of Cancer, $23\frac{1}{3}$
26 degrees north latitude. This is the northern-
27 most point where the sun can be directly over-
28 head. On or about December 21 of each year,
29 the sun reaches the Tropic of Capricorn, $23\frac{1}{3}$
30 degrees south latitude. This is the southernmost
31 point at which the sun can be directly overhead.
32 The polar regions are the coldest parts of Earth
33 because they receive the least direct and, there-
34 fore, the weakest solar radiation. Here, solar

35 radiation strikes at a very oblique angle and
36 thus spreads the same amount of energy over a
37 greater area than in the equatorial regions. A
38 static envelope of air surrounding Earth would
39 produce an extremely hot, uninhabitable equa-
40 torial region, while the polar regions would
41 remain inhospitably cold.

1. Which sentence from the passage best supports
   the author's argument that circulation of the
   atmosphere is vital to life on Earth?
   a. "[The atmosphere] protects Earth from the
      cold of space, from harmful ultraviolet light,
      and from all but the largest meteors."
   b. "The equatorial region is the warmest part
      of Earth because it receives the most direct
      and, therefore, strongest solar radiation."
   c. "The polar regions are the coldest parts of
      Earth because they receive the least direct
      and, therefore, the weakest solar radiation."
   d. "Here, solar radiation strikes at a very
      oblique angle and thus spreads the same
      amount of energy over a greater area than in
      the equatorial regions."
   e. "A static envelope of air surrounding
      Earth would produce an extremely hot,
      uninhabitable equatorial region, while the
      polar regions would remain inhospitably
      cold."

2. Which inference about Earth's biosphere can be
   made from the information provided within
   the passage?
   a. It operates as the home to human beings.
   b. It is responsible for solar energy in the
      atmosphere.
   c. It contributes to the circulation of the
      atmosphere.
   d. It is the uppermost layer of the earth's
      atmosphere.
   e. It is most susceptible to climate change.

3. In the context of the passage, *oblique* (line 35) can be replaced with which word to incur the smallest alteration in meaning?
   a. opaque
   b. obtuse
   c. slanted
   d. perpendicular
   e. straight

4. The first paragraph of the passage deals mainly with which of the following effects of the atmosphere on Earth?
   a. its sheltering effect
   b. its reviving effect
   c. its invigorating effect
   d. its cleansing effect
   e. its warming effect

5. The word *oscillates* as it appears in the passage (line 23) shares the closest meaning with which expression?
   a. rotates around itself
   b. shines brightly
   c. radiates energy
   d. moves back and forth
   e. remains stationary

Use the following passage to answer questions 6 and 7.

1 Plato, the famous Greek philosopher, taught
2 that the things of the world around us are
3 merely copies, or "shadows," of greater, eternal
4 realities. He used a metaphor of people living
5 inside a cave to convey his ideas. The people
6 inside the cave could not see the world outside
7 the cave; they could only see shadows of people
8 and animals as they passed by. Plato was sug-
9 gesting that the shadows would seem very real
10 and alive to the people inside the cave, because
11 that was all they had ever seen of the outside
12 world. But these shadows were not the real, liv-
13 ing creatures of the outside world; they were
14 merely reflections of them. Plato's position was
15 that this temporal world is a narrow picture of
16 some greater, eternal reality.

6. For which reason did the author most likely include the sentence, "The people … passed by" (lines 5–8) in the passage?
   a. to provide concrete evidence for a philosophical truism
   b. to provide a metaphor that will obscure a true meaning
   c. to illustrate a concept using an understandable context
   d. to describe the geographic location and setting of a story
   e. to illustrate a vision of a greater, eternal reality

7. As it appears in the passage, *position* (line 14) most nearly means
   a. situation.
   b. location.
   c. movement.
   d. opinion.
   e. style.

Use the following passage to answer questions 8 and 9.

Far too often artists are pigeonholed into the medium for which they are most famous and the works that are the most lucrative. But for many artists whose talents overflow, it may be the case that no single form can contain their abilities. After all, Pablo Picasso was not only a painter but a sculptor, and Salvador Dali was both a painter and a filmmaker. Emerging artists should never let their output be constrained within a solitary structure, lest their shining brilliance be dulled as a result.

8. The primary concern of this passage is
   a. describing artists who have found success with a variety of art forms.
   b. encouraging artists to experiment beyond their more recognizable media.
   c. suggesting that artists disdain the commercial exploits of their artwork.
   d. recommending that artists focus on their primary and most profitable art forms.
   e. condemning shortsighted people who disregard an artist's secondary works.

9. The author's ideas could be reinforced with the success of which other artist?
   a. Chuck Close, whose paralysis restricts the details of his paintings
   b. Samuel Clemens, whose work was attributed to either Clemens or Mark Twain
   c. Claude Monet, whose paintings varied in style throughout his career
   d. Marc Chagall, whose contributions to art include paintings and stained glass
   e. Paul Simon, who wrote songs in a partnership and as a solo artist

Use the following passage to answer question 10.

Despite what some lawyers might suggest, litigation is not always the only or best way to resolve conflicts. Mediation offers an alternative approach, and it is one that can be quite efficient and successful. Mediation can be faster, less expensive, and can lead to creative solutions not always possible in a court of law. Additionally, mediation focuses on mutually acceptable solutions, rather than on winning or losing.

10. The author of this passage would most likely agree with which of the following statements?
   a. There is too much reliance on litigation in our society.
   b. Litigation is expensive, slow, and limited by its reliance on following the letter of the law.
   c. Mediation is the best way to resolve a conflict.
   d. Compared to litigation, there is a greater chance that mediation satisfies both parties in a conflict.
   e. Lawyers are overly concerned with their earning potential and not the best interest of their clients.

Use the following passage to answer questions 11 and 12.

Recycling is a well-intentioned action to follow responsible Earth stewardship, but its usefulness is greatly overshadowed by the other "R" words: reduce and reuse. **While some materials, such as steel, are easily recyclable, other materials, such as plastic, offer only a minimal reduction in environmental waste or conservation of resources.** When glass or aluminum is recycled, it can be reused as a similar glass or aluminum product. **When plastic is recycled, it cannot be**

used to make the same plastic form—meaning that a brand-new bottle will still need to be manufactured for the next water bottle. Worse still, products made from recycled plastics, such as plastic chairs, are not recyclable. It is for these reasons that plastic is an especially dreadful material. It may feel environmentally conscientious to recycle, but it would be far, far better to avoid the creation of new materials altogether by reducing or reusing existing materials.

11. In the author's argument, what are the functions of the sections of the text in boldface?
    a. The first section supports the transitional conclusion that supports the overall argument's conclusion; the second section lists that transitional conclusion.
    b. The first section contradicts the overall argument; the second section provides support for that overall argument.
    c. The first section provides support for the overall argument of the passage; the second section presents that overall argument.
    d. The first section provides support for the overall argument; the second section contradicts that overall argument.
    e. The first section lists the transitional conclusion that supports the overall argument's conclusion; the second section supports that transitional conclusion.

12. Which sentence from the passage contains an opinion rather than a statement of fact?
    a. "While some materials . . . of resources."
    b. "When glass or . . . aluminum product."
    c. "When plastic is . . . water bottle."
    d. "Worse still, products . . . not recyclable."
    e. "It is for . . . dreadful material."

Use the following passage to answer questions 13–15.

No one is immune to the repercussions of extreme weather conditions. But with age, the body may become less able to respond to long exposure to very hot or very cold temperatures. This explains why older people are more susceptible to hypothermia—a drop in internal body temperature below 95°F—when exposed to cold weather. In fact, the majority of hypothermia victims are senior citizens. Hypothermia can be fatal if not detected and treated, usually through external warming. It is for this reason that the living environments of the elderly should be closely monitored to ensure that their temperatures are maintained within appropriate ranges.

Rate of Hypothermia Deaths in the United States, 2001

Age-adjusted rate* of hypothermia-associated death, by age group—United States, 2001

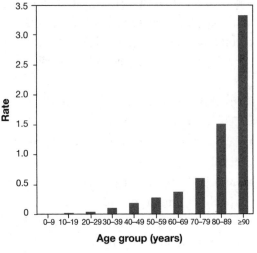

*Per 100,000 population.

13. The passage offers information on each of the following EXCEPT
    a. causes of hypothermia.
    b. prevention of hypothermia.
    c. treatments of hypothermia.
    d. hazards of hypothermia.
    e. symptoms of hypothermia.

14. According to the data in the accompanying bar graph, which conclusion about hypothermia can be fully supported?
  a. The majority of all victims of hypothermia were 90 years old or older.
  b. Children under the age of 10 are not in danger of hypothermia.
  c. The percentage of octogenarians who fell victim to hypothermia was greater than the percentage of septuagenarians who fell victim to hypothermia.
  d. Hypothermia must be detected at an early stage, before its onset affects the body's internal organs, as prevention from death.
  e. Regardless of the age of its victims, hypothermia affects a wide range of people in an equal distribution.

15. It can be concluded from the information in the passage that
  a. older people are less easily able to tolerate cold weather compared to hot weather.
  b. hypothermia is a condition that only affects older people.
  c. fewer than 50% of hypothermia victims are under 60 years old.
  d. older people who live in warm climates are healthier than older people who live in cold climates.
  e. a deteriorating circulation system is responsible for elderly people's susceptibility to hypothermia.

Use the following passage to answer questions 16–19.

1   The success of the immune system in defending
2   the human body relies on a dynamic regulatory
3   communications network consisting of mil-
4   lions and millions of cells. Organized into sets
5   and subsets, these cells pass information back
6   and forth like clouds of bees swarming around
7   a hive. The result is a sensitive system of checks
8   and balances that produces an immune
9   response that is prompt, appropriate, effective,
10   and self-limiting. At the heart of the immune
11   system is the ability to distinguish between self
12   and non-self entities. When immune defenders
13   encounter cells or organisms carrying non-self
14   molecules, the immune troops move quickly to
15   eliminate the intruders. The body's immune
16   defenses do not normally attack its own tissues
17   because of the presence of self-markers, indica-
18   tors unique to the DNA that tell that the cells
19   belong to the host body. Rather, immune cells
20   and other body cells coexist peaceably in a state
21   known as *self-tolerance*. When a normally func-
22   tioning immune system attacks a non-self mol-
23   ecule, the system can remember the specifics of
24   the foreign body. Upon subsequent encounters
25   with the same species of molecules, the
26   immune system reacts accordingly. With the
27   possible exception of antibodies passed during
28   lactation, this so-called immune system mem-
29   ory is not inherited: an immune system must
30   learn from experience with the many millions
31   of distinctive non-self molecules in the sea of
32   microbes in which we live.

16. When a person gets the chicken pox virus for the first time, his or her immune system will most likely be able to
  a. prevent its offspring from infection by the chicken pox virus.
  b. distinguish between its body cells and those of the chicken pox virus.
  c. remember previous experiences with the chicken pox virus.
  d. attack its own tissues.
  e. recall the specifics of the foreign body from ancestors' experiences.

17. Which statement represents a main idea rather than a supporting detail from the passage?

 a. The human body's immune system effectiveness lies in its complex organizational structure.

 b. The basic function of the immune system is to distinguish between self and non-self.

 c. Immune cells and body cells from the host body can coexist due to self-tolerance.

 d. The human body is an extraordinary and complicated mechanism.

 e. The human body presents an opportune habitat for microbes.

18. According to the information in the passage, why might tissue transplanted from father to daughter have a greater risk of being detected as foreign than tissue transplanted between identical twins?

 a. The identical twin's tissue would carry the same self-markers and would, therefore, be less likely to be rejected.

 b. The age of the twins' tissue would be the same and, therefore, be less likely to be rejected.

 c. The difference in the sex of the father and daughter would cause the tissue to be rejected by the daughter's immune system.

 d. The twins' immune systems would remember the same encounters with childhood illnesses.

 e. The immune system would have the previous experience of being transplanted, whereas the father and daughter's system would not.

19. As it appears in the passage, *sensitive* (line 7) most nearly means

 a. responsive.

 b. delicate.

 c. indifferent.

 d. nervous.

 e. sensible.

Use the following passage to answer question 20.

Regardless of the claims that may be made by the companies that manufacture them, there are simply no effective boundaries when it comes to pollutants. Studies have shown that toxic insecticides that have been banned in many countries are riding the wind from countries where they remain legal. Compounds such as DDT and toxaphene, used as a pesticide and an insecticide, respectively, for decades before being banned in the United States, have been found in far-flung places like the Yukon and other Arctic regions.

20. Which statement, if it were true, most significantly weakens the argument in the passage?

 a. Few companies continue to claim that their pollutants remain in the same general geographic location.

 b. Depending on the size of compounds and their relative weight, some pollutants are more stationary than others.

 c. Years after the production of some toxic compounds were banned, their presence can be identified in random ocean samplings.

 d. DDT, once considered one of the most environmentally dangerous pesticides, is now not considered nearly as toxic.

 e. The levels of compounds identified in faraway places are low enough to be considered statistically insignificant.

Use the following passage to answer questions 21–26.

1 Oil, gas, and coal—America's chief sources of
2 power—are among the chief contributors to
3 greenhouse gases. While utilizing nuclear
4 energy does not spew greenhouse gases into the
5 environment, nuclear power plants present
6 safety concerns for many. And as any driver
7 knows, the rising cost of energy is demoralizing
8 for consumers. In an effort to avoid the

9   potentially deleterious consequences of oil, gas,
10 coal, and nuclear power, some companies are
11 investigating new technologies for the potential
12 to generate cheap, clean, safe power. One of
13 these new technologies involves harnessing
14 tidal energies, using the ebb and flow of the
15 ocean's tides to produce electricity. To help
16 determine the effectiveness of this technology, a
17 power company has installed tidal power tur-
18 bines in New York City's East River. The river,
19 technically a tidal strait, features swift currents
20 that can spin the underwater turbine's long
21 blades, which in turn generate electricity. While
22 the capacity of the project can currently only
23 supply a miniscule fraction of the city's power,
24 the potential for a clean energy source within
25 the city's limits is exciting for many of the city's
26 residents. Furthermore, the success of this ini-
27 tial trial in New York City opens up the possi-
28 bilities for the greater use of tidal power at areas
29 of running water across the globe.

21. Which best describes the organization of the
passage?
  a. An untested theory is given, and then it is
proven with appropriate evidence.
  b. A problematic situation is provided, and
then a potential solution is given.
  c. A new technology is introduced, and then its
difficulties are addressed.
  d. The benefits of technologies are explained,
and then their disadvantages are provided.
  e. A series of potential technologies are
compared and contrasted.

22. As it is used in the context of the sentence,
which word best describes the meaning of *deleterious* (line 9)?
  a. disappearing
  b. expensive
  c. important
  d. safe
  e. harmful

23. Which piece of evidence, if true, would most
significantly weaken the author's primary
argument?
  a. Solar energy also provides a clean and
inexpensive source of energy, but it is not yet
efficient enough to power entire cities.
  b. With a 16-foot diameter, the size of the tidal
energy turbines is substantial.
  c. The turbines will be installed on the river
bottom and will therefore not be visible
from the shore.
  d. Due to tidal changes, the speed of the East
River is not always fast enough to generate
electricity.
  e. Given its speed and pollution, the East River
can be dangerous for swimmers in its waters.

24. Which geographic location would provide the
best option for additional experiments with
tidal energies
  a. the Bay of Fundy, a narrow bay on the
Atlantic coast of Maine
  b. the peak of Mount Whitney, the tallest peak
in the continental United States
  c. the Great Salt Lake, the largest natural lake
in the western United States
  d. Death Valley, a low, hot, and dry desert
valley in California
  e. Bullough's Pond, a former mill pond in
suburban Massachusetts

25. What purpose does the author have in mentioning the potential concerns of nuclear power?
  a. to accentuate the benefits of a safe energy source through a contrast
  b. to provide a list of negative features of nuclear power
  c. to make a point about the dangers of greenhouse gases
  d. to stress the financial considerations of alternative energy sources
  e. to downplay the safety issues of renewable energy sources

26. Which information from the passage contains an opinion rather than a fact?
  a. Oil, gas, and coal are America's chief sources of power.
  b. Nuclear energy does not spew greenhouse gases into the environment.
  c. The rising cost of energy is demoralizing for consumers.
  d. A power company installed tidal power turbines in the East River.
  e. The capacity of the project can only supply a miniscule fraction of the city's power.

Use the following passage to answer questions 27–29.

1 The forty-three men who have held the title of
2 U.S. president through 2011 have come from a
3 remarkable variety of fields. Before entering
4 politics, these leaders have been schoolteachers
5 (John Adams), tailors (Andrew Johnson), pea-
6 nut farmers (Jimmy Carter), and even actors
7 (Ronald Reagan). While there are many paths
8 to the presidency, one avenue is less circuitous.
9 Unsurprisingly, most presidents served in the
10 armed forces before becoming commander in
11 chief, including three generals: George Wash-
12 ington, Ulysses S. Grant, and Dwight D. Eisen-
13 hower. In fact, only a dozen U.S. presidents

14 never served in uniform. However, voters lately
15 seem to discount the importance of military
16 service; eight of the 12 presidents in the last 100
17 years, including two of the three presidents
18 from 1993 to 2012, never served at all. More
19 important to voters lately is the president's
20 knowledge of the law; half of the presidents
21 since 1961 have been lawyers at one time,
22 including two of the last three.

27. Which inference can be made from the passage?
  a. Regardless of their backgrounds, all presidents had some experience in politics before attaining the highest office.
  b. Military service is a prerequisite for election as U.S. president.
  c. Only Jimmy Carter had a job as a farmer before becoming U.S. president.
  d. George H. W. Bush, who served as president from 1989–1993, did not serve in the U.S. military.
  e. More than thirty U.S. presidents have served in the U.S. military in some capacity.

28. According to the passage, which occupation will the next U.S. president most likely have had before taking office?
  a. tailor
  b. soldier
  c. lawyer
  d. actor
  e. army general

29. As it is used in the context of the sentence, which word best describes the meaning of *circuitous* (line 8)?
  a. direct
  b. roundabout
  c. mainstream
  d. political
  e. circuslike

Use the following passage to answer questions 30 and 31.

One of the most common fears that people have is that of snakes. However, that fear is not only largely groundless but highly irrational. There are more than 2,500 different species of snakes around the world, but only a small percentage of those species are poisonous. Furthermore, only a few species have venom strong enough to actually kill a human being. Statistically, snakes bite only 1,000–2,000 people in the United States each year, and only ten of those bites (that's less than 1%!) result in death. In fact, in this country, more people die from dog bites each year than from snake bites.

30. Based on the information in the passage, which number could best represent the number of unique species of snakes in the world?
   a. 10
   b. 1,100
   c. 2,000
   d. 2,350
   e. 2,700

31. Which sentence from the passage represents an opinion rather than a fact?
   a. "However, that fear . . . highly irrational."
   b. "There are more . . . are poisonous."
   c. "Furthermore, only a . . . human being."
   d. "Statistically, snakes bite . . . in death."
   e. "In fact, in . . . from snake bites."

Use the following passage to answer questions 32 and 33.

After generations of referring to the creature by its misnomer, marine biologists are now encouraging people to rename all starfish as sea stars. The change in name is more than simply a cosmetic alteration. A fish is defined as an aquatic vertebrate with gills; the marine animals formerly known as starfish are not vertebrates because they have no spine or internal skeleton. The roughly 2,000 species of sea stars belong to a phylum of marine animals called *echinoderms*, and their name should more accurately represent this classification—despite any complications that some people may have with the amendment.

32. Which sentence best summarizes the main point of the passage?
   a. Sea stars are not considered vertebrates because they have no spine or internal skeleton.
   b. It can be difficult, but it is often necessary to change a creature's name based on scientific evidence.
   c. Starfish are not technically fish and should therefore be identified as sea stars.
   d. A fish is defined as an aquatic vertebrate with gills.
   e. Sea stars belong to a phylum of marine animals called *echinoderms*.

33. The author of this passage would most likely agree with which of the following statements?
   a. Sea stars are among the most beautiful creatures in the sea.
   b. Sea stars should be considered in the same classification as vertebrates.
   c. It is not worth the trouble to rename an entire class of roughly 2,000 species.
   d. Jellyfish should be given a new name because they do not have a spine.
   e. Sea stars and starfish are synonyms for the same creature and may be used interchangeably.

Use the following passage to answer questions 34–37.

1   The skyline of St. Louis, Missouri, is fairly
2   unremarkable, with one prodigious exception—
3   the Gateway Arch, which stands on the banks of

4   the Mississippi River. Part of the Jefferson
5   National Expansion Memorial, the Arch is an
6   amazing structure built to honor St. Louis's role
7   as the gateway to the West. In 1947 a group of
8   interested citizens known as the Jefferson
9   National Expansion Memorial Association held
10 a nationwide competition to select a design for
11 a new monument that would celebrate the
12 growth of the United States. Other U.S. monu-
13 ments at the time featured spires, statues, or
14 imposing buildings, but the winner of this con-
15 test was a plan for a completely different type of
16 structure. The man who submitted the winning
17 design, Eero Saarinen, later became a famous
18 architect. In designing the Arch, Saarinen
19 wanted to "create a monument which would
20 have lasting significance and would be a land-
21 mark of our time."
22   The Gateway Arch is a masterpiece of
23 engineering, a monument even taller than the
24 Great Pyramid in Egypt. In its own way, the
25 Arch is at least as majestic as the Great Pyra-
26 mid. The Gateway is shaped as an inverted cate-
27 nary curve, the same shape that a heavy chain
28 will form if suspended between two points.
29 Covered with a sleek skin of stainless steel, the
30 Arch often reflects dazzling bursts of sunlight.
31 In a beautiful display of symmetry, the height
32 of the arch is the same as the distance between
33 the legs at ground level.

34. Which sentence from the passage contains both
a fact and an opinion?
  a. In its own way, the Arch is at least as majestic
  as the Great Pyramid.
  b. In 1947 a group of interested citizens known
  as the Jefferson National Expansion
  Memorial Association held a nationwide
  competition to select a design for a new
  monument that would celebrate the growth
  of the United States.
  c. In designing the Arch, Saarinen wanted to
  "create a monument which would have
  lasting significance and would be a landmark
  of our time."
  d. The Gateway Arch is a masterpiece of
  engineering, a monument even taller than
  the Great Pyramid in Egypt.
  e. The Gateway is shaped as an inverted
  catenary curve, the same shape that a heavy
  chain will form if suspended between two
  points.

35. According to the passage, Saarinen's winning
design was
  a. modeled after other U.S. monuments.
  b. unlike any other existing monument.
  c. part of a series of monuments.
  d. less expensive to construct than other
  monuments.
  e. shaped like the Great Pyramid.

36. What was the author's primary purpose in revealing the material of the Gateway Arch's casing?
   a. to provide a comprehensive description of its metallic components
   b. to describe another astounding quality of the monument
   c. to contrast it with the materials of the Great Pyramid
   d. to illustrate the balanced symmetry of the monument
   e. to offer historic context for the construction of the monument

37. As it is used in the context of the sentence, which word best describes the meaning of *prodigious* (line 2)?
   a. commonplace
   b. talented
   c. extraordinary
   d. timely
   e. lackluster

Use the following passage to answer questions 38–40.

1   The U.S. government has spent more than $10
2   billion each year since 1989 on the National
3   Aeronautics and Space Administration (NASA).
4   Furthermore, the government agency's budget
5   is expected to increase every year, with its
6   annual spending estimated to surpass $20 bil-
7   lion for the first time in the mid-2010s. A hefty
8   fraction of this budget will be spent on space
9   operations, including the construction and
10   maintenance of the International Space Station
11   (ISS). At a time when the country is facing
12   domestic crises with unemployment, energy,
13   and health care, it can be difficult to justify the
14   exorbitant costs of space exploration. Neverthe-
15   less, its indirect benefits are impossible to
16   ignore; the valuable research and development
17   associated with NASA's space program have
18   resulted in an incredibly wide variety of impor-
19   tant everyday technological advancements,
20   ranging from water filters to improved highway
21   safety.

38. How is the key word *nevertheless* used in the last sentence of the passage?
   a. to accentuate the financial concerns of space exploration
   b. to list additional domestic concerns that should receive a higher priority
   c. to suggest that too great a fraction of NASA's budget is spent on space operations
   d. to show that the financial expenditures of the agency have been changing
   e. to provide a contrast with the monetary costs of a government agency

39. As it is used in the context of the sentence, which word best describes the meaning of *exorbitant* (line 14)?
   a. excessive
   b. painful
   c. reasonable
   d. fixed
   e. exciting

40. Which sentence best describes the author's attitude toward the financial cost of the National Aeronautics and Space Administration?
   a. The costs must be curtailed to allow for increased funding for domestic crises.
   b. The costs are very high, but the rewards make the agency a worthwhile expense.
   c. The costs should decrease at a time when the government operates with a financial deficit.
   d. The increasing cost of running the government agency is simply indefensible.
   e. The high costs should only be validated during periods of planetary exploration, such as a trip to Mars.

Skills Test in Mathematics

1. Veronica runs for exercise. The following chart shows how far she ran each day last week. How many miles did Veronica need to run on Saturday in order for her average distance for the week to be 4 miles per day?

DAY OF THE WEEK	NUMBER OF MILES
Sunday	3
Monday	4
Tuesday	5
Wednesday	2
Thursday	5
Friday	4
Saturday	?

   a. 2
   b. 3
   c. 4
   d. 5
   e. 6

2. Which of the following has the greatest value?
   a. $4\frac{3}{4}\%$
   b. 4.09%
   c. $\frac{47}{1,000}$
   d. $\frac{23}{500}$
   e. 0.0408

3. If the following spinner is drawn to scale, what is the probability that the spinner will land on the number 1?

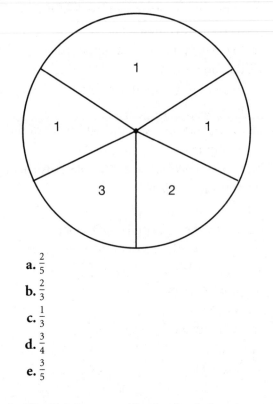

   a. $\frac{2}{5}$
   b. $\frac{2}{3}$
   c. $\frac{1}{3}$
   d. $\frac{3}{4}$
   e. $\frac{3}{5}$

4. The U.S. Bureau of Justice Statistics reported that 7,225,800 people were in prison, on probation, or on parole at the end of 2009. If this number accounted for approximately 3% of the adult U.S. population, what was the U.S. population at the end of 2009?
   a. 216,774
   b. 216,774,000
   c. 2,167,740,000
   d. 240,860,000
   e. 2,408,600,000

5. The following figure is an isosceles right triangle. What is the value of side *h*?

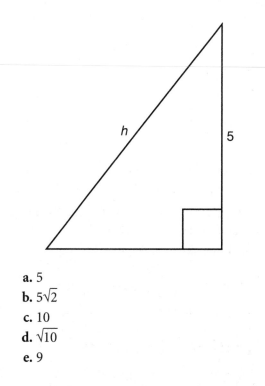

    a. 5
    b. $5\sqrt{2}$
    c. 10
    d. $\sqrt{10}$
    e. 9

6. Ryan and Kimberly spend a combined total of 12 hours to begin the spring landscaping for a friend. The next week Jaime and Janet spend another 18 hours to finish the landscaping job. If Ryan worked three times as many hours as Kimberly, and Jaime worked five more hours than Ryan worked, how many hours did Janet spend on the landscaping?
    a. 3
    b. 9
    c. 14
    d. 4
    e. 7

7. Paula has four friends over to watch the basketball game. They are all hungry, but no one wants to go get food. Just as they are arguing about who should go pick up food, a commercial comes on for a local pizzeria that delivers. The phone number flashes on the screen briefly and they all try to remember it. By the time Paula grabs a pen and paper, each of them recollects a different number. Each of the numbers below is one of the guesses. Which of the numbers is most likely the telephone number of the delivery pizzeria?
    a. 995-9266
    b. 995-9336
    c. 995-9268
    d. 995-8266
    e. 996-8638

8. Marvin wrapped a gift that is in a box that is a perfect cube with each side measuring *d* inches. Maya arrives with a gift that is also in a box that is a perfect cube, but the edge length of each side of her gift is twice as long as Marvin's gift. How many square inches of wrapping paper, in terms of *d*, will Maya need to wrap her gift?
    a. $6d^2$
    b. $12d^2$
    c. $24d^2$
    d. $2d^3$
    e. $12d^3$

9. Jesse ate $\frac{1}{2}$ of a pizza and left the other half in his dorm room. Dennis came by and ate one-quarter of what was left there. How much of the original pie did Dennis eat?
    a. $\frac{1}{16}$
    b. $\frac{1}{6}$
    c. $\frac{1}{4}$
    d. $\frac{1}{8}$
    e. $\frac{3}{4}$

Use the following table to answer questions 10 and 11.

RETIREMENT ACCOUNT BALANCE	
DATE	**BALANCE ON 1ST OF MONTH**
April 1, 2008	$3,360
December 1, 2008	$6,720
December 1, 2009	$11,760
May 1, 2010	$13,860
September 1, 2011	—

10. Frank's employer deposited a consistent amount of money into his retirement account on the last day of each month. Use the table to figure out how much money his employer put into Frank's retirement account each month, rounded to the nearest dollar.
   a. $420
   b. $373
   c. $388
   d. $350
   e. $480

11. It is September 7, 2011, and Frank's wife cannot find his latest bank statement for the 1st of the month. She wants to know how much money is currently in his retirement account. Using the information in the table, calculate what the balance in Frank's retirement account should be as of September 1, 2011.
   a. $20,160
   b. $19,828
   c. $21,000
   d. $20,201
   e. $20,580

12. Find the value of w in terms of p.
   $$2w = 15k + 4$$
   $$3k = 10 - \frac{1}{2}q$$
   $$q = 12p + 8$$
   a. $6 - 6p$
   b. $3 - 3p$
   c. $30 - 30p$
   d. $17 - 15p$
   e. $37 - 15p$

13. A rectangular community garden needs fencing to keep deer from eating the vegetables. If 200 linear feet of fencing is needed to enclose the garden space, which of the following could be the dimensions for the length and width of the garden?
   a. 100 feet long and 100 feet wide
   b. 100 feet long and 20 feet wide
   c. 80 feet long and 20 feet wide
   d. 50 feet long and 40 feet wide
   e. 20 feet long and 10 feet wide

14. The Sunnyside Resort has a pool that is 5 feet deep, 30 feet long, and 20 feet wide. One cubic foot of water is equal to approximately 7.5 gallons. One gallon of water weighs approximately 8.35 pounds. What is the approximate weight, in pounds, of the water held in the pool at the Sunnyside Resort?
   a. 3,000 pounds
   b. 22,500 pounds
   c. 187,875 pounds
   d. 156,563 pounds
   e. 25,050 pounds

Use the following Venn diagram and the information beneath it to answer questions 15 and 16.

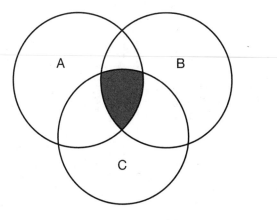

Lonely Star Prep School is offering a summer enrichment program that 80 students are enrolled in. One of the electives students can select is science, and if they choose to take a science class they can chose from Biology, Chemistry, or Physics. Students can enroll for 5 classes for the summer and they can choose 0 to 3 science classes. In the Venn diagram above, A represents the students enrolled in Physics, B represents the students enrolled in Biology, and C represents the students enrolled in Chemistry.

15. Circle A contains 18 students who are enrolled in the Physics class, and circle B contains 26 students who are enrolled in Biology. If 34 students are enrolled in just Physics, just Biology, or both Physics and Biology, how many students are enrolled in both Physics and Biology?
   a. 10
   b. 8
   c. 16
   d. 46
   e. 36

16. Which of the following best describes the students in the shaded region of the Venn Diagram?
   a. the students who are most talented in science
   b. the students who are enrolled in Physics and Biology
   c. the students who decided not to take science
   d. the students who like chemistry the best
   e. the students who are enrolled in three science classes this summer

17. Fifty students at Adams College were asked about the sports in which they participate. Each student participates in at least one sport, and some participate in two sports. The results are shown in the following table. What percent of the students participate in two sports?

SPORT	STUDENTS
Soccer	13
Football	16
Basketball	12
Baseball	10
Hockey	9

   a. 10%
   b. 20%
   c. 50%
   d. 60%
   e. 80%

18. Which of the following triangles could not exist?
   a. an acute equilateral triangle
   b. an obtuse isosceles triangle
   c. a scalene right triangle
   d. an acute isosceles triangle
   e. an obtuse right triangle

19. Which of the following equations was used to construct this input/output table?

x	y
1	7
2	10
3	13
4	16
5	19

a. $y = 3x + 4$
b. $y = 4x + 3$
c. $y = 8x - 1$
d. $y = 5x - 2$
e. $y = x^2 + 6$

20. A dodecahedron is a 12-sided die that has an equal probability of landing on each side. If Chi Chun rolls a dodecahedron one time, what is the probability that she will roll a prime factor of 12?

a. $\frac{1}{6}$
b. $\frac{1}{2}$
c. $\frac{1}{4}$
d. $\frac{1}{12}$
e. $\frac{6}{1}$

21. The following scatter plot shows the population of a city over the last 50 years.

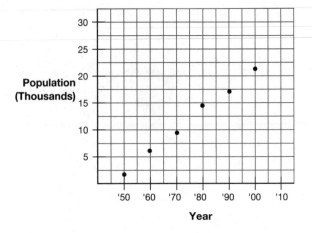

If the population continues to grow at the same rate, what is the best estimate for the population in 2010?

a. 20,000
b. 22,000
c. 25,000
d. 29,000
e. 30,000

22. Josh buys $5\frac{3}{4}$ yards of upholstery fabric to make seat cushions. If he needs to cover two seats with just that material, how many inches of upholstery fabric does he have to use on each seat?

a. 207 inches
b. 192.24 inches
c. 96.12 inches
d. 103.5 inches
e. 34.5 inches

23. Consider the following three facts:

Fact A: Kris said, "Emily and I both have dogs."

Fact B: Emily said, "I don't have a dog."

Fact C: Kris always tells the truth, but Emily sometimes lies.

If the first three statements are facts, which of the following statements must also be a fact?

    I. Emily has a dog.

    II. Kris has a dog.

    III. Emily is lying.

a. II only

b. I and II only

c. I, II, and III

d. II and III only

e. None of the statements is a known fact.

24. A circular table is going to be covered with tile. If the diameter of the table is 10 feet, approximately how many square feet of tile must be purchased to cover the table?

a. 10 square feet

b. 314 square feet

c. 31 square feet

d. 63 feet

e. 79 feet

25. A factory operates 20 machines that make buttons. Each machine can make between 80 and 100 buttons per minute. Which of the following could be the number of buttons produced per hour if all 20 machines are working at the same time?

a. 1,600

b. 4,800

c. 6,000

d. 88,000

e. 100,000

26. Susie types 12 words per minute, and Doug types 22 words per minute. They are dividing up scenes of an independent film and typing up a 68,000-word manuscript for Buffalo Indi Films. After typing it up, it takes them about 20% additional time to proofread it for errors. Lastly, for every 3 hours they work, Doug and Susie *both* get a union break of 30 minutes of paid time which can be billed to Buffalo Indi Films. Rounded to the nearest hour, what is the closest approximation to the total amount of hours that Susie and Doug will be able to bill Buffalo Indi Films for at the end of this project?

a. 33 hours

b. 40 hours

c. 48 hours

d. 53 hours

e. 56 hours

27. The graphs of the dotted line $y = (\frac{1}{4})x$ and the solid line $y = -4x$ form the boundaries of the shaded region. The solution set of which of the following systems of linear inequalities is given by the region with the darkest shading?

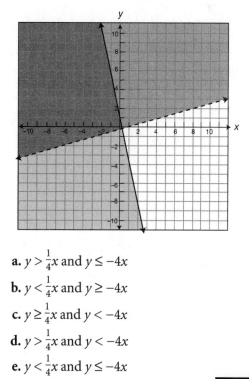

a. $y > \frac{1}{4}x$ and $y \leq -4x$

b. $y < \frac{1}{4}x$ and $y \geq -4x$

c. $y \geq \frac{1}{4}x$ and $y < -4x$

d. $y > \frac{1}{4}x$ and $y < -4x$

e. $y < \frac{1}{4}x$ and $y \leq -4x$

28. If Ψ is divisible by 3 and 10, then 8Ψ must be divisible by all the following EXCEPT

 a. 14.

 b. 15.

 c. 16.

 d. 30.

 e. 32.

The following graph shows the yearly electricity usage for Finnigan Engineering Inc. over the course of three years for three departments. Use it to answer questions 29–31.

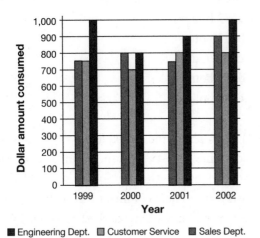

29. How much greater was the electricity cost for Sales during the year 1999 than the electricity cost for Customer Service in 2000?

 a. $800

 b. $50

 c. $150

 d. $250

 e. $0

30. Which of the following statements is supported by the data?

 I. The Sales Department showed a steady increase in the dollar amount of electricity used during the four-year period.

 II. The two departments that have the most similar electricity usage over the four-year period are the Customer Service and Sales Departments.

 III. The Engineering Department showed a steady increase in the dollar amount of electricity used from 2000–2002.

 a. I

 b. II

 c. III

 d. II and III

 e. I, II, and III

31. What was the percent decrease in cost of electricity usage from 1999 to 2000 for the Engineering Department?

 a. 25%

 b. 20%

 c. 12.5%

 d. 10%

 e. 0%

32. Look at the following series and determine which two numbers most logically follow next: 28, 25, 5, 21, 18, 5, 14, …

 a. 11, 5

 b. 10, 7

 c. 11, 8

 d. 5, 10

 e. 10, 5

33. If it takes John h hours to bike k kilometers, how far can he bike in m minutes?

    a. $\frac{m}{60hk}$

    b. $\frac{60h}{mk}$

    c. $\frac{mk}{60h}$

    d. $\frac{60k}{mh}$

    e. $60mhk$

34. 1,200 new nursing students were asked to complete a survey in which they were asked which type of nursing they would like to pursue. The data was used to make the following pie chart.

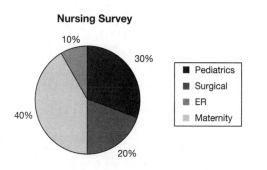

Nursing Survey

If the same color scheme is used, which of the following bar graphs would represent the same data as the pie chart?

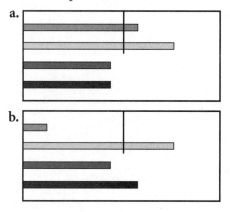

    a.

    b.

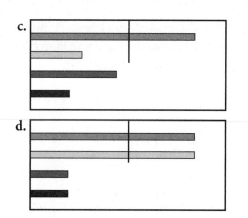

    c.

    d.

    e. Bar graphs cannot be used to represent the data found in pie charts.

35. Belicia drives a compact car that gets, on average, 28 miles for every gallon of gas. If she must drive 364 miles from Los Angeles to San Francisco, and gas costs on average $4.85 per gallon, approximately how much will she spend on gas?

    a. $63

    b. $75

    c. $73

    d. $136

    e. $65

36. *The Independent* is a British newspaper. It ran a headline in January 2001 that read, "Three-quarters of a million to pay higher rate of tax." Which number below is equivalent to three-quarters of a million?

    a. 340,000,000

    b. $\left(\frac{3}{4}\right) \div 1{,}000{,}000$

    c. 750,000

    d. 750,000,000,000

    e. $\frac{3}{4} \times 1{,}000{,}000{,}000$

37. A cylindrical cooling tank holds 150 liters of chemical solution. How many milliliters of solution does the tank hold?

a. 7,500

b. 15,000

c. 75,000

d. 150,000

e. 1,500

38. Shane would like her business to sell an average of $5,000 of jewelry every month; however, her industry is very seasonal, with the end-of-the-year holiday season being the busiest time. In 2010 her sales totaled $35,400 on September 30, 2010. What must her monthly average sales be for October, November, and December if she wants to make her year-end goal of averaging $5,000 a month?

a. $11,800

b. $8,200

c. $5,000

d. $3,933

e. Shane will not be able to make her goal in 2010.

39. What inequality is represented by the following graph?

a. $x \geq -4$

b. $x > -4$

c. $x \leq -4$

d. $x < -4$

e. $10 > x > -4$

40. $\frac{3}{5}$ is equivalent to

a. 0.06

b. 6%

c. 0.60

d. 0.6%

e. 0.35

Skills Test in Writing

Section 1, Part A

Directions: Choose the letter for the underlined portion that contains a grammatical error. If there is no error in the sentence, choose **e**.

1. In the <u>United States</u>, three states—<u>Indiana, Ohio, and Wisconsin</u>—<u>is</u> scenes of fierce debate over
        a   b   c

   <u>legislation</u> aimed at curtailing the power of labor unions. <u>No error</u>
      d   e

2. The audience applauded <u>politely</u> for the <u>actor not</u> feeling <u>well</u>, he hadn't performed to the best of his
                             a   b   c

   ability. <u>No error</u>
           e

3. Juliet did <u>poor</u> in her first dance <u>recital</u>; she was <u>confident</u> she could have done better if she had
           a   b   c

   practiced the routine a <u>few</u> more times. <u>No error</u>
                   d   e

4. <u>Adjectives and adverbs</u> add <u>spice</u> to writing <u>in that they</u> describe, <u>or modify,</u> other words. <u>No error</u>
         a   b   c   d   e

5. I have <u>all ways</u> been <u>enamored</u> with the concept that <u>through</u> computer modeling we can create an
          a   b   c

   <u>executable</u> model to test a complex system. <u>No error</u>
     d   e

6. In my opinion, <u>watching a psychological</u> thriller is <u>less scary than</u> <u>a horror film</u>. <u>No error</u>
                a   b   c   d   e

7. In <u>Disney's</u> *The Pirates of the Caribbean: On Stranger Tides*, Captain Jack Sparrow—<u>played by</u>
      a   b   c

   <u>Johnny Depp</u>—journeys to the fabled <u>Fountain of Youth</u>. <u>No error</u>
     d   e

8. <u>Based on</u> her <u>continuous</u> need to pay her <u>rent,</u> Annabelle decided to offer to teach <u>another</u> yoga class
      a   b   c   d

   on the weekends. <u>No error</u>
                  e

9. Trading <u>elicit</u> drugs <u>(also referred to as trafficking illegal drugs)</u> is one of the <u>largest</u> global
                    a   b   c

markets, valued at over <u>$322 billion.</u> <u>No error</u>
                           d   e

10. The other senators <u>watched</u> their colleague, who frequently <u>launched</u> filibusters to draw
                           a   b

attention to <u>neglected</u> discussion, <u>stood</u> up. <u>No error</u>
               c   d   e

11. Despite the fact that <u>her</u> friends <u>became vegetarian,</u> <u>Darbys</u> position on eating meat <u>hasn't</u> changed.
                            a   b   c   d

<u>No error</u>
e

12. Even though they <u>were</u> admired by some, the innovations of <u>Lewis Carroll's</u> later novels <u>were not as</u>
                        a   b   c

well received <u>as his *Alice's Adventures in Wonderland*.</u> <u>No error</u>
                            d   e

13. At the Belmont, on <u>June 9, 1973,</u> Secretariat won <u>by:</u> an astonishing 31 <u>lengths,</u> claiming the first
                          a   b   c

Triple Crown in <u>25 years.</u> <u>No error</u>
                  d   e

14. Introduced by the International Olympic Committee in the <u>Vancouver 2010 Winter Olympics Games,</u>
                                                                     a

<u>they</u> allow future host cities <u>access</u> to draw on the knowledge and experience of previous <u>Games</u>
b   c   d

hosts. <u>No error</u>
         e

15. Dawn, <u>an administrative assistant with extensive experience working in human resources,</u> <u>was looking</u>
                                               a   b

for a position in an office where she <u>would be respected</u> for her knowledge and experience,
                                     c

would be looked upon as a professional, and <u>within an easily commutable distance.</u> <u>No error</u>
                                                   d   e

16. The sign at the <u>cash register</u> in the <u>supermarket</u> was <u>grammatically</u> correct: It read, "15 Items or
                           a   b   c

<u>Less."</u> <u>No error</u>
d   e

17. <u>Screaming</u> and shouting to <u>cheer on</u> the <u>team,</u> <u>the day ended with everyone having a sore throat.</u> <u>No error</u>
     a   b   c   d   e

18. As the term is <u>intrinsically</u> linked to the process of writing personalized communications on paper,
                          a

the usage and marketing of <u>stationary</u> is a <u>niche industry</u> that is increasingly threatened by electronic
                                  b   c

<u>media.</u> <u>No error</u>
 d   e

19. The following artifacts are the <u>Seven Wonders</u> of the Ancient <u>World:</u> The Great Pyramid at Giza,
                                  a   b

the Hanging Gardens of Babylon, the Temple of Artemis at Ephesus, the <u>Statue of Zeus at Olympia,</u>
                                                                    c

the Pharos Lighthouse near Alexandria, the Mausoleum of Halicarnassus, <u>and the Colossus of</u>
                                                                    d

<u>Rhodes.</u> <u>No error</u>
        e

20. <u>Believe it or not,</u> several of our most loved and revered artists, <u>such as Michelangelo and Leonardo</u>
     a   b

DaVinci, lived and created <u>their</u> masterpieces during the <u>Middle Ages.</u> <u>No error</u>
                              c   d   e

21. Of all the <u>people</u> running for governor, Samuels was <u>less</u> likely to win <u>based on</u> his <u>progressive</u>
              a   b   c   d

<u>views.</u> <u>No error</u>
      e

Section 1, Part B
Directions: Choose the best replacement for the underlined portion of the sentence. If no revision is necessary, choose **a**, which always repeats the original phrasing.

22. My instinct was to take my time to figure out the <u>problem, but</u> I only had one hour to finish the whole test.
  a. problem, but
  b. problem but
  c. problem; but
  d. problem: but
  e. problem, but,

23. <u>No one had no</u> idea where to find the book.
  a. No one had no
  b. No one had not
  c. No one had any
  d. Any one had any
  e. Any one had no

24. The school budget not only provided for three new school <u>buses but also sets aside</u> enough funds to hire a second fourth-grade teacher.
  a. buses but also sets aside
  b. buses, but also set aside
  c. buses, but also sets aside
  d. buses but also set aside
  e. buses but also provides

25. <u>There are several reasons why there concerned about there grades.</u>
  a. There are several reasons why there concerned about there grades.
  b. They're are several reasons why there concerned about their grades.
  c. Their are several reasons why they're concerned about there grades.
  d. There are several reasons why they're concerned about their grades.
  e. There are several reasons why they're concerned about they're grades.

26. When it comes to running a marathon, a person has to run at <u>their own pace.</u>
  a. their own pace.
  b. there own pace.
  c. her own pace.
  d. his own pace.
  e. his or her own pace.

27. The teacher looked <u>skeptical when</u> the student said she left her homework on the bus.
  a. skeptical when
  b. skeptically when
  c. skeptical, when
  d. skeptically, when
  e. skeptically, when,

28. The school held a reunion for all the <u>alumnus of the Class of 1975.</u>
  a. alumnus of the Class of 1975.
  b. alumnus of the class of 1975.
  c. alumni of the Class of 1975.
  d. alumni of the Class of Nineteen Seventy-Five.
  e. alumnus of the Class of Nineteen Hundred Seventy-Five.

29. I saw a long, black snake <u>following a frog that was slithering slowly toward the rocks in my garden.</u>
  a. following a frog that was slithering slowly toward the rocks in my garden.
  b. slithering slowly toward the rocks in my garden following a frog.
  c. following a frog toward the rocks in my garden that was slithering slowly.
  d. toward the rocks slithering in my garden following a frog slowly.
  e. following a frog slithering slowly in my garden toward the rocks.

30. Every day before I go to work, I <u>fed the dogs, watered the garden, and then run three miles.</u>
  a. fed the dogs, watered the garden, and then run three miles.
  b. feed the dogs, watered the garden, and then run three miles.
  c. feed the dogs, water the garden, and then ran three miles.
  d. feed the dogs water the garden and then run three miles.
  e. feed the dogs, water the garden, and then run three miles.

31. Stressed about the deadline she had committed to meet, <u>it was difficult for Ann to concentrate on the project.</u>
  a. it was difficult for Ann to concentrate on the project.
  b. Ann found it difficult to concentrate on the project.
  c. concentrating on the project was difficult for Ann.
  d. it was difficult to concentrate on the project for Ann.
  e. Ann concentrated on the difficult project.

32. To see the <u>good view of the lake, better</u> than anywhere else, you have to climb to the top of that hillside.
  a. good view of the lake, better
  b. good view of the lake, best
  c. better view of the lake, better
  d. better view of the lake, best
  e. best view of the lake, better

33. It was evident that the school had insufficient funds for technology; students <u>didn't hardly have no</u> computers available to use.
  a. didn't hardly have no
  b. did hardly have no
  c. hardly had any
  d. hardly had no
  e. didn't hardly have any

34. <u>Even though</u> he ate the Thanksgiving dinner off the table, the dog was sent to his kennel crate for the night.
  a. Even though
  b. Although
  c. After
  d. Furthermore
  e. As

35. Out of all the courses I've taken, this one is definitely the <u>easiest.</u>
  a. easiest.
  b. easier.
  c. easy.
  d. more easier.
  e. most easiest.

36. <u>Crisis</u> place an enormous strain on our resources as embassy personnel focus on assisting U.S. citizens affected by them.
  a. Crisis
  b. Crisese
  c. Crisses
  d. Crisises
  e. Crises

37. <u>Since the ancient city of Ashur, capital of the powerful Assyrian Empire, because it will soon be flooded to make more water available for today's Iraqi settlers and farmers.</u>
  a. Since the ancient city of Ashur, capital of the powerful Assyrian Empire, because it will soon be flooded to make more water available for today's Iraqi settlers and farmers.
  b. The ancient city of Ashur, capital of the powerful Assyrian Empire, will soon be flooded to make more water available for today's Iraqi settlers and farmers.
  c. Since the ancient city of Ashur, capital of the powerful Assyrian Empire, because today's Iraqi settlers and farmers will flood more water.
  d. Since it will soon be flooded to make more water available for today's Iraqi settlers and farmers, since the ancient city of Ashur, capital of the powerful Assyrian Empire.
  e. Because it will soon be flooded to make more water available for today's Iraqi settlers and farmers, since the ancient city of Ashur, capital of the powerful Assyrian Empire.

38. The carpenter did a very <u>good job building the garden shed; it</u> was spacious and had a strong foundation and roof.
  a. good job building the garden shed; it
  b. well job building the garden shed; it
  c. good job building the garden shed, it
  d. well job building the garden shed, it
  e. good job building the garden shed: it

Section 2, Essay Writing

Carefully read the essay topic that follows. Plan and write an essay that addresses all points in the topic. Make sure that your essay is well organized and that you support your central argument with concrete examples. Allow 30 minutes for your essay.

In an effort to reduce juvenile violence and crime, many towns have chosen to enforce curfews on minors under the age of 18. These curfews make it illegal for any minor to loiter, wander, stroll, or play in public streets, highways, roads, alleys, parks, playgrounds, or other public places between the hours of 10:00 P.M. and 5:00 A.M. Supporters of the curfew believe that it will reduce community problems such as violence, graffiti, and drugs. Those who oppose curfews for minors claim these laws violate Fourteenth Amendment rights to equal protection and due process for U.S. citizens. They also believe that such curfews stereotype minors by presupposing that citizens under the age of 18 are the only people who commit crimes.

In your essay, take a position on this question.

You may write about either of the two points of view given, or you may present a different point of view on the topic. Use specific reasons and examples to support your position.

Answers

Skills Test in Reading

1. e. The sentence in choice **e** explains that conditions would be inhospitable at the equator and the polar regions without the circulation of the atmosphere; therefore, it is the best choice to support the author's argument that circulation of the atmosphere is vital to life on Earth. The sentence in choice **a** describes how the atmosphere protects Earth, but it does not speak of the circulation of the atmosphere; therefore, it cannot be correct. The sentences in choices **b** and **c** deal with solar radiation, not with circulation of the atmosphere, so they are incorrect. The fact that solar radiation is spread over a greater area, choice **d**, does not directly explain how the circulation of the atmosphere is vital to life on Earth; a different sentence better makes the connection to the author's argument.

2. a. The passage states that the biosphere is the region of Earth capable of sustaining life. Therefore, you can infer that human beings must live within the biosphere, making choice **a** correct. If you read the passage carefully, you will see that it is the solar energy that is responsible for the creation of the biosphere, not the other way around. Therefore, choice **b** cannot be correct. According to the passage, a combination of Earth's rotation and solar radiation causes the atmosphere to circulate. Because the passage does not mention the atmosphere as one of the causes, you can eliminate choice **c**. There is no indication in the passage that the biosphere is the uppermost layer of Earth's atmosphere or the most susceptible to climate change, so choices **d** and **e** are incorrect.

3. c. The word *oblique* as it appears in line 35 refers to the angle of the solar radiation on Earth. If you read the sentence before the one in which *oblique* appears, you will see that the radiation strikes the polar regions where the solar radiation is *least direct*. Therefore, the meaning of oblique will also mean least direct; *slanted* describes this perfectly. *Opaque* sounds similar to oblique, but its meaning is dense or unclear. An angle cannot be described as opaque, so choice **a** is not correct. An *obtuse* angle is an angle with a measure greater than 90 degrees. However, it cannot be inferred that the measure of the angle at which radiation hits Earth must be greater than 90 degrees, so choice **b** is not correct. *Perpendicular* lines form right angles, such as the *x*- and *y*-axes of a coordinate plane. The oblique angle referred to in this sentence is describing the way that the solar radiation strikes the polar regions of Earth. This striking of the radiation is also called *not direct* in the previous sentence. Perpendicular lines are perfectly direct, so choice **d** cannot be correct. Similarly, the striking of the radiation is also referred to as *not direct* in the passage. *Straight* means direct, so choice **e** cannot be correct either.

4. a. The very first sentence of the first paragraph sums up the main effect of the atmosphere on Earth—to create a *protective envelope around Earth*. This can be described as a sheltering effect because it shelters Earth from most dangers other than large meteors. There is no mention in the first paragraph of any *reviving* or *cleansing* effect of the atmosphere on Earth. Therefore, choices **b** and **d** are not correct. In a sense, enabling Earth to sustain life is *invigorating*; however, there is a better choice than choice **c** because the first two sentences talk about how the atmosphere specifically *protects* Earth from harmful forces. The first paragraph mentions ways in which the solar energy warms the planet, not the atmosphere itself. The heat in the atmosphere may be spread across Earth through circulation, but that is not the same as suggesting that the focus of the paragraph is the atmosphere's warming effect on Earth; therefore, choice **e** is incorrect.

5. d. The word *oscillate* means to move back and forth, making choice **d** correct. The sun may indeed shine brightly or radiate energy, choices **b** and **c**, but that is not the meaning of the word in the context of the passage. The word is not suggesting that the sun rotates around itself or remains stationary, meaning choices **a** and **e** are also not correct.

6. c. The sentence that precedes this line in the text suggests that Plato used a metaphor to convey his ideas. This sentence then provides details of the metaphor, describing the visions of the people inside the cave as seeing only the shadows of those that passed by. The concept of living in a world of shadows may be difficult to grasp without a description to give it some perspective. The illustrative concept of living within the walls of the cave *does* provide an understandable context, meaning that choice **c** represents the author's function for including the sentence. Keep in mind that the sentence is still a description of a metaphor; the sentence does *not* provide any sort of concrete evidence—no indisputable proof or confirmation—that Plato's philosophical idea was, in fact, true. Therefore, choice **a** cannot be correct. Also note that the sentence illustrates the metaphor but does not itself provide a metaphor, making choice **b** incorrect. The description of a cave is not to provide a setting for a story, and it is actually obscuring the eternal reality, so choices **d** and **e** are not correct.

7. d. The word *position* has several meanings. In the context of this sentence, however, it is describing Plato's argument that the world is only a picture of a greater reality. This is his point, his *opinion*. The word *position* can mean *situation*, a specific *location*, or *style*. However, if you substitute those terms for *position* in the given sentence, you will see that they do not fit very well in the provided context; therefore, choices **a**, **b**, and **e** are incorrect. The word *position* in this sentence describes Plato's main point; if anything, this point is unmoving and static, so choice **c** is not correct.

8. b. The passage focuses on a suggestion that artists should not *let their output be constrained within a solitary structure*, meaning that he or she should experiment with media other than the one that they're most well known for using. That's choice **b**, and the opposite of choice **d**. The author describes two successful artists, but that is not the primary concern of the passage, so choice **a** is not correct. The focus is also not specifically on the rejection of commercial exploits or on people who disregard artists' non-primary art forms, making choices **c** and **e** incorrect.

9. d. Because the author's primary idea is that talented artists can and should experiment with multiple art forms, the description of Marc Chagall—who paints and creates stained glass—best fits that idea. Nothing about the description of Chuck Close or Samuel Clemens suggests that they've experimented with multiple media, making choices **a** and **b** incorrect. Claude Monet may have experimented with different styles, but those styles were all within the painting medium. Likewise, Paul Simon recorded songs in a partnership and as a solo artist, but that description still limits him to a single art form: songwriting. Therefore, choices **c** and **e** are incorrect.

10. d. The passage states that mediation *focuses on mutually acceptable solutions*, which suggests that both parties could be satisfied by the resolution of a conflict. Since litigation results in "winning or losing," it is fair to presume that the author would agree with the statement in choice **d**. The statement in choice **a** may be felt by some people, but it is not supported by the passage. It is too broad to be correct. Choice **b** is incorrect; the author states that mediation can be faster, less expensive, and can lead to more creative solutions than litigation. However, that is not the same thing as suggesting that litigation is expensive, slow, and limited by its reliance on following the letter of the law. The author might not agree that litigation is expensive or slow—just that mitigation can be faster and cheaper. Choice **c** might seem attractive, but the passage does not say that mediation is the best way to resolve a conflict—simply that it is an alternative way that might prove effective. The dependent clause that begins the passage hints at the idea that the author thinks that lawyers prefer litigation to resolve conflicts. However, it cannot be deduced from that little information that lawyers are overly concerned with their earning potential; this is beyond the scope of the information provided, making choice **e** incorrect.

11. e. The overall conclusion of this short passage is that recycling is not entirely efficient. The first section in boldface suggests a transitional conclusion to that larger conclusion: that some materials don't offer much reduction in waste. The second section in boldface supports that transitional conclusion by explaining that plastic cannot be recycled to make the same object. The first section does not provide the support for the second section in boldface, so choices **a**, **c**, and **d** are not correct. The first section does not contradict the other section either, so choice **b** cannot be correct.

12. e. An opinion is a statement that cannot be verified. Whether or not plastic is a "dreadful" material is not a statement that can or cannot be verified. The statements in sentences 2 through 6 each contain facts that can be verified, such as that an aluminum product can be recycled as a similar aluminum product or that recycled plastics are frequently not recyclable; therefore, choices **a**, **b**, **c**, and **d** represent facts instead of opinions and are not correct.

13. e. The passage describes many attributes of hypothermia, but never are the symptoms of hypothermia—such as shaking or sluggishness—provided. The passage states that the cause of hypothermia is exposure to cold weather, so choice **a** is incorrect. The passage does not explicitly say how to prevent hypothermia, but it does say that the living environments of the elderly should be closely monitored to ensure that their temperatures are maintained within appropriate ranges. The reason for this is to avoid hypothermia in the elderly, an approach to prevention; therefore, choice **b** is incorrect. External warming is listed as a type of treatment, so choice **c** cannot be correct. By stating that hypothermia can be fatal, the passage does indicate its most grave hazard; choice **d** is therefore not correct.

14. c. The bar graph shows the number of Americans, per 100,000, who fell victim to hypothermia in 2001. Because each bar is taller than the previous bar, the percentage of 80-year-olds who fell victim to it was greater than the percentage of 70-year-olds, choice **c**. Choice **a** is wrong because the bar graphs show a rate, not a total number, meaning that you cannot confirm that the majority of all hypothermia victims were 90 years old or older. Similarly, children under 10 have the lowest rate of hypothermia, but that does not mean that there are no dangers to them. The graph provides no indication that choice **d** is correct. The statement in choice **e** is contradicted by the different-sized bars in the bar graph, so it cannot be correct either.

15. c. The passage states that *the majority of hypothermia victims are senior citizens.* That must mean that a minority, or less than 50%, of all other cases are from people who are not senior citizens, including those under 60 years of age. The passage says that older people are less easily able to tolerate cold weather compared to younger people. However, it also says that the elderly are less able to respond to long exposure to very hot *or* very cold temperatures, so choice **a** cannot be supported. The statement in choice **b** is an overgeneralization that is not supported by the passage. The majority of sufferers of hypothermia are older people, but younger people can be affected as well. It may be the case that older people living in warmer climates are less likely to suffer from hypothermia, but that does not necessarily make them *healthier*, so the statement in choice **d** is not supported. No explanation for elderly people's susceptibility to hypothermia is provided in the given text. It may or may not be a result of a deteriorating circulation system; however, without the support from the passage, choice **e** cannot be the correct answer.

16. b. The passage mentions that the immune system is capable of distinguishing between body cells and non-body cells, so the statement in choice **b** is correct. Every individual's immune system must learn to recognize and deal with non-self molecules through experience. Therefore, no one is able to prevent their offspring from getting an infection, making choices **a** and **e** incorrect. The passage also explains how the body is able to remember the specifics of a foreign body, such as the chicken pox virus; however, because this is the first encounter with the virus, the body's immune system will not yet be able to remember previous experiences with the virus, making choice **c** incorrect. A normally functioning immune system will *not* attack its own tissues, so choice **d** is not right either.

17. b. According to the passage, the ability to distinguish between self and non-self is the heart of the immune system. This topic is set up in the first half of the passage and further elucidated throughout the body. The passage begins with a description of the complexity of the immune system, choice **a**; however, the rest of the passage does not support that statement as a major point since it does not focus on the structure of the immune system specifically, so that choice is not correct. The point in choice **c** is provided in the passage, but it represents only a very minor point about the balance between self cells and non-self cells. It does not represent the major point of the passage, so it is incorrect. On the other hand, the point in choice **d** is *too* general to be considered correct for the given passage. A major point could be that the human body's *immune system* is an extraordinary and complicated mechanism, but the focus is not on the human body's capabilities in general. The final sentence of the passage suggests that the human body is exposed to a sea of microbes, but that does not mean that that point is the focus of the passage. In fact, the passage is more about the immune system as a whole instead of the fact that the body is a habitat for microbes, so choice **e** is not right either.

18. a. The passage states that self-markers are unique to DNA, meaning that identical twins would have the same self-markers. Because self-markers are responsible for preventing the body's immune system from attacking its own tissues, the explanation in choice **a** makes the most sense. There is no indication in the passage that the age of tissues would have any relevance to whether a body identifies it as self or non-self; therefore, there is no support for choice **b**. The passage does not suggest that the sex of the host body plays any role in whether an immune system identifies a cell or tissue as self or non-self, making choice **c** incorrect. Of greater importance is the presence of self-markers, which are unique to each person's DNA. Choice **d** is incorrect; previous illnesses, even if both were shared by the twins during childhood, would not set precedent for tissues being shared between the people. The passage states that the immune system can recall the specifics of a foreign body, such as a virus. However, the transplant of tissue is not something that would have necessarily occurred beforehand—and that does not explain why the twins would have a more likely chance of success at a transplant than the father and daughter—so choice **e** is incorrect.

19. a. The word *sensitive* has several definitions. In the context of this passage, it is being used to describe the immune system—specifically, its ability to react quickly and effectively. In that sense, it can be considered *responsive*, choice **a**. The word *sensitive* can mean *delicate or nervous*, choices **b** and **d**, but those meanings do not make sense in the context of the sentence in the passage. The word *indifferent* is an antonym of *sensitive*, so choice **c** cannot be correct. There is no indication that the word means *sensible*, so choice **e** is incorrect.

20. e. The main argument of the passage is that there are no boundaries when it comes to pollutants. Only the statement in choice **e** weakens the argument by suggesting that the levels of the pollutants found are so low as to be "statistically insignificant." That doesn't mean that the compounds aren't there at all, but that the levels are so low that the argument is weakened. The statements in the other answer choices do not significantly weaken the argument. For choice **a**, the main argument of the passage is not about the companies' claims about their pollutants. Whether or not companies make claims about them, the author's main argument—that there are no boundaries when it comes to pollutants—is not weakened. The statement in choice **b** would suggest that some compounds travel better than others. That doesn't necessarily weaken the main argument that pollutants are not constrained by boundaries, however. If the sentence in choice **c** were true, the author's argument would be *strengthened*, not *weakened.* This is suggesting that even years after a compound stops being created, it can be found throughout the planet's oceans. The statement in choice **d** would weaken the author's argument if the chief argument were that DDT causes significant damage. However, the chief argument is simply that there are no boundaries when it comes to pollutants. This statement, even if it were true, does not address that issue.

21. b. The passage begins by pointing out the concerns about getting energy from oil, gas, coal, or nuclear sources. It then introduces a potentially clean, safe, and efficient energy as a solution to the problems of these other sources. Therefore, choice **b** provides the best organization of the passage. Because the passage begins with the drawbacks of some energy technologies, choice **d** is not correct. No untested theory is introduced at the beginning of the passage, so choice **a** is not correct. While a new technology is introduced in the passage, it is not how the passage begins; furthermore, its difficulties are not listed in detail, so choice **c** is not correct. The organization of the passage is not built around the comparison or contrast between technologies, making choice **e** incorrect.

22. e. Given that the dangerous effects of gas, oil, coal, and nuclear energy are described in the beginning of the passage, it would make sense that *deleterious* would have a negative meaning. That eliminates choices **c** and **d**, which have words with positive meanings. While the word contains the prefix *delet-*, *deleterious* does not mean deleting or *disappearing*, choice **a**. It has nothing to do with cost, so choice **b** is not correct either.

23. d. Because the East River does not always flow quickly, the tidal energy turbines cannot always generate electricity. This would detract from the author's argument that tidal energy is a clean, safe, and efficient energy source. The statements in choices **a** and **e** have little relevance on the author's argument about tidal energy; the statements neither weaken nor strengthen the argument. The statement in choice **b** could introduce a negative factor of the turbines, but there is another choice that more significantly weakens the point that they are effective generators of electricity. The statement in choice **c** actually strengthens the case for tidal energy; detractors of wind energy complain that the large windmills are eyesores, so an invisible turbine would be a positive development.

24. a. Tidal energy requires the movement—the ebb and flow—of the tides. The Bay of Fundy, as part of the Atlantic Ocean, is known for its massive tidal flows. Choices **b** and **d** cannot be correct since they do not involve water. Neither the Great South Lake, choice **c**, nor Bullough's Pond, choice **e**, involve waterways that would be influenced much by tides. Because they are smaller bodies of water that are not related to the oceans, they are not as good an option for tidal energy experiments as a location by the Bay of Fundy.

25. a. The author describes the concerns of nuclear energy before describing the advantages of tidal energy; this contrast accentuates its benefits, making choice **a** correct. This is the opposite of choice **e**, which states that the safety of renewable energy sources would be downplayed, so choice **e** is wrong. No other negative feature of nuclear power is provided, so choice **b** cannot be correct. In fact, the passage states that nuclear energy does *not* create greenhouse gases, meaning that choice **c** is not correct. The mention of safety concerns does not involve financial considerations, so choice **d** is not correct.

26. c. The only statement from the answer choices that cannot be verified as fact is listed in choice **c**, because whether an event is "demoralizing" is not a verifiable statement. The statements in choices **a**, **b**, **d**, and **e** can all be proven and are therefore facts, not opinions.

27. e. The passage states that all but a dozen U.S. presidents served in uniform. That means that 31 presidents have served in some capacity, making choice **e** correct. The fact that twelve men become president with no military experience also means that choice **b** cannot be correct. The statements in choices **a, c,** and **d** are neither confirmed nor denied based on the information in the passage; therefore, they are not correct.

28. c. The end of the passage states that voters are most concerned now with their presidents' knowledge of the law. Therefore, based on the passage, a lawyer is the best prediction for the next president's former occupation (choice **c**). The passage mentions that at least one president was a tailor, choice **a**, and one was an actor, choice **d**, but there is nothing to indicate that that is the most likely occupation of the next U.S. president. While many presidents were previously soldiers, not as many lately have served in the military, so choice **b** is not the best answer. Only three presidents were generals, so choice **e** is not the best answer either.

29. b. The passage mentions that the U.S. presidents have had a variety of occupations before holding the highest office. To contrast those varying paths to the presidency, the passage mentions the clearer path from the U.S. military to the presidency. Therefore, the path was being described as indirect, or *roundabout* (choice **b**). *Direct*, choice **a**, has the opposite meaning of *circuitous*. Similarly, *mainstream* (choice **c**) could also be considered an antonym of *circuitous*. There is nothing in the passage to suggest that the route would be *political* or *circuslike*, so choices **d** and **e** are not correct either.

30. e. There are several numbers given in this passage, but the only one that matters for this question is that there are *more than 2,500 difference species of snakes around the world*; therefore, choice **e** is correct. Choice **a** refers to the approximate number of snake bite fatalities in the United States each year, so it is not correct. Choices **b** and **c** could refer to the number of annual snake bites in the United States, so they are not correct. Choice **d** is less than 2,500, so it cannot be correct either.

31. a. An opinion cannot be proven with facts or statistics. The statement in the second sentence, choice **a**, cannot be proven because there is no way to show definitively whether someone is or is not irrational. On the other hand, the statements in choices **b**, **c**, **d**, and **e** each contain statements that can be verified—making them statements of fact rather than opinion. Therefore, those answer choices cannot be correct.

32. c. The passage begins with the proposed name change from starfish to sea stars, and then the rest of the passage provides support for this change. Therefore, the statement in choice **c** best summarizes the passage. The statements in choices **a**, **d**, and **e** are all correct, but they act as supporting details that reinforce the main point of the idea: that the name should be changed. The statement in choice **b** is also correct, but the main idea of the passage is not the difficulties in changing a name but how and why the starfish should be changed to the sea star specifically. Therefore, there is a better choice than choice **b**.

33. d. The author makes it clear that the name *starfish* is factually incorrect and should therefore be revised to something more scientifically accurate. Given that information, it would also make sense that the author would agree that jellyfish should also have their name changed if they are also not technically fish (choice **d**). The author may agree that sea stars are beautiful, choice **a**, but that cannot be verified from any information in the passage; the author is interested in naming the marine creatures appropriately, but that does not necessarily mean that he or she finds them attractive. The author would likely disagree with the statements in choices **b**, **c**, and **e** since he or she clearly states that sea stars are *not* vertebrates, and they should therefore not be referred to as "fish"—and it *is* worth the trouble to rename them.

34. d. Calling a monument a masterpiece is an opinion because it cannot be verified with facts or statistics; whether it is taller than a pyramid, however, is a fact because it can be verified with measurements. Therefore, choice **d** contains both a fact and an opinion. The statement in choice **a** contains only an opinion and no verifiable facts. The statements in choices **b** and **e** contain only facts and no opinions, so they are not correct either. The quote in choice **c** is a fact because it can be proven that Saarinen said those words, and it does not contain the author's opinion.

35. b. The passage states that the winner of the contest was a plan for a completely different type of structure. Therefore, this describes a design that was like any other existing monument (choice **b**). This is the opposite of the statement in choice **a**, so that choice is not correct. There is no evidence in the passage that Saarinen's design was part of a series of monuments or less expensive than other monuments, making choices **c** and **d** incorrect. The shape of the arch is considerably different from the shape of the Great Pyramid, so choice **e** is not correct.

36. b. The author in the passage reveals the material of the arch's casing by saying that it is stainless steel. As a result, *the Arch often reflects dazzling bursts of sunlight.* Therefore, the purpose of including this information was to describe another astounding quality of the monument (choice **b**). No other information about the metallic components of the arch is given, so choice **a** is not correct. Similarly, no materials are listed for the Great Pyramid, so choice **c** cannot be correct. The following sentence in the passage describes the arch's symmetry, but the information about the stainless steel skin does nothing to illustrate the symmetry; therefore, choice **d** is incorrect. The information also does not provide any historical context for the monument, meaning that choice **e** is incorrect as well.

37. c. The initial sentence of the passage describes the skyline of St. Louis as unremarkable with one prodigious exception. The word *prodigious* must therefore have the opposite meaning as unremarkable. The best choice is *extraordinary* (choice **c**). *Commonplace* and *lackluster*, choices **a** and **e**, have similar meanings as unremarkable, so they cannot be correct. The exception is not being described as *talented* or *timely*, so choices **b** and **d** are incorrect as well.

38. e. The word *nevertheless* is generally used to provide a contrasting transition. In this passage, it is used to contrast the high costs of NASA with the important technological advancements; therefore, choice **e** is correct. Because the key transition word is changing the direction of the passage up to that point, choices **a** and **b** cannot be correct. There is nothing about this key word to suggest that space operations specifically make up too great a fraction of NASA's budget, so choice **c** is incorrect. Choice **d** is likewise incorrect because the financial expenditures of the agency have not changed too much over the past decade or so; the annual budget has steadily increased each year.

39. a. The passage focuses on the high cost of the government agency NASA. Therefore, the meaning of *exorbitant* must reflect these high costs: *excessive*, choice **a**, is the best word to describe its meaning. The high costs may be *painful* for taxpayers, but that is not the meaning of the word, so choice **b** is incorrect. Choice **c**, *reasonable*, has the opposite meaning as *exorbitant*; exorbitant spending is *unreasonable*, so choice **c** is incorrect. The budget continues to rise, so choice **d** cannot be correct. Space travel may be *exciting*, but there is nothing in the passage to suggest that the costs are exciting, making choice **e** incorrect.

40. b. The author mentions the high costs for operating NASA, but he or she ends the passage with a declaration of support for the agency's valuable research and development. This is summed up by the statement in choice **b**. The author says that it may be difficult to justify the expense at a time of domestic crises, but he or she uses *nevertheless* to suggest that it's still justifiable; this eliminates choices **a** and **d**. There is no specific support in the passage to suggest that the author would want the costs to decrease during a time of deficit, choice **c**, or only during times of planetary exploration, choice **e**.

The following is a chart of the different skills assessed by the questions in this practice PPST; you can use it to identify your strengths and weaknesses in this subject to better focus your study.

READING SKILLS STUDY CHART FOR PRACTICE EXAM 2	
LITERAL COMPREHENSION SKILLS	**QUESTIONS**
Main Ideas	8, 17, 32
Supporting Ideas	13, 30, 35
Organization	4, 11, 21, 38
Vocabulary in Context	3, 5, 7, 19, 22, 29, 37, 39
CRITICAL AND INFERENTIAL COMPREHENSION SKILLS	
Evaluation	1, 6, 12, 20, 23, 25, 31, 34, 36
Inferential Reasoning	2, 10, 15, 16, 26, 27, 33, 40
Generalization	9, 14, 18, 24, 28

Skills Test in Mathematics

1. d. To find the average of a set of data, first add all the data numbers together and then divide that sum by the number of data pieces. In this case, if the average for 7 days is 4 miles, then Veronica must have run a total of 28 miles, since $28 \div 7 = 4$. Her Sunday through Friday mileage totals 23 miles, so Veronica needed to run 5 miles on Saturday. Choices **a**, **b**, **c**, and **e** would all give a sum that is different from 28 miles, so the resulting average would not have been 4.

2. a. In order to compare percentages, fractions, and decimals it is easiest to convert them all into decimals. The $\frac{3}{4}$ in choice **a** is equivalent to 0.75, so $4\frac{3}{4}\%$ is the same as 4.75%. When working with percentages, remember that they mean "out of 100." Therefore, in order to turn them into decimals you need to divide them by 100, which simply moves the decimal point two places to the left. So in this case, 4.75% is the same as 0.0475. Next, turn choice **b** into a decimal the same way: 4.09% becomes 0.0409. Choice **c**, $\frac{47}{1,000}$, is equivalent to 0.047 (move the decimal three times to the left). Choice **d**, $\frac{23}{500}$, is the same as $\frac{46}{1,000}$ or 0.0460. Choice **e** is already in decimal form for us, 0.0408. Once they are all in decimal form and you are looking for the largest value, follow these steps: compare the numbers' tenths place, looking for the highest number. If all the numbers have the same value in the tenths place, then move to the hundredths place and exclude any decimals whose value in the hundredths place is smaller than the rest. Next move to the thousandths place, still looking for the largest number, and so on. Of all these choices, **a** has the largest value.

3. b. It is important to notice that although the markings on this spinner only show that it is divided into 5 sections, the pie-shaped section labeled "1" on top is actually equivalent to any of the other two sections combined. That means that there are actually six equal sections, four of them having a "1" in them, one with a "2," and one with a "3." To find the probability of an event happening, put the number of desired events possible over the total number of events. In this case, there are four "desired events" (or number "1" sections) and six total events (or sections on the board). $\frac{4}{6}$ can be reduced to $\frac{2}{3}$. Choice **a** incorrectly gives the probability of the spinner *not* landing on a "1" with the incorrect assumption that there are 5 equal chances. Choice **c** is the probability of not getting a 1 since there are two chances out of six to not land on a 1, and $\frac{2}{6} = \frac{1}{3}$. Choice **d** is not valid because there are not four equal chances on the board, so four should not be in the denominator. Choice **e** incorrectly gives the probability of the spinner landing on a "1" with the incorrect assumption that there are 5 equal chances and three chances for "1."

4. d. This question is asking "7,225,800 is 3% of what number, x?" In order to set this up, set up a proportion that has "part" in the numerator and "whole" in the population ratio and $\frac{3}{100}$ in the percentage ratio. Set these two ratios equal to one another in a proportion and solve:

$$\frac{part}{whole} = \frac{7{,}225{,}800}{\text{U.S. Population}} = \frac{3}{100}$$

$7{,}225{,}800 \times 100 = (\text{U.S. Population}) \times 3$

$722{,}580{,}000 = 3x$

$x = 240{,}860{,}000$

Choice **a** is 7,225,800 *divided* by 3, but percentages always need to be turned into decimals first, and in this instance, a proportion needs to be used. Choice **b** is 7,225,800 *multiplied* by 30, but in this instance, a proportion needs to be used. Choice **c** is 7,225,800 *multiplied* by 300, which yields a population that is unrealistic for the United States. Choice **e** is the answer when using the correct method listed above, but incorrectly including $\frac{0.03}{100}$ as the percentage fraction instead of $\frac{3}{100}$.

5. b. An isosceles triangle has exactly two equal sides. Since the hypotenuse of a right triangle is always the longest side, the base of the triangle must be equal to the height, or 5. Use the Pythagorean theorem to find the value of h:

$a^2 + b^2 = c^2$

$(5)^2 + (5)^2 = h^2$

$25 + 25 = h^2$

$50 = h^2$

$\sqrt{50} = h$

Because $\sqrt{50}$ is not one of the choices, simplify the radical to arrive at $h = \sqrt{25 \times 2} = 5\sqrt{2}$. Choice **a**, 5, cannot be correct because this is not an equilateral triangle, which has equal sides. In an isosceles triangle, only the legs have equal lengths. Choice **c**, 10, would be correct if 5 were the *shortest* side in a 30-60-90 triangle because in those special triangles the hypotenuse is twice the length of the shortest side. Choice **d**, $\sqrt{10}$, is an incorrect way to write $5\sqrt{2}$. Choice **e**, 9, cannot be possible because in any triangle the sum of any two sides must be greater than the third side, and in this case the sum of the two legs is 10.

6. d. First, represent the work that Ryan and Kimberly did by letting Kimberly's hours be k and Ryan's hours be $3k$. Their combined work would be represented as $3k + k = 12$. So $4k = 12$ and $k = 3$. Therefore Kimberly worked 3 hours (which is the incorrect choice **a**), and Ryan worked $3k$, or 9 hours (which is the incorrect choice **b**). If Jaime worked 5 more hours than Ryan, that means he worked 14 hours (which is the incorrect choice **c**). Because Jaime and Janet worked a total of 18 hours, that means that Janet worked 4 hours. Choice **e**, 7, is the answer when subtracting the 5 more hours that Jaime worked from the 12 total hours that Ryan and Kimberly worked, which does not show how many hours Janet worked.

7. a. In order to solve this problem you need to look at how many people recalled the same digit for each of the seven numbers in the phone number. Choice **e** is out of the running right away because only one person recalled 996 as the first three digits. Looking at the fourth digit, three of the friends recalled a 9 versus the two who recalled an 8, so answer choice **d** is ruled out. Next, look at the fifth digit: three friends remembered a 2 there, and the other two friends recalled different numbers, so since choice **b** has a 3 in the fifth place, you can rule this one out. Lastly, looking at the sixth and seventh places, a 6 and another 6 are the most commonly recalled digits in those places, making choice **a** a better choice than choice **c**.

8. c. The concepts to be considered here are area and surface area. The amount of paper needed to cover a cube is equivalent to the surface area of a cube. The surface area of a cube is the area of each face $(d \times d) \times 6$, which is $6d^2$ (incorrect choice **a**). Although it is tempting to just double $6d^2$ to $12d^2$ (incorrect choice **b**), that will not work because it doesn't take into consideration that *each* side length has doubled. Instead, you must consider that Maya's gift has a side length of $2d$, which will, in turn, have 6 faces that are each $4d^2$ in area. The total surface area of Maya's gift will be $6 \times 4d^2 = 24d^2$. Choice **d**, $2d^3$, is a mistake made by taking the volume, $l \times w \times h$, of Marvin's gift and doubling that. Choice **e**, $12d^3$, comes from a combination of errors made by confusing volume, surface area, and how the doubling of an edge length affects either of these measures.

9. d. The question being asked here is "What is $\frac{1}{4}$ of $\frac{1}{2}$?" The word *of* in math is normally an indication that multiplication is required. To multiply fractions, multiply straight across their numerators and straight across their denominators: $\frac{1}{4} \times \frac{1}{2} = \frac{1}{8}$. Choice **a**, $\frac{1}{16}$, is one-quarter of *one-quarter*, not one-quarter of *one-half*. Choice **b**, $\frac{1}{6}$, is the answer when $\frac{1}{2}$ and $\frac{1}{4}$ are incorrectly added by keeping the numerator the same and adding the denominators. Choice **c**, $\frac{1}{4}$, is $\frac{1}{2}$ minus $\frac{1}{4}$, but they need to be multiplied, not subtracted. Choice **e**, $\frac{3}{4}$, is the correct sum of $\frac{1}{2}$ and $\frac{1}{4}$, but is not the correct way to answer this question.

10. a. To see what amount of money Frank's employer was putting into his retirement account each month, isolate any two dates in the table, find out how much money was deposited during that period, and then divide by the number of *full* months in that period. The answer in all cases is $420. From April 1, 2006 to December 1, 2006, there were eight full months. There was $3,360 deposited in that period (this is known from $6,720 − $3,360 = $3,360). Because $3,360 ÷ 8 = $420, it is clear that Frank's employer contributed $420/month into his retirement account. Choice **b** comes from dividing $3,360 by 9 months, thinking that the month of December counts, but it doesn't since the deposit only gets posted on the last day of the month. Similarly, choice **c** comes from incorrectly dividing the $5,040 deposited from December 1, 2006 to December 1, 2007 by 13 months, and choice **d** comes from incorrectly dividing the $2,100 deposited from December 1, 2007 to May 1, 2008 by 6 months. Choice **e** comes from dividing $3,360 by 7 months.

11. e. Using the information in the table and the method employed in question 10, Frank's wife knows that his employer deposited $420 into his retirement account every month. There are 16 full months between May 1, 2010, and September 1, 2011. $420 × 16 = $6,720, which is what Frank's employer has deposited since May 1, 2010, so add this to the May 1st balance: $13,860 + $670 = $20,580. Choice **a** is incorrect because it only multiplies the $420 by 15 months, and choice **c** is incorrect because it multiplies the $420 by 17 months. Choices **b** and **d** are both wrong because they use the incorrect monthly deposit amount of $373 combined with 16 months and 17 months, respectively.

12. d. To solve this problem, you need to work backward, starting with q, and use substitution: Because $q = 12p + 8$, put $12p + 8$ in for q in the equation $3k = 10 − \frac{1}{2}q$. Doing this, $3k = 10 − \frac{1}{2}q$ can be written as $3k = 10 − \frac{1}{2}(12p + 8)$. Here it is essential to remember to distribute the negative sign with the $\frac{1}{2}$ as you multiply it by the $12p$ and 8 in the parentheses: $3k = 10 − \frac{1}{2}(12p) − \frac{1}{2}(8) = 10 − 6p − 4 = 6 − 6p$. Because $3k = 6 − 6p$, the incorrect answer choice **a** is then incorrectly divided by 2 to get incorrect answer choice **b**. Next, seeing that the first equation has $15k$ in it, you need to multiply all the terms in $3k = 6 − 6p$ by 5 so that you get $15k = 30 − 30p$ (the incorrect answer choice **c**). Now you can substitute $30 − 30p$ in for the $15k$ in $2w = 15k + 4$. $2w = 30 − 30p + 4$, which yields $2w = 34 − 30p$, and dividing both sides by 2 gives $w = 17 − 15p$ (correct choice **d**). The answer choice for **e** is what will happen if there is a mistake distributing the negative sign in the first substitution resulting in $14 − 6p$; following the next steps with the $14 − 6p$ would yield $37 − 15p$.

13. c. Because the garden needs 200 feet of linear fencing to enclose it, the distance around the garden (the perimeter) is 200 feet. The formula for calculating the perimeter of a rectangle is 2 × length + 2 × width. Because 2 × 80 + 2 × 20 = 200, the dimensions of the garden could be 80 feet long and 20 feet wide. Choice **a** seems like it might work since the length and width add up to 200 feet, but because there are *two* lengths and widths it would yield 2 × 100 + 2 × 100 = 400 feet of linear fencing. Choice **b** would yield 240 feet of linear fencing, choice **d** would yield 180 feet of linear fencing, and choice **e** would yield just 60 feet of linear fencing.

14. c. First, calculate the volume of the pool by multiplying length × width × height: 5 × 20 × 30 = 3,000 cubic feet (which is the incorrect answer choice **a**). Then, in order to find out how many gallons 3,000 cubic feet is, multiply 3,000 by 7.5: 3,000 × 7.5 = 22,500 (which is the incorrect answer choice **b**). Next, because each gallon weighs 8.35 pounds, multiply the number of gallons by 8.35: 22,500 × 8.35 = 187,875 (correct choice **c**). Choice **d** is incorrect because in the first step, the width and length of 20 and 30 are incorrectly multiplied to 500 to get a mistaken volume of 2,500. Multiplying that by 7.5 followed by 8.35 yields 156,563 pounds. Choice **e** is the incorrect result when the volume of 3,000 cubic feet is just multiplied by the 8.35 pounds per gallon without first converting to gallons.

15. a. Adding the 18 students who are in Physics to the 26 students who are enrolled in biology sums to 44 students. Because only 34 students are enrolled in either one or both of these classes, and there are a total of 44 registrations, 10 students must be in both Physics and Biology. Choice **b**, 8, is the answer to 34 − 26, but this does not take into account the students who are in Physics. Choice **c**, 16, is the answer to 34 − 18, but this does not take into account the students who are in Biology. Choice **d**, 46, subtracts the 34 students enrolled in just Physics, just Biology, or both from the entire student body of 80; however, not all the students have to take a science class, so the 80 students is not relevant. Choice **e**, 36, subtracts the headcount of 44 students from the entire student body of 80; however, not all the students have to take a science class, so the 80 students is not relevant.

16. e. In Venn diagrams, the overlapping sections of the circles represent subsets of the data that belong to two separate categories. If any single point inside a Venn diagram is in just one circle, that means that this data point only falls into one category (like "just Physics"). If a point inside a Venn diagram is in two circles, then this data point falls into two categories (like "Physics and Biology"). Similarly, when a point inside a Venn diagram is contained in three circles, then this data point falls into three categories (like "Physics, Biology, *and* Chemistry"). Therefore, the shaded section represents the students who are enrolled in three science classes this summer. While choice **a** may be true, it is not guaranteed. Choice **b** is not the best answer because these students are also in Chemistry. Choice **c** is illogical because all the students represented in the Venn diagram are taking science classes. While some of the students in the shaded region may like Chemistry the best (choice **d**), the Venn diagram is not indicating preference of subject—just class enrollment.

17. b. In order to find the total number of students who chose two sports, find the number of sports indicated and subtract 50, the total number of students, from that sum. The total number of sports played is 13 + 16 + 12 + 10 + 9 = 60. Therefore, 10 of the students reported 2 sports. The percentage of students who play two sports is $\frac{10}{50}$ = 20%. Choice **a**, 10%, would be correct if the survey had resulted in 56 selections and only 6 students played two sports Choice **c**, 50%, would have needed 25 students to report two sports, which would have been a survey with 75 results. Choices **d** and **e**, 60% and 80%, would have also required a survey result of more than 75 answers.

18. e. First you must keep in mind that the interior angles of all triangles sum to 180°. First consider choice **a**: all equilateral triangles have three 60° angles and an acute angle is an angle less than 90°. Acute triangles are triangles that do not have an angle greater than 89°; therefore, all equilateral triangles are acute, and the triangle in choice **a** exists. An obtuse angle is an angle that is greater than 90° but less than 180°, and an obtuse triangle is a triangle that has one obtuse angle. An isosceles triangle has two equal base angles and one unique vertex angle; a triangle could have one obtuse angle and two acute angles that would sum to 180°, so choice **b** works. A scalene triangle has three unique angles and since it is possible that a triangle could have one 90° angle and two other different angles, choice **c** also works. Choice **d** works because an isosceles triangle can have three angles that are all less than 90°. An obtuse right triangle is impossible because a right triangle has one 90° angle and two acute angles, while an obtuse triangle must have at least one angle greater than 90°.

19. a. To test each equation, sub $x = 1$ into each equation to see if the output $y = 7$ is obtained. For example, for choice **a** you would get $y = 3(1) + 4 = 7$. Using this method the equations in choices **b** and **c** also work with the point $x = 1$ and $y = 7$, but the equations in choices **d** and **e** do not work. Next, sub $x = 2$ into the equation in choices **a**, **b**, and **c** to see if the output $y = 10$ is obtained. Only the equation $y = 3x + 4$ in choice **a** yields 10 for y, so this is the only possible solution.

20. a. The six factors of 12 are 1, 2, 3, 4, 6, and 12. A prime number is any number greater than 1, whose only factors are 1 and itself. Therefore, the prime factors of 12 are 2 and 3, so there are two chances out of 12 to roll a prime factor of 12 when rolling a dodecahedron: $\frac{2}{12} = \frac{1}{6}$ (choice **a**). Ignoring the requirement for these factors to be prime would result in incorrect choice **b**, since $\frac{6}{12} = \frac{1}{2}$. It is a common mistake to think that 1 is a prime number, but it is not. This would lead to thinking that three out the 12 numbers were prime, which results in $\frac{3}{12} = \frac{1}{4}$ (choice **c**). It is also a common mistake to think that 2 cannot be a prime number because it is even; however, 2 is the only prime number that *is* even. This error leads to thinking that only one of the 12 numbers is prime, which results in $\frac{1}{12}$ (choice **d**). Choice **e** is the reciprocal of choice **a**, but probabilities must always be a number between 0 and 1.

21. c. The points on the scatter plot create an almost perfect line, and extending that imaginary line would result in a population of 25,000 in 2010. Choice **a** is actually lower than the population in the year 2000, which would oppose the demonstrated trend. Choice **b** is only slightly larger than the population in the year 2000 and is probably a better estimate for the year 2005 than for 2010. Choices **d** and **e** are both way too large to match the trend shown in the scatter plot.

22. d. To begin, remember that 1 yard = 3 feet and that each foot has 12 inches in it. So, first, recall or calculate that 1 yard is 3×12, or 36 inches long. Because Josh bought $5\frac{3}{4}$ yards, which is a mixed fraction, turn that into an improper fraction by multiplying 5 by the denominator and adding that to the numerator, while keeping the denominator the same: $5\frac{3}{4} = 2\frac{3}{4}$. Next, multiply $2\frac{3}{4}$ by 36 inches: $2\frac{3}{4} \times \frac{36}{1}$ becomes $\frac{23}{1} \times \frac{9}{1}$ after some diagonal cross-canceling. $\frac{23}{1} \times \frac{9}{1}$ results in 207 inches (incorrect choice **a**). Then because there are two seats, dividing 207 results in 103.5 inches of fabric for each chair. Choice **b**, 192.24, incorrectly translates the mixed fraction $5\frac{3}{4}$ to 5.34 before multiplying it by 3 feet and next by 12 inches. (This choice forgets to divide it by two seats, but incorrect choice **c** is $192.24 \div 2 = 96.12$) Choice **e**, 34.5, forgets to apply that there are 3 feet in a yard, and only multiplies $5\frac{3}{4}$ by 12 inches before dividing it by two.

23. c. If Kris always tells the truth, then both Emily and Kris have dogs (statements I and II). If Emily has a dog, then Emily is lying (statement III). This means that all three statements are true, and choice **c** is the only possible correct answer.

24. e. In order to know how many square feet of tile are needed to cover the table, the area of the table must be calculated. The area of a circle is calculated with the formula, $A = \pi r^2$. The diameter of the table is 10 feet, and therefore the radius is 5 feet (the radius is always half the diameter). So the area of the tabletop will be $\pi \times 5^2 = 3.14 \times 25 = 78.5$ square feet. The closest approximation of 78.5 is 79 square feet. Choice **a** is only the diameter of the table; it is not the area. Choice **b** mistakenly uses the diameter of 10 as r in the formula $A = \pi r^2$. Choice **c** uses the circumference formula $C = 2\pi r$ instead of the area formula: $C = 2 \times 3.14 \times 5 = 31.4$ feet. Choice **d** also uses the circumference formula but mistakenly puts the diameter in for the radius: $C = 2 \times 3.14 \times 10 = 62.8$ feet.

25. e. The smallest number of buttons that one machine could make in one hour would be $80(60 \text{ minutes}) = 4{,}800$ (which is incorrect choice **b**). The largest number of buttons that one machine could make in one hour would be $100(60 \text{ minutes}) = 6{,}000$ (which is incorrect choice **c**). Because one machine will make from 4,800 to 6,000 buttons in one hour, multiply both of these numbers by 20 to see how many buttons can be made by 20 machines in one hour; the range is from 96,000 to 120,000 buttons, and 100,000 (correct choice **e**) falls within that range. Choice **a** is incorrectly arrived at by multiplying 20 machines times 80 buttons, forgetting that 80 is buttons per *minute*. Choice **d** is just below the number of buttons that all 20 machines would make if they were operating at their slowest capacity.

26. d. If Susie and Doug are both working on typing the manuscript, that means that together, they are typing at a rate of 34 words per minute ($12 + 22 = 34$). Since the manuscript is 68,000 words long, divide 68,000 by 34 to see how many minutes this will take them. $68,000 \div 34 = 2,000$ minutes. (Incorrect choice **a** only considers these 2,000 minutes and divides 2,000 by 60 to get 33.3 hours.) Because it takes Susie and Doug 20% of additional time to proofread their work, add 20% of 2,000 (which is 400 minutes) onto 2,000 to get 2,400. (Incorrect choice **b** only considers these 2,400 minutes and divides 2,400 by 60 to get 40 hours.) So *together* Susie and Doug have worked 40 hours, but for each 3 hours, they were *both* given a 30-minute, billable break. There are 13 sets of 3 in 40 hours ($13 \times 3 = 39$), so they *each* got 13 breaks of 30 minutes, which results in another 13 billable hours. (Incorrect choice **c** considers only 30 minutes for each 3-hour period, forgetting that they *both* got a break. This choice reflects 40 hours plus 7.5 hours, which rounds to 48 hours.) The correct answer, choice **d**, is 40 hours plus their 13 break hours, which gives Susie and Doug 53 billable hours.

27. a. In graphs of inequalities, a dotted line symbolizes that the equation is not part of the solution, so a < or > symbol is used. A *solid* line symbolizes that the equation *is* part of the solution, so a ≤ or ≥ symbol is used. Because the dotted line was using the equation $y = \frac{1}{4}x$, it must have a < or > in the answer to the system of equations to show that the line is NOT included in the answer. And because the graph is shaded *above* the dotted line, the solution for that equation will be $y \leq \frac{1}{4}x$. The solid line for $y = -4x$ will include the line in its answer and is shaded *to the left* of the line, so the correct equation to model that is $y < 4x$. All the answer choices have incorrect combinations of inequalities except for answer choice **a**, which is correct.

28. a. Because Ψ is divisible by 3 and 10, then 8Ψ must be divisible by any of the factors of the product of 3, 10, and 8. Since $3 \times 10 \times 8 = 240$, any factors of 240 will also be factors of 8Ψ. To find all the potential factors of 240, break it down into its prime factorization by breaking it into factors until all the factors are prime: $240 = 24 \times 10 = (6 \times 4) \times (5 \times 2) = (3 \times 2) \times (2 \times 2) \times 5 \times 2$ is the prime factorization of 240. Any number that is a product of two or more of the factors of 240 will also divide into 240 as well as 8Ψ. Answer choices **b** through **e** are all products of two or more of the prime factors above; 14, choice **a**, is the only number that cannot be the product of any of the prime factors of 240.

29. b. In 1999, the Sales Department had an electricity cost of $750, and in 2000, the Customer Service Department had an electricity cost of $700, so their difference is $50. Choice **a** is the cost of electricity for the Sales Department in 2000, not the increase in electricity costs. Choice **c**, $150, is the difference between the Sales Departments in 2002 and 1999 ($900 − $750). Choice **d** is the difference between the Sales and Engineering Departments in 1999 ($1,000 − $750). Choice **e** is a comparison of the two departments in 1999 when they both had the same electricity costs.

30. d. The first statement, I, is not true, because the Sales Department's increase was not steady since it declined from 2000 to 2001. The second statement is true because in every year other than 2000, the Engineering Department's electricity usage was at least $100 more than the second-highest user. The Customer Service and Sales Departments were the same in 1999, and in 2000–2002 their electricity usages were more similar to each other's than to the Engineering Department's. The third statement is true since the Engineering Department's electricity usage increased by $100 each year from 2000 to 2002.

31. b. The Engineering Department's electricity usage decreased $200, from $1,000 to $800, in the period from 1999 to 2000. To calculate the percentage decrease between two numbers, divide the difference between the two numbers by the original number. So $\frac{\$200}{\$1,000} = \frac{20}{100}$, which is 20%. Choice **a**, 25%, is the increase of $200 from $800 to $1,000 in 2000 to 2002, but these were not the dates in question. Choice **c**, 12.5%, is the increase of $100 from $800 to $900 in 2001 to 2002, but these were not the dates in question. Choice **d**, 10%, is the decrease in the Engineering Department's electricity usage between the years 1999 and 2001, when it went from $1,000 to $900. Choice **e**, 0%, is the decrease in the Engineering Department's electricity usage between the years 1999 and 2002, when they were both $1,000.

32. a. In this series there is a pattern of pairs with a difference of three that is interrupted every third term by a "5." Looking at the first two terms, you can see that they are decreasing by 3 (28 − 25 = 3), as is the second pair of numbers (21 − 18 = 3). The jump "over the 5" from one pair to the next pair is decreased by four each time since 25 − 21 = 4 and 18 − 14 = 4. Because the pairs themselves are decreased by 3 and then followed by a random 5, it follows that the next two numbers would be 11 and 5. Choices **b** and **e** decrease 14 by 4 to get 10, which does not follow the decrease in the first two pairs' patterns. Choice **c** does not have the spacer "5," and choice **d** has the spacer "5" in the wrong place.

33. c. The formula for distance is *distance = rate × time*, and in this case, the distance is *k* kilometers and the time is *h* is hours, so putting this into the formula gives *k* = rate × *h*. Solving for rate gives rate = *k* ÷ *h*. Time in this formula usually represents hours, but since we are now introducing minutes, it is necessary to express the hours in terms of minutes. *m* minutes can be translated into hours by dividing by 60, so time can be written as *m* ÷ 60. Putting these two equivalents into the formula distance = rate × time, one gets distance = $\frac{k}{h} \times \frac{m}{60} = \frac{mk}{60h}$. Choice **a** incorrectly puts the kilometers in the denominator. Choice **b** is the reciprocal of the correct answer, so the terms were mistakenly flip-flopped during the calculations. Choice **d** puts 60 *over* minutes, which will not correctly translate into hours. Choice **e** will also not correctly convert minutes into hours since it is *multiplying* the minutes by hours.

34. b. Looking at the pie chart, you can see that the darkest section, the Pediatrics, is slightly bigger than the next darker section, Surgical; about three times bigger than the ER section; and slightly smaller than the lightest section, Maternity. Looking at the bar graphs, choices **a** and **d** have bars that are equal, so those two graphs are disqualified as being equivalent to the pie chart. The chart in choice **c** shows Pediatrics as less than Surgical, which is not accurate, so this answer can also be disqualified. That leaves only choices **b** and **e**. The data represented in choice **b** achieves the relative breakdown displayed in the pie chart, and choice **e** is wrong because bar graphs *can* be used to represent the data found in pie charts.

35. a. The first calculation needed is how many gallons of gas Belicia's car will consume on the 364-mile trip. Because her car gets 28 miles for every gallon of gas, divide 364 by 28: 364 miles ÷ 28 miles per gallon = 13 gallons of gas needed. Because gas costs $4.85 per gallon, calculate the total cost by multiplying 13 gallons of gas by $4.85: 13 × $4.85 = $63.05. Choice **b** incorrectly divides the 364-mile trip by the $4.85 cost of gas per gallon while ignoring the 28 miles per gallon that Belicia's car gets. Choice **c** makes the same error as in choice **b**, but in addition to this error, it also rounds the $4.85 to $5 before dividing 364 miles. Choice **d** incorrectly multiplies the $4.85 cost of gas per gallon with the 28 miles per gallon that Belicia's car gets—it ignores that the trip is 364 miles. Choice **e** correctly calculates 13 gallons needed for the trip, but rounds the $4.85 per gallon to $5 per gallon *before* multiplying it to the 13 gallons. The rounding should be done *after* this product is found, not beforehand.

36. c. Three-quarters is written as $\frac{3}{4}$, which is equivalent to 0.75. One million is 1,000,000, and the word *of* in math means to multiply, so 0.75 × 1,000,000 gives 750,000, which is seven hundred fifty thousand. Choice **e** almost does this correctly, but it multiplies $\frac{3}{4}$ by one *billion* and not one *million*. Choice **b** also almost does this correctly, but it *divides* instead of *multiplying* the $\frac{3}{4}$ by 1,000,000. Choice **a** mistakes $\frac{3}{4}$ as 34 and multiplies it by one hundred million, and not by one million. Choice **d** is 750 *billion* and not 750 *million*.

37. d. The prefix *milli-* means 1,000. It is found in words such as millipede (the insect) and millimeter, the unit of linear measurement. In this case, there are 1,000 milliliters in each liter of solution. Therefore, in 150 liters of solution there are $150 \times 1,000 = 150,000$ milliliters. Choices **b** and **e** incorrectly use 100 milliliters per liter and 10 milliliters per liter, respectively, in their calculations. Choice **a** incorrectly uses 50 milliliters per liter in its calculation, and choice **c** incorrectly uses 500 milliliters per liter in its calculation.

38. b. Because Shane would like to average $5,000 per month, that means she would like to sell $5,000 \times 12$ months = $60,000 over the course of the year. Since she has already sold $35,400, Shane needs to sell $24,600 over the last three months of the year to make her year-end goal. Therefore, the average per month that she needs to sell will be $24,600 ÷ 3 = $8,200. Choice **a** is Shane's sales of $35,400 divided by three months: $35,400 ÷ 3 = $11,800. Choice **c** is the average per month that she wants, but her average per month during the holiday season must be much higher than this in order to compensate for the slower first 9 months of the year. Choice **d** is the average of Shane's monthly sales for the first nine months: $35,400 ÷ 9 = $3,933.

39. a. With graphs of inequalities, it is important to notice if the endpoint is an empty circle or if it is filled in. If it is empty, then the point that the circle is on is not part of the solution set. If the endpoint is filled in, then that number exists in the solution set. In this case, the circle above −4 is filled in, so this equation must include −4 and will have a ≤ symbol, which means "less than or equal to," or a ≥ symbol, which means "greater than or equal to." Because the shading points to the right, it is shading values that are greater than or equal to −4, so the appropriate inequality to represent the graph is $x \geq -4$. Choices **b** and **d** cannot be correct because $x > -4$ and $x < -4$ do not include −4. Choice **c** cannot be correct because $x \leq -4$ represents the points that are *less than* or equal to −4. Choice **e** cannot be correct because the solution set extends past the 10 as indicated by the shading and arrow, and the given inequality, $10 > x > -4$, does not include −4.

40. c. Remember that percentages are always out of 100. Therefore, in order to convert a fraction to a percent, change the denominator to 100 by multiplying the denominator and the numerator by the factor that will convert the denominator into 100: $\frac{3}{5} \times \frac{20}{20} = \frac{60}{100}$ We see that $\frac{3}{5}$ is equivalent to 60%, so choices **b** and **d** are both incorrect. The next way to approach this problem is to change $\frac{3}{5}$ to a decimal by dividing the numerator, 3, by the denominator, 5; $3.00 ÷ 5 = 0.60$. This rules out choices **a** and **e** and shows that choice **c** is the correct answer.

The following is a chart of the different skills assessed by the questions in this practice PPST; you can use it to identify your strengths and weaknesses in this subject to better focus your study.

MATH SKILLS STUDY CHART FOR PRACTICE EXAM 2	
NUMBER AND OPERATIONS SKILLS	**QUESTIONS**
Order	2
Equivalence	40
Numeration and Place Value	36
Number Properties	28
Operation Properties	—
Computation	1, 9, 26, 35
Estimation	21
Ratio, Proportion, and Percent	4, 17, 31
Numerical Reasoning	23
ALGEBRA SKILLS	
Equations and Inequalities	12, 25, 39
Algorithmic Thinking	6, 15
Patterns	32
Algebraic Representations	8, 27
Algebraic Reasoning	33
GEOMETRY AND MEASUREMENT	
Geometric Properties	5, 18, 24
The xy-Coordinate Plane	19
Geometric Reasoning	13
Systems of Measurement	22, 37
Measurement	8, 14
DATA ANALYSIS AND PROBABILITY SKILLS	
Data Interpretation	10, 11, 16, 29
Data Representation	34
Trends and Inferences	7, 30
Measures of Center and Spread	38
Probability	3, 20

Skills Test in Writing—Section 1, Part A

1. c. This sentence contains a subject-verb agreement error. The subject *states* is plural and takes a plural verb, such as *are*.

2. b. This run-on sentence needs to be split into two separate sentences. A semicolon should be inserted after the word *actor*.

3. a. Here, *poor* is being used to describe how Juliet did. It is describing the verb, so *poor* is an adverb. Adverbs end in *–ly*. The sentence should read *Juliet did poorly*.

4. e. Because there are no grammatical, idiomatic, logical, or structural errors in this sentence, choice **e** is the best answer.

5. a. *All ways* refers to every method, while *always* means forever. In this sentence, the wrong word has been used. The author means that he has been enamored forever, so he should use the word *always*.

6. d. This sentence compares two activities, so the form, or part of speech, of the two entities must match. As it reads, a verb and a noun are being compared. To be correct, we can change "a horror film" to the verb phrase "sitting through a horror film." This matches "watching a psychological thriller."

7. e. Because there are no grammatical, idiomatic, logical, or structural errors in this sentence, choice **e** is the best answer.

8. b. *Continuous*—meaning uninterrupted in time—should be replaced with *continual* in this sentence. Annabelle's need to pay rent recurs regularly or frequently, which is the definition of *continual*, but she doesn't pay continuously. So, the correct word choice is *continual*.

9. a. This sentence has an error in word choice. *Elicit* means to stir up. *Illicit* means illegal. The correct word choice is *illicit*.

10. d. This sentence has a verb error. The senators watched their colleague *stand* up. Another possible correct answer would be that they watched the colleague *as she stood* up.

11. c. The position belongs to Darby; therefore, an apostrophe is required to indicate possession. The sentence should read ". . . Darby's position. . . ."

12. d. This error has an error in comparison. The sentence compares *the innovations* of Carroll's later novels with the book *Alice's Adventures in Wonderland*. The comparison becomes parallel when you simply compare Lewis Carroll's later novels with his early book. Another way to make the sentence parallel would be to compare the innovations of the later novels with the innovations of the early book.

13. b. There is no grammatical reason to use a colon here.

14. b. It is unclear to what the ambiguous pronoun *they* refers as there is no apparent antecedent. However, the sentence makes sense when we replace the pronoun with *Olympic Games Knowledge Management (OGKM) resources*.

15. d. This error is in parallel construction. The series of phrases must all be consistent in structure, so the last phrase should begin, like the other two, with a verb. In this case, we could change it to *would have an easy commute*.

16. d. *Less* describes singular nouns that represent a quantity or a degree. So, in this case we should use *fewer*, which describes plural nouns or things that can be counted.

17. d. This sentence contains a dangling modifier because the opening phrase mistakenly modifies the wrong noun. Here, it sounds like the day was screaming and shouting. The underlined portion of the sentence could be changed to *everyone ended the day with a sore throat*.

18. b. *Stationery* (with an *e*) is the writing material the context of this sentence requires. *Stationary* (with an *a*) means still or not moving.

19. e. Because there are no grammatical, idiomatic, logical, or structural errors in this sentence, choice **e** is the best answer.

20. e. Because there are no grammatical, idiomatic, logical, or structural errors in this sentence, choice **e** is the best answer.

21. b. When comparing Samuels to *all the people*, Samuels is least likely to win. *Least* is the superlative form for comparisons. Superlative is used when comparing more than two items. *Less* is the comparative form and used when comparing only two items.

Skills Test in Writing—Section 1, Part B

22. a. To separate independent clauses joined by a coordinating conjunction, such as *but*, use a comma before the conjunction. Choices **b** through **d** do not use a comma. Choice **e** uses a comma before and after *but*; however, one is not needed after *but*.

23. c. *No one* is considered a negative; in this sentence there are two negatives. Avoid double negatives in a sentence. Choices **a** and **b** have double negatives. Choices **d** and **e** do not make sense.

24. d. This sentence contains an error in parallel construction because the phrases before and after *but also* do not match. Choice **d** uses the past tense verb *set* to match *provided*. Choices **a**, **c**, and **e** use present tense verbs that do not match *provided*. Choices **b** and **c** introduce a comma, which is not needed here because these are not two complete sentences joined by a conjunction.

25. d. Choice **d** is the only one that uses all three pronouns in the correct places. *Their* means belonging to them; *they're* is the contraction for "they are"; *there* describes where an action takes place.

26. e. When referring to a single person of unknown gender, use *his or her*, not *their*.

27. a. Choices **b**, **d**, and **e** use *skeptically*, which is an adverb. This sentence requires the adjective *skeptical* because it is describing the teacher, not how she looked (i.e., not the verb). Choices **c**, **d**, and **e** introduce commas, which are not needed in this sentence.

28. c. *Alumni* is the plural form of *alumnus*, so choices **a**, **b**, and **e** are incorrect. Choice **d** is incorrect because dates should not be spelled out.

29. b. Choice **a** sounds like the frog was slithering rather than the snake. Choices **c**, **d**, and **e** contain misplaced modifiers that are confusing and unclear. Only choice **b** is arranged in an order that is clear.

30. e. The series of events must all have parallel construction. That is, they must be in the same tense and have the same structure. Choice **e** has parallel construction in that each item begins with the same tense verb. Choices **a** through **d** do not consistently use the same verb tenses.

31. b. The introductory clause must refer to the subject of the sentence. Choice **b** refers to Ann as the subject, which is correct. Choices **a**, **c**, and **d** do not connect directly to the subject, Ann. Choice **e** changes the meaning of the sentence.

32. e. The comparative terms for *good* are *good*, *better*, and *best*. In choice **e**, we're comparing all the views first (best); then we're saying that the best view, as compared to anywhere else, is better. *Better* is used when comparing two things; *best* is used when comparing more than two things. The other choices do this incorrectly.

33. c. Choices **a**, **b**, **d**, and **e** contain double negatives. Choice **c** is the only one that does not contain double negatives and is, therefore, correct.

34. c. In choice **c** the conjunction *after* sets up a contrast between the two clauses that makes sense. None of the other choices make sense.

35. a. Choice **a** shows the superlative form of the comparison. This is correct, and the other choices are incorrect because we are comparing more than three items. Also, in choices **d** and **e** we don't use both most/ more and the comparative/superlative form of an adjective.

36. e. The plural for *crisis* is *crises*. We know it is plural because the pronoun used (them) is plural.

37. b. Choices **a**, **c**, **d**, and **e** contain errors in subordination. These sentences have two subordinate clauses but no independent clause; therefore, they are not correct.

38. a. Choices **b** and **d** are incorrect because *well* is an adverb, but here *good* is describing the noun *job*. Choices **c** and **d** are incorrect because of the punctuation. If we went with choice **c**, we'd have a run-on sentence. If we used choice **d**, we'd need to add a conjunction.

The following is a chart of the different skills assessed by the questions in this practice PPST; you can use it to identify your strengths and weaknesses in this subject to better focus your study.

SKILLS TEST IN WRITING STUDY CHART FOR PRACTICE EXAM 2	
GRAMMATICAL RELATIONSHIP SKILLS	**QUESTIONS**
Identify Errors in Adjectives	27, 32, 35
Identify Errors in Adverbs	3, 16, 38
Identify Errors in Nouns	28, 36
Identify Errors in Pronouns	14, 25, 26
Identify Errors in Verbs	1, 10
STRUCTURAL RELATIONSHIP SKILLS	
Identify Errors in Comparison	6, 12, 21
Identify Errors in Coordination	34
Identify Errors in Correlation	17, 29, 31
Identify Errors in Negation	23, 33
Identify Errors in Parallelism	15, 24, 30
Identify Errors in Subordination	37
WORD CHOICE AND MECHANICS SKILLS	
Identify Errors in Word Choice	5, 8, 9, 18
Identify Errors in Mechanics	2, 11, 13, 22
Identify Sentences Free from Error	4, 7, 19, 20

Skills Test in Writing—Section 2, Essay Writing

Following are sample criteria for scoring a PPST essay.

A score "6" writer will:

- create an exceptional composition that appropriately addresses the audience and given task
- organize ideas effectively, include very strong supporting details, and use smooth transitions
- present a definitive, focused thesis and clearly support it throughout the composition
- include vivid details, clear examples, and strong supporting text to enhance the themes of the composition
- exhibit an exceptional level of skill in the usage of the English language and the capacity to employ an assortment of sentence structures
- build essentially error-free sentences that accurately convey intended meaning

A score "5" writer will:

- create a commendable composition that appropriately addresses the audience and given task
- organize ideas, include supporting details, and use smooth transitions
- present a thesis and support it throughout the composition
- include details, examples, and supporting text to enhance the themes of the composition
- generally exhibit a high level of skill in the usage of the English language and the capacity to employ an assortment of sentence structures
- build mostly error-free sentences that accurately convey intended meaning

A score "4" writer will:

- create a composition that satisfactorily addresses the audience and given task
- display satisfactory organization of ideas, include adequate supporting details, and generally use smooth transitions
- present a thesis and mostly support it throughout the composition
- include some details, examples, and supporting text that typically enhance most themes of the composition
- exhibit a competent level of skill in the usage of the English language and the general capacity to employ an assortment of sentence structures
- build sentences with several minor errors that generally do not confuse the intended meaning

A score "3" writer will:

- create an adequate composition that basically addresses the audience and given task
- display some organization of ideas, include some supporting details, and use mostly logical transitions
- present a somewhat underdeveloped thesis but attempt to support it throughout the composition
- display limited organization of ideas, have some inconsistent supporting details, and use few transitions
- exhibit an adequate level of skill in the usage of the English language and a basic capacity to employ an assortment of sentence structures
- build sentences with some minor and major errors that may obscure the intended meaning

A score "2" writer will:

- create a composition that restrictedly addresses the audience and given task
- display little organization of ideas, have inconsistent supporting details, and use very few transitions
- present an unclear or confusing thesis with little support throughout the composition

- include very few details, examples, and supporting text
- exhibit a less-than-adequate level of skill in the usage of the English language and a limited capacity to employ a basic assortment of sentence structures
- build sentences with a few major errors that may confuse the intended meaning

A score "1" writer will:

- create a composition that has a limited sense of the audience and given task
- display illogical organization of ideas, include confusing or no supporting details, and lack the ability to effectively use transitions
- present a minimal or unclear thesis
- include confusing or irrelevant details and examples, and little or no supporting text
- exhibit a limited level of skill in the usage of the English language and little or no capacity to employ basic sentence structure
- build sentences with many major errors that obscure or confuse the intended meaning

Sample 6 Essay

Imagine yourself as a teenager. Were you running around vandalizing movie theaters and ripping off ice cream parlors? Every previous American generation has enjoyed parties and late-night diner runs as much as the youth of today. They were not out to scandalize their communities; they simply wanted to enjoy life. Yet now, these same freedom-loving adults want to suppress a teenager's freedom by enforcing a law that would prevent any teen from attending parties or working late to earn a little extra money. A curfew for minors under the age of 18 will not only have little effect on crime rates, but it will also wrongly restrict the social life and employability of many teens.

According to supporters of this legislation, enforcing a curfew on children under the age of 18 would "reduce community problems such as violence, graffiti, and drugs." There are many problems with this statement. For instance, violence does not take place in a community only at night. Violence can take place in broad daylight, and the root of this violence can sometimes begin at home. While graffiti is ugly and destructive, it is not done only in "alleys, parks, or playgrounds." There are scribbling and drawings on many of the desks and textbooks in schools, yet they were done in the daylight and are just as destructive. Similarly, drugs are a problem in every community and do not discriminate against any type of student or time of day. It is unfortunate but true that a student can sell drugs just as easily in school as he or she can in a park at midnight. This law is not eliminating problems. It is simply shifting them to different public places during different times of the day.

One argument of those opposed to this legislation is that "curfews stereotype minors by presupposing that citizens under the age of 18 are the only people who commit crimes." This is true. While many community problems can be attributed to minors, the same problems can also be attributed to adults. This fact is supported by the large numbers of men and women over the age of 18 in our prison system. The community may save money by keeping a few young vandals or drug dealers out of juvenile prison, but they will certainly continue to pay for those mature men and women who have chosen to support themselves by selling drugs to minors in the first place. While a curfew may keep minors from loitering and causing destruction, there is a group of young adults between the ages of 18 and 21 who cannot legally drink alcohol but still do. The curfew will do nothing to stop the destruction of property or even loss of lives that may result from this action.

A curfew like this would only restrict the positive outlets many teenagers have, such as healthy interaction with their peers and work. Many teens have long days filled with school and after-school activities such as sports or clubs, chores, and homework. It isn't until 9:00 or 10:00 p.m. that many teens go out and see a movie or visit with friends. This curfew would all but prevent most teens from being able to socialize with other teens in person. Teenagers would be relegated to online and phone friendships. The curfew would also make it difficult for many teenagers to hold a job and earn money for college. Social interaction and work are both healthy experiences that make teens into good, productive community members.

Obviously, by encouraging this legislation, the supporters of this curfew feel they are protecting their rights as well as those of the community. Perhaps instead of trying to contain troublesome youth with a curfew, we could find the root of the crime, violence, and drug problems. Together, adults and minors can make our community a better place.

Sample 4 Essay

Curfews for minors are a bad idea. Curfews make it illegal for minors to be out in public between the hours of 10 pm and 5 am. These curfews are a bad idea for several reasons. If a minor is out after 10 pm, it does not mean that this minor is comiting a crime. People over the age of 18 commit crimes too. Sometimes it is necessary for a minor to be out after 10 pm for work and for friends. Also, just because a minor is out after 10 pm doesn't mean he's a bad kid. He shouldn't get in trouble for not really doing anything bad.

The people who want to create a curfew think that it'll create less crime in the community. It might do that with some kids, sure, but it won't stop crime all together. If a kid knows he has to be in by 10 pm he might decide not to write graffiti on the walls or hang out and do drugs, but that doesn't mean that other people won't. Old people commit crimes, too. Also, a kid can do drugs after school at a friends house. He doesn't have to do it at night. He can draw or write on the sides of buildings before 10 pm too. In the wintertime, it is dark outside at 7 pm. Kids

will do the same things, they will just do them earlier in the day.

Sometimes, too, a minor needs to be out after 10 pm. For example a kid might have a job that doesn't get out until 10 pm and than the kid needs to drive home. If he gets caught driving, he could get in trouble. Or what if he is at a friends house and they are just having a fun time or doing there homework, not doing anything wrong or anything, but just hanging out? If he forgets what time it is and he leaves a little too late he could get in trouble. That is not fair if he is a good kid.

This brings me to my last point. If a minor gets in trouble for staying out after the curfew it could ruin his reputation. He might be a good student who wants to get a scholarship to college. He can't get a scholarship with a police record. He was probably out late studying anyway if he's a smart kid. Maybe the people who create these curfews could make some guidelines to follow so that kids could stay out later if there is a special event or for work or studying. That would make it easier to follow and good kids wouldn't get in trouble.

In conclusion, I think that curfews are a bad idea. They don't change anything and don't make kids stop doing inapropriate things.

Sample 1 Essay

I'm getting very tired of adults not trusting teenagers. This curfew idea just adds to the problem. It's a terrible idea.

People who want this curfew think that all teenagers are out to vandalize and cause trouble. That's not true. Some teens are trouble-makers but most aren't. As a student teacher I've found that most teens are good kids. They want to go out at night to have fun, not cause trouble. If we had a curfew teens would probably not be able to have much fun. They would have to go in their houses so early that they wouldn't be able to really do anything. The curfew might keep the bad teens from doing bad things but it punishes the good teens at the same time and that's not fair.

The curfew would make it practically impossible for teens to have jobs and that also wouldn't be fair. Teens can't really get a job at McDonalds if they can't work passed 10:00 P.M.

The whole problem is that adults don't trust teens and they should. Most teens are fine. Maybe only teens that have been bad should have the curfew instead of everyone.

5 ▶ PRAXIS I: POWER PRACTICE EXAM 3

CHAPTER SUMMARY
Here is a full-length test based on the three elements of the Praxis I, the Pre-Professional Skills Tests (PPSTs) of Reading, Mathematics, and Writing.

The exam that follows is made up of three tests: a Reading test (multiple-choice questions), a Mathematics test (multiple-choice questions), and a Writing test (multiple-choice questions and one essay).

With this practice exam, you should simulate the actual test-taking experience as closely as you can. Find a quiet place to work where you won't be disturbed. Set a timer or stopwatch for each part of the exam to guide your pace.

When you have completed the exam, use the answer explanations to learn more about the questions you missed, and use the scoring guide in Chapter 8 to figure out how you did.

LEARNINGEXPRESS ANSWER SHEET

SKILLS TEST IN READING

1. (a) (b) (c) (d) (e)
2. (a) (b) (c) (d) (e)
3. (a) (b) (c) (d) (e)
4. (a) (b) (c) (d) (e)
5. (a) (b) (c) (d) (e)
6. (a) (b) (c) (d) (e)
7. (a) (b) (c) (d) (e)
8. (a) (b) (c) (d) (e)
9. (a) (b) (c) (d) (e)
10. (a) (b) (c) (d) (e)
11. (a) (b) (c) (d) (e)
12. (a) (b) (c) (d) (e)
13. (a) (b) (c) (d) (e)
14. (a) (b) (c) (d) (e)
15. (a) (b) (c) (d) (e)
16. (a) (b) (c) (d) (e)
17. (a) (b) (c) (d) (e)
18. (a) (b) (c) (d) (e)
19. (a) (b) (c) (d) (e)
20. (a) (b) (c) (d) (e)
21. (a) (b) (c) (d) (e)
22. (a) (b) (c) (d) (e)
23. (a) (b) (c) (d) (e)
24. (a) (b) (c) (d) (e)
25. (a) (b) (c) (d) (e)
26. (a) (b) (c) (d) (e)
27. (a) (b) (c) (d) (e)
28. (a) (b) (c) (d) (e)
29. (a) (b) (c) (d) (e)
30. (a) (b) (c) (d) (e)
31. (a) (b) (c) (d) (e)
32. (a) (b) (c) (d) (e)
33. (a) (b) (c) (d) (e)
34. (a) (b) (c) (d) (e)
35. (a) (b) (c) (d) (e)
36. (a) (b) (c) (d) (e)
37. (a) (b) (c) (d) (e)
38. (a) (b) (c) (d) (e)
39. (a) (b) (c) (d) (e)
40. (a) (b) (c) (d) (e)

SKILLS TEST IN MATHEMATICS

1. (a) (b) (c) (d) (e)
2. (a) (b) (c) (d) (e)
3. (a) (b) (c) (d) (e)
4. (a) (b) (c) (d) (e)
5. (a) (b) (c) (d) (e)
6. (a) (b) (c) (d) (e)
7. (a) (b) (c) (d) (e)
8. (a) (b) (c) (d) (e)
9. (a) (b) (c) (d) (e)
10. (a) (b) (c) (d) (e)
11. (a) (b) (c) (d) (e)
12. (a) (b) (c) (d) (e)
13. (a) (b) (c) (d) (e)
14. (a) (b) (c) (d) (e)
15. (a) (b) (c) (d) (e)
16. (a) (b) (c) (d) (e)
17. (a) (b) (c) (d) (e)
18. (a) (b) (c) (d) (e)
19. (a) (b) (c) (d) (e)
20. (a) (b) (c) (d) (e)
21. (a) (b) (c) (d) (e)
22. (a) (b) (c) (d) (e)
23. (a) (b) (c) (d) (e)
24. (a) (b) (c) (d) (e)
25. (a) (b) (c) (d) (e)
26. (a) (b) (c) (d) (e)
27. (a) (b) (c) (d) (e)
28. (a) (b) (c) (d) (e)
29. (a) (b) (c) (d) (e)
30. (a) (b) (c) (d) (e)
31. (a) (b) (c) (d) (e)
32. (a) (b) (c) (d) (e)
33. (a) (b) (c) (d) (e)
34. (a) (b) (c) (d) (e)
35. (a) (b) (c) (d) (e)
36. (a) (b) (c) (d) (e)
37. (a) (b) (c) (d) (e)
38. (a) (b) (c) (d) (e)
39. (a) (b) (c) (d) (e)
40. (a) (b) (c) (d) (e)

SKILLS TEST IN WRITING

1. (a) (b) (c) (d) (e)
2. (a) (b) (c) (d) (e)
3. (a) (b) (c) (d) (e)
4. (a) (b) (c) (d) (e)
5. (a) (b) (c) (d) (e)
6. (a) (b) (c) (d) (e)
7. (a) (b) (c) (d) (e)
8. (a) (b) (c) (d) (e)
9. (a) (b) (c) (d) (e)
10. (a) (b) (c) (d) (e)
11. (a) (b) (c) (d) (e)
12. (a) (b) (c) (d) (e)
13. (a) (b) (c) (d) (e)
14. (a) (b) (c) (d) (e)
15. (a) (b) (c) (d) (e)
16. (a) (b) (c) (d) (e)
17. (a) (b) (c) (d) (e)
18. (a) (b) (c) (d) (e)
19. (a) (b) (c) (d) (e)
20. (a) (b) (c) (d) (e)
21. (a) (b) (c) (d) (e)
22. (a) (b) (c) (d) (e)
23. (a) (b) (c) (d) (e)
24. (a) (b) (c) (d) (e)
25. (a) (b) (c) (d) (e)
26. (a) (b) (c) (d) (e)
27. (a) (b) (c) (d) (e)
28. (a) (b) (c) (d) (e)
29. (a) (b) (c) (d) (e)
30. (a) (b) (c) (d) (e)
31. (a) (b) (c) (d) (e)
32. (a) (b) (c) (d) (e)
33. (a) (b) (c) (d) (e)
34. (a) (b) (c) (d) (e)
35. (a) (b) (c) (d) (e)
36. (a) (b) (c) (d) (e)
37. (a) (b) (c) (d) (e)
38. (a) (b) (c) (d) (e)

Skills Test in Reading

Directions: Read the following passages and answer the questions that follow.

Use the following passage to answer questions 1–3.

1   One of the most unusual creatures on Earth,
2   the sloth of Central and South America is
3   famous for its sluggish speed. In fact, its name
4   is actually a form of a word frequently used to
5   describe it: slow. However, don't mistake the
6   sloth's lack of speed for simple laziness. The
7   creature's languid motion developed out of a
8   necessity to avoid predators. For example, by
9   moving so slowly in the trees they call home,
10   sloths have adapted a self-defense against harpy
11   eagles who might be attracted to obvious
12   movements. As seen from above or below a
13   tree, a sloth can therefore easily be mistaken for
14   vegetation. In fact, its fur is specialized to grow
15   algae, thus adding to the creature's camouflage.
16   Combined with its renowned languid pace, the
17   sloth appears much more like hanging foliage
18   than an appetizing snack.

1. Which inference can be made from the information provided within the passage?
   a. The sloth is the slowest creature on Earth.
   b. The sloth never leaves the protection of the trees.
   c. The algae that grow on the sloth's fur are dangerous to other animals.
   d. The eagle is a natural predator to the sloth.
   e. Deforestation of the Americas is endangering the sloth.

2. In the context of the passage, *renowned* (line 16) can be replaced with which word to incur the smallest alteration in meaning?
   a. lethargic
   b. incredibly
   c. dangerous
   d. hurried
   e. legendary

3. What was the author's purpose in describing the sloth's fur?
   a. to accentuate the effectiveness of the sloth's speed as a self-defense mechanism
   b. to describe the uniqueness of the sloth among all other animals
   c. to further describe the sloth's protective adaptations in self-defense
   d. to describe an appealing attribute to sloths' potential predators
   e. to describe its warming effect

Use the following passage to answer questions 4–6.

1   Wilma Rudolph, the crippled child who became
2   an Olympic running champion, is an inspira-
3   tion for us all. Born prematurely in 1940,
4   Wilma spent her childhood battling illness,
5   including measles, scarlet fever, chicken pox,
6   pneumonia, and polio, a crippling disease
7   which at that time had no cure. At the age of
8   four, she was told she would never walk again.
9   But Wilma and her family refused to give up.
10   After years of special treatment and physical
11   therapy, 12-year-old Wilma was able to walk
12   normally again. But walking wasn't enough for
13   Wilma, who was determined to be an athlete.
14   Before long, her talent earned her a spot in the
15   1956 Olympics, where she earned a bronze
16   medal. In the 1960 Olympics, the zenith of her
17   career, she won three gold medals.

4. Which statement provides the best summary of the main idea of the reading selection?

   a. Wilma Rudolph was very sick as a child.

   b. Wilma Rudolph was an Olympic champion.

   c. Wilma Rudolph is someone to admire.

   d. With special treatment, anyone can overcome a handicap.

   e. Polio was a crippling disease in the mid-twentieth century.

5. Which situation is most similar to the scenario provided in the passage?

   a. After contracting what was believed to be polio at age 39, President Franklin Roosevelt was paralyzed from the waist down and had to spend much of the rest of his life in braces or a wheelchair.

   b. Diagnosed with the degenerative nervous system disorder Parkinson's disease in 1991, actor Michael J. Fox retired from full-time acting in 2000.

   c. Following his fall from a horse in 1995, actor Christopher Reeve was confined to a wheelchair until his death in 2004.

   d. Nicknamed the "Iron Horse" for his durability, New York Yankee Lou Gehrig retired at age 36 due to advancement of amyotrophic lateral sclerosis (ALS).

   e. Although he suffered from severe asthma as a child, Theodore Roosevelt became not only a U.S. president but also an avid outdoorsman and an expert hunter.

6. In the context of the passage, the word *zenith* (line 16) most nearly means

   a. peak.

   b. nadir.

   c. conclusion.

   d. epilogue.

   e. midpoint.

Use the following passage to answer questions 7 and 8.

The following passage is an advertisement for Mercury Shoes.

Help your feet take flight! Mercury Shoes promises you high quality and can save you from the aches and pains that runners often suffer.

Running magazine has awarded Mercury Shoes its "High Quality" rating for our breakthrough in shoe technology! By studying the feet of track-and-field champions and ultra-marathoners, we have developed a revolutionary sole construction that offers complete support for dedicated runners. Our unique combination of gel and air cushioning provides greater stability and incredible comfort.

Three types of Mercury Shoes are now available:

- **Cheetah:** A racing shoe that combines light weight with real support.
- **Mountain Goat:** A superior trail-running shoe with great traction and stability even on muddy or slick trails.
- **Gray Wolf:** A shoe that gives maximum support in order to minimize common injuries caused by mile after mile of training runs on hard pavement.

7. Which of the following is presented as a *fact* in the ad?

   a. Mercury Shoes can save you from the aches and pains that runners often suffer.

   b. *Running* magazine has awarded Mercury Shoes its "High Quality" rating.

   c. Mercury Shoes has developed a revolutionary sole construction.

   d. Mountain Goats are superior trail-running shoes.

   e. The construction of Mercury Shoes provides incredible comfort.

8. Which is the most likely reason that Mercury Shoes named one of its models the Cheetah?
   a. The shoes will make you run faster.
   b. The shoes are designed to look like cheetah skins.
   c. The shoes provide extra support.
   d. The shoes are for those who like to run wild.
   e. The shoes can help prevent injury.

Use the following passage to answer questions 9–15.

1   Two of the most famous and popular authors
2   in the field of children's literature are Eric Carle
3   and Theodor Seuss Geisel, the latter author
4   more commonly recognized as Dr. Seuss. Each
5   author has published more than 60 books dur-
6   ing his storied career, and many of those titles
7   have been translated into multiple languages.
8   Not only have Seuss and Carle written dozens
9   of famous books but they have illustrated them
10   as well. Both authors were born in the north-
11   eastern United States, raised by parents of Ger-
12   man descent.
13   Carle uses a unique collage process to
14   illustrate his books, including arguably his most
15   famous book, *The Very Hungry Caterpillar.* To
16   create the collages, he cuts brightly painted
17   paper and uses the pieces to form recognizable
18   shapes. Seuss, on the other hand, mostly cre-
19   ated the illustrations for his books, such as the
20   legendary *The Cat in the Hat,* by drawing car-
21   toons by hand. Regardless of the process used
22   to illustrate their books, the end result was the
23   same for Seuss's and Carle's creations: millions
24   of children loved the stories and were inspired
25   to read as a result.

9. Why does the author of the passage most likely mention the heritage of the two children's book authors?
   a. to show that the best children's authors always come from Germany
   b. to explain the ways in which Eric Carle created his illustrations
   c. to demonstrate the importance of a strong family life
   d. to show another way in which the two writers were alike
   e. to illustrate the degree of talent that originated from a geographic area

10. According to the passage, which supporting detail is NOT given about both Eric Carle and Dr. Seuss to compare their lives and careers?
   a. They both wrote and illustrated children's books.
   b. They both were born in the United States.
   c. They both drew the illustrations for their books by hand.
   d. They both inspired millions of children with their books.
   e. They both had their publications translated into other languages.

11. The author most likely mentions the collage process of Eric Carle in order to
   a. show students an easy and fun way to create beautiful artwork.
   b. give an example of Eric Carle's level of brilliance as an artist.
   c. compare the similar styles of comparable artists.
   d. show the reasons for the wild success of *The Very Hungry Caterpillar.*
   e. demonstrate the difference between the illustrating styles of Carle and Seuss.

12. Which best describes the organization of the passage?

   a. The accomplishments of one artist are listed, and then the accomplishments of another are provided.

   b. A comparison of two artists is given, and then a difference of the artists is provided.

   c. The story of two artists is told in chronological order through their careers.

   d. Two authors are described in detail, and then the features of two illustrators are explained.

   e. A series of children's book authors is provided, and then the readers' responses are given.

13. In the context of the passage, the word *storied* (line 6) most nearly means

   a. fictional.

   b. celebrated.

   c. infamous.

   d. elaborative.

   e. imaginative.

14. Which summary best describes the main idea of the passage?

   a. Eric Carle and Dr. Seuss are nearly identical children's book authors.

   b. To create his collages, Eric Carle cuts brightly painted paper and uses the pieces to form recognizable shapes.

   c. Children's book authors can use different styles to inspire their readers.

   d. Both Eric Carle and Dr. Seuss are known for authoring and illustrating a variety of children's books.

   e. Eric Carle and Dr. Seuss may use different processes, but they are both successful and inspiring artists.

15. Which word or term from the passage best serves to create a distinction between the two authors?

   a. on the other hand

   b. as well

   c. regardless

   d. such as

   e. as a result

Use the following bar graph to answer question 16.

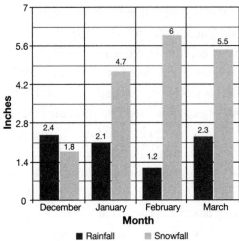

16. Which conclusion about the precipitation in Springfield is supported by the information in the preceding bar graph?

   a. The only months during the year in which there was any snowfall was December, January, February, and March.

   b. There was more combined precipitation, in inches, in February then there was in March.

   c. Each winter month featured a decreasing amount of rainfall, in inches.

   d. There was less snowfall, in inches, in December and January combined than there was in February.

   e. The only winter month in which there was a greater amount of rain than snow, in inches, was December.

Use the following passage to answer questions 17–22.

1   In A.D. 79, the volcano Mount Vesuvius
2   erupted, showering the nearby city of Pompeii
3   with ash for hours until the once-thriving
4   town—and hundreds of its cosmopolitan
5   inhabitants—were completely buried. So much
6   ash fell on the city that it remained completely
7   hidden until the 18th century. Unfortunately
8   for the residents who live in the Bay of Naples,
9   Italy, in the shadows of Mount Vesuvius, the
10   eruption was not a onetime event. In fact, the
11   volcano has erupted at least thirty times since
12   the deadly 1st-century eruption that obliterated
13   Pompeii. The only active volcano on mainland
14   Europe, Mount Vesuvius has been atypically
15   dormant since its last eruption in 1944. Citizens
16   have mistaken this relative peace as an invita-
17   tion to live near to Mount Vesuvius again; more
18   than half a million people live within 4.3 miles
19   of the volcano's mouth. It is for this reason that
20   the Italian government is stepping in to
21   improve the safety of its residents. In 1995, gov-
22   ernment officials declared the uppermost part
23   of the volcano a national park, thus preventing
24   further construction near the danger zone.
25   Recently, the government has even offered to
26   pay thousands of families living on the slopes
27   of Mount Vesuvius to move to safer areas, thus
28   improving the ease of the evacuation and limit-
29   ing casualties when the next major eruption
30   occurs.

17. Which statement could be concluded from the information in the passage?
  a. Mount Vesuvius is expected to erupt at some point in the next 20 years.
  b. Few families took advantage of the government's offer to pay for them to move away from Mount Vesuvius.
  c. None of the Mount Vesuvius eruptions following A.D. 79 resulted in fatalities.
  d. The eruption of Mount Vesuvius in A.D. 79 was the world's most catastrophic volcano event.
  e. Mount Etna, an active volcano in Europe, resides off the European mainland.

18. In the context of the passage, *dormant* (line 15) can be replaced with which word to incur the smallest alteration in meaning?
  a. dangerous
  b. inactive
  c. threatening
  d. overdeveloped
  e. explosive

19. For which reason does the author most likely describe the events of the A.D. 79 eruption of Mount Vesuvius?
  a. to illustrate the raw power of mother nature
  b. to demonstrate the measures that the government is taking to increase safety
  c. to emphasize the hazards of living near the volcano
  d. to provide a historical description of ancient Italy
  e. to accentuate the frequency of the volcano's major eruptions

20. Which best describes the general organization of the passage?

    a. A historical anecdote is provided, and then its modern implications are considered.

    b. The dangers of an area are described, and then several safety measures are presented.

    c. The history of a geological formation is described in a chronological sequence.

    d. A geological formation is defined, and then its causes and effects are detailed.

    e. A warning is presented, and then the justifications for the warning are described.

21. Which statement, if it were true, would most significantly strengthen the author's central argument?

    a. The majority of the world's active volcanoes exist in the Pacific Rim, along the edges of the Pacific Ocean.

    b. Predictive technologies can predict an eruption several weeks in advance, allowing for a proper evacuation.

    c. The amount that the Italian government was prepared to offer families to move was €25,000, or about $35,000 USD.

    d. Geologists predict that Mount Vesuvius is overdue for a major eruption within the next 10–15 years.

    e. The residents of ancient Pompeii had warning of the impending eruption and ample time to flee the approaching devastation.

22. Which specific detail from the passage supports the primary purpose of the selection the least?

    a. A Mount Vesuvius eruption nearly 2,000 years ago buried an entire city with ash.

    b. There has not been an eruption at Mount Vesuvius since 1944.

    c. Mount Vesuvius has erupted at least thirty times since AD 79.

    d. Mount Vesuvius is the only active volcano in mainland Europe.

    e. The area near the mouth of Mount Vesuvius is densely populated.

Use the following passage to answer questions 23 and 24.

For many students juggling a heavy scholarly workload and numerous extracurricular activities, school is tough enough without having to worry about what to wear and how to look cool every day. Much of what students choose to wear to school on their own accord, such as oversized jeans or revealing shirts, can be a distraction within the classroom's walls. Furthermore, allowing students the freedom to select their own attire presents an outward inequality; students who have the ability to show off designer-labeled clothes will frequently do so, revealing the students' financial disparity.

23. Which adjective best describes the author's attitude toward an enforced student dress code?

    a. resistant

    b. cautious

    c. ambivalent

    d. concerned

    e. sympathetic

24. Which statement, if it were true, would most significantly weaken the author's main argument?
  a. An education study recently demonstrated that a dress code increases students' ability to learn.
  b. A school that employs a stringent dress code is a safer educational environment.
  c. Restricting students' ability to choose their clothes limits their independence and creativity.
  d. Tolerance across ethnic and social groups is improved with the use of a formal dress code.
  e. Different schools frequently differ on the style and color of a mandatory school uniform.

Use the following passage to answer questions 25–30.

1   At the age of six, Goran Kropp climbed his first
2   mountain. Twenty-three years later, he tackled
3   the highest mountain in the world, Mount
4   Everest. His journey to the top shows just how
5   independent, persistent, and determined this
6   remarkable man is. While most people arrive at
7   the foothills of Mount Everest using modern
8   vehicles, Kropp bicycled 7,000 miles from his
9   home in Sweden. Traveling that kind of dis-
10 tance by bike is not easy. Bumpy, rough roads
11 caused mechanical problems for Kropp, and he
12 stopped many times to repair his bike. In addi-
13 tion, he was chased by dogs, stung by hornets,
14 and drenched by rain many times before he
15 arrived at the base of the mountain. Kropp
16 chose to climb Mount Everest the same way he
17 traveled to the mountain: without the help of
18 others and without modern conveniences.
19   Unlike most others, Kropp climbed Ever-
20 est without a guide or helper. He did not bring
21 bottled oxygen to help him breathe at high
22 altitudes, and he carried all his gear himself in a
23 pack that weighed about 140 pounds. It took
24 Kropp two tries to reach the summit. The first
25 time, he had to turn back only 350 feet from
26 the top because the weather was too dangerous.
27 Just a few days earlier, at that same level, eight
28 climbers died when a sudden snowstorm hit the
29 mountain. Kropp waited out the storm, rested,
30 and tried again a few days later. This time, he
31 was successful. After he descended the moun-
32 tain, Kropp got back on his bike and rode the
33 7,000 miles back home.

25. Which sentence summarizes the information from the passage?
  a. Goran Kropp climbed his first mountain at age six, then later climbed Mount Everest.
  b. Goran Kropp is able to ride a bicycle for incredibly long distances.
  c. Goran Kropp did not bring oxygen to his ascent of Mount Everest.
  d. Goran Kropp is a reckless and thoughtless adventurer.
  e. Goran Kropp is an independent and determined adventurer.

26. What purpose does the phrase *In addition* serve in lines 12 and 13 of the passage?
  a. to provide additional ways that Goran Kropp was an accomplished climber
  b. to emphasize Goran Kropp's unwillingness to work in a team
  c. to describe additional ways that Goran Kropp was a cautious adventurer
  d. to illustrate further hardships that Goran Kropp had to endure on his journey
  e. to provide additional occurrences where Goran Kropp needlessly risked his life

27. Goran Kropp's unique Everest adventure is most similar to which other adventurer's exploit?

    a. John Fairfax, a British rower who in 1969 became the first person to row across an ocean by himself

    b. Sir Edmund Hillary, a New Zealand mountaineer who first climbed Mount Everest in 1953, with the help of Sherpa Tenzing Norgay

    c. Neil Armstrong, an American aviator who, along with Buzz Aldrin in 1969, guided *Eagle* to the first manned landing on the Moon

    d. George Washington, a general during the Revolutionary War and the first President of the United States

    e. Amelia Earhart, a pioneering American pilot whose plane disappeared over the Pacific Ocean in 1937

28. Which sentence contains a statement of opinion rather than fact?

    a. At the age of six, Goran Kropp climbed his first mountain.

    b. While most people arrive at the foothills of Mount Everest using modern vehicles, Kropp bicycled 7,000 miles from his home in Sweden.

    c. Traveling that kind of distance by bike is not easy.

    d. It took Kropp two tries to reach the summit.

    e. After he descended the mountain, Kropp got back on his bike and rode the 7,000 miles back home.

29. For which reason does the author most likely mention that Goran Kropp had to *turn back only 350 feet from the top* on his initial attempt to reach the summit of Mount Everest?

    a. to paint a picture of Kropp as a resolute but careful adventurer

    b. to further enhance Kropp's daredevil attitude

    c. to demonstrate the difficulties of mountain climbing

    d. to show that climbers must be aware of changing weather patterns

    e. to support the idea that climbing Mount Everest is the world's greatest challenge

30. Which structure best describes the general organization of the entire passage?

    a. compare and contrast

    b. problem and solution

    c. order of importance

    d. cause and effect

    e. chronological order

Use the following passage to answer questions 31 and 32.

The official end of the school days should be extended until 4:00 P.M. As it is now, the majority of students go home after school to an empty house. These "latchkey children" are often alone for hours until their parents come home from work. A recent survey in a school district found that more than 60% of middle-school students are home alone for two or more hours a day. Of those students, furthermore, more than half watch television while waiting for their parents to come home.

31. Which sentence from the passage contains an opinion rather than a fact?

    a. The official end of the school days should be extended until 4:00 P.M.

    b. As it is now, the majority of students go home after school to an empty house.

    c. These "latchkey children" are often alone for hours until their parents come home from work.

    d. A recent survey in a school district found that more than 60% of middle-school students are home alone for two or more hours a day.

    e. Of those students, more than half watch television while waiting for their parents to come home.

32. Which implication is most supported by the information in the passage?

    a. Students should be involved in more after-school activities.

    b. Working parents do not generally get home until after 6:00 P.M.

    c. It is not safe for students to be at home by themselves.

    d. Students should be given additional homework from the classes.

    e. Television is not an effective use of a student's time.

Use the following passage to answer questions 33–35.

1   One of the greatest scientific minds in human
2   history, Albert Einstein advanced the world of
3   physics through his numerous achievements in
4   the field. But despite a multifarious array of sig-
5   nificant discoveries, it is perhaps his theory of
6   special relativity that earned him the greatest
7   celebrity and reverence. Einstein's theory
8   described the structure of spacetime using a
9   deceptively simple equation, $E = mc^2$, which
10   revolutionized physics by relating speed (the

11   speed of light, *c*) and mass (*m*) to energy (*E*) in
12   a way that had never before been defined and,
13   as a result, transformed the way we understood
14   the universe forever.

33. The primary concern of the passage is

    a. describing the myriad discoveries of a noted scientist.

    b. relating how the speed of light, mass, and energy are all related.

    c. analyzing the potentially harmful effects of a groundbreaking discovery.

    d. balancing the potential benefits and drawbacks of a scientific innovation.

    e. discussing a particular discovery that altered an entire branch of science.

34. Which key transition word or phrase from the reading selection most helps focus the content on Einstein's most important discovery from general information about him?

    a. one of

    b. but despite

    c. deceptively simple

    d. by relating

    e. as a result

35. Which word shares the closest meaning to the word *multifarious* (line 4) as it appears in the passage?

    a. multitalented

    b. varied

    c. nefarious

    d. groundbreaking

    e. unique

Use the following passage to answer questions 36–38.

The Cambrian Period was a period on Earth when life diversified from mostly single-cell organisms to more complex animal groups, some of which still exist today. Ranging from about 488 to 542 million years ago, the period represented an explosion of innovative life-forms. In fact, the term *Cambrian explosion* is often used to describe the rapid diversification of species on our planet. Although scientists are enthralled by this evolutionary epoch, they don't agree on the reasons for the immense increase of life.

36. The most likely reason that the author included the first sentence of the passage was to
  a. provide readers with a comparison of similar life forms.
  b. describe the evolution of life on Earth through the present.
  c. contrast different periods in Earth's history.
  d. provide the definition of a scientific term.
  e. explain the origin of life on Earth.

37. Which conclusion could be made from the material in the reading selection?
  a. The Jurassic Period, which featured the dominance of large reptiles including dinosaurs, came after the Cambrian Period.
  b. A variety of shark species originated at some point during the Cambrian Period.
  c. There was a greater variety of life on planet Earth during the Cambrian Period than during any other period.
  d. The lack of available fossils from the ancient Cambrian Period is the reason for the unknown cause of the increase of life.
  e. The length of the Cambrian Period, in years, was the longest period in Earth's history.

38. The role of the final sentence in the reading selection is to
  a. explain a scientific phenomenon.
  b. mention an unexplained aspect of a period.
  c. provide additional information about a time period.
  d. disprove a common claim about a scientific theory.
  e. present an introduction to the following time period.

Use the following passage to answer questions 39 and 40.

1　The United States is one of the most culturally
2　diverse nations on Earth. It is one of the most
3　climatically diverse nations as well. The climate
4　of the United States ranges from the frigid to
5　the torrid. Some areas of Alaska rarely get
6　warm enough to melt an ice cube. The weather
7　in Hawaii is perfect all year long. A temperature
8　once recorded in northern Alaska was −79.8°F,
9　while Hawaii has never recorded a sub-zero
10　temperature.

39. Which of the following sentences from the passage is an example of an opinion?
  a. "The United States . . . nations on Earth."
  b. "The climate of . . . to the torrid."
  c. "Some areas of . . . an ice cube."
  d. "The weather in . . . all year long."
  e. "A temperature once . . . sub-zero temperature."

40. In the context of the passage, *torrid* (line 5) can be replaced with which word to incur the smallest alteration in meaning?
  a. sweltering
  b. dissimilar
  c. glacial
  d. lukewarm
  e. uncomfortable

Skills Test in Mathematics

1. A dormitory now houses 30 men and allows 42 square feet of space per man. If five more men are put into this dormitory, each man will have how much less space?

  a. 36 square feet

  b. 5 square feet

  c. 6 square feet

  d. 7 square feet

  e. 8 square feet

2. Sea Horse Pool Servicing Professionals charge by the gallon. They charge a $75 flat fee for delivery and then 12¢ per gallon. The delivery fee for Penny's Pool Services is a flat $25 and their fill water is 15¢ per gallon. If Rosary is making a fishpond that needs 3,800 gallons of water, which company should she use and how much money will she save?

  a. Sea Horse Pool Servicing Professionals; $531

  b. Penny's Pool Services; $595

  c. Sea Horse Pool Servicing Professionals; $64

  d. Penny's Pool Services; $64

  e. Penny's Pool Services; $11,350

3. Two hundred customers in a mall were surveyed to determine their favorite flavors of ice cream. Seventy-five people said their favorite flavor was vanilla. If the survey is expanded to 1,200 similar customers, what is the best prediction of how many people would choose vanilla as their favorite flavor?

  a. 75

  b. 450

  c. 525

  d. 600

  e. 1,075

4. If 14Q is divisible by 48, then Q must be divisible by all of the following EXCEPT

  a. 2.

  b. 3.

  c. 8.

  d. 14.

  e. 24.

Use the following information to answer questions 5 and 6.

A forest fire engulfed the Wildlife Preserve in Blackhill County in 2008. Since then, park rangers have kept track of the number of animals living in the forest. Below is a graph of how many deer, foxes, and owls were reported during the years following the fire.

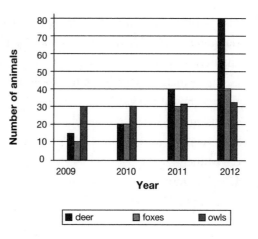

5. Which of the following statements appears to be true for the years shown?

  a. The fox population doubled every year from 2009 to 2012.

  b. The deer population doubled every year from 2010 to 2012.

  c. The owl population showed neither a steady nor rapid increase since the 2008 fire.

  d. Choices **a, b,** and **c** are all true.

  e. Choices **b** and **c** are both true.

6. Which statement about the owl population might explain the data presented in the graph?

   a. The owl population was greatly reduced by the fire, and, thus, the trend shows a steady increase in this population during the years of recovery.

   b. The owls were able to fly away from the fire, thus, the owl population does not show the pattern of recovery that the deer and fox populations exhibit.

   c. Factors independent of the fire are causing a slow decline in the owl population.

   d. A steadiness in the owl population can be attributed to illness.

   e. Because owls feed on foxes, their population suffered until the foxes recovered.

7. Miss Sweet has a flower vase that is a regular triangular prism. The vase is a foot and a half tall and its triangular base has a surface area of 16 square inches. What is the total volume in cubic inches of the vase?

   a. 288 inches^2

   b. 24 inches^2

   c. 144 inches^2

   d. 256 inches^2

   e. 320 inches^2

8. Which number is equal to 6%?

   a. $\frac{2}{3}$

   b. 0.60

   c. $\frac{3}{50}$

   d. 6.00

   e. $\frac{6}{1,000}$

For questions 9 and 10, consider the following graph and assume that ABCD is a square.

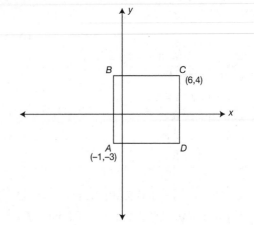

9. What are the coordinates of point *D*?

   a. (6,−4)

   b. (−6,4)

   c. (−1,4)

   d. (−4,6)

   e. (6,−3)

10. What is the area of square *ABCD* in the graph?

   a. 24 square units

   b. 36 square units

   c. 49 square units

   d. 81 square units

   e. 25 square units

11. After a computer is discounted by 20%, its price is $960. What was the original price of the computer before the discount?

   a. $768

   b. $1,160

   c. $1,152

   d. $1,200

   e. $1,220

12. In the following Venn Diagram, circle A represents all numbers that can be written in the form $2x + 1$, where x is all integers greater than or equal to 0. Circle B represents all factors of 24. How many numbers are contained in section C, which is contained both in circle A and circle B?

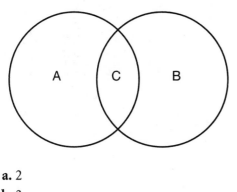

a. 2
b. 3
c. 4
d. 6
e. 8

13. Two less than four times the square of a number can be represented as which of the following?
a. $2 - 4x^2$
b. $4x^2 - 2$
c. $(4x)^2 - 2$
d. $2 - 4\sqrt{x}$
e. $4\sqrt{x} - 2$

14. The breakdown of the girls' lacrosse team's budget for 2007 is shown in the following pie chart. If their transportation expenses were $550 more than their uniform expenses, what was the total budget for the team in 2007?

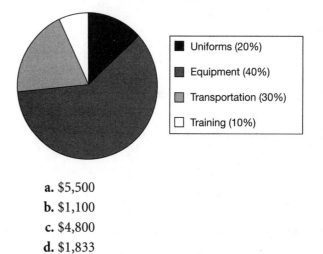

a. $5,500
b. $1,100
c. $4,800
d. $1,833
e. $2,750

15. Which of the following correctly shows the inequality $-1.4 \leq x \leq 2$?

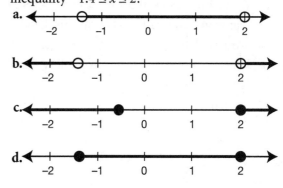

e. None of the above closely model $-1.4 \leq x \leq 2$.

16. Philana, Zosia, and Emily each have white ribbons to use to decorate a room. Philana's ribbon is 11 and a half yards. Zosia's is 30 feet. Emily's ribbon is two-thirds as long as Zosia's. Together, how many inches of ribbon do they have?

a. 84.5 inches

b. 1,014 inches

c. 414 inches

d. 798 inches

e. 1,262 inches

17. If the prime factorization of f contains a 3 and the prime factorization of g contains a 2, then which of the following statements is NOT correct?

a. $f \times g$ must be divisible by 4.

b. $f \times g$ must be divisible by 3.

c. $f \times g$ must be divisible by 2.

d. $f \times g$ must be divisible by 6.

e. $f \times g$ can be divisible by 5.

18. The Astoria Main Street Fair is raffling off a weeklong stay at a summer art camp. Sohail buys 4 raffle tickets for his son, Asad, and three times as many raffle tickets for his daughter, Amara. If a total of 80 raffle tickets are sold for the art camp, what is the probability that Asad or Amara will win?

a. 0.05

b. 0.15

c. 0.20

d. 0.25

e. 0.09

19. It takes six painters 12 hours to paint a house. At the same rate, how long would it take eight painters to paint the same house?

a. 4 hours

b. 6 hours

c. 10 hours

d. 9 hours

e. 16 hours

Use the following bar graph to answer questions 20–22.

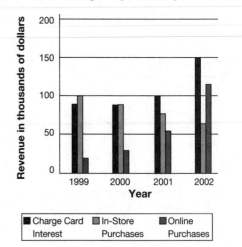

20. Based on the chart, which answer choice represents a true statement?

a. Online Purchases have increased, whereas Charge Card Interest has decreased over the course of the four years shown.

b. Charge Card Interest has increased, whereas Online Purchases have decreased over the course of the four years shown.

c. In-Store Purchases have increased, whereas Charge Card Interest has decreased over the course of the four years shown.

d. Online Purchases have increased, whereas In-Store Purchases have decreased over the course of the four years shown.

e. The increase in Online Purchases is probably because of the decrease in the profits in the other two categories.

21. If all the information on the previous graph were converted into a table, which of the following tables would correctly display the data (with revenue in thousands of dollars)?

a.

	1999	2000	2001	2002
Charge Card Interest	$90	$90	$100	$150
In-Store Purchases	$80	$90	$ 80	$ 70
Online Purchases	$15	$60	$ 30	$120

b.

	1999	2000	2001	2002
Charge Card Interest	$80	$90	$100	$120
In-Store Purchases	$80	$80	$ 80	$ 70
Online Purchases	$15	$60	$ 60	$120

c.

	1999	2000	2001	2002
Charge Card Interest	$ 80	$90	$100	$150
In-Store Purchases	$100	$90	$ 80	$ 70
Online Purchases	$ 15	$30	$ 60	$120

d.

	1999	2000	2001	2002
Charge Card Interest	$80	$90	$100	$150
In-Store Purchases	$90	$80	$ 90	$ 70
Online Purchases	$15	$30	$ 60	$120

e. None of the tables correctly display the data.

22. If Charge Card Interest profits were $40,000 in 1997 and $150,000 in 2002 (data not shown in bar graph), what was the percentage increase in Charge Card Interest profits from 1997 to 2002?
a. 275%
b. 150%
c. 110%
d. 73.3%
e. 100%

Use the following illustration to answer questions 23 and 24.

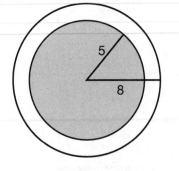

23. A boutique hotel has a circular pool with a 5-yard radius. The hotel staff will be putting a 3-yard-wide tile-work pattern around the circumference of the pool. What equation best represents the square yards of tile that will be needed to put a 3-yard-wide border around the pool?

  a. 64π square yards

  b. 25π square yards

  c. 39π square yards

  d. 89π square yards

  e. 9π square yards

24. The area of the 3-yard-wide border is determined to be $w\pi$ square yards. The manager needs to order tile, but it is only sold by the square *foot* and not by the square *yard*. Which expression correctly represents the number of square feet of tile the manager would need to order to complete the job?

  a. $12w\pi$ square feet

  b. $3w\pi$ square feet

  c. $144w\pi$ square feet

  d. $9w\pi$ square feet

  e. $6w\pi$ square feet

25. A local phone company offers a long-distance plan that costs $6.95 per month and includes 100 free long-distance minutes. After the first 100 long-distance minutes, each additional long-distance minute costs 5¢. If John uses 240 long-distance minutes in March, how much will his long-distance bill be?

  a. $7.00

  b. $12.00

  c. $13.95

  d. $15.50

  e. $76.95

26. What is the value of $5 + 3 \times 2^4$?

  a. 29

  b. 1,301

  c. 128

  d. 64

  e. 53

27. A girl is 4 feet tall and casts a 6-foot shadow. How long of a shadow does a tree that is 24 feet tall cast?

  a. 6 feet

  b. 36 feet

  c. 16 feet

  d. 22 feet

  e. 28 feet

28. Midori is a manager at Kaychan Toys, which produces fine hand-made wooden animals. She has an Assembly Department receive the hand-made parts and assemble them into the final product. Use their rates in the following table to determine the median assembly rate of Midori's employees.

ASSEMBLY DEPARTMENT	
NAME	**TOYS ASSEMBLED PER HOUR**
Tom	6
Kaoru	4
Kai	13
Hope	11
Arata	6
Takashi	8

a. 8
b. 6
c. 7
d. 4
e. 12

29. Estimate the sum of the following numbers when they are all rounded to the nearest hundred before adding: 152; 2,812; 245; 8,459
a. 11,900
b. 12,000
c. 12,100
d. 11,700
e. 11,860

30. Which of the following expressions is equal to 52,801 plus 4,157?
a. 50,000 + 3,000+ 300 + 50 + 8
b. 90,000 + 3,000+ 300 + 70 + 1
c. 90,000 + 4,000+ 300 + 70 + 1
d. 50,000 + 6,000+ 900 + 50 + 8
e. 50,000 + 4,000+ 100 + 50 + 7

31. For all x, $(3x - 4)^2 =$
a. $6x - 8$.
b. $9x^2 + 16$.
c. $9x^2 - 16$.
d. $9x^2 - 12x + 16$.
e. $9x^2 - 24x + 16$.

32. Simplify the expression:
$3x^2 + 4ax - 8a^2 + 7x^2 - 2ax + 7a^2$.
a. $21x^2 - 8ax - 56a^2$
b. $10x^2 + 2a^2x^2 - a^2$
c. $10x^4 - 2a^2x^2 - a^4$
d. $10x^2 - a^2 + 2ax$
e. The expression cannot be simplified further.

33. The school cafeteria offers the lunch menu shown below on Tuesday. If Betty chooses one meat, one vegetable, and one dessert, how many different lunches can she choose?

MEAT	VEGETABLE	DESSERT
Hamburger	Salad	Cake
Chicken	Broccoli	Pie
	Beans	Cookies
		Pudding

a. 9
b. 16
c. 18
d. 24
e. 36

34. Tyler has an extension cord that measures five and three-quarters meters long. How many centimeters of extension cord does Tyler have?
a. 575 centimeters
b. 534 centimeters
c. 5,750 centimeters
d. 5,340 centimeters
e. 57,500 centimeters

35. Jake is playing a card game in which there are nine cards. Two cards are red, and the rest are black. Jake is instructed to select two cards. Jake draws two cards and flips over the first card. The color on the first card is red. What is the probability that the second card is red?

 a. $\frac{1}{9}$

 b. $\frac{1}{8}$

 c. $\frac{1}{4}$

 d. $\frac{7}{8}$

 e. $\frac{7}{9}$

36. Each of the following polygons can have a line of symmetry EXCEPT

 a. hexagon.

 b. rectangle.

 c. isosceles triangle.

 d. rhombus.

 e. scalene triangle.

37. Which of the following statements best describes the relationship among the data points shown on the scatter plot?

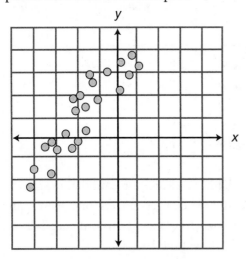

 a. There is a positive correlation.

 b. There is a negative correlation.

 c. There is an inverse relationship.

 d. There does not appear to be any correlation.

 e. It cannot be determined without knowing the values of the data points.

38. Which of the following numbers is NOT between −0.02 and 1.02?

 a. −0.15

 b. −0.015

 c. 1.002

 d. 0

 e. 1.010

39. Which of the following equations is correct?

 a. $\sqrt{36} + \sqrt{64} = \sqrt{100}$

 b. $\sqrt{25} + \sqrt{16} = \sqrt{41}$

 c. $\sqrt{9} + \sqrt{25} = \sqrt{64}$

 d. $\sqrt{16} + \sqrt{4} = \sqrt{20}$

 e. There is no correct equation.

40. Rodney needs a grade of C or higher in Geometry in order to receive his undergraduate degree. His final grade will be the average of the five unit exams his professor has given over the course of the semester. Any average from 74 to 77 is considered a C. If his first 4 test scores are 64, 72, 68, and 76, what is the lowest grade he can get on his last unit exam in order to receive his undergraduate degree?

 a. 70

 b. 78

 c. 80

 d. 85

 e. 90

Skills Test in Writing

Section 1, Part A

Directions: Choose the letter for the underlined portion that contains a grammatical error. If there is no error in the sentence, choose **e**.

1. Recently, 23.6-inches-tall Junrey Balawing of the Philippines not only turned 18 years old
   a   b
   but also receives the title of the world's shortest man from officials at the *Guinness Book of World*
        c   d
   Records. No error
            e

2. In 2007, Trouble an eight-year-old Maltese dog made headlines all over the world when he
               a
   inherited $12 million from his New York billionaire owner Leona Helmsley. No error
             b   c   d   e

3. Even though she had already purposely lied to him, he was very foolish enough to trust her again. No
        a   b   c   d
   error
   e

4. Conservationists at the Russian Wildfowl and Wetlands Trust and Birds are desperately trying
                            a   b
   to save one of the world's rarest birds, the Spoon-Billed Sandpiper. No error
                        c   d   e

5. Several states have statewide dog leash laws that prohibit dog owners from letting
                        a   b   c
   their dog lose under certain conditions. No error
             d   e

6. Would you rather be swimming in the blue-green waters of Hawaii or a catamaran in Calcutta? No
        a   b   c   d
   error
   e

7. I tried to run for cover from the pouring rain, but there were too many people crowding the sidewalk.
                                     a   b   c   d
   No error
   e

8. Beside the fact that he invented cubism, what made Pablo Picasso such a great artist? No error
   a   b   c   d   e

9. Before becoming a dog <u>owner</u>, you have to <u>commit</u> to <u>walking, feeding, and caring</u> for your dog
                          a   **b**   **c**

everyday—not just when you feel like it. <u>No error</u>
d   **e**

10. The <u>major</u> newspapers <u>covering</u> the story <u>throughout</u> the <u>year because</u> of the controversy. <u>No error</u>
       a   **b**   **c**   **d**   **e**

11. The <u>first-year</u> teachers in the <u>Altamont Central School District</u> <u>are:</u> Ann, Jill, Kelly, <u>Dawn, Mark,</u>
          a   **b**   **c**   **d**

and Rita. <u>No error</u>
        e

12. If I <u>were</u> a movie <u>star</u>, my life would be <u>more</u> <u>perfect</u>. <u>No error</u>
       a   **b**   **c**   **d**   **e**

13. <u>Childrens'</u> ability to learn a second language at a young age is <u>amazing;</u> <u>however</u>, this ability
     a   **b**   **c**

becomes <u>more difficult</u> as people age. <u>No error</u>
             d   **e**

14. The event <u>doubles</u> as a <u>fundraiser</u>, and <u>they</u> <u>showcase</u> the surfing skills of canines. <u>No error</u>
            a   **b**   **c**   **d**   **e**

15. The office manager <u>was</u> <u>someone</u> who was <u>efficient</u>, skilled, and <u>communicated well</u>. <u>No error</u>
                   a   **b**   **c**   **d**   **e**

16. Investors in the stock market fear the market might decline even <u>farther</u> <u>than</u> it <u>already</u> <u>has</u> in the
                                                       a   **b**   **c**   **d**

past year. <u>No error</u>
         e

17. <u>Relieved</u> <u>that</u> her report <u>finally</u> was done, <u>quickly out came</u> her basketball and sneakers. <u>No error</u>
     a   **b**   **c**   **d**   **e**

18. "Why do I <u>always</u> <u>overdue</u> it when I start an exercise <u>program and</u> make myself so sore the next
               a   **b**   **c**

day?" Daniqua wondered. <u>No error</u>
    d   **e**

19. On <u>Friday, September 10,</u> over 100 cities across the globe <u>will participate</u> in the second
　　　　　　a　　　　　　　　　　　　　　　　　　　　　　　　　　　b

annual Fashion's Night Out, a global initiative organized by <u>*Vogue* magazine</u> and the Council of
　　　　　　　　　　　　　　　　　　　　　　　　　　　　　　　　c

Fashion Designers of <u>America, to</u> promote retail shopping and celebrate fashion. <u>No error</u>
　　　　　　　　　　　　d　　　　　　　　　　　　　　　　　　　　　　　　　　　　　　　　e

20. <u>Yes, it</u> is a highly unusual <u>career;</u> but Kobi Levi is a young designer who creates humorous
　　　　a　　　　　　　　　　　b

depictions of <u>real-life</u> objects and people in the form of <u>shoes!</u> <u>No error</u>
　　　　　　　c　　　　　　　　　　　　　　　　　　　　d　　　e

21. Is the <u>Statue of Liberty</u> in <u>New York</u> Harbor <u>taller than</u> in <u>France?</u> <u>No error</u>
　　　　　　a　　　　　　　　　　b　　　　　　　c　　　　　d　　　e

Section 1, Part B

Directions: Choose the best replacement for the underlined portion of the sentence. If no revision is necessary, choose **a**, which always repeats the original phrasing.

22. Alternative <u>medicine which includes massage and yoga, has</u> become increasingly appealing to Americans.
　　a. medicine which includes massage and yoga, has
　　b. medicine, which includes massage and yoga has
　　c. medicine, which includes massage and yoga, has
　　d. medicine that includes massage and yoga, has
　　e. medicine that includes massage and yoga has

23. <u>Nobody could hardly</u> believe that the United States was attacked that dreadful day.
　　a. Nobody could hardly
　　b. Nobody couldn't hardly
　　c. No body could hardly
　　d. No body couldn't hardly
　　e. Nobody could

24. <u>Reading is more fun than television.</u>
　　a. Reading is more fun than television.
　　b. Reading is more fun than watching television.
　　c. Reading is funner than television.
　　d. Reading is more fun then television.
　　e. Reading is more fun than televising.

25. The dog wagged <u>its tail when its</u> owner's car pulled into the driveway.
　　a. its tail when its
　　b. it's tail when its
　　c. it's tale when it's
　　d. its tail when it's
　　e. its tale when it's

26. <u>Although the car hit the tree, it wasn't damaged.</u>
　　a. Although the car hit the tree, it wasn't damaged.
　　b. The car hit the tree, it wasn't damaged.
　　c. The car hit the tree but did not damage it.
　　d. Although the car hit the tree, it was damaged.
　　e. Even though the car hit the tree, it wasn't damaged.

27. Surely, he meant to say he was sorry.
    a. Surely, he meant to say he was sorry.
    b. Sure that he meant to say he was sorry.
    c. He meant sure to say that he was sorry.
    d. I meant surely to say that he was sorry.
    e. I am surely he meant to say he was sorry.

28. If a base number raised to a power appears in parenthesis and is raised to another power, you should multiply the exponents together.
    a. parenthesis and is raised to another power, you
    b. parentheses and is raised to another power, you
    c. parenthesis, and is raised to another power you
    d. parentheses, and is raised to another power you
    e. parenthesis, and is raised to another power, you

29. Jake sleeping in his bed, not realizing the danger he was in.
    a. Jake sleeping in his bed, not realizing the danger he was in.
    b. Jake sleeping in his bed. Not realizing the danger he was in.
    c. Jake sleeping in his bed; not realizing the danger he was in.
    d. Jake asleep in his bed; not realizing the danger he was in.
    e. Jake was sleeping in his bed, not realizing the danger he was in.

30. Many people think the actress Sandra Bullock is beautiful and has intelligence.
    a. is beautiful and has intelligence.
    b. is more beautiful and has intelligence.
    c. has beautiful intelligence.
    d. is beautiful and intelligent.
    e. has beauty and is intelligent.

31. Although the Russian aerocar is the ultimate machine on air, sea, and land.
    a. Although the Russian aerocar is the ultimate machine on air, sea, and land.
    b. Although the Russian aerocar is the ultimate machine on air sea and land.
    c. Although the russian aerocar is the ultimate machine on air, sea, and land.
    d. The Russian aerocar is the ultimate machine on air, sea, and land.
    e. The russian aerocar is the ultimate machine on air, sea, and land.

32. The circumstances surrounding the death of the salesperson were unusual and strangely.
    a. unusual and strangely.
    b. unusually and strangely.
    c. unusual and strange.
    d. unusually strange.
    e. usual and strange.

33. Neither of the sisters could do nothing when they saw their long-lost brother get off the plane.
    a. Neither of the sisters could do nothing
    b. Neither of the sisters couldn't do anything
    c. Either of the sisters could do anything
    d. Neither of the sisters could do anything
    e. Neither of the sisters couldn't do nothing

34. Although he felt ill, the doctor gave him a prescription.
    a. Although he felt ill, the doctor gave him a prescription.
    b. The patient felt ill, so the doctor gave him a prescription.
    c. Although he felt ill, the doctor gave the patient a prescription.
    d. He felt ill, the doctor gave him a prescription.
    e. He felt ill although the doctor gave him a prescription.

35. I felt <u>really bad</u> when I dropped my friend's antique vase.
  a. really bad
  b. real bad
  c. really badly
  d. real badly
  e. reel badly

36. Scientists use <u>phenomenon to refine hypotheses and disprove theories.</u>
  a. phenomenon to refine hypotheses and disprove theories.
  b. phenomena to refine hypotheses and disprove theories.
  c. phenomenon to refine hypothesis and disprove theories.
  d. phenomena to refine hypothesis and disprove theories.
  e. phenomenon to refine hypothesis and disprove theorys.

37. <u>Since the beginning of June, because I've been on summer break.</u>
  a. Since the beginning of June, because I've been on summer break.
  b. Since the beginning of June, therefore, I've been on summer break.
  c. Since the beginning of June, I've been on summer break.
  d. The beginning of June, because I've been on summer break.
  e. The beginning of June, therefore, I've been on summer break.

38. <u>"Are we nearly there?" asked the impatient child.</u>
  a. "Are we nearly there?" asked the impatient child.
  b. "Are we nearly there," asked the impatient child?
  c. "Are we near there?" asked the impatient child.
  d. "Are we near there." asked the impatient child?
  e. "Are we nearly their?" asked the impatient child.

Section 2, Essay Writing

Carefully read the essay topic that follows. Plan and write an essay that addresses all points in the topic. Make sure that your essay is well organized and that you support your central argument with concrete examples. Allow 30 minutes for your essay.

A student activist group on your school campus is protesting the use of animals for dissection in science classes. The group claims that animals have basic rights to life and happiness, and that purposely destroying them for use in classes is cruel. Many of the science students disagree, stating that animals are useful in educating people about important medical and health issues and that eliminating their use in the classes would severely harm students' education.

In your essay, take a position on this question. You may write about either of the two points of view given, or you may present a different point of view on the topic. Use specific reasons and examples to support your position.

Answers

Skills Test in Reading

1. **d.** The passage states that the sloth has developed a self-defense to its predators, and then it provides an example of the sloth avoiding the harpy eagle with its adaptation. Therefore, it can be inferred that the eagle is a natural predator to the sloth, choice **d**. The passage states repeatedly that the sloth is very slow, but never does it suggest that the sloth is the slowest creature on Earth, choice **a**. Furthermore, the passage says that the sloth lives in the trees, but it cannot be inferred that it never leaves the protection of the trees, choice **b**. The sloth's algae protects it from being seen, but the passage does not suggest that it is dangerous to other animals, so choice **c** cannot be correct. The statement in choice **e** is not supported by the passage at all.

2. **e.** The slow pace of the sloth is famous, and the word *renowned* is being used to describe that well-known attribute; therefore, choice **e**, *legendary*, makes the most sense in the context of the passage. The sloth can be described as *lethargic*, but that is what the word *languid* accomplishes in this sentence; therefore, choice **a** is incorrect. The word *incredibly* is not describing how slow the sloth is, so choice **b** is incorrect. Choices **c** and **d** are incorrect as well because the sloth is not described in the passage as either *dangerous* or *hurried*.

3. **c.** The passage describes the sloth's movement as a self-defense mechanism. Then it adds that the fur also serves as camouflage to protect it, matching the purpose listed in choice **c**. The fur does nothing to aid or detract from the sloth's speed specifically, so choice **a** is not correct. While the fur does make the sloth unique, that is not the author's purpose in including that information; therefore, choice **b** is incorrect. The fur is described as a protective trait of the sloth, not something that appeals to predators in particular; therefore, choice **d** is not correct. Choice **e** is not correct because the passage does not mention or imply that the sloth's fur is warming.

4. **c.** The statement in choice **c** summarizes the idea the paragraph adds up to; it's what holds all the information in the paragraph together and is therefore correct. The statements in choices **a** and **b** describe details about Wilma Rudolph, but they do not summarize the main idea of the passage, so they are not correct. The statements in choices **d** and **e** also contain details from the passage, but since they do not reflect the entire paragraph, they cannot be correct.

5. **e.** The fact that Theodore Roosevelt suffered from severe asthma as a child but overcame it as an adult is most similar to the story of Wilma Rudolph. While the situation listed in choice **a** regarding Franklin Roosevelt is also similar, the fact that he acquired his illness as an adult makes it less comparable. The situations listed in choices **b**, **c**, and **d** do not present analogous scenarios of a child overcoming a debilitating illness to become a highly successful professional as an adult, so they are not correct answer choices.

6. a. The passage states that at the 1960 Olympics, Rudolph won three gold medals. This is the greatest accomplishment that Rudolph achieved as a runner; therefore, it was her *zenith*, or *peak*, choice **a.** Choice **b,** *nadir*, has the opposite meaning, and would suggest that that was the low point of her career. Choice **c** is close, but suggests that it was the end of Rudolph's career. The passage doesn't suggest that Rudolph stopped running after that, so this choice is incorrect. Because an *epilogue* occurs after an event and a *midpoint* occurs directly in the middle, choices **d** and **e** must be incorrect; neither statement is supported by the passage.

7. b. Answers **a, c, d,** and **e** offer opinions about the quality and benefits of the shoes. Answers **c** and **d** use clear, evaluative words—*revolutionary* and *superior*—to show they are stating an opinion. The statement in choice **a** doesn't provide any evidence for this claim about the benefits of the shoes. It is difficult to prove with facts that a shoe provides *incredible comfort*, meaning that choice **e** provides an opinion rather than a fact. Only the statement in choice **b** states a fact; this is the only statement here that is not debatable.

8. a. Cheetahs are the fastest four-footed animals on Earth, reaching speeds of up to 60 miles per hour when they run. The name of the shoe, therefore, suggests that the shoe is built for speed and that if you wear them, you'll be able to run faster. Therefore, the statement in choice **a** is the most likely reason for the naming of that particular shoe model. None of the other choices present as likely a prediction for its naming, given the qualities most commonly associated with a cheetah.

9. d. The first paragraph mentions many similarities between two of the most popular children's book authors. The author includes the fact that their families were German to show another way that they were alike, choice **d.** Choice **a** suggests that the best children's authors *always* come from Germany, which is not correct. The heritage of the authors does not tell about the way Eric Carle created his illustrations, so **b** is incorrect. The reason is also not to stress a strong family life, choice **c.** Because the passage is about the talent from Germany specifically, choice **e** cannot be correct.

10. c. This question asks for the one attribute of Seuss and Carle that is NOT mentioned in the passage as a similarity between the two writers. The passage says that both men wrote and illustrated children's books (choice **a**), were born in the United States (choice **b**), inspired children to read with their stories (choice **d**), and had their books translated into other languages (choice **e**). Dr. Seuss drew his illustrations by hand; Eric Carle uses pieces of colored paper to create collages for his illustrations. Therefore, choice **c** is correct.

11. e. The second paragraph of the passage tells about Eric Carle's collage process. The author does this primarily to contrast with the process that Dr. Seuss uses to create his illustrations, choice **e.** The explanation of the collage process may tell students a way to create artwork (choice **a**), to show why a book was popular (choice **d**), or see another way that Carle was very talented (choice **b**), but those are not the most likely reasons why the author mentioned the collage process. The collage process is unique to Carle's books, so choice **c** cannot be correct.

12. b. The passage is structured neatly with the comparisons of two artists given in the first paragraph and then a difference, the style of the artwork, explained in the second paragraph. The organization does not relay the accomplishments of one artist and then another, so choice **a** is incorrect. Likewise, the passage does not describe the careers of two artists in chronological order, making choice **c** incorrect. The passage does not describe artists and then illustrators, nor does it give any readers' responses, making choices **d** and **e** incorrect.

13. b. The word *storied* is a positive word that most nearly means *celebrated*, choice **b**. While the word seems to have "story" in it, the meaning has little to do with the elements of a story, including whether it is *fictional*, *elaborative*, or *imaginative*, choices **a**, **d**, or **e**. *Infamous*, choice **c**, has a negative connotation that would not be associated with a word with a positive connotation, such as *storied*.

14. e. The passage presents comparisons and contrasts between Eric Carle and Dr. Seuss, but the main idea is that both are successful and ultimately inspire their young readers. Therefore, choice **e** best summarizes the passage. The statements in choices **a** and **c** are too general to reflect the entire passage, and choices **b** and **d** include only supporting details for the main idea.

15. a. To create a distinction, a word or phrase needs to act as a transition and change the direction of the text. The term *on the other hand* does this, so choice **a** is correct. *As well* provides an additional similarity, so choice **b** is not correct. *Regardless*, choice **c**, may change direction, but in the context of the passage it only acts to disregard the illustration method and not to create a distinction between the authors. Choices **d** and **e** are not correct because neither *such as* nor *as a result* creates a distinction between the two authors.

16. e. The statement in choice **e** can be supported because the winter months January, February, and March all show more snowfall, in inches, than rainfall. None of the other statements can be supported. Choice **a** is incorrect because the graph only shows the winter months, and you cannot determine whether there was any snowfall in the other months of the year. Choices **b**, **c**, and **d** can all be disproven with the sizes of the bars in the graph.

17. e. The passage refers to Mount Vesuvius as "The only active volcano on mainland Europe." Therefore, any other active volcanoes in Europe must reside off the mainland; Mount Etna can be found in Sicily, an island off of Italy. The statements in choices **a** and **b** are not supported by information in the passage, so they cannot be concluded to be correct. The passage makes no mention of the severity of the post-A.D. 79 eruptions, so the statement in choice **c** cannot be supported. The eruption of Mount Vesuvius in A.D. 79 was certainly catastrophic, but it cannot be determined from the passage that it was the *most* catastrophic in the world, making choice **d** incorrect as well.

18. b. Though Mount Vesuvius has traditionally been a very active volcano, the passage describes it as *atypically dormant* since 1944. Therefore, the meaning of *dormant* must be the opposite of active, which is *inactive*, choice **b**. Though the volcano may be *dangerous*, *threatening*, and *explosive*, the word *dormant* is not being used to describe the volcano in those terms, making choices **a**, **c**, and **e** incorrect. The area near the mouth of the volcano may be *overdeveloped*, but *dormant* does not have this meaning, so choice **d** is incorrect.

19. c. The passage begins with a description of the A.D. 79 eruption of Mount Vesuvius. The purpose of this description is to show how dangerous the volcano is, making choice **c** the most likely reason. While the description of the event illustrates the power of nature and provides some history of ancient Italy (choices **a** and **d**), those are not the author's primary reasons for providing the information; he or she is trying to make a specific point about Mount Vesuvius. The information about the A.D. 79 eruption does not do anything to describe the government's measures to increase safety, choice **b**, nor to accentuate the frequency of the volcano's major eruptions, choice **e**.

20. a. The passage begins with the famous A.D. 79 eruption of Mount Vesuvius, and then the author uses that historical event to frame the importance of safety in the current-day Bay of Naples, which he or she then describes. While the dangers of the volcano are initially provided (choice **b**), the organization of the passage does not then present safety measures. The sentences in choices **c** and **d** focus too much on the geology of the volcano to describe the entire passage, so they are incorrect. For choice **e**, no specific warning is presented at the beginning of the passage, so it cannot be correct.

21. d. The author's central argument in the passage is that Mount Vesuvius is very dangerous, and that people should not live so close to its mouth. This argument would be most strengthened if it were predicted that the volcano would have another major eruption in the next decade or two (choice **d**). The statement in choice **a** is irrelevant to the central argument and neither strengthens nor weakens it. The statements in choices **b** and **e** make Mount Vesuvius seem less dangerous, so they would weaken the argument and are therefore not correct. The precise amount offered to the families living near Mount Vesuvius does not significantly alter the author's argument either, so choice **c** is incorrect as well.

22. d. The primary purpose of the passage is to express the dangers of Mount Vesuvius. The fact that it is the only active volcano in mainland Europe does not specifically make it more or less dangerous, so choice **d** is the best answer. The details provided in choices **a** and **c** help show how potentially dangerous the volcano is by showing its power and frequency, so those choices are not correct. The statement that Mount Vesuvius has not erupted since 1944 might make it seem like the volcano is less dangerous, but that belies the fact that it is still active and hazardous; therefore, choice **b** is incorrect. The passage mentions how many people live close to the volcano's mouth to accentuate the specific danger to many people who live in the area, making choice **e** incorrect as well.

23. e. *Sympathetic* can be defined as favorably inclined. Because the author presents details that support the need for a student dress code, *sympathetic* best describes his or her attitude. The author is supportive of a dress code, so choice **a** is incorrect. Because he or she seems convinced about the effectiveness of a dress code, choices **b** and **c** are incorrect as well. The author may be concerned about students' well-being, but that is not the same as being concerned about a dress code. The best adjective should present a positive spin on a dress code, so choice **d** is not the best answer.

24. c. The author's main argument is that a dress code is a good idea. The only statement in the answer choices that weakens this argument is given in choice **c**, because restricting students' independence would not be a positive result. The statements in choices **a**, **b**, and **d** would all strengthen the author's main argument because each choice adds further support that a dress code is a good idea. The statement in choice **e** is not relevant to the author's argument and neither weakens nor strengthens it.

25. e. The third sentence of the passage provides its main idea. The sentence in choice **e** is a rewording of that sentence and is therefore the best summary of the passage. The sentences in choices **a**, **b**, and **c** are all supporting details that back up the main idea that Goran Kropp is an independent and determined adventurer. Based on the details from the story, Kropp was *not* reckless and thoughtless, so choice **d** could not be correct.

26. d. The part of the passage where the author uses the phrase "In addition" comes where Goran Kropp's journey to Mount Everest is described. Specifically, it refers to the difficulties Kropp faced in riding his bicycle to the base of the mountain, making choice **d** correct. The phrase did not relate specifically to Kropp's mountain-climbing abilities, so choice **a** is not correct. It also does not refer to Kropp's decision to adventure independently or cautiously, making choices **b** and **c** incorrect. Kropp may have put himself in danger with his bicycle ride, but the statement in choice **e** is too extreme; Kropp does not exactly risk his life by getting chased by dogs, stung by wasps, or drenched by the rain.

27. a. The passage focuses on Kropp's unique desire to travel alone and without the aid of modern technology. That description best suits the description of John Fairfax, who rowed across an ocean (which uses only his own manpower) and did his adventure alone. The adventurers listed in choices **b** and **c** did not accomplish their feats alone, so those are not the best choices. George Washington is not especially known for solo adventures, so choice **d** is not correct. Amelia Earhart may have done things by herself, but her use of airplanes means that she relied on technology—and therefore was not as similar to Kropp as Fairfax, according to the passage.

28. c. An opinion cannot be supported with actual evidence. Whether an action is easy or difficult cannot be supported; it is a matter of opinion, making choice **c** correct. Each of the statements presented in choices **a**, **b**, **d**, and **e** contains information that can be verified. Therefore, those statements are all facts, and those choices are therefore incorrect.

29. a. Throughout the passage the author depicts Kropp as a determined adventurer; even after having to turn back from the summit of Everest, he returned two days later after the storm passed. Therefore, the justification given in choice **a** is the most likely reason that the author included this information. The fact that Kropp did *not* continue climbing through the bad weather is indicative that he is not simply a daredevil, making choice **b** not the best option. The inclusion of that information was specific to Kropp and not about mountain climbing in general, so choices **c** and **d** cannot be correct. Likewise, choice **e** is too general and not supported by the passage either, making it an incorrect choice.

30. e. The passage begins with an event that occurred when Goran Kropp climbed his first mountain at age six. It then continues through his adventure to Mount Everest, and ends when he rode his bike home after reaching the summit. Therefore, the best description of the organization of the passage is in chronological order (choice **e**). The organization is not structured using compare and contrast, problem and solution, or cause and effect, so choices **a**, **b**, and **d** are not correct. If choice **c** were correct, the most important details would appear in the beginning of the passage. Because that's not the case, choice **c** is not correct.

31. a. An opinion cannot be proven. The statement in choice **a** is an opinion because it cannot be proven. The statements in choices **b**, **c**, **d**, and **e** each contain information that could be proven in some way. For that reason, each of those statements contain facts instead of opinions; choices **b**, **c**, **d**, and **e** are therefore incorrect.

32. e. The final sentence of the passage insinuates that because so many students watch television, it is another reason why the school day should be extended; therefore, the inference is that television is not an effective use of a student's time (choice **e**). The passage does not specify that students should be involved in more after-school activities, just that the school day should be extended; choice **a** is therefore incorrect. While the passage says that students frequently must wait for two hours, it doesn't say when students get home; therefore, it cannot be deduced when the parents get home, making choice **b** incorrect. Nowhere in the passage is it mentioned that being at home is unsafe or that students should be given extra homework, so choices **c** and **d** are likewise incorrect.

33. e. The passage discusses Albert Einstein's theory of special relativity and how and why it so greatly affected the world of physics. Therefore, the statement in choice **e** most closely describes the primary concern of the passage. The passage focuses only on Einstein's theory of special relativity, so choice **a** is not correct. While the passage does relate the speed of light, mass, and energy, this is only a detail of the passage and not its primary concern; therefore, choice **b** is not correct. The passage does not discuss harmful effects or potential drawbacks of the discovery, making choices **c** and **d** incorrect.

34. b. The beginning of the passage mentions that Einstein had many discoveries. However, it then goes on to focus on one particularly important discovery; the phrase *but despite* is used to help make that transition from the general to the specific. The phrase *one of* does not focus the content on one specific discovery, so choice **a** is not correct. The phrase *deceptively simple* describes the equation from the theory of special relativity, but it does not focus the passage on the specific discovery, so choice **c** is not correct. The phrase *by relating* does not act as a transition, and *as a result* describes the consequences of the discovery; neither phrase serves to focus the content of the passage on a specific discovery, so choices **d** and **e** are not correct.

35. b. The previous sentence from the sentence that contains the word *multifarious* describes Einstein's *numerous achievements*. The *multifarious array of significant discoveries* also describes the numerous discoveries; therefore, *varied* shares the closest meaning. There were many significant discoveries, but the discoveries themselves were not *multitalented* or *nefarious* (meaning evil) themselves, thus making choices **a** and **c** incorrect. While the discoveries were certainly *groundbreaking* and *unique*, the word *multifarious* is not being used to describe them in those ways; therefore, choices **d** and **e** are also not correct.

36. d. The first sentence of the passage provides readers with a meaning of the Cambrian Period, so the sentence does provide a definition (choice **d**). Nothing is being compared or contrasted in this initial sentence, so choices **a** and **c** are not correct. The sentence describes the evolution of life only within the Cambrian Period, not the entire history through the present, so choice **b** cannot be correct. While there was an explosion of growth during the Cambrian Period, the sentence does not explain the origin of life on the planet, making choice **e** incorrect as well.

37. a. The passage states that life on Earth advanced from single-celled organisms to more complex animal groups during the Cambrian Period. It is for that reason that the Jurassic Period, with its massively complex creatures, must have followed the Cambrian Period. There is no indication that sharks originated during the Cambrian Period, even though "some" of the more complex organisms still exist. Additionally, although there was an explosion of life during this period, there is no evidence that there was a greater variety of life on planet Earth during the Cambrian Period than during any other period, so choices **b** and **c** are not correct. While the reason for the increase of life during the Cambrian Period is unknown, it cannot be concluded that it is because of a lack of available fossils. In fact, there are fossils from the Cambrian Period, so choice **d** must be incorrect. The passage tells you the length of the Cambrian Period (about 54 million years), but you cannot use that information to determine that it was the longest period in Earth's history. Choice **e** is therefore incorrect.

38. b. The author tells the readers in the last sentence of the passage that scientists don't agree on why life diversified so greatly during the Cambrian Period. Therefore, choice **b** makes the most sense. The author does not explain a scientific phenomenon or disprove a claim in the final sentence, so choices **a** and **d** are not true either. Because the author is simply saying that scientists don't exactly know why the explosion of life occurred, no other information is being provided, making choices **c** and **e** incorrect.

39. d. An opinion is a statement that cannot be proven. It can be proven that the United States is culturally diverse and that its climate ranges from freezing to hot—or that some areas are so cold that an ice cube will rarely melt. However, *perfect* weather is a matter of opinion. Some people might like cold weather. Some people might like hot weather. That's why the fourth sentence in the passage is an example of an opinion. Each of the other sentences from the passage, represented by choices **a**, **b**, **c**, and **e**, are examples of facts instead of opinions.

40. a. The passage contrasts the climate extremes in the United States, comparing the frigid to the torrid. Therefore, *torrid* must have the opposite meaning of frigid, such as hot; the best word to describe that opposite is *sweltering* (choice **a**). The temperatures may be *dissimilar*, but the word *torrid* is describing how they are dissimilar, so choice **b** is not correct. *Glacial* and *lukewarm* do not describe the weather as *hot*, so choices **c** and **d** are incorrect. While a torrid temperature may be uncomfortable, the word *torrid* cannot be replaced with *uncomfortable* in the passage and keep the same meaning; therefore, choice **e** cannot be correct.

The following is a chart of the different skills assessed by the questions in this practice PPST; you can use it to identify your strengths and weaknesses in this subject to better focus your study.

READING SKILLS STUDY CHART FOR PRACTICE EXAM 3	
LITERAL COMPREHENSION SKILLS	**QUESTIONS**
Main Ideas	4, 14, 25, 33
Supporting Ideas	10, 22
Organization	12, 15, 20, 26, 30, 34, 36
Vocabulary in Context	2, 6, 13, 18, 35, 40
CRITICAL AND INFERENTIAL COMPREHENSION SKILLS	
Evaluation	3, 7, 9, 11, 19, 21, 24, 28, 29, 31, 38, 39
Inferential Reasoning	1, 16, 17, 23, 32
Generalization	5, 8, 27, 37

Answers

1. c. If 30 men each have 42 square feet, then the dormitory has $30 \times 42 = 1,260$ square feet in total. $1,260 \div 35 = 36$ square feet, which is the amount of square footage each man will now have, but this does not yet answer the question (incorrect choice **a**). Because the men now have 42 square feet, subtract 36 to get how much less square footage he will have: $42 - 36 = 6$, so each man will have 6 fewer square feet. Choices **b**, **d**, and **e** all do this last step of subtraction incorrectly.

2. c. To determine the cost of 3,800 gallons of water from each company, multiply 3,800 by the cost per gallon and then add the flat fee. So Sea Horse Pool Servicing Professionals would cost $531 ($3,800 \times 0.12 + \$75 = \$531$), which is the incomplete answer and incorrect choice **a**. Penny's Pool Services would cost $595 ($3,800 \times 0.15 + \$25 = \$595$), which is the incomplete answer and incorrect choice **b**. Because $595 - \$531 = \$64$, Sea Horse Pool Servicing Professionals would be $64 cheaper. Choice **d** lists the right savings, but the wrong company. Choice **e** almost uses the correct equations but forgets to turn the 15¢ and 12¢ into dollars by moving the decimal point two places to the left: $(3,800 \times 15 + \$25) - (3,800 \times 12 + \$75) = \$11,350$.

3. b. If 200 customers were surveyed at first and then 1,200 were surveyed, the best way to predict how many people would choose vanilla ice cream would be to multiply the results of the first survey by 6, since $200 \times 6 = 1,200$. Because the original survey had 75 votes for vanilla, multiply 75 by 6 to get 450. Choice **a** could not work because that is how many people chose vanilla out of just 200 people, so it would not be the same number when surveying 1,200 people. Choice **c** was the closest, but 525 is 75 times 7, and the sample size was only 6 times as big as the original. Similarly, choice **d** is 75 times 8, but the sample size was not 200×8 people large. Choice **e** cannot be correct because that is almost the entire sample size, and in the first survey of 200 customers, less than half chose vanilla.

4. d. The factors of 14 are 7 and 2, and because $14Q$ is divisible by 48, Q must be divisible by 24 (the 2 factor from 14 would have to multiply by a factor of Q to get 48, and $2 \times 24 = 48$). Because Q must be divisible by 24, then Q is also divisible by all factors of 24. The only answer choice that is not a factor of 24 is 14.

5. e. The fox population doubled from 10 to 20 from 2009 to 2010, but after that it did not double for the next two years, so choices **a** and **d** cannot be true. The deer population doubled from 20 to 40 and then from 40 to 80 from 2010 to 2012, so choice **b** is true. Choice **c** is also true; the owl population increase was neither rapid nor steady since it stayed the same in 2009 and 2010, and again remained unchanged from 2011 to 2012. Choice **e** contains both of the true statements, **b** and **c**.

6. b. The trend of the owl population does not show a steady increase, which rules out choice **a**. Choice **c** mentions a decline in the owl population, but it did not decrease at all during this four-year period. Choice **d** does not make sense since an illness in the owl population would lead to decline, not to steadiness. Choice **e** is not supported by the data—the recovery of the fox population does not affect the change in the owl population. Choice **b** is a reasonable hypothesis to why the owl population did not show the same recovery growth as the other two groups.

7. a. In order to find the volume of any regular prism, multiply the surface area of the bottom or top face by the height of the prism. In this case, the area of the triangular base is given in square *inches*, but the height of the vase is given in *feet*. When 16 square inches is multiplied by 18 inches (which is 1.5 feet), then the correct answer is 288 inches^2, which is answer choice **a**. Finding the area of the vase by incorrectly adding 16 square inches and 18 inches would give 24 inches^2, which is incorrect answer choice **b**. Finding the area for triangles involves taking half of the base and multiplying that by the height. Therefore, one error possible to make when answering this question is taking half of the area of the base before multiplying it by 18 inches: $(\frac{1}{2})(16) \times 18 = 144$ square inches (incorrect answer choice **c**). This is incorrect because the area of the base has already been calculated and does not need to be divided by 2 again. Choices **d** and **e** both used incorrect translations of a foot and a half into inches: $16 \times 16 = 256$ (choice **d**) and $16 \times 20 = 320$ (choice **e**).

8. c. To compare percentages, fractions, and decimals, it is easiest to convert them all into fractions. "Percent" means out of 100, so 6% means six out of 100, or $\frac{6}{100}$, which reduces to $\frac{3}{50}$ when you divide the numerator and denominator by two (choice **c**). The fraction in choice **a** is equal to the repeating decimal 0.666 . . . which is $66\frac{2}{3}$%. The answer in choice **b** is equal to the $\frac{60}{100}$, which is 60%. Choice **d** cannot work because percentages are always represented in decimals that are between 0 and 1, with 1 being 100%, so 6.00 would be 600% and not 6%. Choice **e** does not work because the six is over *one thousand* and not *one hundred*, so $\frac{6}{1,000}$ would be 0.06% and not 6%.

9. e. On the *xy*-plane, points are plotted in coordinate pairs. A coordinate pair consists of the *x-coordinate* first, which shows the horizontal location of a point. The *x*-coordinate will be positive when a point is to the right of the origin (the origin is the place where the *x*- and *y*-axis cross). An *x*-coordinate is negative when a point is to the left of the origin. The second coordinate in a pair is the *y*-coordinate, which shows the vertical location of a point. The *y*-coordinate will be positive when the point is above the origin and negative when the point is below the origin. Using point *C*, you can see that its *x*-coordinate is 6. Because point *D* is directly below it, point *D* will also have an *x*-coordinate of 6. This rules out answer choices **b, c,** and **d.** Looking at point *A*, which has a *y*-coordinate of −3, you can see that point D will also have a *y*-coordinate of −3. Therefore, choice **e** is the coordinate pair that has the correct *x*- and *y*-coordinates, (6,−3). Choice **a** has a *y*-coordinate of −4, which would be one space directly below point *D*. Choice **c**, (−1,4), would be the correct answer for point B.

10. c. The formula for the area of a square is $A = s^2$ where *s* is the side length. Because squares are symmetrical with all equal sides, you just need to find the length of one side. In this case, the side length of $\overline{AD}$ is 7 because the *x*-coordinate goes from −1 at point *A* to 6 at point *C*. Because $7 \times 7 = 49$, the square has an area of 49 square units. Choice **a** incorrectly multiplies the coordinates of 6 and 4 in point *C*. Choice **b** squares just the 6 *x*-coordinate in point *C*. Choice **d** incorrectly determines that the side length is 9 by incorrectly combining coordinates 6 and 3: $9 \times 9 = 81$. Choice **e** incorrectly determines that the side length is 5 by incorrectly combining coordinates 6 and −1 or coordinates 4 and −1: $5 \times 5 = 25$.

11. d. Use the relationship, "Discounted Price = Original Price − Amount of Discount." Let *p* = the Original Price. Then the Amount of Discount would equal $(0.20)(p)$. This can be used in the equation as follows: $960 = p − (0.20)(p)$. Therefore, $960 = 1p − (0.20)(p) = 0.80p$. Because $960 = 0.80p$, divide both sides by 0.80 to get $p = \$1,200$. Choice **a** is unreasonable since $768 is already lower than the price *after* the computer was discounted. ($768 would be the price after removing 20% from the already discounted price of $960.) Choice **b** assumes that 20% is the same as $200, and it adds $200 to $960 to get $1,160. This is incorrect because 20% of $1,160 will be more than $200. A common mistake is to take 20% of $960, which would be $192, and then add $192 to $960 to get $1,152. This is wrong because 20% of $1,200 will be greater than $192, so the sale price after taking 20% of $1,152 would not be $960, ruling out choice **c.**

12. a. Because circle A represents all numbers that can be written in the form $2x + 1$, where x is all integers greater than or equal to 0, circle A contains all odd numbers, since odd numbers can always be expressed in the form $2x + 1$. Because circle B represents all factors of 24, circle B contains 1, 2, 3, 4, 6, 8, 12, and 24. The only overlap of the points that are in circles A and B are the two numbers, 1 and 3. Choice **b** is an odd factor of 24, but this answer forgets the odd factor 1. Choice **c** is the sum of the two odd factors of 24. Choice **d** is the number of factors of 24, with the exception of 1 and 24. Choice **e** is the total number of factors of 24.

13. b. An important thing when translating "less than" into an algebraic expression is to remember that the order of the algebraic terms must be swapped. So in this case, the two must come after the subtraction sign. This rules out choices **a** and **d** as being possible. Another crucial translation is writing the square of a number as x^2 and not as $\sqrt{x}$ (which is the "square root of x"). This additional detail rules out choice **e**. The remaining choices are **b** and **c**. $(4x)^2$ is actually "the square of the product of four times a number" and $4x^2$ is four times the square of a number. Therefore, $4x^2 - 2$ (choice **b**) is the proper translation.

14. a. The uniforms were 20% of the budget and transportation was 30% of the budget, so allow the budget to be x and express the difference between transportation and uniforms: $0.30x - 0.20x = \$550$. This simplifies to $0.10x = \$550$, so $x = \$5,500$. Choice **b** accidentally adds the percentages and uses this equation $0.30x + 0.20x = \$550$ to get $x = \$1,100$. Choice **c** only divides the $550 by 30%, ignoring the 20% of the uniforms. Choice **d** only divides the $550 by 20%, ignoring the 30% of the transportation.

15. d. When modeling inequalities on a number line, an open circle symbolizes that this number is *not* part of the solution (so a < or > symbol is reflected by an open circle). Conversely, a closed circle is used to model part of the solution (so a ≤ or ≥ symbol is reflected by a closed circle). Because the solution set includes both of the endpoints −1.4 and 2, the circles must be filled in as well as the data points in between. Therefore, choice **d** best models $-1.4 \le x \le 2$. Choice **a** models the inequality $-1.4 < x < 2$. Choice **b** models the inequality $-1.4 > x > 2$. Choice **c** models the inequality $-1.4 \ge x \ge 2$.

16. b. Because the ribbon lengths are given in yards and feet, first see how each girl's ribbon translates into feet: Philana's 11 and a half yards will be 33 feet + $1\frac{1}{2}$ feet, because 11 yards is 11×3 feet and half of a yard is $1\frac{1}{2}$ feet. Philana's ribbon totals $34\frac{1}{2}$ feet. Since Emily has $\frac{2}{3}$ of Zosia's 30 feet, multiply those to see how many feet Emily has: $(\frac{2}{3})(\frac{30}{1}) = \frac{60}{3}$, which is 20 feet. Together the three girls have $34.5 + 30 + 20 = 84\frac{1}{2}$ feet. Because the answer calls for inches, multiply $84\frac{1}{2}$ feet by 12 to get 1,014 inches. Choice **a** confuses $84\frac{1}{2}$ feet with $84\frac{1}{2}$ inches. Choice **c** turns the $11\frac{1}{2}$ yards into inches and then forgets to consider the other two girls' lengths of ribbon. Choice **d** forgets to turn the $11\frac{1}{2}$ yards into feet first and combines $11\frac{1}{2}$ with 30 feet and 20 feet, getting $66\frac{1}{2}$ feet, which is 798 inches. Choice **e** turns Emily's ribbon into $\frac{2}{3}$ *more* ribbon than Zosia's ribbon and wrongly concludes that Emily has $30\frac{2}{3}$ feet of ribbon: $(34\frac{1}{2} + 40 + 30\frac{2}{3})(12) = 1,262$ inches.

17. a. $f \times g$ must be divisible by 2, 3, and by 6, since $6 = 2 \times 3$, so choices **b**, **c**, and **d** are all correct. It *is* possible that $f \times g$ is divisible by 5 (for example, 30 is divisible by 2, 3, and 5), so statement **e** is correct. $f \times g$ does not have to be divisible by 4 (for example, 6 is divisible by 2 and 3, but not by 4), so statement **a** is not correct.

18. c. Because Sohail bought 4 raffle tickets for Asad and three times that for Amara, he bought $4 \times 3 = 12$ tickets for Amara, which means there were 16 tickets in total between the two of them. To find the probability of an event happening, the number of desired events must be put over the total number of events. In this case, there are sixteen "desired events" (tickets belonging to Asad or Amara) and 80 total events (total number of tickets). Probability can be written as a fraction or as a decimal (between 0 and 1). In this case all the answers are given in decimal form, so $\frac{16}{80}$ must be turned into a decimal. Using long division to do this, 0.20 is the correct quotient. Choice **a** is the probability that Asad alone will win: $\frac{4}{80} = 0.05$. Choice **b** is the probability that Amara alone will win: $\frac{12}{80} = 0.05$. Choice **d** is the probability that Asad and Amara would win if they had 20 tickets between them: $\frac{20}{80} = 0.25$. Choice **e** is the probability that Asad and Amara would win if they only had 7 tickets between them: $\frac{7}{80} = 0.0875$, which rounds to 0.09.

19. d. This is an example of indirect variation because as the number of painters increases, the time in hours decrease. With indirect variation, a proportion is used by setting a ratio of the independent variables equal to the dependent variables. It is essential to position the dependent information in the right place so that when the independent increases, the dependent will decrease. (In this case the painters are "independent" because *they* are determining how long the painting will take, and not vice versa). The proportion of $\frac{6 \text{ painters}}{8 \text{ painters}}$ is equal to $\frac{\text{new hours}}{12 \text{ hours}}$ will work because the unknown hours will be less than the 12 hours it would take 6 painters to do the job. Cross-multiply $\frac{6}{8} = \frac{\text{new hours}}{12}$ to get $8(\text{new hours}) = 72$, and *new hours* $= 9$. Choice **c**, 10 hours, incorrectly assumes that because there are two more painters it will take 2 fewer hours to complete the job; this does not consider the rate per hour at which the painters all work. Choice **e** mistakenly sets up the proportion as $\frac{6}{8} = \frac{12}{\text{hours}}$ which doesn't make sense because then 8 painters are taking more time to finish the job than the 6 painters would have.

20. d. Choices **a**, **c**, and **e** are not correct since Charge Card Interest has *increased* over the four years shown, not *decreased*. Choice **b** is not correct since Online Purchases have *increased* over the four years shown, not *decreased*. Choice **d** is correct since Online Purchases have increased *and* In-Store Purchases have decreased over the four years shown.

21. e. First, notice that Charge Card Interest was exactly $100 in 2001 and $150 in 2002. The only table that does not display these two points correctly is **b**, so rule that one out. Next, notice that Charge Card Interest was the same in 1999 and 2000, perhaps around $80 or $90. Charts **c** and **d** display different amounts for Charge Card Interest in 1999 and 2000, so those cannot be correct. The only possibilities now are **a** or **e**, so check the rest of the data in table **a**. In-Store Purchases show a regular decline in the bar graph, but in table **a** they show an increase from 1999 to 2000, so this table is not fully accurate and the correct answer is **e**.

22. a. If Charge Card Interest profits were $150,000 in 2002 and $40,000 in 1997, they experienced an increase of $110,000. To calculate the percentage increase between two numbers, divide the difference between the two numbers (found using subtraction) by the original number. So in this case it would be $\frac{110}{40}$. There are several ways that this could be translated to a percentage, but we will use long division and then multiply it by 100. (To change a decimal to percentage you *multiply* by 100, but to change a percentage to a decimal, you *divide* it by 100.) In this case $110 \div 40 = 2.75 = 275\%$, choice **a**. Choice **b** mistakes the Charge Card Interest profits of $150,000 in 2002 for the percentage increase. Choice **c** mistakes the difference of $150,000 and $40,000 to be the percentage increase, but it is just the dollar amount of the increase. Choice **d** mistakenly puts the $110,000 increase in profits over the new profits of $150,000 instead of over the original profits of $40,000: $\frac{110}{150} = 0.7333$. Choice **e** cannot be correct because if profits only increased by 100%, then they would have doubled by 2002 and been only $80,000, not $150,000.

23. c. To find the area of the non-shaded part of the drawing, subtract the area of the smaller circle from the area of the larger circle. The formula for the area of a circle is $A = \pi r^2$. Using this, the area of the entire pool and border space is $A = \pi(8^2)$, which is 64π (incorrect answer **a**). Using the area formula again, the area of just the pool is $A = \pi(5^2)$, which is 25π (incorrect answer **b**). Subtracting 25π from 64π gives 39π (correct answer **c**). Choice **d** adds 25π to 64π to get 89π. Incorrect answer **e** subtracts the radii of 5 and 8 *before* applying each radius in the area formula, and this cannot work because each radius must be squared *before* subtracting them (the correct order of operations must be respected): $A = \pi(8-5)^2 = 9\pi$.

24. d. A square yard is 3 feet by 3 feet, which is 9 square feet. Therefore, to calculate the square feet of tile needed, the square yardage needs to be multiplied by 9. The manager needs to order $w\pi$ square yards of tile, which is $9w\pi$ square feet. Choice **a** incorrectly uses a multiple of 12, thinking that the 12 inches in a foot need to be multiplied by the square yardage of $w\pi$. Choice **b** incorrectly uses a multiple of 3, thinking that the 3 feet in a yard need to be multiplied by the square yardage of $w\pi$, but really the 3 feet need to be squared first. Choice **c** incorrectly squares 12 (because area was being calculated) and then uses 144 as the multiple of $w\pi$. Choice **e** incorrectly doubles the 3 feet in a yard and then uses 6 as the multiple of $w\pi$.

25. c. John's first 100 minutes will be free because they are included in the monthly price of $6.95. That leaves 140 minutes at $0.05 per minute, which will cost $140 \times \$0.05 = \$7$ in addition to the $6.95, which is $13.95. Choice **a** is just the cost of the additional 140 minutes. Choice **e** uses 0.50 for the cost per minute to incorrectly calculate that the additional 140 minutes cost $70 instead of $7. Choices **b** and **d** are close approximations to the correct answer, but are not based on the correct method outlined here.

26. e. The acronym PEMDAS is helpful when doing problems that deal with order of operation. Parentheses come first, followed by exponents. Then multiplication and division are done simultaneously in the order of left to right. Addition and subtraction follow, and are also done simultaneously in the order of left to right. Remember, that 2^4 is $2 \times 2 \times 2 \times 2$, not 2×4. Using these pieces of information, $5 + 3 \times 2^4 = 5 + 3 \times 16 = 5 + 48 = 53$. Choice **a** makes the mistake of performing 2^4 as 2×4: $5 + 3 \times 8 = 5 + 24 = 29$. Choice **b** makes the mistake of performing 3×2 before using the exponent: $5 + 6^4 = 5 + 1,296 = 1,301$. Choice **c** makes the mistake of adding 5 plus 3 before multiplying by 2^4: $5 + 3 \times 16 = 8 \times 16 = 128$. Choice **d** makes a combination of the mistakes made in **b** and **c**: $5 + 3 \times 8 = 8 \times 8 = 64$.

27. b. This is a problem that can be solved by drawing similar triangles and then writing a proportion to solve. Make two different ratios, each one representing $\frac{height}{shadow}$: $\frac{4}{6} = \frac{24}{x}$, where $x =$ length of tree's shadow. Since the numerator 24 is 6 times larger than the numerator of 4, you can multiply the denominator of 6 by 6 also, and then the fractions will make a correct proportion: $\left(\frac{4}{6}\right)\left(\frac{6}{6}\right) = \frac{24}{36}$, so $x = 36$ and the shadow will be 36 feet long. Choices **a** and **c** do not make sense since both of those shadow lengths are shorter than the 24-foot tree. Because the 4-foot girl cast a shadow longer than herself, the 24-foot tree must also cast a shadow longer than itself. Choice **c** comes from setting the proportion up incorrectly by having $\frac{height}{shadow}$ in one fraction and $\frac{shadow}{height}$ in the other fraction.

28. c. The median measure in a set of data is the middle number when the data are listed from smallest to largest. In this case there are six pieces of data, so there is not *one* middle data entry, but *two* entries that must be averaged: 4, 6, <u>6</u>, <u>8</u>, 11, 13. The average of the two middle numbers is 7, so 7 is the median. Choice **a** is incorrect because it is the average (arithmetic mean) of all the data entries: $4 + 6 + 6 + 8 + 11 + 13 = 48$ and $48 \div 6 = 8$. Choice **b** is incorrect because 6 is the mode, or data entry that occurs most frequently in the data set. Choice **d** is incorrect because 4 is the minimum of the data set. Choice **e** is incorrect because 12 is the average of the two data entries that are in the middle in the table (11 and 13), but the two middle entries need to be taken from the ordered list of data from smallest to greatest.

29. a. To round numbers to the nearest hundred, look at the tens place: if the tens digit is 5 or higher, round the next number to the nearest hundred. If the tens digit is less than 4, round down. 152 becomes 200; 2,812 becomes 2,800; 445 becomes 400; 8,451 becomes 8,500; and the sum of 200 + 2,800 + 400 + 8,500 is 11,900. Choice **b** is 11,900 rounded to the nearest thousand. Choice **c** incorrectly rounds every number up, not looking at the tens place in each one: 200 + 2,900 + 500 + 8,500. Choice **d** incorrectly rounds every number down, not looking at the tens place in each one: 100 + 2,800 + 400 + 8,400. Choice **e** incorrectly rounds every number to the nearest ten, not to the nearest one hundred: 150+ 2,810 + 450 + 8,450.

30. d. To solve this, isolate each of the equivalent places in each number and find the sum for that place. If necessary, you may have to carry over a digit to the next place. The correct answer combines the ones places to get: 1 + 7 = 8; the tens places to get 50 + 00 = 50; the hundreds places to get 100 + 800 = 900; the thousands places to get 4,000 + 2,000 = 6,000; and the ten thousands places to get 50,000 + 00,000 = 50,000. Combined, these terms are 50,000 + 6,000 + 900 + 50 + 8, choice **d**. Choices **b** and **c** accidentally tack a zero onto 4,157 so that it would have as many digits at 52,801. Choice **b** is an incorrect addition of 41,570 and 52,801 that forgets to carry a one from the hundreds to the thousands place. Choice **c** is the correct addition of 41,570 and 52,801 but the incorrect answer to this problem. Incorrect choice **e** only combines the 50,000 from the 52,801 with 4,157.

31. e. There are two ways this problem can be solved. First, you can use the acronym FOIL (Firsts, Outsides, Insides, Lasts) to remember the order of multiplication that needs to happen between the following pairs of terms to expand the binomial: $(3x - 4)^2 = (3x - 4)(3x - 4) = 9x^2 - 12x - 12x + 16 = 9x^2 - 24x + 16$. The second way to do this is to work backward by plugging in a value for x and seeing which expression gives you the same value. For example, $(3x - 4)^2 = 16$ when $x = 0$, because $(3 \times 0 - 4)^2 = (-4)^2 = 16$. This disqualifies choice **a**, which gives -8 when $x = 0$. It also disqualifies **c**, which gives -16 when $x = 0$. Next, investigate what happens when $x = 1$: $(3 \times 1 - 4)^2 = (3 - 4)^2 = (-1)^2 = 1$. Choice **b** yields 25 when $x = 1$, so this cannot be correct. Choice **d** yields 3 when $x = 1$, so this cannot be correct. Choice **e** yields 1 when $x = 1$, so this must be the correct solution.

32. d. The most important thing to remember when combining algebraic terms with exponents is that terms with the same exact variables and exponents ("like terms") can be added and subtracted. (Although not needed for this question, algebraic terms with different variables and exponents can be multiplied and divided.) Write the expression so that the like terms are grouped together (when moving terms, you must keep the sign to the left of each term with that term). Once like terms are grouped together, add or subtract the coefficients and keep the terms separate. $3x^2 + 7x^2 - 8a^2 + 7a^2 - 2ax + 4ax = 10x^2 - a^2 + 2ax$ (choice **d**). Choice **a** multiplies all the coefficients together instead of adding and subtracting them. Choice **c** almost performs these steps correctly, but here the exponents in each of the like-term groupings are added. Choice **b** also adds the exponents, but just of the middle terms, $-2ax$ and $4ax$.

33. d. For each of the two meat choices there are three vegetable choices, so there are 6 combinations of meat and vegetable (for hamburger, there will be three combinations with each of the different vegetables and for chicken there will also be three pairings). There are four dessert options to be paired with each of those 6 meat/vegetable combinations. Therefore there are 24 different combinations. This is calculated by performing $2 \times 3 \times 4 = 24$. Choice **a** is $2 + 3 + 4 = 9$. Choice **c** would have been appropriate if there were 2 meat, 3 vegetable, and only 3 dessert options because $2 \times 3 \times 3 = 18$.

34. a. Each meter has 100 centimeters in it, so you need to multiply the total number of meters by 100 centimeters. $5\frac{3}{4}$ is the same as 5.75, so 5.75 meters will have $5.75 \times 100 = 575$ centimeters in it. Choice **b** confuses $5\frac{3}{4}$ for 5.34 and then multiplies 5.34 by 100. Choices **c** and **e** make mistakes converting meters into centimeters, multiplying 5.75 by 1,000 and 10,000, respectively. Choice **d** combines the errors found in choices **b** and **d**.

35. b. Before he draws the first card, Jake has 2 red cards, 7 black cards, and 9 cards in total. After he flips the first card, which is red, there are still 1 red card, 7 black cards, and 8 cards in total. To find the probability of an event happening, the number of desired events must be put over the total number of events. In this case, there is one "desired event" (red card) and 8 total events (total number of cards). Therefore the probability that Jake's second card will be red is $\frac{1}{8}$. Choice **a** mistakenly compares the 1 red card left to the total number of cards there were to begin with. Choice **c** mistakenly compares the 2 red cards to the remaining number of cards; however, after the first card was flipped, we know that only 1 and not 2 red cards are left. Choice **d** is the probability that the second card will be black, because there are 7 black cards left out of the 8 that remain. Choice **e** is the probability that the second card will be black, but forgets that there are no longer 9 cards left, and therefore, compares the 7 black cards to 9.

36. e. A line of symmetry is a line that divides a shape into two symmetrical halves. Rectangles and hexagons can be divided in half by connecting the midpoints of opposite sides. A rhombus is a 4-sided figure whose four sides all have the same length. A rhombus often looks like a kite and can be divided into two halves by connecting its opposite vertices. An isosceles triangle has two equal base angles and its line of symmetry exists from the midpoint of the base side to the vertex angle. A scalene triangle has 3 angles and 3 sides that are all unique and does not have a line of symmetry.

37. a. This scatter plot shows a positive correlation because the general trend models an increase in the y values as the x values are increasing. It does not show a negative correlation (choice **b**), as that would be a downward-sloping collection of points, not upward sloping as shown. An inverse relationship (choice **c**) is when the dependent variable (y) decreases as the independent variable (x) increases, so the graph would have a negative slope. Choice **d** is not correct because there is an obvious trend, and a trend line could be drawn to model the trend shown. Choice **e** is not correct because the values of the x- and y-coordinates are unimportant when determining the general type of relationship.

38. a. To compare decimals, add zeros to the right of the decimal point so that all the numbers have the same number of places to the right of the zero. In this case, every number should be extended to the thousandths place: -0.150; -0.015; 1.002; 0; and 1.010 will be compared to -0.020 and 1.020. -0.150 has a larger absolute value than -0.020, which means that since it is negative, it is less than -0.02, so choice **a** is correct. -0.015 has a smaller absolute value than -0.020, which means it is larger than -0.02 because it is negative; therefore, choice **b** is not correct. 1.002 has only two thousandths, so it is smaller than 1.020, which has 20 thousandths, thus eliminating choice **c**. Zero is always between any negative and positive numbers, so choice **d** is eliminated. You can see that 1.010 is smaller than 1.020, so choice **e** is eliminated.

39. c. Square roots are treated like exponents and must be dealt with before the other operations of addition and subtraction. You have to take the square roots of the individual numbers before adding them. You cannot add or subtract numbers that are in square root symbols. This means that choices **a**, **b**, and **d** contain incorrect statements. Investigating choice **c**, we see that $\sqrt{9} = 3$; $\sqrt{25} = 5$; and $\sqrt{64} = 8$. Because $3 + 5 = 8$ is a true statement, this choice is correct.

40. e. In order to graduate, Rodney needs at least an average of 74 in his Geometry class. The average of five pieces of data is found by adding them all up and dividing that sum by five. In this case we do not have the fifth piece, so we take a different approach. Because Rodney needs to earn an average of 74 over 5 tests, that means that the sum of his five tests must be $(74)(5) = 370$. This is true because $370 \div 5 = 74$. His first four tests sum to 280: $64 + 72 + 68 + 76 = 280$. This is 90 points shy of the sum of 370 he needs, which means that he must score a 90 on his fifth test in order to have an average of 74. Choice **a** is the average of his first four tests because $280 \div 4 = 70$. Choice **b** is wrong because it supposes that the average of the first four tests (which is 70) must average with the fifth test to be 74: $\frac{70 + 78}{2} = 74$. This is not correct because it is a weighted average that gives the score of the fifth exam as much weight in the final score as all the other tests combined. This is not how this professor will determine the average. A fifth test score of 80 would give a final average of 72, so choice **c** is not correct. A fifth test score of 85 would give a final average of 73, so choice **d** is not correct.

The following is a chart of the different skills assessed by the questions in this practice PPST; you can use it to identify your strengths and weaknesses in this subject to better focus your study.

MATH SKILLS STUDY CHART FOR PRACTICE EXAM 3	
NUMBER AND OPERATIONS	**QUESTIONS**
Order	38
Equivalence	8
Numeration and Place Value	30
Number Properties	4, 17, 39
Operation Properties	26
Computation	1, 31
Estimation	29
Ratio, Proportion, and Percent	14, 22
Numerical Reasoning	33
ALGEBRA	
Equations and Inequalities	15, 19, 27
Algorithmic Thinking	2, 25
Patterns	19, 32
Algebraic Representations	13
Algebraic Reasoning	11
GEOMETRY AND MEASUREMENT	
Geometric Properties	23, 24
The xy-Coordinate Plane	9, 10
Geometric Reasoning	36
Systems of Measurement	16, 34
Measurement	7
DATA ANALYSIS AND PROBABILITY	
Data Interpretation	5, 6, 12, 20
Data Representation	21
Trends and Inferences	3, 37
Measures of Center and Spread	28, 40
Probability	18, 35

Skills Test in Writing—Section 1, Part A

1. c. Verb tense should be consistent throughout a sentence. If a sentence describes an event in the past, its verbs should all be in the past tense. *Receives* should be *received.*

2. a. Commas are needed to set off the appositive phrase *an eight-year-old Maltese dog.*

3. d. *Enough* cannot be modified by *very.*

4. e. Because there are no grammatical, idiomatic, logical, or structural errors in this sentence, choice **e** is the best answer.

5. d. *Loose* is an adjective that means the opposite of tight or restrained. *Lose* is a verb and means to miss something. In this case, the correct word choice is *loose* because the dogs must be restrained.

6. d. This sentence contains an error in comparison. A writer can compare two nouns or two verb phrases but should not compare a noun with a verb phrase. Choice **c** is a verb phrase, so choice **d** must also be a verb phrase. The underlined portion could read *riding on a catamaran in Calcutta.*

7. e. Because there are no grammatical, idiomatic, logical, or structural errors in this sentence, choice **e** is the best answer.

8. a. *Beside* means next to, and *besides* means in addition to. Therefore, in this case, the sentence should read *Besides the fact....*

9. d. When used as an adjective, *everyday* is one word. However, in this case it should be two words (*every day*) because it is not being used to describe a noun.

10. b. The *–ing* form of the verb *covering,* in this case, needs a helping verb to make sense. Helping verbs include *is, has, has been, was, had, had been,* and so on. *The major newspapers have been covering the story . . .* would make sense in this sentence.

11. c. Use a colon to introduce a list when the clause before the colon can stand as a complete sentence. In this sentence, it doesn't make sense if you end the sentence after the verb *are,* so the colon should be deleted.

12. c. Perfect is in its superlative form. Some words represent qualities that are either present or absent. A life can be perfect or not perfect. There is no condition of being a degree of perfect.

13. a. *Children* is a plural noun even though it does not end in *–s.* We add an *'s* to plural words not ending in *–s* to show possession.

14. c. The pronoun *they* does not agree with the antecedent *event. Event* is singular; *they* is plural.

15. d. This sentence lacks parallel construction. The items in the series list must all be in the same form or part of speech. *Efficient* and *skilled* are adjectives; *communicated* is a verb form.

16. a. *Farther* refers to distance; it is the comparative form of *far* when referring to distance. *Further* means to a greater degree. This sentence implies the stock market will decline to a greater degree; therefore, the correct word choice is *further.*

17. d. This sentence contains a dangling modifier. It mistakenly modifies the wrong noun. To be correct, modifying phrases at the beginning of a sentence should describe the subject of the sentence that directly follows the comma. To correct the sentence, we could finish the sentence with ". . . Maria quickly took out her basketball and sneakers."

18. b. *Overdue* means late, such as having an overdue library book. *Overdo* refers to doing too much. In this case, *overdo* is the correct word choice.

19. e. Because there are no grammatical, idiomatic, logical, or structural errors in this sentence, choice **e** is the best answer.

20. e. Because there are no grammatical, idiomatic, logical, or structural errors in this sentence, choice **e** is the best answer.

21. d. This sentence contains an error in comparison. When comparing two items, we need to match the form of the two entities. To correct this sentence, we could end it with . . . *taller than the Eiffel Tower in France?*

Skills Test in Writing—Section 1, Part B

22. c. *Which includes massage and yoga* is a nonessential clause. The meaning of the sentence is not changed when it is deleted. Commas set off nonessential clauses. Choices **a** and **b** are missing the commas to offset the clause. Choices **d** and **e** have changed the nonessential clause to an essential clause by using *that*.

23. e. Using *nobody* and *hardly* in the same sentence makes it a double negative; therefore, choice **e** is correct. *No body* would refer to there being no physical body, so choices **c** and **d** do not make sense.

24. b. To give this sentence parallel construction, we have to make both entities match in form. Changing *television* to *watching television* matches it to *reading*. Choice **c** uses *funner,* which is not a word. Choice **d** uses *then,* which is not the correct word choice to compare things. Choice **e** uses *televising,* which changes the meaning of the sentence.

25. a. Choice **a** is correct because it is the only choice that uses *its* in both cases. *Its* shows possession, while *it's* is the contraction for *it is.* Also, *tale* refers to a story; *tail* refers to the part of the dog that wags.

26. c. In choices **a, b, d,** and **e,** we aren't sure if it was the car or the tree that was or wasn't damaged. The pronoun *it* does not identify which noun was damaged. Choice **c** clearly states that the tree was not damaged.

27. a. *Sure* is an adjective; *surely* is an adverb. In this case, *surely* acts as a sentence-adverb by telling how or what he *meant* (verb). Choice **b** is a sentence fragment. Choice **c** incorrectly uses *sure* (an adjective) to describe *meant* (the verb). Choices **d** and **e** change the meaning of the sentence.

28. b. Choices **a, c,** and **e** misspell the plural noun *parentheses.* Choice **d** needs a comma to offset the introductory phrase ending with *power* and doesn't need the comma after *parentheses.*

29. e. All the choices are sentence fragments except choice **e.** *Sleeping* needs a helping verb.

30. d. *Beautiful* and *intelligent* are both adjectives, so choice **d** contains parallel construction. None of the other choices are parallel because the entities do not match.

31. d. Choices **a, b,** and **c** are all sentence fragments. In choice **e,** *Russian* is a proper adjective and should be capitalized.

32. c. In choice **c,** both words are the correct adjective forms needed to allow the sentence to make sense. The other choices do not consistently use the adjective form of the intended words.

33. d. Choice **d** is correct because it is the only choice that does not contain double negatives.

34. b. In choices **a** and **c,** we don't know if the doctor was ill or the patient. Choice **d** is a run-on sentence. Choice **e** changes the meaning of the sentence. Choice **b** is correct because it is clear that the patient felt ill, not the doctor.

35. a. Choices **c**, **d**, and **e** are incorrect because they use *badly* (an adverb that would imply how I *felt*) instead of *bad* (describing the noun *I*). Imagine feeling around with your hands and doing a bad job at it, perhaps because you are being too rough as you feel around—that's feeling badly. Also, *really* is an adverb describing the adjective *bad*.

36. b. Choice **b** correctly uses these plural nouns: *phenomena*, *hypotheses*, and *theories*. All the other choices incorrectly use at least one of the plural nouns.

37. c. The original sentence (**a**) and choices **b**, **d**, and **e** contain errors in subordination because they have two subordinate clauses. By deleting *because*, the sentence makes sense. So, choice **c** is correct.

38. a. Choices **b** and **d** contain incorrect punctuation. Choices **c** and **d** incorrectly use *near* (an adjective) instead of *nearly* (an adverb). Choice **e** uses the wrong *there*.

The following is a chart of the different skills assessed by the questions in this practice PPST; you can use it to identify your strengths and weaknesses in this subject to better focus your study.

WRITING STUDY CHART FOR PRACTICE EXAM 3	
GRAMMATICAL RELATIONSHIP SKILLS	**QUESTIONS**
Identify Errors in Adjectives	27, 32, 35
Identify Errors in Adverbs	3, 16, 38
Identify Errors in Nouns	28, 36
Identify Errors in Pronouns	14, 25, 26
Identify Errors in Verbs	1, 10
STRUCTURAL RELATIONSHIP SKILLS	
Identify Errors in Comparison	6, 12, 21
Identify Errors in Coordination	34
Identify Errors in Correlation	17, 29, 31
Identify Errors in Negation	23, 33
Identify Errors in Parallelism	15, 24, 30
Identify Errors in Subordination	37
WORD CHOICE AND MECHANICS SKILLS	
Identify Errors in Word Choice	5, 8, 9, 18
Identify Errors in Mechanics	2, 11, 13, 22
Identify Sentences Free from Error	4, 7, 19, 20

Skills Test in Writing—Section 2, Essay Writing

Following are sample criteria for scoring a PPST essay.

A score "6" writer will:

- create an exceptional composition that appropriately addresses the audience and given task
- organize ideas effectively, include very strong supporting details, and use smooth transitions
- present a definitive, focused thesis and clearly support it throughout the composition
- include vivid details, clear examples, and strong supporting text to enhance the themes of the composition
- exhibit an exceptional level of skill in the usage of the English language and the capacity to employ an assortment of sentence structures
- build essentially error-free sentences that accurately convey intended meaning

A score "5" writer will:

- create a commendable composition that appropriately addresses the audience and given task
- organize ideas, include supporting details, and use smooth transitions
- present a thesis and support it throughout the composition
- include details, examples, and supporting text to enhance the themes of the composition
- generally exhibit a high level of skill in the usage of the English language and the capacity to employ an assortment of sentence structures
- build mostly error-free sentences that accurately convey intended meaning

A score "4" writer will:

- create a composition that satisfactorily addresses the audience and given task

- display satisfactory organization of ideas, include adequate supporting details, and generally use smooth transitions
- present a thesis and mostly support it throughout the composition
- include some details, examples, and supporting text that typically enhance most themes of the composition
- exhibit a competent level of skill in the usage of the English language and the general capacity to employ an assortment of sentence structures
- build sentences with several minor errors that generally do not confuse the intended meaning

A score "3" writer will:

- create an adequate composition that basically addresses the audience and given task
- display some organization of ideas, include some supporting details, and use mostly logical transitions
- present a somewhat underdeveloped thesis but attempt to support it throughout the composition
- display limited organization of ideas, have some inconsistent supporting details, and use few transitions
- exhibit an adequate level of skill in the usage of the English language and a basic capacity to employ an assortment of sentence structures
- build sentences with some minor and major errors that may obscure the intended meaning

A score "2" writer will:

- create a composition that restrictedly addresses the audience and given task
- display little organization of ideas, have inconsistent supporting details, and use very few transitions
- present an unclear or confusing thesis with little support throughout the composition

- include very few details, examples, and supporting text
- exhibit a less-than-adequate level of skill in the usage of the English language and a limited capacity to employ a basic assortment of sentence structures
- build sentences with a few major errors that may confuse the intended meaning

A score "1" writer will:

- create a composition that has a limited sense of the audience and given task
- display illogical organization of ideas, include confusing or no supporting details, and lack the ability to effectively use transitions
- present a minimal or unclear thesis
- include confusing or irrelevant details and examples, and little or no supporting text
- exhibit a limited level of skill in the usage of the English language and little or no capacity to employ basic sentence structure
- build sentences with many major errors that obscure or confuse the intended meaning

Sample 6 Essay

Picture your beloved pet—a dog, cat, bird, or hamster—being killed, then shipped to one of thousands of schools to be dissected by students, many of whom are just taking the course for credit and who have no real interest in learning about health or biology. Now picture an unknown animal. Does the fact that the animal wasn't someone's pet make it any different? Your pet has emotions; it shows love, loyalty, fear, and pain. Obviously, these attributes are not unique to animals that are pets. All animals have these feelings. That is why using any animal for dissection is cruel, a violation of the animals' rights, and completely unnecessary.

The use of animals for dissection in schools is cruel. No matter how "humanely" the animals are put to death, they are still losing their lives. Some of them lose their lives quite young—before they even have a chance to live. Some schools use piglets as dissection animals in classes. Beyond that, some of these animals are specifically bred for dissection purposes. They live their lives in cages basically only being provided the bare necessities until they are put to sleep. Not only does this make their death cruel; it makes their lives cruel as well.

Animals have rights. Just like humans, animals have the right to live their lives and pursue happiness. Many animals enjoy their lives. You can tell when an animal is happy. Whether it be a dog that runs and plays and wags its tail, a cat that contentedly curls up on your lap, a horse that prances in the field, or a bird that sings—all animals show their enjoyment of life. We have no right to take that life away just because we are bigger or stronger or have more power than they do. This is the worst form of bullying. Opponents to this idea cite survival of the fittest or the biblical tradition of having dominion over the Earth to support the use of animals in this way. However, simply because humans have advanced technological knowledge does not necessarily mean that the human species is morally or emotionally better than other animals. Therefore, we should not simply use animals for our purposes.

Finally, the use of animals for dissection in school classes is completely unnecessary. Because we as humans have advanced knowledge of technology, we should use it. It is now entirely possible to recreate the internal and external images of animals (and humans) via computer technology. Rather than continuing to take the lives of innocent animals, students should use the information already gained and catalogued in computer programs to study scientific issues. Not only does this save the lives of animals, it is probably safer for students because now they do not have to be concerned with contracting a disease while dissecting an infected animal.

We have been destroying animals for our own selfish purposes long enough. It's time to use the brains we were given (or have developed) to make the world a better place for all its inhabitants, not just humans.

Sample 4 Essay

I have been brought up to believe that all life is precious and that the life of an animal is not to be taken unless it's for a very good reason. I love all animals and I am very upset about the animal dissections that occur in science classes. I think this is cruel both for the animals and for the students.

Dissecting an animal is cruel for the animal itself. Even though the animals are already dead when they are dissected, I still think the whole process is cruel. The poor animals that are used in science class are bred just for dissection purposes. It's like they don't even have a real life. As soon as they're big and old enough, they are killed and shipped to schools for dissection. Even the dissection is cruel. Sure the animal is dead, but now instead of being able to just rest in peace, the poor thing is cut up and all its parts are taken out. Think about your favorite pet. Would you like it if your cat or dog died and then someone came in and started cutting it all apart?

The whole process of dissection is also cruel for students. Some students actually get sick from the smell and from having to handle the insides of an animal. I've been in classes where students had to stop dissecting because they felt faint and nauseas. Emotionally, it is hard on some students to have to deal with death. They see something that was once alive, and it is now dead. It reminds them of pets or even people who have died. This can be very upsetting to some students.

There are also other students like me who simply become upset when they think about how these animals died for no reason. Some students may even have moral or religious ideas that state that killing a living thing is wrong. The school should not force these students to go against their beliefs by making them handle a dead animal.

School should be an enjoyable place for students to learn. Cutting up animals makes school an uncomfortable place and a place that brings up a lot of bad feelings in some students. School should be a place where values are supported, especially the value of life.

Sample 1 Essay

There are some students in this school who refuse to dissect animals. They say they feel sorry for the animals. I think they are wrong. Dissecting animals is part of what we have to do for our grade, and the animals are allready dead so they don't know what's going on.

Dissecting animals gives us the chance to see some really cool things. Seeing stuff in a book is not the same as seeing it in real life. Its important for students to have experiances like this in life. We will learn and remember stuff better if we see it and do it for ourselves. Learning about pigs or frogs will help us learn more about ourselves and how our body works.

Another thing is that the animals are dead allready, so we don't have to kill them. They do it in a humane way, which means the animals do not feel anything, they just die. Once their dead, they don't feel anything, so cutting them up is not a problem. Plus, its not like were just going to hack them to pieces.

We are going to carefully cut and remove some of the organs. You could think of it as the animals are doing a good thing in their life by helping us learn. I don't feel sorry for the animals. That's part of what their there for, to help students learn. I think dissecting them is fine and students shouldn't worry so much about the animals.

PRAXIS I: POWER PRACTICE EXAM 4

CHAPTER SUMMARY

Here is a full-length test based on the three elements of the Praxis I, the Pre-Professional Skills Tests (PPSTs) of Reading, Mathematics, and Writing.

The exam that follows is made up of three tests: a Reading test (multiple-choice questions), a Mathematics test (multiple-choice questions), and a Writing test (multiple-choice questions and one essay).

With this practice exam, you should simulate the actual test-taking experience as closely as you can. Find a quiet place to work where you won't be disturbed. Set a timer or stopwatch for each part of the exam to guide your pace.

When you have completed the exam, use the answer explanations to learn more about the questions you missed, and use the scoring guide in Chapter 8 to figure out how you did.

SKILLS TEST IN READING

1. (a) (b) (c) (d) (e)
2. (a) (b) (c) (d) (e)
3. (a) (b) (c) (d) (e)
4. (a) (b) (c) (d) (e)
5. (a) (b) (c) (d) (e)
6. (a) (b) (c) (d) (e)
7. (a) (b) (c) (d) (e)
8. (a) (b) (c) (d) (e)
9. (a) (b) (c) (d) (e)
10. (a) (b) (c) (d) (e)
11. (a) (b) (c) (d) (e)
12. (a) (b) (c) (d) (e)
13. (a) (b) (c) (d) (e)
14. (a) (b) (c) (d) (e)
15. (a) (b) (c) (d) (e)
16. (a) (b) (c) (d) (e)
17. (a) (b) (c) (d) (e)
18. (a) (b) (c) (d) (e)
19. (a) (b) (c) (d) (e)
20. (a) (b) (c) (d) (e)
21. (a) (b) (c) (d) (e)
22. (a) (b) (c) (d) (e)
23. (a) (b) (c) (d) (e)
24. (a) (b) (c) (d) (e)
25. (a) (b) (c) (d) (e)
26. (a) (b) (c) (d) (e)
27. (a) (b) (c) (d) (e)
28. (a) (b) (c) (d) (e)
29. (a) (b) (c) (d) (e)
30. (a) (b) (c) (d) (e)
31. (a) (b) (c) (d) (e)
32. (a) (b) (c) (d) (e)
33. (a) (b) (c) (d) (e)
34. (a) (b) (c) (d) (e)
35. (a) (b) (c) (d) (e)
36. (a) (b) (c) (d) (e)
37. (a) (b) (c) (d) (e)
38. (a) (b) (c) (d) (e)
39. (a) (b) (c) (d) (e)
40. (a) (b) (c) (d) (e)

SKILLS TEST IN MATHEMATICS

1. (a) (b) (c) (d) (e)
2. (a) (b) (c) (d) (e)
3. (a) (b) (c) (d) (e)
4. (a) (b) (c) (d) (e)
5. (a) (b) (c) (d) (e)
6. (a) (b) (c) (d) (e)
7. (a) (b) (c) (d) (e)
8. (a) (b) (c) (d) (e)
9. (a) (b) (c) (d) (e)
10. (a) (b) (c) (d) (e)
11. (a) (b) (c) (d) (e)
12. (a) (b) (c) (d) (e)
13. (a) (b) (c) (d) (e)
14. (a) (b) (c) (d) (e)
15. (a) (b) (c) (d) (e)
16. (a) (b) (c) (d) (e)
17. (a) (b) (c) (d) (e)
18. (a) (b) (c) (d) (e)
19. (a) (b) (c) (d) (e)
20. (a) (b) (c) (d) (e)
21. (a) (b) (c) (d) (e)
22. (a) (b) (c) (d) (e)
23. (a) (b) (c) (d) (e)
24. (a) (b) (c) (d) (e)
25. (a) (b) (c) (d) (e)
26. (a) (b) (c) (d) (e)
27. (a) (b) (c) (d) (e)
28. (a) (b) (c) (d) (e)
29. (a) (b) (c) (d) (e)
30. (a) (b) (c) (d) (e)
31. (a) (b) (c) (d) (e)
32. (a) (b) (c) (d) (e)
33. (a) (b) (c) (d) (e)
34. (a) (b) (c) (d) (e)
35. (a) (b) (c) (d) (e)
36. (a) (b) (c) (d) (e)
37. (a) (b) (c) (d) (e)
38. (a) (b) (c) (d) (e)
39. (a) (b) (c) (d) (e)
40. (a) (b) (c) (d) (e)

SKILLS TEST IN WRITING

1. (a) (b) (c) (d) (e)
2. (a) (b) (c) (d) (e)
3. (a) (b) (c) (d) (e)
4. (a) (b) (c) (d) (e)
5. (a) (b) (c) (d) (e)
6. (a) (b) (c) (d) (e)
7. (a) (b) (c) (d) (e)
8. (a) (b) (c) (d) (e)
9. (a) (b) (c) (d) (e)
10. (a) (b) (c) (d) (e)
11. (a) (b) (c) (d) (e)
12. (a) (b) (c) (d) (e)
13. (a) (b) (c) (d) (e)
14. (a) (b) (c) (d) (e)
15. (a) (b) (c) (d) (e)
16. (a) (b) (c) (d) (e)
17. (a) (b) (c) (d) (e)
18. (a) (b) (c) (d) (e)
19. (a) (b) (c) (d) (e)
20. (a) (b) (c) (d) (e)
21. (a) (b) (c) (d) (e)
22. (a) (b) (c) (d) (e)
23. (a) (b) (c) (d) (e)
24. (a) (b) (c) (d) (e)
25. (a) (b) (c) (d) (e)
26. (a) (b) (c) (d) (e)
27. (a) (b) (c) (d) (e)
28. (a) (b) (c) (d) (e)
29. (a) (b) (c) (d) (e)
30. (a) (b) (c) (d) (e)
31. (a) (b) (c) (d) (e)
32. (a) (b) (c) (d) (e)
33. (a) (b) (c) (d) (e)
34. (a) (b) (c) (d) (e)
35. (a) (b) (c) (d) (e)
36. (a) (b) (c) (d) (e)
37. (a) (b) (c) (d) (e)
38. (a) (b) (c) (d) (e)

Skills Test in Reading

Directions: Read the following passages and answer the questions that follow.

Use the following passage to answer questions 1–7.

1 Sharks have layers of sharp teeth in their
2 mighty jaws that allow them to cut through a
3 fish's bones or a shellfish's hard shell. The shark
4 will eat almost every creature found in the
5 ocean, from crabs and turtles to seals and pen-
6 guins. If an animal is too big, a shark will sim-
7 ply tear it into smaller chunks before eating it.
8 This ancient fish has been patrolling Earth's
9 waters for more than 400 million years and can
10 now be found in all the planet's seas, from the
11 surface to a depth of below a mile. Species of
12 sharks can be massive, with a length of up to 46
13 feet, and some can be swift, with bursts of
14 speed of up to 30 miles per hour.
15   Despite all the impressive physical charac-
16 teristics of the shark that would make it seem
17 especially treacherous to humans, on average
18 fewer than 5 people in the world are killed each
19 year by sharks—fewer than are killed by wasps
20 or lightning. By contrast, an estimated 100 mil-
21 lion sharks are killed by fishermen each year. In
22 addition to this overfishing, sharks suffer from
23 habitat loss due to coastal development and the
24 impact of water pollution; some species are fac-
25 ing severe population decline as a result. Many
26 people share a groundless fear of shark attacks;
27 perhaps they should instead be fearful of losing
28 one of the planet's most remarkable creatures
29 to extinction.

1. Which statement, if it were true, would most significantly strengthen the author's argument?
   a. The smallest shark in the world reaches only a length of about 8 inches when fully grown.
   b. Of the nearly 400 species of sharks in the world, only four have been known to be dangerous to humans.
   c. Swimming in a group is safer than swimming alone because sharks are less likely to attack an individual.
   d. Other than humans, sharks have very few natural predators.
   e. The bull shark, known for its aggressive and often unpredictable nature, can often be found in shallow waters near beaches.

2. In the context of the passage, *groundless* (line 26) can be replaced with which word to incur the smallest alteration in meaning?
   a. sound
   b. aquatic
   c. terrifying
   d. justifiable
   e. unwarranted

3. The author's attitude toward sharks could be best described as
   a. reverential.
   b. frightened.
   c. ambivalent.
   d. quarrelsome.
   e. cautionary.

4. Which sentence best describes the organization of the two paragraphs of the passage?
 a. A detailed description of the creature is provided, and then common perceptions of it are supported.
 b. The evolution and history of an animal is illustrated, and then its present-day status is defined.
 c. The intimidating physical characteristics are listed, and then a defense of the creature is given.
 d. A series of harmless attributes are defined, and then a list of hazardous characteristics is described.
 e. The distinguishing features of an organism are provided, and then those features are described in further detail.

5. Which creature shares a similar relationship to humans as sharks to humans?
 a. killer whales, also called orcas, because they reside in all the oceans and lack natural predators
 b. frogs, because, despite their attractive appearance, they are among the most toxic animals on Earth
 c. caterpillars, because they go through a series of life stages during their complete metamorphosis
 d. deer, because they generally have a fear of humans and frequently will run away when approached
 e. snakes, because many people fear them despite the fact that very few species are venomous

6. Which detail from the passage would best support the idea that sharks should benefit from the protection of a conservation bill from Congress?
 a. More people are killed each year by wasps or lightning than by shark attacks.
 b. The shark will eat almost every creature found in the ocean.
 c. The shark can be found in all the planet's seas.
 d. Some species are facing severe population loss.
 e. Many people share a groundless fear of shark attacks.

7. Which sentence from the passage contains an opinion from the author?
 a. "Sharks have layers . . . hard shell."
 b. "The shark will . . . and penguins."
 c. "The ancient fish . . . a mile."
 d. "By contrast, an . . . each year."
 e. "Many people share . . . to extinction."

Use the following double bar graph to answer question 8.

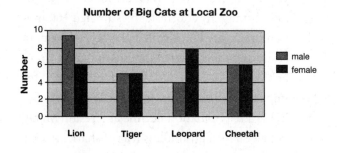

8. Which conclusion can be made from the information presented in the double bar graph above?

    a. Lions are the most popular big cats at the local zoo.

    b. The zoo has an equal number of female cheetahs and female lions.

    c. Tigers are more difficult to contain in captivity.

    d. The zoo has more male leopards than female leopards.

    e. The cheetah is the fastest animal on Earth.

Use the following passage to answer questions 9–11.

Although the Pacific island nation was populated by the Maori people more than 700 years earlier, the Dutchman Abel Tasman is generally credited with being the first European to discover New Zealand in 1642. Though Tasman described the place as "a very fine land," the Dutch did not continue their exploration of New Zealand; not until the Englishman James Cook captained a scientific voyage there in 1770 did another European visit New Zealand. In two subsequent voyages during the 1770s, Cook helped map the land and explore the unexplored oceans around New Zealand. Thanks to his thorough charting of the land and his respectful treatment of the native Maoris, Cook opened the door for further explorers and navigators of New Zealand. Eventually, Europeans settled in the "fine land," setting up the country's first capital, Russell, with the partnership of the Maoris in 1840.

9. Which organization best describes the structure of the passage?

    a. order of importance

    b. compare and contrast

    c. problem and solution

    d. classification

    e. chronological order

10. The passage is primarily focused on

    a. the means and methods for the exploration of New Zealand.

    b. the explorers Abel Tasman and James Cook.

    c. the initial European discovery of New Zealand.

    d. the first capital of New Zealand.

    e. the early history of New Zealand.

11. Which conclusion can be determined with certainty based on the information in the passage?

    a. The Maori people were living in New Zealand by AD 1000.

    b. The Dutch found no financial incentives to return to New Zealand.

    c. The Europeans and the Maori people have enjoyed a long, peaceful relationship.

    d. James Cook made significant scientific discoveries on his voyages to New Zealand.

    e. Russell is still the capital of New Zealand today.

Use the following passage to answer questions 12–16.

1   From early on in his administration, Abraham
2   Lincoln was pressured by abolitionists and radi-
3   cal Republicans to issue an Emancipation Proc-
4   lamation. In principle, Lincoln approved, but
5   he postponed action against slavery until he
6   believed he had wider support from the Ameri-
7   can public. The passage of the Second Confisca-
8   tion Act by Congress on July 17, 1862, which
9   freed the slaves of everyone in rebellion against
10   the government, consequently provided the

11 desired signal. Not only had Congress relieved
12 the administration of considerable strain with
13 its limited initiative on emancipation, it dem-
14 onstrated an increasing public abhorrence
15 toward slavery. Lincoln had already drafted
16 what he termed his "Preliminary Proclama-
17 tion." He read his initial draft of the Emancipa-
18 tion Proclamation to Secretaries William H.
19 Seward and Gideon Welles on July 13, 1862.
20 For a moment, both secretaries were speechless.
21 Quickly collecting his thoughts, Seward sug-
22 gested possible anarchy in the South and for-
23 eign intervention, but with Welles apparently
24 too confused to respond, Lincoln let the
25 matter drop.
26   Nine days later, Lincoln raised the issue in
27 a regularly scheduled Cabinet meeting. The
28 reaction was mixed. Secretary of War Edwin M.
29 Stanton, correctly interpreting the Proclama-
30 tion as a military measure designed to deprive
31 the Confederacy of slave labor and bring addi-
32 tional men into the Union Army, advocated its
33 immediate release. Conversely, Montgomery
34 Blair, the Postmaster General, foresaw defeat in
35 the fall elections. Attorney General Edward
36 Bates, a conservative, opposed civil and political
37 equality for blacks but gave his qualified sup-
38 port. Fortunately, President Lincoln only
39 wanted the advice of his Cabinet on the style of
40 the Proclamation, not its substance. The course
41 was set. The Cabinet meeting of September 22,
42 1862, resulted in the political and literary
43 refinement of the July draft, and on January 1,
44 1863, Lincoln composed the final Emancipa-
45 tion Proclamation. In the end, it was the
46 crowning achievement of his administration.

12. The passage suggests which of the following
about Lincoln's Emancipation Proclamation?
  a. Abolitionists did not support such an
  executive order.
  b. The draft proclamation was unanimously
  well received by Lincoln's cabinet.
  c. Congressional actions influenced Lincoln
  and encouraged him to issue it.
  d. The proclamation was not part of a military
  strategy.
  e. The first draft needed to be edited because
  Lincoln made numerous grammatical errors.

13. The description of the reaction of Secretaries
Seward and Welles to Lincoln's draft proclamation in lines 20–25 is used to illustrate
  a. Lincoln's lack of political acumen.
  b. that Lincoln's advisors did not anticipate his
  plan.
  c. the incompetence of Lincoln's advisors.
  d. Seward and Welles's disappointment that
  Lincoln did not free all slaves at that time.
  e. that most members of Lincoln's
  administration were abolitionists.

14. In line 37, *qualified* most nearly means
  a. adept.
  b. capable.
  c. limited.
  d. eligible.
  e. certified.

15. The author's attitude to the issuing of the
Emancipation Proclamation is one of
  a. informed appreciation.
  b. reluctant admiration.
  c. ambiguous acceptance.
  d. conflicted disapproval.
  e. personal dislike.

16. Which word or phrase from the passage helps illustrate that Lincoln's proposed proclamation was not universally supported?
 a. consequently (line 10)
 b. not only (line 11)
 c. conversely (line 33)
 d. fortunately (line 38)
 e. in the end (line 45)

Use the following passage to answer questions 17–21.

1   Thirty years ago, the northern spotted owl was
2   one of the most common owls in the Pacific
3   Northwest. However, these owls live in old-
4   growth forest, and much of their habitat has
5   been lost to logging and natural disasters. In
6   1991 the federal government passed laws to
7   protect the land where the owls live. Now,
8   though, the owls face a new threat—competi-
9   tion with the barred owl. Barred owls are larger
10   and more aggressive, and they scare the spotted
11   owls away from nesting and hunting grounds.
12   Scientists have tried several ways to protect this
13   endangered bird. Some track the owl nests to
14   monitor when their eggs hatch. Some scientists
15   have even tried to reduce the population of
16   barred owls. Environment specialists are work-
17   ing hard to protect this species, but more
18   research is needed. In addition to the myriad
19   other dangers, the northern spotted owl is also
20   threatened by climate change and competition
21   with other birds of prey. Given all these signifi-
22   cant hazards, scientists must do whatever they
23   can to save the northern spotted owl species.

17. Which is NOT suggested by the passage as a threat to the northern spotted owl?
 a. logging
 b. scientific research
 c. forest fires
 d. climate change
 e. barred owls

18. Which sentence from the passage represents an opinion rather than a fact?
 a. "Thirty years ago . . . Pacific Northwest."
 b. "In 1991 the . . . owls live."
 c. "Barred owls are . . . hunting grounds."
 d. "Some track the . . . eggs hatch."
 e. "Given all these . . . owl species."

19. What purpose does the phrase *Now, though* (lines 7 and 8) serve in the context of the passage?
 a. to contrast the author's opinion with the actual facts
 b. to reverse the decision that a species must be protected
 c. to question the reasonability of a government bill
 d. to contrast an earlier protection with current threats
 e. to compare a variety of threats to an endangered species

20. Which sentence provides the best summary of the reading selection?
 a. The northern spotted owl suffers from a loss of habitat.
 b. The northern spotted owl faces severe threats and must be protected.
 c. Scientists are struggling to identify ways to protect the northern spotted owl.
 d. The northern spotted owl used to be common in the Pacific Northwest.
 e. The northern spotted owl is an endangered species.

21. Which sentence from the reading selection provides the least amount of support for the main idea?
  a. However, these owls live in old-growth forest, and much of their habitat has been lost to logging and natural disasters.
  b. Now, though, the owls face a new threat—competition with the barred owl.
  c. Barred owls are larger and more aggressive, and they scare the spotted owls away from nesting and hunting grounds.
  d. Some track the owl nests to monitor when their eggs hatch.
  e. In addition to the myriad other dangers, the northern spotted owl is also threatened by climate change and competition with other birds of prey.

Use this passage to answer question 22.

Paradoxical as it may seem, Theodore Roosevelt was once of America's most well-known hunters and also one of the pioneers of the twentieth-century environmental movement. A passionate game hunter, Roosevelt took frequent trips to the Dakota Badlands. As U.S. president at the start of the century, Roosevelt enlarged and expanded the national park system, designating large swaths of the American West as territories protected from development.

22. According to the passage, Theodore Roosevelt
  a. established the U.S. national park system.
  b. was responsible for the conservation of large amounts of land.
  c. killed some of the largest animals on the North American continent.
  d. was not a successful president because of his passion for hunting.
  e. initiated significant climate change legislature.

Use the following passage to answer questions 23–25.

1 If you frequently feel drowsy during the day or
2 fall asleep within five minutes of lying down,
3 you may have sleep deprivation. Microsleeps,
4 very brief episodes of sleep in an otherwise
5 awake person, are another mark of sleep depri-
6 vation. The widespread practice of "burning the
7 candle at both ends" in Western industrialized
8 societies has created so much sleep deprivation
9 that what is really abnormal sleepiness is now
10 almost the norm.
11   Studies prove that sleep deprivation is
12 dangerous. Sleep-deprived people tested with a
13 driving simulator perform as badly as or worse
14 than those who are intoxicated. Driver fatigue is
15 responsible for an estimated 100,000 motor
16 vehicle accidents and 1,500 deaths each year.
17 Since drowsiness is the brain's last step before
18 falling asleep, drowsy driving can often lead to
19 disaster. The National Sleep Foundation says
20 that if you have trouble keeping your eyes
21 focused, can't stop yawning, or can't remember
22 driving the last few miles, you are too drowsy to
23 drive safely.

23. The primary purpose of the passage is to
  a. offer preventive measures for sleep deprivation.
  b. explain why sleeplessness has become a common state in Western cultures.
  c. recommend the amount of sleep individuals need at different ages.
  d. alert readers to the signs and risks of not getting enough sleep.
  e. discuss the effects of alcohol on a sleep-deprived person

24. The author uses the phrase *burning the candle at both ends* (lines 6–7) most likely to refer to

a. an unrelenting schedule that affords little rest.

b. an ardent desire to achieve.

c. the unavoidable conflagration that occurs when two forces oppose each other.

d. a latent period before a conflict or collapse.

e. a state of extreme agitation.

25. In line 10, the term *norm* could be replaced with which of the following words to result in the most minimal change of meaning?

a. outlier

b. standard

c. danger

d. anomaly

e. ideal

Use the following passage to answer questions 26–32.

1   The mounting conflict between the colonies
2   and England in the 1760s and 1770s reinforced
3   a growing conviction that Americans should be
4   less dependent on their mother country for
5   manufactures. The manufacture of homespun
6   cloth was encouraged as a substitute for English
7   imports. But manufacturing of cloth outside
8   the household was associated with relief of the
9   poor. Houses of Industry employed poor fami-
10 lies at spinning for their daily bread.
11   Such practices made many pre-
12 Revolutionary Americans dubious about man-
13 ufacturing. After independence there were a
14 number of unsuccessful attempts to establish
15 textile factories. Americans needed access to the
16 British industrial innovations, but England had
17 passed laws forbidding the export of machinery
18 or the emigration of those who could operate
19 it. Nevertheless, an English immigrant, Samuel
20 Slater, introduced British cotton technology to
21 America.

22   Slater had worked his way up from
23 apprentice to overseer in an English factory.
24 Drawn by American bounties for the introduc-
25 tion of textile technology, he passed as a farmer
26 and sailed for America with details of a revolu-
27 tionary cloth-making machine committed to
28 memory. In December 1790, he started the first
29 permanent American cotton spinning mill in
30 Rhode Island. Employing a workforce of nine
31 children between the ages of seven and twelve,
32 Slater successfully mechanized the carding and
33 spinning processes.
34   A generation of millwrights and textile
35 workers trained under Slater was the catalyst
36 for the rapid proliferation of textile mills in the
37 early nineteenth century. From Slater's first
38 mill, the industry spread across New England.
39 For two decades, before mills modeled after
40 Francis Cabot Lowell's factory system offered
41 competition, the "Rhode Island System" of
42 small, rural spinning mills set the tone for early
43 industrialization.

26. The primary purpose of the passage is to

a. account for the decline of rural America.

b. contrast political views held by the British and the Americans.

c. summarize British laws forbidding the export of industrial machinery.

d. describe the introduction of textile mills in New England.

e. make an argument in support of industrial development.

27. The passage refers to Houses of Industry (line 9) to illustrate
  a. a highly successful and early social welfare program.
  b. the perception of cloth production outside the home as a social welfare measure.
  c. the preference for the work of individual artisans over that of spinning machines.
  d. the first textile factory in the United States.
  e. the utilization of technological advances being made in England at the time.

28. It can be inferred from the passage that early American manufacturing was
  a. entirely beneficial.
  b. politically and economically necessary.
  c. symbolically undemocratic.
  d. environmentally destructive.
  e. spiritually corrosive.

29. The author most likely included the description of Slater's immigration to the American colonies (lines 24–28) primarily in order to
  a. demonstrate Slater's craftiness in evading British export laws.
  b. show the attraction of farming opportunities in the American colonies.
  c. explain the details of British manufacturing technologies.
  d. illustrate American efforts to block immigration to the colonies.
  e. describe the willingness of English factories to share knowledge with the colonies.

30. Lines 30–33 infer that Slater viewed child labor as
  a. an available workforce.
  b. a necessary evil.
  c. an unpleasant reality.
  d. an immoral institution.
  e. superior to adult labor.

31. The author implies that *the catalyst* (line 35) behind the spread of American textile mills in the early 1800s was
  a. Slater's invention of a groundbreaking cloth-making machine.
  b. the decline in the ideal of the self-sufficient American farm family.
  c. the expertise of the workforce trained in Slater's prototype mill.
  d. an increased willingness to employ child laborers.
  e. the support of British manufacturers who owned stock in American mills.

32. In line 39, *modeled* most nearly means
  a. posed.
  b. displayed.
  c. arranged.
  d. illustrated.
  e. fashioned.

Use the following passage to answer questions 33–35.

1 The running of the bulls, a practice where men
2 and women test their bravado by dodging bulls
3 rampaging through city streets, is one of the
4 more famous Spanish traditions. The most
5 popular running of the bulls is held during the
6 San Fermin Festival in Pamplona, Spain, where
7 a crowd of greater than a million people gathers
8 to avoid the charging and observe the wild
9 event. The entertainment is not innocuous,
10 however; each year several hundred people are

11 injured from the run, and 15 people have been
12 killed by bulls during the last century. On the
13 flipside, the Spanish La Tomatina festival offers
14 a much safer way to enjoy an incredibly unique
15 tradition. Held in the Spanish town of Buñol,
16 participants throw tomatoes at each other in a
17 massive food fight. For an hour, tens of thou-
18 sands of participants hurl up to 100 tons of
19 tomatoes, even swimming in the tomato paste.
20 There have been no reported casualties from La
21 Tomatina.

33. Which organization best describes the structure
of the reading selection?
   a. classification
   b. compare and contrast
   c. problem and solution
   d. chronological order
   e. order of importance

34. In line 9, the word *innocuous* most nearly
means
   a. dangerous.
   b. customary.
   c. harmless.
   d. fun.
   e. harmful.

35. For which reason did the author most likely
include the last sentence of the passage?
   a. to compare personal experiences of two
Spanish festivals
   b. to criticize the dangers of the misuse of food
products
   c. to accentuate the dangers of a particular
festival
   d. to downplay potentially grave concerns of
one festival
   e. to contrast one festival's safety with the
dangers of another

Use the following passage to answer questions 36–38.

An ecosystem is a grouping of animals and
plants living in a specific region and interacting
with one another and with their physical environment. Ecosystems include physical and
chemical components such as soils, water, and
nutrients. These components support the
organisms living in the ecosystem. Ecosystems
can also be thought of as the interactions
among all organisms in a given habitat. These
organisms may range from large animals to
microscopic bacteria and may work together in
various ways. For example, one species may
serve as food for another. Human activities,
such as housing developments and trash dis-
posal, can greatly harm or even destroy local
ecosystems. Proper ecosystem management is
crucial for the overall health and diversity of
our planet. We must find ways to protect local
ecosystems without stifling economic
development.

36. Which sentence best expresses the main idea of
this passage?
   a. Our actions can have a great impact on our
ecosystems.
   b. Ecosystems have been badly managed in the
past.
   c. Humans must clean up their trash.
   d. Ecosystems interact with one another.
   e. Trash disposals can greatly harm local
ecosystems.

37. Which relationship best describes the activities
within an ecosystem?
   a. predator-prey relationships
   b. interactions among all members
   c. human-animal interactions
   d. human relationship with the environment
   e. destroyer-preserver relationships

38. The author of the reading selection would most likely define an ecosystem as

    a. a specific place.

    b. a community of plants and animals.

    c. a group of animals working together.

    d. a protected environment.

    e. a threatened setting.

Use the following passage to answer question 39.

It may be difficult to envision with today's technologies and comforts, but the early European expeditions to the Americas were incredibly arduous; the journey took several months, during which time the travelers faced extreme isolation, limited supplies due to space constraints, and a somewhat mysterious concept of what to expect upon arrival.

39. Which journey would be most similar to the early European expeditions to the Americas?

    a. a luxury cruise across the Atlantic

    b. a solo skydive

    c. an unmanned probe to Venus

    d. a jet flight to Asia

    e. a manned trip to Mars

Use the following double bar graph to answer question 40.

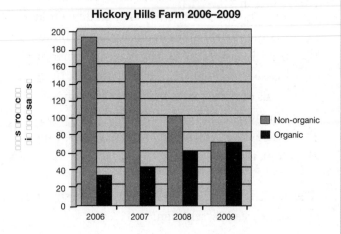

40. Which conclusion is supported from the information presented in the double bar graph?

    a. The year in which Hickory Hills Farm produced the most eggs was 2006.

    b. Hickory Hills Farm makes more money selling organic eggs than non-organic eggs.

    c. More customers are buying organic produce than ever before.

    d. The first year that Hickory Hills Farm produced more organic eggs than non-organic eggs was 2010.

    e. Hickory Hills Farm will no longer be producing non-organic eggs by 2020.

Skills Test in Mathematics

1. Joel wants to purchase a CD for $16.25. The clerk tells him he must pay a sales tax equal to 8% of his purchase. What is the total amount Joel must pay for his CD?

  a. $1.30
  b. $14.95
  c. $17.05
  d. $17.55
  e. $16.33

2. The following chart shows the cost for different categories of UTP cabling. If Athena needs to buy 100 feet of UTP cable that can send data at a speed of 65 megabytes per second, 30 feet of UTP cable that can send data at a speed of 18 megabytes per second, and 10 feet of UTP cable that can send data at a speed of 12 megabytes per second, how much will she spend?

3. A cube with sides of length x centimeters has a surface area of $6x^2$ cm^2. If the length of each side of the cube is tripled, what will the surface area be of the resulting cube?

  a. $9x^2$ cm^2
  b. $54x^2$ cm^2
  c. $18x^2$ cm^2
  d. $6(x + 2)^2$ cm^2
  e. $216x^6$ cm^2

4. Jean Marie heads to the grocery store and makes the following purchases: bread for $3.20, eggs for $2.65, salmon for $12, four mangos that are $1.50 each, and a piece of candy for a quarter. There is no tax on her food purchase. If she pays for the items with a $50 bill, how much change will Jean Marie receive?

  a. $24.10
  b. $25.90
  c. $26.10
  d. $5.65
  e. Jean Marie should have only paid with a $20 bill.

CATEGORY	CHARACTERISTICS	PRICE PER FOOT
Category 1	Does not support data transmission	75¢
Category 2	Supports data transmission speeds up to 4 megabytes per second	$1.00
Category 3	Supports data transmission speeds up to 16 megabytes per second	$1.75
Category 4	Supports data transmission speeds up to 20 megabytes per second	$2.50
Category 5	Supports data transmission speeds up to 100 megabytes per second	$3.00

  a. $362.50
  b. $312.50
  c. $385.00
  d. $1,015.00
  e. $392.50

5. The stem-and-leaf plot shows the scores on the last test in Mr. O'Brien's Spanish class. Which statement about the scores is true?

STEM	LEAF
9	8 5 2
8	9 7 7 4 3 1 0 0
7	8 8 5
6	6 3
5	2

   a. More than 50% of the class scored above an 80.
   b. The highest score was a 92.
   c. The median score was an 80.
   d. The range of the scores was 50.
   e. The only mode is 80.

6. The city of Santa Barbara is considering a new sales tax on alcohol that is $\frac{1}{9}$ of the purchase price on all alcoholic beverages. If this passes at the next Santa Barbara City Council meeting, what would be the percentage of sales tax charged on all alcoholic beverages?
   a. 9%
   b. 9.19%
   c. 11.11%
   d. 10%
   e. 1.9%

7. Ken earns a bonus to work on Saturdays. The bonus is $1\frac{1}{2}$ times his standard hourly pay for the first four hours he works on Saturday and then for any time worked *over* four hours, Ken earns twice his standard pay. If his standard hourly pay is $12.50, how much bonus pay does Ken earn when he works six hours on a Saturday?
   a. $75.00
   b. $100.00
   c. $112.50
   d. $125.00
   e. $150.00

8. KCRW is giving away tickets to go see a special performance of Amos Lee at the Henry Fonda Theater. One month before the date of the show they gave away 16 tickets. A week before the show they gave away another 8 tickets. On the day of the show, KCRW gave away 6 more tickets. If the Henry Fonda Theater only released 200 tickets in total for this special performance, what is the probability that a person at that Amos Lee concert received a free ticket from KCRW?
   a. $\frac{1}{10}$
   b. $\frac{2}{25}$
   c. $\frac{17}{20}$
   d. $\frac{3}{50}$
   e. $\frac{3}{20}$

9. An isosceles right triangle has a base that measures 8 inches. What is the sum of the two legs of the triangle?
   a. $\sqrt{32}$ inches
   b. $2\sqrt{32}$ inches
   c. 32 inches
   d. 64 inches
   e. 16 inches

10. Which is the best estimate of $\sqrt{181}$?
   a. 9
   b. 11
   c. 12
   d. 13
   e. 14

11. At her party, Mackenzie put out a bowl containing 360 jellybeans. Marina came by and ate $\frac{1}{12}$ of the original total of jellybeans, Christina ate $\frac{1}{4}$ of the original total of jellybeans, Athena ate $\frac{1}{5}$ of the original total of jellybeans, and Jade ate $\frac{1}{8}$ of the original total of jellybeans. How many jellybeans were left?

    a. 273

    b. 168

    c. 237

    d. 108

    e. 123

12. The following table shows the total number of Full-Time Psychology Faculty at Canadian Universities as well as the percentage of that faculty that was female. By rounding the Full-Time Psychology Faculty data to the nearest hundred and the percentages to the nearest ten, estimate how many more female professors were there in the period from 2002–2003 than in the period from 2006–2007?

YEAR	FULL-TIME PSYCHOLOGY FACULTY	% FEMALE
2000–2001	1,545	94.91
2001–2002	1,563	96.68
2002–2003	1,588	97.83
2003–2004	1,578	27.95
2004–2005	1,566	28.54
2005–2006	1,588	29.41
2006–2007	1,533	30.40
2007–2008	1,510	31.85
2008–2009	1,477	39.77

    a. 1,280

    b. 480

    c. 500

    d. 1,250

    e. 1,150

13. This graph shows the number of inches of rain for five towns in Suffolk County during the spring of 2009.

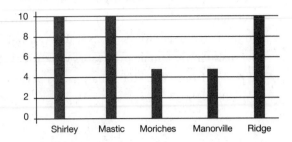

What was the average (arithmetic mean) number of inches of rain for the spring of 2009?

a. 5
b. 7.5
c. 8
d. 9
e. 10

14. The dimensions of Ash and Hala's living room are represented below. They are shopping for cork flooring that is sold by the square meter, but they have measured their living room out in centimeters. What is the approximate amount of money they will pay to cover their floor with cork that is on sale for $12 per square meter?

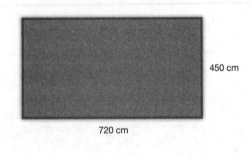

450 cm

720 cm

a. $389.00
b. $1,555.00
c. $3,240.00
d. $38,880.00
e. $280.00

15. Carol works part time at the movie theater. Her schedule for the next three weeks lists the number of hours Carol will work each day. What is the median number of hours Carol will work over the next three weeks?

SUNDAY	MONDAY	TUESDAY	WEDNESDAY	THURSDAY	FRIDAY	SATURDAY
0	7	0	4	4	5	0
0	4	6	5	3	2	0
0	5	4	3	6	5	0

a. 0 hours
b. 3 hours
c. 4 hours
d. 4.5 hours
e. 5 hours

16. Determine the function that best explains the relationship between the *x* and *y* values shown in the following table:

x	y
−2	8
−1	6
0	4
1	2
2	0

a. $y = x^2 + 4$
b. $y = 2x + 4$
c. $y = -4x$
d. $y = -2x + 4$
e. $y = -(x^2 - 4)$

17. If lines *CD* and *GH* are perpendicular and ∠4 is congruent to ∠7, which of the following is NOT true?

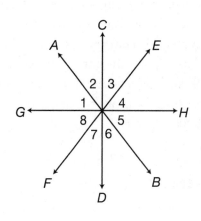

a. $m\angle 4 = m\angle 3$
b. $m\angle 2 = m\angle 3$
c. $m\angle 8 = m\angle 3$
d. $m\angle 7 = m\angle 3$
e. $m\angle 7 = m\angle 8$

18. Consider the following information and determine which statement below *must* be true:

Ten new television shows appeared during the month of September. Five of the shows were sitcoms, three were hour-long dramas, and two were news-magazine shows. By January, only seven of these new shows were still on the air. Five of the shows that remained were sitcoms.

a. Only one of the news-magazine shows remained on the air.

b. Only one of the hour-long dramas remained on the air.

c. At least one of the shows that was canceled was an hour-long drama.

d. Television viewers prefer sitcoms over hour-long dramas.

e. None of the statements above *must* be true.

19. An organism initially contained 100 cells. The number of cells in the organism is tripling every 5 hours. The expression $100 \cdot 3^{\frac{h}{5}}$ can be used to calculate the number of cells in the organism after h hours. How many cells will the organism contain after 20 hours?

a. 1,200

b. 700

c. 1,500

d. 8,100

e. 12,000

20. If y is the square root of 9, which of the following best represents y?

a. 81 only

b. 81 and −81

c. 3 only

d. 3 and −3

e. 36

21. At Smith Advertising Company, a standard 1-minute commercial can be broken down into a 5-second intro, a 40-second endorsement, and a 15-second conclusion. If Derek accidentally got a fingerprint on one frame of a 1-minute commercial, what is the probability that this frame is part of the concluding segment?

a. $\frac{1}{12}$

b. $\frac{3}{4}$

c. $\frac{1}{4}$

d. $\frac{2}{3}$

e. $\frac{11}{12}$

22. Which of the following contains the correct ordering of $\frac{17}{20}, \frac{5}{7}, \frac{3}{4}, \frac{11}{14}$ and $\frac{4}{5}$ from *least* to *greatest*?

a. $\frac{17}{20}, \frac{4}{5}, \frac{11}{14}, \frac{3}{4}, \frac{5}{7}$

b. $\frac{3}{4}, \frac{4}{5}, \frac{5}{7}, \frac{11}{14}, \frac{17}{20}$

c. $\frac{5}{7}, \frac{3}{4}, \frac{11}{14}, \frac{17}{20}, \frac{4}{5}$

d. $\frac{17}{20}, \frac{11}{14}, \frac{5}{7}, \frac{4}{5}, \frac{3}{4}$

e. $\frac{5}{7}, \frac{3}{4}, \frac{11}{14}, \frac{4}{5}, \frac{17}{20}$

23. If $\triangle ABC$ is rotated 90° counterclockwise about •A, the result is $\triangle A'B'C'$, what are the coordinates of $\triangle A'B'C'$?

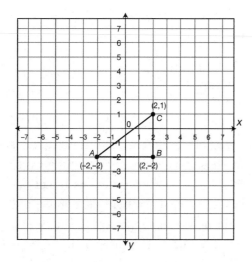

a. $A' = (-2,-2); B' = (-2,-6); C' = (1,-6)$
b. $A' = (-2,2); B' = (-2,-2); C' = (-5,-2)$
c. $A' = (2,2); B' = (2,6); C' = (1,6)$
d. $A' = (-2,-2); B' = (-2,2); C' = (-5,2)$
e. $A' = (-2,-2); B' = (-2,-2); C' = (-5,-2)$

24. It takes 4 gardeners 9 hours to do the landscaping each week at Anne's estate. Anne is having a party and needs the gardening done more quickly this Friday, so she asks the landscaping company to send two more gardeners who work at the same rate as the four who normally take care of her property. How long should it take the increased team of gardeners to finish the landscaping at Anne's estate?
a. 6 hours
b. 4.5 hours
c. 18 hours
d. 7 hours
e. 6.75 hours

25. If z is even and v is odd, which of the following must be true?
a. $2z > 0$
b. v is prime.
c. $3z$ is odd.
d. z is a composite number.
e. none of the above

26. If the following multiplication problem is correctly calculated, what digit does R represent?

$$
\begin{array}{r}
8\ 3 \\
\times\ \ Q\ P \\
\hline
Q\ 1\ \ P \\
3\ 3\ 2\ \ \\
\hline
3\ R\ 3\ \ P
\end{array}
$$

a. 4
b. 5
c. 6
d. 7
e. 1

27. $\angle A$, $\angle B$, and $\angle C$ meet the following conditions.
1. $\angle A$ and $\angle B$ are complementary (they add to 90°).
2. $\angle B = \frac{1}{2}\angle C$.
3. $\angle C = \angle A + 30°$.
Which choice satisfies all three conditions?
a. $\angle A = 40°, \angle B = 50°, \angle C = 100°$
b. $\angle A = 40°, \angle B = 140°, \angle C = 10°$
c. $\angle A = 50°, \angle B = 40°, \angle C = 25°$
d. $\angle A = 50°, \angle B = 40°, \angle C = 100°$
e. $\angle A = 50°, \angle B = 40°, \angle C = 80°$

28. Which of the following graphs represents the solution set for $(\frac{3}{4})y + 6 \geq 3x$?

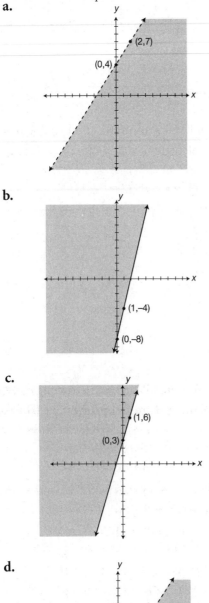

a.

b.

c.

d.

e. None of the above graphs correctly represents $(\frac{3}{4})y + 6 \geq 3x$.

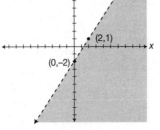

29. A recipe calls for $5\frac{1}{4}$ cups of apples for six servings. How many cups of apples would be required to make nine servings?

a. $7\frac{3}{4}$ cups

b. $7\frac{7}{8}$ cups

c. $8\frac{1}{4}$ cups

d. 9 cups

e. $10\frac{1}{2}$ cups

30. A glass bowl is full of just nickels, dimes, and quarters. It has twice as many quarters as it does dimes. The bowl contains a total value of $8.15. Letting d represent the number of dimes in the bowl and n represent the number of nickels in the bowl, which equation properly expresses the relationship of coins in the bowl?

a. $0.05n + 0.10d = \$8.15$

b. $0.55n + 0.10d = \$8.15$

c. $0.05n + 0.45d = \$8.15$

d. $0.05n + 0.60d = \$8.15$

e. $0.55n + 0.45d = \$8.15$

31. What is the measure of B in the following diagram?

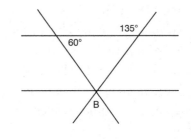

a. 45°

b. 60°

c. 75°

d. 105°

e. 135°

Use the following chart to answer questions 32 and 33.

NAME	SCORE
Darin	95
Miguel	90
Anthony	82
Christopher	90
Samuel	88

32. What is the mode of the five scores in the table?
   a. 82
   b. 90
   c. 89
   d. 13
   e. 95

33. If Anthony's score was incorrectly reported as an 82 when his actual score on the test was a 90, which of the following statements would be true when his actual score is used in the calculations?
   a. The mean, median, range, and mode will change.
   b. The mean, median, and range will change; the mode will remain the same.
   c. Only the mean and median will change.
   d. The mean and range will change; the median and mode will remain the same.
   e. None of the above.

34. If $R = -3k$ and $B = -2k - 4$, then what will the value of $6R - 5B$ be in terms of k?
   a. $-8k + 20$
   b. $-8k - 20$
   c. $8k + 20$
   d. $8k - 20$
   e. $-18k - 20$

35. As a person walks, the distance from the heel print of one foot to the heel print of the other foot is defined as one step, which averages about two feet. Renatta would like to use the number of steps she takes when she walks to school to estimate the distance she travels. Which unit of measurement would be best to estimate this distance?
   a. millimeters
   b. centimeters
   c. meters
   d. decimeters
   e. kilometers

36. Solve the following inequality for r:
   $10 - 3(r - 4) > -14$
   a. $r < 12$
   b. $r > 12$
   c. $r > -12$
   d. $r < 4$
   e. $r > 4$

37. Erik is buying a dress shirt that regularly costs $68 and pants that regularly cost $52. If the store is having a 30% off sale, what will the total price of Erik's shirt and pants be after the discount is taken and a 5% sales tax is applied to his purchase?
   a. $90.00
   b. $84.00
   c. $95.00
   d. $94.50
   e. $88.20

38. If the annual sales for A Stone's Throw follow the same trend that is modeled in the following table, what is a good estimate for A Stone's Throw's annual sales in 2012?

A STONE'S THROW ANNUAL SALES	
YEAR	ANNUAL SALES
2006	$30,000
2007	$36,000
2008	$43,000
2009	$52,000
2010	$62,000
2011	$75,000
2012	—

a. $81,000
b. $83,000
c. $88,000
d. $90,000
e. $97,000

39. If $\dfrac{6}{-y-1} = \dfrac{10}{-2y-3}$, what is the value of y?
a. -4
b. 4
c. 14
d. -14
e. $\dfrac{9}{11}$

40. Consider the following three facts:
Fact A: Some pens don't write.
Fact B: All blue pens write.
Fact C: Some writing utensils are pens.
If the first three statements are facts, which of the following statements must also be a fact?
I. Some writing utensils don't write.
II. Some writing utensils are blue.
III. Some blue writing utensils don't write.
a. II only
b. I and II only
c. I, II, and III
d. II and III only
e. None of the statements is a known fact.

Skills Test in Writing

Skills Test in Writing—Section 1, Part A

Directions: Choose the letter for the underlined portion that contains a grammatical error. If there is no error in the sentence, choose **e**.

1. According to researchers at the <u>World Health Organization</u>, radiation from exposure <u>to</u> <u>cell</u> phones
                   a   **b** **c**

   <u>could associated</u> with some risk for brain cancer. <u>No error</u>
         d   **e**

2. <u>When it comes</u> to teaching <u>children</u>, we would agree that <u>everyones</u> ability level <u>should be</u>
       a   **b**   **c**   **d**

   considered. <u>No error</u>
             e

3. The contractor <u>was impressed</u> <u>with</u> the way the new employee <u>worked</u>; she worked <u>hardly</u> and never
                   a   **b**   **c**   **d**

   complained. <u>No error</u>
              e

4. <u>Earthquakes</u> <u>are extremely difficult</u> to <u>predict</u>; <u>that's</u> why most scientific investigations occur after
       a   **b**   **c**   **d**

   earthquakes occur. <u>No error</u>
                    e

5. Don't be so <u>incredible</u>; I <u>really</u> did see a <u>flying saucer</u> in the sky last <u>night</u>! <u>No error</u>
                 a   **b**   **c**   **d**   **e**

6. <u>Based on</u> my experience <u>with</u> having done both, <u>running a marathon</u> is easier than <u>a triathlon</u>. <u>No</u>
      a   **b**   **c**   **d**

   <u>error</u>
   e

7. <u>Memorial Day</u> has the special honor of marking the informal start of <u>summer</u>; more <u>importantly</u>,
      a   **b**   **c**

   however, it is the day Americans reflect on the sacrifices made by the over one million people on active

   military duty <u>nationally</u> and internationally. <u>No error</u>
                d   **e**

8. Just <u>between</u> the three of <u>us</u>, we made a big <u>mistake</u>; <u>however</u>, our error will be officially
           a   **b**   **c**   **d**

   recorded as a computer error. <u>No error</u>
                              e

9. The <u>principal</u> of the <u>conservation of matter</u> states that matter cannot be created <u>or</u> <u>destroyed;</u> it
      a   b   c   d

can only be changed from one form to another. <u>No error</u>
                                              e

10. If I <u>was</u> a billionaire, I can <u>assure</u> you that I would <u>quit</u> my job tomorrow and fly away to
        a   b   c

<u>Italy</u>. <u>No error</u>
 d   e

11. <u>Although</u> <u>Queen's</u> most recognized song is <u>"Bohemian Rhapsody"</u>, my
     a   b   c

favorite song is <u>"Made in Heaven."</u> <u>No error</u>
               d   e

12. <u>Brewing sun tea</u> in the <u>summertime</u> is <u>more enjoyable</u> <u>than instant</u> tea from a jar. <u>No error</u>
        a   b   c   d   e

13. <u>James</u> enjoys reading *A Christmas Carol* by <u>Charles Dickens</u> each <u>winter, it</u> is his favorite
     a   b   c   d

book. <u>No error</u>
     e

14. The teacher told the student to get his <u>backpack</u> and books because <u>their</u> mother had arrived
                                      a   b

to pick <u>him</u> up for a <u>doctor's</u> appointment. <u>No error</u>
       c   d   e

15. <u>For his birthday,</u> Coleman wanted <u>to have his friends over to go swimming,</u> <u>to get ice cream</u>
          a   b   c

<u>at his favorite ice cream parlor,</u> <u>and his father to come home</u> from Iraq. <u>No error</u>
                                   d   e

16. She <u>knew</u> perfectly <u>good</u> that it was her turn to do the <u>dishes;</u> <u>yet,</u> right after dinner she made
        a   b   c   d

up an excuse for having to go out. <u>No error</u>
                             e

17. He was fully <u>capable to</u> changing the <u>baby, but</u> he was waiting for <u>someone else</u> to come
                 a   b   c

home to take care of the <u>newborn's</u> needs. <u>No error</u>
                   d   e

18. It's hard to believe that <u>its</u> only been 50 years <u>since</u> 400 courageous African-American
                                        a   **b**

youths took a stand to desegregate interstate buses in the deep <u>South</u> by participating in the
                                                                        c

<u>Freedom Rides</u>. <u>No error</u>
    d   **e**

19. Through an interactive message board called Massively Multiplayer Online War Game Leveraging the
Internet <u>(MMOWGLI)</u>, the <u>U.S. Navy</u> <u>is employing</u> the <u>video-gaming public</u> to
                a   **b**   **c**   **d**

track and fight pirates. <u>No error</u>
                      e

20. <u>Although</u> it <u>began</u> as a fatal plague <u>three decades ago</u>, acquired immune deficiency syndrome
    a   **b**   **c**

(AIDS) <u>has become</u> a treatable chronic disease in many countries. <u>No error</u>
          d   **e**

21. Some people believe <u>it's</u> <u>more important</u> to be happy doing your job <u>than</u> <u>earn lots of money</u>.
                         a   **b**   **c**   **d**

<u>No error</u>
 e

Section 1, Part B

Directions: Choose the best replacement for the underlined portion of the sentence. If no revision is necessary, choose **a**, which always repeats the original phrasing.

22. According to this Global Positioning System (GPS), I have to drive <u>north then east</u> to get to the lake.
    a. north then east
    b. North then east
    c. north then East
    d. North then East
    e. North than East

23. Mark, Roger, and Maurice went looking for Jill and Kelly last night, but <u>no one could find the girls nowhere.</u>
    a. no one could find the girls nowhere.
    b. no one could find the girls anywhere.
    c. anyone could find the girls anywhere.
    d. anyone could find the girls nowhere.
    e. no one could find the girls no where.

24. Before leaving for their two-week vacation in the Adirondacks, the Tenaces cancelled their newspaper delivery, <u>asking the postal service to hold their mail,</u> and brought their two dogs to the boarding kennel.
    a. asking the postal service to hold their mail,
    b. asking the Postal Service to hold their mail,
    c. asking the postal service to hold there mail,
    d. asked the postal service to hold there mail,
    e. asked the postal service to hold their mail,

25. Planet Earth has billions of inhabitants, <u>and it</u> is destroying our natural resources.
a. and it
b. and they
c. and the pollution they create
d. and the earth
e. and Earth

26. Each of the athletes on the <u>men's basketball team believed their team would win;</u> unfortunately, one team would lose.
a. men's basketball team believed their team would win;
b. mens basketball team believed their team would win;
c. mens' basketball team believed their team would win,
d. men's basketball team believed their team would win,
e. men's basketball team believed his team would win;

27. We were all down on our hands and knees searching <u>careful threw the grains</u> of sand on the beach for Juan's missing ring.
a. careful threw the grains
b. carefully threw the grains
c. carefully through the grains
d. careful through the grains
e. carefully through the granes

28. According to behavior modification theory, discriminative <u>stimuli control behaviors and tell</u> people or animals how to act or what to do.
a. stimuli control behaviors and tell
b. stimuli controls behaviors and tells
c. stimuli controls behaviors and tell
d. stimulus control behaviors and tell
e. stimulus controls behaviors and tell

29. To improve his results, <u>the experiment was repeated</u> with more control of the variables.
a. the experiment was repeated
b. he repeated the experiment
c. repeating the experiment
d. the experiment was repeating
e. he is experimenting

30. His speech not only cost him the support of his own political party <u>but enraging</u> his opponents to the point of causing demonstrations.
a. but enraging
b. by enraging
c. yet enraging
d. and enraging
e. but enraged

31. <u>Spreading</u> mothballs around in the vegetable garden to keep chipmunks from eating the plants and seeds.
a. Spreading
b. Spread
c. Because spreading
d. Although spreading
e. Yet, spreading

32. Her <u>vivid description of the murder facilitated the detectives'</u> ability to find the murderer.
a. vivid description of the murder facilitated the detectives'
b. vividly description of the murder facilitated the detectives'
c. more vivider description of the murder facilitated the detectives
d. most vividest description of the murder facilitated the detectives
e. most vividly description of the murder facilitated the detectives'

33. Neither of the men scarcely knew nobody at the reception.
   a. Neither of the men scarcely knew nobody
   b. Neither of the men knew anybody
   c. Neither of the men knew scarcely anybody
   d. Neither of the men scarcely knew anybody
   e. Neither of the men knew anybody scarcely

34. The young woman took the dog for a walk with no shoes.
   a. took the dog for a walk with no shoes.
   b. took the dog with no shoes for a walk.
   c. for a walk with no shoes, took the dog.
   d. who took the dog for a walk with no shoes.
   e. with no shoes took the dog for a walk.

35. We enjoyed the deliciously meal that the chef had prepared perfect.
   a. deliciously meal that the chef had prepared perfect.
   b. delicious meal that the chef had prepared perfectly.
   c. deliciously meal that the chef had prepared perfectly.
   d. delicious meal who the chef had prepared perfectly.
   e. meal deliciously that the chef had prepared perfectly.

36. On her first day of college classes, she received five course syllabi and bought nine textbooks.
   a. syllabi and bought nine textbooks.
   b. syllabi, and bought nine textbooks.
   c. syllabus and bought nine textbooks.
   d. syllabus, and bought nine textbooks.
   e. syllabus and bought 9 textbooks.

37. Taking a drastic step to end its overpopulation problems, because China's government started a One Child Policy.
   a. Taking a drastic step to end its overpopulation problems, because China's government started a One Child Policy.
   b. Because China's government started a One Child Policy, taking a drastic step to end its overpopulation problems.
   c. China's government started a One Child Policy, taking a drastic step to end its overpopulation problems.
   d. Since China's government started a One Child Policy, taking a drastic step to end its overpopulation problems.
   e. Even though taking a drastic step to end its overpopulation problems, because China's government started a One Child Policy.

38. If the world population predictions come to fruition, the country of India will overtake China as the more populated country in the world around the year 2040.
   a. more populated
   b. more population
   c. most populated
   d. most population
   e. more populous

Section 2, Essay Writing

Carefully read the essay topic that follows. Plan and write an essay that addresses all points in the topic. Make sure that your essay is well organized and that you support your central argument with concrete examples. Allow 30 minutes for your essay.

Parents and school board members have become increasingly concerned about the use of the Internet in school. Many people report that students have either purposely visited or inadvertently been exposed to websites that display text and images that are inappropriate for teenagers. These people want to set up a school Intranet that would allow access to only a few preapproved websites. Opponents of this idea state that this is censorship and does not give students enough access to valuable information on the Internet.

In your opinion, should the school create an Intranet that would limit the websites students could visit, or do you think this is censorship that would deny students access to valuable information?

In your essay, take a position on this question. You may write about either of the two points of view given, or you may present a different point of view on the topic. Use specific reasons and examples to support your position.

Answers

Skills Test in Reading

1. b. The author's chief argument is that, despite the public perception, sharks are not especially dangerous to humans. If only 1% of shark species were dangerous to humans, that would strengthen the argument. The statements about sharks in choices **a** and **d** are not relevant to the author's argument, so are not correct. The statement in choice **c** provides a potential way to avoid a shark attack, but it does nothing to either weaken or strengthen the author's argument. The statement in choice **e**, however, would make sharks seem more dangerous to people, thereby weakening the author's argument. Choice **e** is therefore incorrect.

2. e. The author explains throughout the second paragraph that fatal shark attacks are exceedingly rare, then refers to the fear of them as *groundless*, which would mean without support or *unwarranted*. Because no genuine reason is provided for the fear, choices **a** and **d** are not correct. Sharks may be *aquatic* or *terrifying*, but that is not the meaning of the word *groundless* as it appears in the passage, so choices **b** and **c** are incorrect as well.

3. a. The author describes the shark as *massive, swift*, and *impressive*, then refers to it as *one of the planet's most remarkable creatures*. Therefore, he or she is treating the shark with reverence (choice **a**). The author explains that the fear is largely unwarranted, so choices **b** and **d** are not correct. The author has a strong positive opinion about sharks, so the attitude would not be best described as *ambivalent*, choice **c.** The author's attitude toward sharks would not be best described as *cautionary*, though perhaps that would describe his or her attitude toward the protection of sharks; therefore, choice **e** is not the best answer.

4. c. The first paragraph of the passage describes the physical characteristics of the shark, such as its size and speed and its jaws. The passage depicts the shark as a dangerous animal, but the second paragraph then defends the shark as a relatively harmless creature. Therefore, the sentence in choice **c** best describes the organization of the passage. Common perceptions of the shark are not supported in the second paragraph, nor are features of the shark described in further detail, so choices **a** and **e** could not be correct. While the passage briefly mentions the history of the animal, its evolution and present-day status is not the focus of the organization of the passage, thus making choice **b** incorrect. The organization describes more of the shark's hazardous characteristics before attempting to defray the dangers, so choice **d** is backward and cannot be correct either.

5. e. The author points out that many people are scared of sharks even though sharks do not pose a great danger to them. Similarly, many people fear snakes, even though most snakes are not dangerous. Therefore, choice **e** represents the most similar relationship that sharks share with humans. Killer whales may share some attributes as sharks, but they do not have a similar relationship to humans, so choice **a** is not correct. People do not fear frogs or caterpillars, making choices **b** and **c** incorrect. Deer may fear people, but people do not have an unnatural fear of deer, so choice **d** is not the best choice.

6. d. The detail that best supports the idea of a conservation bill would show that the shark's population numbers are declining; this is best shown in choice **d**. The details listed in choices **b** and **c** describe the shark in some way but do not directly support the idea for the protection of the shark; therefore, these choices cannot be correct. The details in choices **a** and **e** might provide a reason to not want to kill sharks, but they do not provide great support to show that sharks are deserving of our protection.

7. e. An opinion cannot be supported by concrete evidence and represents the author's personal beliefs. When the author suggests that people should *be fearful of losing one of the planet's most remarkable creatures,* he or she is providing an opinion. Each of the other sentences listed in answer choices **a, b, c,** and **d** contain facts because they can be supported with concrete evidence. Even though an estimate, such as the one in choice **d,** cannot be verified precisely, the estimate itself can still be a fact.

8. b. According to the graph, the zoo has 6 female lions and 6 female cheetahs; therefore, the conclusion in choice **b** can be supported. The conclusions in choices **a** and **c** cannot be proven or disproven by the data in the graph because the graph does not represent an animal's popularity or the difficulty of keeping a particular big cat in captivity. The graph shows that the zoo has 8 female leopards and only 4 male leopards, so choice **d** is incorrect. While the statement in choice **e** may seem correct, it cannot be concluded from the information in the graph; in fact, the cheetah is not as fast as many birds. Regardless, choice **e** cannot be supported, so it cannot be correct.

9. e. The passage begins with the first European explorer to reach New Zealand and then describes some of the important milestones in the country's history until its formation of a capital in 1840. Because the information is given in order of the year the events occurred, the passage is in chronological order. The information is not provided in terms of most important to least important, so choice **a** is not correct. The passage also does not use a compare/contrast or problem/solution structure, so choices **b** and **c** are not correct. A classification structure would organize the passage into specific categories; because the passage does not do this, choice **d** is incorrect.

10. e. Because the passage describes the initial populating of New Zealand through the formation of its first capital, it focuses mostly on the early history of the country, choice **e**. While it describes the exploration, it does not focus primarily on why and how the exploring was done, making choice **a** incorrect. The passage mentions Abel Tasman and James Cook as important explorers of New Zealand, but the passage is mostly about New Zealand itself and not any specific explorer; therefore, choice **b** is not the correct answer. While the passage mentions the initial European discovery of New Zealand and its first capital, those are only details that support the primary purpose. Therefore, choices **c** and **d** are also not correct.

11. a. The first sentence of the passage states that the Maori people populated New Zealand more than 700 years before Abel Tasman visited New Zealand. Therefore, the Maoris must have been living in New Zealand before A.D. 1000. The passage states that the Dutch did not seek to return to New Zealand, but it did not suggest why, meaning that the statement in choice **b** cannot be concluded with certainty. While James Cook treated the Maoris with respect and visited New Zealand on a scientific voyage, there is no evidence to support the statements in either choice **c** or choice **d** with absolute certainty. Likewise, while Russell was the New Zealand capital in 1840, it cannot be concluded from the passage that it is still the country's capital. In fact, Wellington is the current capital, so choice **e** is incorrect.

12. c. According to the passage, the Second Confiscation Act passed by Congress in 1862 *provided the desired signal* (lines 10 and 11), encouraging him to pursue his plan of a proclamation. Abolitionists supported the proclamation, so choice **a** is incorrect. Some members of Lincoln's cabinet objected to it, so choice **b** is incorrect. The Secretary of War correctly interpreted the Proclamation as a military measure, so choice **d** is not correct. There is no specific support in the passage that suggests the proclamation had numerous grammatical errors, making choice **e** incorrect as well.

13. b. The speechless reaction of Secretaries Seward and Welles implies that they were surprised by the plan and were concerned about its political and military consequences. The purpose of the reaction is not to describe Lincoln as lacking political acumen or to show the advisors as incompetent, making choices **a** and **c** incorrect. There is no support in the passage to show that Seward and Welles wanted Lincoln to free all slaves at once, **d**, or that most members of Lincoln's administration were abolitionists, choice **e**.

14. c. One meaning of *qualified* is fitted by training or experience for a given purpose ("he is qualified for the job"). Another meaning is having complied with specific requirements ("she qualified for the marathon"). In this context, *qualified* means limited or modified in some way. The words in answer choices **a**, **b**, **d**, and **e** do not accurately describe the meaning of the word as it appears in the passage.

15. a. The author calls the Emancipation Proclamation the *crowning achievement* (line 43) of Lincoln's administration. Therefore, it can be concluded that the author appreciates the issuing of the Emancipation Proclamation. Each of the other answer choices contain some negative or non-positive attitude; because the author is clearly in support of the issuing, choices **b**, **c**, **d**, and **e** cannot be correct.

16. c. The word *conversely* is being used to contrast Montgomery Blair's disapproval of the proclamation with Secretary of War Edwin M. Stanton's support. It is the only word or phrase among those listed in the answer choices that helps show that there were some people who were against Lincoln's proposed proclamation. Therefore, choices **a**, **b**, **d**, and **e** are not correct.

17. b. The passage mentions that more research is needed to try to protect the northern spotted owl, but the research itself is not a direct threat to the owl. Forest fires are not mentioned explicitly in the passage as a threat to the northern spotted owl, but the passage does mention that much of the owl's habitat has been lost to logging and natural disasters—and forest fires are a natural disaster. Therefore, choices **a** and **c** are incorrect. Climate change and barred owls are mentioned explicitly as threats to the northern spotted owl, so choices **d** and **e** are incorrect as well.

18. e. The passage contains many facts that can be proven. The final sentence of the passage, however, includes a sentence that cannot be proven; that sentence is an opinion, making choice **e** correct and choices **a**, **b**, **c**, and **d** incorrect.

19. d. When it appears in the context of the passage, the phrase *Now, though* is used to describe an additional threat to the northern spotted owl, despite the protection from a 1991 law. This contrast means that choice **d** demonstrates the most likely purpose. The phrase is not used to contrast opinions with facts, reverse or question the government bill, or compare different threats, so choices **a**, **b**, **c**, and **e** are not correct.

20. b. The crux of the passage is about the many threats that the northern spotted owl faces, and the need for the protection of the species is stated clearly in the final sentence of the passage. The sentence in choice **b**, therefore, provides the best summary. The sentences in choices **a**, **c**, and **d** all provide support for the summary. The sentence in choice **e** is too general to summarize the passage; it is not just about the owl being endangered but that it faces many threats and should be protected. Therefore, choice **e** is not the best answer.

21. d. The main idea of the passage is that the northern spotted owl faces many threats and should be protected. The sentence from the passage in choice **d** shows that scientists are trying to monitor the owls' nests; this alone does not support the main idea. The sentences listed in choices **a**, **b**, **c**, and **e** all list more specific ways that the northern spotted owl faces significant threats; as a result, they cannot be correct answer choices.

22. b. By enlarging and expanding the national park system, which protects land from development, Theodore Roosevelt was indeed responsible for the conservation of large amounts of land. There is nothing in the statement to suggest that Theodore Roosevelt established the U.S. national park system, only that he enlarged and expanded it; therefore, choice **a** is not correct. Roosevelt was a hunter, but it cannot be concluded that he killed some of the largest animals on the continent or that his hunting interfered with his job as president, making choices **c** and **d** incorrect. While Roosevelt is called a pioneer of the twentieth-century environmental movement, the statement does not suggest that he initiated any climate change legislature; climate change was likely not a concern during his presidency, and choice **e** is incorrect.

23. d. The first paragraph of this short passage deals with the symptoms of sleep deprivation, and the second paragraph discusses the dangers of not getting enough sleep. Choices **b** and **e** are too specific to be the passage's primary purpose. Choices **a** and **c** are not supported by the passage.

24. a. The image of *burning the candle at both ends* connotes a state of working hard without adequate rest. While people with an ardent desire to achieve may burn the candle at both ends, the expression itself does not mean an ardent desire, making choice **b** incorrect. The definitions of the term in choices **c**, **d**, and **e** also do not accurately describe the expression.

25. b. The word *norm* most nearly means custom or normal. Therefore, choice **b** would result in the most minimal change of meaning. Because the *norm* is a normal, the words in choices **a** and **d** have the opposite meaning and cannot be correct. While sleep deprivation is dangerous, the word in choice **c** does not share a similar meaning as *norm*. Similarly, abnormal sleepiness is not likely *ideal*, so choice **e** is incorrect as well.

26. d. The passage describes the introduction of British cotton technology to America, specifically to New England. It does not account for the decline of rural America, contrast political views, or argue in support of industrial development; therefore, choices **a**, **b**, and **e** are not correct. While it does mention British laws forbidding the export of industrial machinery (choice **c**), that is only a supporting detail in the passage.

27. b. The passage mentions the Houses of Industry in line 9 as an example of the association of cloth manufacturing with *relief of the poor* (lines 8–9). It is not meant to illustrate an early social welfare program (choice **a**), a first textile factory (choice **d**), or the utilization of technological advances in England (choice **e**). There was no stated preference for the work of individual artisans in the passage, so choice **c** is not supported either.

28. b. The *mounting conflict between the colonies and England* described in the very first sentence of the passage suggests that America had political and/or economic reasons for developing its own textile industry. It is not suggested in the passage that the early American manufacturing was symbolically undemocratic, environmentally destructive, or spiritually corrosive, so choices **c**, **d**, and **e** are not correct. While there were certainly beneficial results from the manufacturing, it cannot be inferred that there were no negative effects, thus making choice **a** incorrect.

29. a. The description of Samuel Slater's immigration to America shows the deceptive measures necessary to evade British export laws and introduce cotton technology to the colonies. Slater posed as a farmer in order to immigrate to America and *committed to memory* the cotton technology he learned in an English factory. The justification for including this information was not primarily to show the attraction of farming opportunities in the American colonies or explain the details of British manufacturing technologies, so choices **b** and **c** are incorrect. And because it was the British who were attempting to prevent the knowledge from being shared with the colonies, choices **d** and **e** are also incorrect.

30. a. The author does not offer Slater's personal viewpoint on child labor, only the fact that Slater hired nine children between the ages of seven and twelve to work in his Rhode Island mill. Therefore, he used the labor as an available workforce. Because there is no opinion given, it cannot be inferred that Slater identified the labor as *evil*, *unpleasant*, *immoral*, or *superior*, making choices **b**, **c**, **d**, and **e** incorrect.

31. c. According to the passage, the knowledge and training acquired in Slater's mill of a generation of millwrights and textile workers provided the catalyst for the spread of cotton mills in New England. Therefore, it was the expertise of the workforce, choice **c**. It was not the machine itself, choice **a**, or child laborers, choice **d**. There is no support in the passage that the spread of American textile mills was a result of a decline in the ideal of the American family or the support of British manufacturers, so choices **b** and **e** are incorrect.

32. e. One meaning of *to model* is to display by means of wearing, using, or posing. In this context, *to model* means to construct or *fashion* after a pattern. The words in the other choices do not have as close a meaning, so choices **a**, **b**, **c**, and **d** are incorrect.

33. b. The general organization of the passage compares and contrasts two unique traditions in Spain, making choice **b** the best answer. A classification structure would organize the passage by specific categories; because the passage does not classify any content into specific categories, choice **a** is not correct. No problem is given, so choice **c** is not the best choice. The passage is not arranged in order of when events happened, so choices **d** and **e** cannot be correct.

34. c. The author says that the running of the bulls is *not innocuous* and then describes some details that would paint a picture of the festival as dangerous. Therefore, the definition of the word would mean *harmless*, making choice **c** correct. For that reason, choices **a** and **e** must be incorrect. The words in choices **b** and **d** do not reflect the meaning of the word.

35. e. The first part of the passage describes the running of the bulls, including the number of injuries and fatalities from it. The second part describes La Tomatina; by referring to the fact that it has had no casualties, its safety is contrasted with that of the running of the bulls. No personal experiences are provided, so choice **a** is not correct. Similarly, the passage is not concerned about the misuse of food products, so choice **b** is not correct. Because the sentence serves to contrast two festivals, choices **c** and **d** are not as good as choice **e** to describe the author's most likely reasoning.

36. a. The author defines an ecosystem and then uses the last few sentences of the passage describing the main idea: that our actions can have a great impact on our ecosystems and that we must protect our ecosystems. The sentences in choices **b**, **c**, and **e** are details that support the main idea. The sentence in choice **d** adds to the definition of an ecosystem but does not define the main idea of the entire passage.

37. b. The author describes several relationships within an ecosystem, covering everything from water and soil to large animals. Therefore, the detail that describes the activities within an ecosystem refers to all the members. Because it involves all members, choices **a**, **c**, and **d** are incorrect. Choice **e** is not correct because other relationships exist within an ecosystem other than entities which either destroy or preserve.

38. b. The passage states in the first sentence that an ecosystem is a grouping of animals and plants. While they may exist in a specific region, an ecosystem is also the interactions among all organisms in a given habitat, making choice **a** incorrect. Choice **c** is not correct because an ecosystem involves plants as well as animals. An ecosystem is not necessarily protected nor threatened, so choices **d** and **e** are not correct.

39. e. Because a manned trip to Mars would take a long time, it would expose astronauts to extreme isolation. The size of the spacecraft would also limit the available supplies. Because man had not yet stepped foot on another planet, it's fair to say that the astronauts would not know entirely what to expect. A luxury cruise or a jet flight would both provide its passengers with comfort and/or expediency, neither of which was provided during the early European expeditions to the Americas; therefore, choices **a** and **d** are not correct. A solo skydive, choice **b**, may be similarly scary, but it would not take a considerable amount of time and is therefore not so similar to the early European expeditions to the Americas. Choice **c** is incorrect as well; an unmanned probe would also not reflect the early European expeditions to the Americas because there would be no explorer to undergo the stress and difficulties of the journey.

40. a. The graph shows that each year from 2006 to 2009 Hickory Hills Farm produced fewer non-organic eggs and more organic eggs. However, the number of non-organic eggs being produced each year is declining very steeply each year. The number of organic eggs produced each year only goes up by a little each year. Therefore, the year in which the farm produced the most eggs was 2006 (choice **a**). The conclusion in choice **d** may be correct based on the trend of the data in the graph, but it cannot be known for certain. The conclusions in choices **b**, **c**, and **e** may also be correct but are not supported by the data in the graph.

The following is a chart of the different skills assessed by the questions in this practice PPST; you can use it to identify your strengths and weaknesses in this subject to better focus your study.

READING SKILLS STUDY CHART FOR PRACTICE EXAM 4	
LITERAL COMPREHENSION SKILLS	**QUESTIONS**
Main Ideas	10, 20, 23, 26, 36
Supporting Ideas	6, 21, 37
Organization	4, 9, 16, 19, 33
Vocabulary in Context	2, 14, 25, 32, 34
CRITICAL AND INFERENTIAL COMPREHENSION SKILLS	
Evaluation	1, 7, 13, 18, 24, 27, 29, 31, 35
Inferential Reasoning	3, 8, 12, 15, 17, 22, 28, 30, 38, 40
Generalization	5, 11, 39

Skills Test in Mathematics

1. d. Calculate 8% of $16.25 by turning 8% into a decimal (dividing 8 by 100) and then multiplying 0.08 by $16.25 (the word *of* in math stands for multiplication). (0.08)($16.25) = $1.30 is the amount of tax Joel must pay (incorrect answer choice **a**). Add the sales tax to the original price to get $17.55. Choice **b** accidentally subtracts the sales tax from the original price instead of adding it. Choice **c** adds just $0.80 to the original price instead of finding 8% of the original price. Choice **e** adds just $0.08 to the original price instead of finding 8% of the original price.

2. e. Because all the categories of cable in the chart support data "up to" a transmission of 4, 16, 20, and 100 megabytes per second, Athena needs to round the speed that she needs up to the closest benchmark of 4, 16, 20, or 100 to see which cable she needs to buy. The 100 feet of cable that must send 65 megabytes per second will only be supported by the cable that sends up to 100 megabytes per second: 100 feet × $3 per foot = $300.00. The 30 feet of cable that must send at 18 megabytes per second will only be supported by the cable that sends up to 20 megabytes

per second: 30 feet × $2.50 per foot = $75.00. The 10 feet of cable that must send at 12 megabytes per second will only be supported by the cable that sends up to 16 megabytes per second: 10 feet × $1.75 per foot = $17.50. The sum of all these is $392.50. Answer **b** uses the category that is one cheaper for each length of cable: 100 × $2.50 + 30 × $1.75 + 10 × $1.00 = $312.50. Choice **d** incorrectly adds all the lengths of cable together first and then multiplies that by the sum of the costs of each category: (100 + 30 + 10) × ($3.00 + $2.50 + $1.75) = $1,015.00. Choice **c** uses the correct category for the first two lengths of cable, but uses category 2 cable for the last 10 feet. Choice **a** makes a similar mistake.

3. b. The surface area of a cube is the area of each face ($x \times x$) times 6. The original cube has a side length of x, so after it is tripled, the side length will by $3x$. A cube with a side length of $3x$ will have six faces that each have an area of $9x^2$ ($3x \times 3x = 9x^2$). This is the incomplete and incorrect answer choice **a**. The surface area will be $6(9x^2)$ cm^2 = $54x^2$ cm^2. Although it is tempting to just triple $6x^2$ cm^2 to $18x^2$ cm^2 (the incorrect choice **c**), that will not work because it does not take into consideration that *each* side length has tripled. Choice **d** incorrectly increases the side length by just 2 cm with addition instead of doubling every side with multiplication. Choice **e** incorrectly cubes the original surface area of $6x^2$ to become $216x^6$.

4. b. For this question is it essential to line up the decimal points when adding. To make this easiest, write everything out in dollars and cents. For example, write twelve dollars as $12.00 and a quarter as $0.25. The four mangos at $1.50 each will cost $6.00 because $4 \times \$1.50 = \$6$. Now to find the sum, stack the numbers so that all their decimals are directly lined up over each other. The total cost of the groceries is $24.10 (incomplete and incorrect answer **a**). To find Jean Marie's change from paying with a $50 bill, subtract $24.10 from $50.00 to get $25.90. Choice **c** incorrectly subtracts $24.10 from $50.00, by subtracting $24 from $50 and then just tacking on the leftover ten cents to get $26.10. Choice **d** incorrectly adds the 25-cent piece of candy as $25.00 instead of as $0.25. This makes the total cost $44.35 and Jean Marie's change $5.65. Choice **e** would be correct if only *one* mango at $1.50 is used, since then the groceries would add up to $19.60.

5. a. Stem-and-leaf plots are visual ways of showing a larger set of data points. The numbers in the stem column represent the tens place, and the numbers in the leaf column each represent a ones digit to go with the tens digit in that row. Therefore, the top row of this stem-and-leaf plot represents the three data points 98, 95, and 92. Count all the entries in the leaf column to see how many data points are being displayed. There are 17 data points represented here. Three of them are in the 90s and six of them are above 80, so 9 out of the 17 points are greater than 80. Because half of 17 is 8.5 and there are 9 grades greater than 80, that means that more than 50% of the class scored above an 80, so choice **a** is correct. Choice **b** is incorrect because the highest score was actually a 98. Choice **c** is incorrect since the median of 17 data points will be the 9th data point, which in this case is 87. Choice **d** is incorrect since the range is from 52 to 98. Choice **e** is incorrect since there are three modes in this data set: 87, 80, and 88.

6. c. To find the decimal equivalent of a fraction, first change it to decimal form by dividing the numerator by the denominator: $1 \div 9 = 0.1111$. To change this decimal into a percentage, multiply 0.1111 by 100, which is the same as moving the decimal point two spaces to the right. This results in 11.11%. Choice **a** mistakes $\frac{1}{9}$ as 9%. Choice **b** mistakes $\frac{1}{9}$ as 9.19%. Choice **d** rounds $\frac{1}{9}$ to $\frac{1}{10}$, which is 10%. Choice **e** mistakes $\frac{1}{9}$ as being the same as 1.9%.

7. d. First determine what $1\frac{1}{2}$ of Ken's normal pay is: $\frac{1}{2}$ of Ken's regular pay is \$6.25, which when added to his regular pay equals a $1\frac{1}{2}$ rate of \$18.75. Because Ken's bonus pay is $1\frac{1}{2}$ times his regular pay for his first 4 hours, during those 4 hours he will earn $4 \times \$18.75 = \$75.00$ (the incomplete and incorrect answer choice **a**). For the next 2 hours Ken would earn 2 times his standard pay, which is $2 \times \$12.50 = \$25.00$ per hour. Therefore for those extra two hours Ken will earn $2 \times \$25.00 = \$50.00$. Adding his pay for the first 4 hours worked plus the next 2 hours shows that Ken's pay for 6 hours on a Saturday would be: $\$75.00 + \$50.00 = \$125.00$. Choice **c** incorrectly multiplies all 6 of Ken's hours by his $1\frac{1}{2}$ pay rate of \$18.75/hour. Choice **e** incorrectly multiplies all 6 of Ken's hours by his double pay rate of \$25.00/hour.

8. e. To find the probability of an event happening, the number of desired events must be put over the total number of events. In this case, there are 30 "desired events" ($16 + 8 + 6 = 30$ KCRW tickets) and 200 total events (total number of tickets released). $\frac{30}{200}$ reduces to $\frac{3}{20}$. Choice **a** reflects the probability of only 20 tickets given away ($\frac{20}{200} = \frac{1}{10}$). Choice **b** considers only the first 16 tickets given away ($\frac{16}{200} = \frac{2}{25}$). Choice **c** gives the probability that a person does *not* have a free ticket from KCRW, since 170 tickets were not given away by KCRW and $\frac{170}{200} = \frac{17}{20}$. Choice **d** gives the probability given that KCRW gave away 12 free tickets ($\frac{12}{200} = \frac{3}{50}$), which is not correct.

9. b. Because this is an isosceles right triangle, you know that the vertex angle must be 90 degrees (a triangle's interior angles sum to 180 degrees and therefore cannot have two base angles measuring 90 degrees each). The 90-degree vertex angle is opposite the 8-inch base. The two legs of the triangle will be congruent (since it is an isosceles triangle). Because this is a right triangle, you can use the Pythagorean theorem. When using $a^2 + b^2 = c^2$, a and b are the legs and c is the hypotenuse (which in this case is the base of 8). Substitute 8 in for the hypotenuse, and since each leg is the same length, let each leg be equal to a:

$$a^2 + a^2 = 8^2$$
$$2a^2 = 64$$
$$a^2 = 64 \div 2$$
$$a^2 = 32$$
$$a = \sqrt{32} \text{ (incorrect choice } \mathbf{a})$$

So the sum of both legs will be $2\sqrt{32}$. Choice **c** forgets to take the square root of $a^2 = 32$ and also forgets to double it to get the sum of *both* legs. Choice **d** forgets to take the square root of $a^2 = 32$ and then doubles it to get the sum of both legs. Choice **e** mistakes an isosceles triangle for an equilateral triangle and assumes that the two legs each measure 8 inches.

10. d. In order to answer this question, find the answer whose square is the closest to 181. $14^2 = 196$ and $13^2 = 169$. 13^2 is only 12 away from 181, and 14^2 is 15 away from 181; therefore, 13 is a better estimate of $\sqrt{181}$. The answers in choices **a**, **b**, and **c** all have squares that are very far from 181: 81, 121, and 144.

11. e. All the girls ate a fraction of the *original* total of jellybeans, so each fraction gets multiplied by x: Marina ate $\frac{1}{12}$ of 360, which is $360 \times \frac{1}{12} = 30$; Christina ate $\frac{1}{4}$ of 360, which is $360 \times \frac{1}{4} = 90$; Athena ate $\frac{1}{5}$ of 360, which is $360 \times \frac{1}{5} = 72$; and Jade ate $\frac{1}{8}$ of 360, which is $360 \times \frac{1}{8} = 45$. Together they all ate 237 jellybeans, so there were 123 left. Choice **a** is incorrect because 273 is the total amount eaten, not the total amount left. Choice **b** is the number of jellybeans left *before* Jade came to eat $\frac{1}{8}$ of the original number of jellybeans. Choice **d** is the number of jellybeans that would be left if Jade ate $\frac{1}{6}$ and not $\frac{1}{8}$ of the original number of jellybeans.

12. e. First, round the Full-Time Psychology Faculty from 2002–2003 to the nearest hundred: 1,588 becomes 1,600. Next, round the percentage of females for that timeframe to the nearest ten: 97.83% becomes 100%. Do the same for the 2006–2007 timeframe: 1,533 becomes 1,500 and 30.40% becomes 30%. Now take 100% of 1,600 : $1.00 \times 1,600 = 1,600$. Next take 30% of 1,500: $0.30 \times 1,500 = 450$. Since $1,600 - 450 = 1,150$, there were approximately 1,150 more female Full-Time Psychology Faculty in 2002–2003 than there were from 2006–2007. Choice **d** does the percentages correctly but there is an error in the subtraction: $1,600 - 450$ does not equal 1,250. Choice **c** accidentally rounds 1,150 to the nearest hundred, but the question did not ask for that. Choice **b** rounds the 1,533 female faculty in 2006–2007 to 1,600 instead of to 1,500, calculating that 30% of 1,600 is 480 and the increase is $1,600 - 480 = 1,120$. Choice **a** makes the same mistake as in letter **b**, then also incorrectly subtracts 480 from 1,600.

13. c. Calculate the mean by adding up the data points for the five different towns and then divide that sum by 5: $(10 + 10 + 5 + 5 + 10) \div 5 = 40 \div 5 = 8$. Choice **a** is not the mean, but the minimum. Choice **b** is just the average of either 5 and 10 inches, or of two towns of 5 inches and two towns of 10 inches. Choice **d** is not any of the critical measures of center. Choice **e** is not the mean, but the maximum.

14. a. Since there are 100 cm in 1 meter, the length of the room is $720 \div 100 = 7.2$ m and the width of the room is $450 \div 100 = 4.5$ m. The area of the rectangular room is length $\times$ width, which is $7.2 \times 4.5 = 32.4$ m^2. Since each square meter costs \$12, $\$12 \times 32.4$ m^2 = \$388.80, which rounds up to \$389.00. Choice **b** mistakes that there are only 50 centimeters in a meter, and only divides 720 and 450 each by 50 before calculating the area of the room. Choice **c** multiplies 720×450 and then divides it by 100, but each dimension needed to be divided by 100 *before* multiplying them to find the area. By that mistake, it seems like the area is 3,240 m^2. Incorrect choice **d** multiplies the incorrect area in answer choice **c** by \$12.00 to get \$38,880.00. Choice **e** is the *perimeter* of 23.4 meters multiplied by \$12.00 per square meter, but the *area* needs to be multiplied by the price per square meter.

15. c. There are 21 days in 3 weeks and the median work shift will be the central, or eleventh, term when the data points are listed out from least to greatest. When putting each day of Carol's hours in order of length, 4 hours is the eleventh term. Choice **a** is the mode, or piece of data that occurs most frequently in the data set. Choice **b** is the arithmetic mean of the data set, since all Carol's answers add up to 63, which when divided by the total number of days, 21, gives an average of 3 hours. Choice **d** ignores all the zeros (which must be used) and organizes the remaining 14 days in order, averaging the two middle terms, 4 and 5, to get 4.5. Choice **e** is the "middle" term in the table, since it is in the middle day (Wednesday) and the middle row (the second week), but it is not an official measure of the median.

16. d. The first fact to notice is that x is changing consistently, increasing by one each time. This means that if this is a linear equation (where x does not have an exponent), then the increases in y should also be consistent. Since y is consistently decreasing by 2 for each 1 increase in x, it is a linear function with a slope of -2. This rules out choices **a** and **e**. Even though they are true for the first coordinate pair $(-2,8)$, the other coordinate pairs do not satisfy these two equations. Choice **b** does not work for the first point since $8 \neq 2(-2) + 4$. Choice **c** works for the first point, but not for the second point, since $6 \neq 2(-1) + 4$. This leaves choice **d**, which does have a slope of -2 (the constant number next to the x is always the slope), and this equation holds true for all the coordinate pairs contained in the table.

17. b. Vertical angles are the non-adjacent angles that are formed when two lines intersect. Vertical angles are always congruent, or equal in measure. Angles 3 and 7 are vertical angles, so their measures are equal (and choice **d** is ruled out). Angles 4 and 8 are also vertical angles, so their measures are also equal. Because angles 4 and 7 are congruent, and angles 4 and 8 are congruent, angles 7 and 8 must be congruent (which rules out choice **e**). In the same way, because angles 4 and 7 are congruent and angles 3 and 7 are congruent, angles 3 and 4 must be congruent (ruling out choice **a**). Angles 3, 4, 7, and 8 are all congruent (ruling out choice **c**). Furthermore, because angles 3 and 4 are complementary (they add up to 90°) and angles 7 and 8 are also complementary, the four angles 3, 4, 7, and 8, each measure 45°. However, nothing is known about angles 1, 2, 5, and 6. Therefore, it cannot be stated that $\angle 2 = \angle 3$.

18. c. If there were 7 shows left and 5 were sitcoms, this means that only 2 of the shows could possibly be dramas and at least 1 of them had to have been canceled. Therefore choice **c** must be true. Choices **a** and **b** *may* be true, but there is no evidence to indicate either of these as facts: in addition to the 5 sitcoms, there could be 2 news-magazine shows left, 2 hour-long dramas left, or 1 news-magazine show and 1 hour-long drama. The fact that all the sitcoms remained does not necessarily mean that viewers prefer sitcoms (choice **d**). Instead, it could be that the sitcoms were well done and the hour-long dramas offered that season were poor in quality.

19. d. The expression is already given to calculate the number of cells based on the number of hours, so simply substitute 5 hours for h and compute by following PEMDAS, which indicates that the exponent must be calculated before the multiplication:
$$100 \cdot 3^{\frac{20}{5}} = 100 \cdot 3^4 = 100 \cdot 81 = 8{,}100$$
It is important to remember that $3^4 = 3 \times 3 \times 3 \times 3 = 81$ and not $3 \times 4 = 12$. Making that mistake would lead to incorrect answer choice **a**. If 3^4 was misconstrued as 3 *plus* 4, then one would get $100 \times 7 = 700$, which is answer choice **b**. Answer choice **c** would be obtained by ignoring h, performing 3^5 incorrectly to get 15, and then multiplying 15 by 100. It is a common error to perform the multiplication first, before the exponent, and in that case one would get 300^4, and an error from there could be to perform 300×4 incorrectly by adding an extra zero to get 12,000 (answer choice **e**).

20. d. The square root of a number is the number that can be multiplied by itself to get the original number. So the square root of 9 will be *both* 3 and −3 since $3 \times 3 = 9$ and $(-3) \times (-3) = 9$. Answer choice **c** is incomplete since it is missing −3. Choices **a** and **b** are not feasible since they contain the *square* of 9 and not the *square root*. Incorrect choice **e** is obtained by multiplying 9 by 4, a misinterpretation of "square root."

21. c. To find the probability of an event happening, the number of desired events must be put over the total number of events. In this case "desired" is not "desirable" since it is a bad thing to have fingerprints on the negatives, but "desired" means the object you are calculating the probability for. In this situation, there are 15 "desired events" (since the conclusion is 15 seconds) and 60 total events (total number of seconds in the commercial). Therefore, the probability that Derek's fingerprint is on the conclusion is $\frac{15}{60} = \frac{1}{4}$. Choice **a** is the probability that Derek's fingerprint is on the 5-second intro, since $\frac{5}{60} = \frac{1}{12}$. Choice **b** is the probability that Derek's fingerprint is *not* on the 15-second conclusion, since $\frac{45}{60} = \frac{3}{4}$. Choice **d** is the probability that Derek's fingerprint is on the 40-second endorsement, since $\frac{40}{60} = \frac{2}{3}$. Choice **e** is the probability that Derek's fingerprint is on the 40-second endorsement or 15-second conclusion since $\frac{55}{60} = \frac{11}{12}$.

22. e. The fastest way to compare each of these fractions is to turn them all into decimals. Since several of these are not rational numbers and do not terminate, begin by calculating each decimal to the hundredths place. If any of the fractions are the same value to the hundredths place, then you can go one more step and divide them to the thousandths place. Just dividing to the hundredths place yields: $17 \div 20 = 0.85$; $5 \div 7 = 0.71$; $3 \div 4 = 0.75$; $11 \div 14 = 0.78$; and $4 \div 5 = 0.80$. Therefore the correct order is $\frac{5}{7}, \frac{3}{4}, \frac{11}{14}, \frac{4}{5}, \frac{17}{20}$. Choice **a** is listed from greatest to least, not from *least* to *greatest*. Choice **b** has the numerators and *denominators* in increasing order. Choices **c** and **d** are in the wrong order without any correct pattern.

23. d. Because the triangle is being rotated around point A, point A' will stay the same. This fact narrows your choices down to **a** and **d**, because the other choices have a changed coordinate pair for point A'. Because the triangle is moving *counterclockwise* by 90 degrees, points B' and C' will be in Quadrant II. Line segment AB is 4 units long, so when segment AB is rotated from being horizontal to being vertical, point B' will be 4 vertical units above point A'. Therefore, the coordinates of point B' will be $(-2,2)$, so **d** is the only possible answer.

24. a. This is an example of indirect variation: as the number of gardeners increases, the time in hours decreases. With indirect variation, a proportion is used by setting a ratio of the independent variables equal to the dependent variables. It is essential to position the dependent information in the right place so that when the independent increases, the dependent will decrease. (In this case the gardeners are "independent" since *they* are determining how long the landscaping will take, and not vice versa.) The proportion of $\frac{4 \text{ gardeners}}{6 \text{ gardeners}} = \frac{new\ hours}{9 \text{ hours}}$ will work because the unknown hours will be fewer than the 9 hours it would take 4 painters to do the job. Cross-multiply to get $6(new\ hours) = 36$. Next, divide both sides by 6 to get *new hours* $= 6$. Choice **b** incorrectly assumes that since half as many gardeners are being added, the job will then take half the time of 9 hours. Choice **c** uses the incorrect proportion, $\frac{4 \text{ gardeners}}{6 \text{ gardeners}} = \frac{9 \text{ hours}}{(new\ hours)}$, which yields $72 = 4(new\ hours)$, and after dividing by 4, *new hours* then $= 18$. Choice **d** just subtracts two hours from the 9 hours it normally takes. Choice **e** divides 9 hours by 4 gardeners to get 2.25, and then subtracts this from the original 9 hours.

25. e. None of the given statements must be true. Starting with choice **a**, we do not know that z is positive; in the case that z is negative, then $2z$ will not be > 0, so choice **a** does not have to be true. Not all odd numbers are prime; for example, 15 is not a prime number. This rules out choice **b**. Since z is even, $3z$ will also always be even, so choice **c** is never true. Composite numbers are numbers that have more factors than just 1 and themselves (they are the opposite of prime numbers). 2 is not a composite number; it is the only even, prime number, which makes **d** false. Since none of these statements must be true, choice **e** is the answer.

26. d. In this equation it is not essential to figure out what P is. This is because, as long as you can determine Q with certainty, you will be able to determine the value of R. To find the value of Q, the fastest method is to look at the fourth row that reads 332 and determine what number times 83 would give you 332. Dividing 332 by 83 yields 4, so Q must be 4. Therefore, R must be 7. Choice **a** is the value of Q, not of R. Choices **b** and **e** could be mistaken as the answer since they are possible values for P when just looking at the right-most column of numbers. Choice **c** is not correct because that would mean that Q would have to equal 3, and 3×83 yields 249, which does not match the 332 in the second row of multiplication.

27. e. Condition 1 rules out answer choice **b** since $\angle A + \angle B = 180°$, instead of 90°. Condition 2 rules out answer choices **a** and **c** since $\angle B$ is not half of $\angle C$ in those two groupings. In choice **d**, $\angle C$ is 50 degrees more than $\angle A$, so it fails condition 3. In choice **e**, though, $\angle C$ is 30 degrees more than $\angle A$, so choice **e** is correct.

28. b. In order to consider the inequality $(\frac{3}{4})y + 6 \geq 3x$, it must first be algebraically manipulated so that it is in $y = mx + b$ form:

$$\frac{3}{4}y + 6 \geq 3x$$
$$\frac{3}{4}y \geq 3x - 6$$
$$4(\frac{3}{4}y) \geq 4(3x - 6)$$
$$3y \geq 12x - 24$$
$$y \geq 4x - 8$$

Since y is "greater than or equal to" the rest of the equation, the graph must be shaded above the line, and the line must be solid to represent that the points on the line are included in the solution. These requirements rule out answer choices **a** and **d**. The line $y = 4x - 8$ will have a y-intercept of -8 and a slope of positive 4. Choice **b** illustrates these properties and also has the correct shading, so this graph correctly represents the solution set for $(\frac{3}{4})y + 6 \geq 3x$.

29. b. First convert the mixed number $5\frac{1}{4}$ into an improper fraction. To do this, multiply the whole number 5 by the denominator 4 to get the product 20. Add 20 to the numerator 1 and put that quantity over the existing denominator of 4: $\frac{21}{4}$. Notice that we are increasing the size from 6 servings to 9 servings. Since this is $\frac{9}{6}$ larger than the size that the recipe calls for, we can multiply $\frac{9}{6}$ by $\frac{21}{4}$ cups of apples. First reduce $\frac{9}{6}$ to $\frac{3}{2}$ and then multiply straight across: $\frac{3}{2} \times \frac{21}{4} = \frac{63}{8}$. 8 divides into 63 7 times and has a remainder of 7, which goes over the existing denominator: $7\frac{7}{8}$. Choice **a** incorrectly translates $\frac{63}{8}$ to $7\frac{6}{8}$, which reduces to $7\frac{3}{4}$. Choice **c** just adds 3 cups (one cup for every additional serving) to the original recipe. Choice **e** cannot be correct since $10\frac{1}{2}$ cups doubles the apples needed for 6 people and would make enough for 12 people.

30. d. In short, let n = number of nickels, d = number of dimes, and $2d$ = number of quarters (since there are twice as many quarters as there are dimes). Multiply each coin's algebraic representation by the value for that coin: $n(0.05) + d(0.10) + 2d(0.25) = 8.15$. This will simplify to $0.05n + 0.10d + 0.50d$. Combine like terms to get $0.05n + 0.60d = 8.15$. Choice **a** ignores the quarters in the equation, only including the expressions for nickels and dimes. Choice **b** accidentally writes an equation with twice as many quarters as *nickels* instead of *dimes*: $n(0.05) + d(0.10) + 2n(0.25) = 0.55n + 0.10d = \$8.15$. Choice **c** accidentally represents the dimes as being twice the number of quarters, rather than the other way around: $n(0.05) + 2d(0.10) + d(0.25) = 0.05n + 0.45d = \$8.15$. Choice **e** combines the errors made in choices **b** and **c**.

31. c. This diagram contains three important concepts: straight angles, which are adjacent angles that together make a straight line and sum to 180°; vertical angles, which are the opposite non-adjacent and congruent angles that are formed when two lines cross; and a triangle, which has three interior angles that sum to 180°. First, using straight angles, you can ascertain that the adjacent angle to 135° that is contained in the triangle will be 180° − 35° = 45° (incorrect choice **a**). Next, use the sum of the interior angles of the triangle. 60° + 45° = 105° (incorrect choice **d**). Since the triangle contains a total of 180°, this leaves 75° for the third angle that is at the bottom of the triangle and is a vertical angle to angle B. Since vertical angles are congruent, the measure of angle B is 75°. Choices **b** and **e** could be misleading if the rules for the congruencies of angles with parallel lines and transversals are incorrectly applied. The horizontal lines are not marked as being parallel, and this cannot be assumed.

32. b. The mode is the piece of data that occurs most frequently in a data set. In this case the mode is 90 since that score occurs twice. Choice **a** could be mistaken as the median of the data set since it is the middle number in the table, but it is not the true median since the median is the middle number when the data is arranged from least to greatest. Choice **c** is the average, or arithmetic mean, of this data set. Choice **d** is the range since the data goes from 82 to 95 and has a spread of 13. Choice **e** is the maximum of this data set, not the mode.

33. d. If Anthony's score changes from an 82 to a 90, the mean will definitely change since the sum of the class's test scores will increase by 8, and when divided by 5, this will increase the average by a little more than a point. All the choices acknowledge this fact. The median of the original scores is 90 because when the scores are listed in order the middle score is 90: 82, 88, 90, 90, 95. When Anthony's 82 changes to a 90, the median is still 90: 88, 90, 90, 90, 95. This rules out choices **a**, **b**, and **c**. The range will change from 13 to 7, and the mode will still be 90; therefore, choice **d** is correct.

34. a. Replace $6R - 5B$ with the expressions given for R and B, and then distribute while remembering to also distribute the negative sign:

$$6(-3k) - 5(-2k - 4)$$
$$-18k - 5(-2k) - (-5)(4) \text{ (here the negative must move with the } -5 \text{ when it is distributed)}$$
$$-18k + 10k - (-20) = -8k + 20 \text{ (here the two negatives in front of the 20 cancel each other out)}$$

Choice **b** forgets that the distributed -5 must stay negative, which will cancel out the minus sign that is in front of the 4. Choice **c** incorrectly does the subtraction between $-18k + 10k$ to equal $8k$. Choice **d** incorrectly does the subtraction between $-18k + 10k$ *and* forgets to distribute the negative sign with the 4, resulting in 20 instead of -20. Choice **e** incorrectly does the subtraction between $-18k + 10k$ to equal $-18k$.

35. c. Two feet is approximately $\frac{2}{3}$ of a meter, so meters would be the best measure for Renatta's distance to school. Millimeters and centimeters are both too small to measure strides, and decimeters and kilometers are too large.

36. a. To solve this inequality, treat it as you would a regular algebraic equation, but be careful if you have to divide or multiply by a negative number. When inequalities are multiplied or divided by negative numbers, you must switch the direction of the inequality sign:

$$10 - 3(r - 4) > -14$$
$$10 - 3(r) - (-3)(4) > -14 \text{ (the negative must stay with the 3 when it is distributed)}$$
$$10 - 3r - (-12) > -14$$
$$10 - 3r + 12 > -14$$
$$-3r + 22 > -14$$
$$-3r > -36$$
$$r < 12 \text{ (here the inequality sign had to change directions since it was divided by } -3)$$

In choice **b**, the direction of the inequality sign is not changed when it is divided by a negative number. Choice **c** makes the same mistake and incorrectly divides -36 by -3 to get -12. Choice **d** switches the direction of the inequality sign correctly, but incorrectly distributes the -3 and ends up with $-3r > -12$, which is simplified to $r < 4$. Choice **e** makes the same mistake while distributing the -3 and also forgets to flip the direction of the inequality sign when dividing by a negative.

37. e. The shirt and pants together would regularly cost $120, and the discount will be 30% of that: $30\% \times \$120 = \$36$. The combined sale subtotal for the two items will therefore be $84, since $120 - \$36 = \$84$ (incorrect answer choice **b**). The 5% tax is calculated by multiplying 0.05 by $84, which gives $4.20. $4.20 + \$84 = \$88.20$. Choice **a** adds $68 to $52 to get $120, and then subtracts $30 instead of 30% from that price and forgets to consider the tax. Choice **c** uses the $90 incorrectly found in choice **a** and then adds $5 tax onto the $90, instead of 5% tax. Choice **d** uses the $90 incorrectly found in choice **a** and adds 5% tax to that to get $94.50.

38. d. Looking at the growth from 2006 to 2007, you can see that A Stone's Throw's annual sales increased from $30,000 to $36,000. This is an increase of $6,000; when this is compared to $30,000, $\frac{6}{30}$ is equal to 20%. Check this trend during the other years. 20% growth of $36,000 is approximately $7,000, and that would result in sales the following year of $43,000, which is what was reported. Looking at 2009, 20% growth of $52,000 is approximately $10,000, and that would result in sales the following year of $62,000, which is what was reported in 2010. Lastly, 20% growth of the $62,000 reported in 2010 is approximately $12,400, and that would result in sales the following year of $74,400, which is very close to what was reported. In 2011, 20% of the $75,000 sales would be $15,000, so a reasonable estimate based on the trend in the chart would be around $90,000. Choice **a** only adds on $6,000, which was the growth from 2006 to 2007, but sales are increasing by much more from 2011 to 2012. Choice **b** only adds on $9,000, which was the growth from 2008 to 2009, but sales are increasing more quickly from 2011 to 2012. Choice **c** still does not reflect the faster growth of sales: it only adds on $13,000, which was the same amount of growth from the year before. This is not reasonable, since no two years in the table have the same dollar amount of growth. Choice **e** is not reasonable because $97,000 in 2012 would be an increase of 30%, which is much greater than the increases of the other years shown.

39. a. Algebraic proportions are solved by cross-multiplication. Multiply diagonally and then get y alone on one side of the equation:
$$\frac{6}{-y-1} = \frac{10}{-2y-3},$$
$$(6)(-2y-3) = (10)(-y-1),$$
$$-12y - 18 = -10y - 10,$$
$$-2y - 18 = -10,$$
$$-2y = 8,$$
$$y = -4.$$
Choice **b** forgets the negative sign. Choice **c** does not perform opposite operations in the last step and combines -18 and -10 to get -28, ending with $-2y = -28$, so $y = 14$. Choice **d** makes the same mistake as choice **c**, but also makes an error with the final negative sign. Choice **e** combines the like terms on opposite sides of the equation without using opposite operations to move them, resulting in $-22y = -18$. This simplifies to $\frac{9}{11}$.

40. b. Since some pens don't write, some writing utensils don't write (so statement I is true). Since there are blue pens and since pens are writing utensils, some writing utensils are blue (so statement II is true). There is not enough information to support statement III since nothing is said about blue writing utensils, so choice **b** is the correct answer.

The following is a chart of the different skills assessed by the questions in this practice PPST; you can use it to identify your strengths and weaknesses in this subject to better focus your study.

MATH SKILLS STUDY CHART FOR PRACTICE EXAM 4

NUMBER AND OPERATIONS SKILLS	QUESTIONS
Order	22
Equivalence	6
Numeration and Place Value	4, 10
Number Properties	20, 25
Operation Properties	34
Computation	11, 19
Estimation	12
Ratio, Proportion, and Percent	1, 5, 29, 37
Numerical Reasoning	40
ALGEBRA SKILLS	
Equations and Inequalities	7, 36, 39
Algorithmic Thinking	26
Patterns	16, 24
Algebraic Representations	28, 30
Algebraic Reasoning	18
GEOMETRY AND MEASUREMENT	
Geometric Properties	9, 31
The xy-Coordinate Plane	23
Geometric Reasoning	17, 27
Systems of Measurement	14, 35
Measurement	3
DATA ANALYSIS AND PROBABILITY SKILLS	
Data Interpretation	2
Data Representation	—
Trends and Inferences	38
Measures of Center and Spread	13, 15, 32, 33
Probability	8, 21

Skills Test in Writing—Section 1, Part A

1. **d.** The verb in this sentence is not complete. In this case, *could* needs the helping verb *be*.

2. **c.** Add *'s* to indefinite pronouns that show ownership. In this sentence, *everyone's* should have an apostrophe for possession.

3. **d.** *Hard* can be an adjective or an adverb. In this case, if we used *hardly* to describe how she worked, it would sound like she didn't work much. *Hard* is an irregular adverb.

4. **e.** Because there are no grammatical, idiomatic, logical, or structural errors in this sentence, choice **e** is the best answer.

5. **a.** This sentence contains an incorrect word choice. *Incredible* is an adjective that means astonishing or beyond belief. In this sentence *incredible* should be replaced with *incredulous*, which means disbelieving.

6. **d.** This sentence contains an error in comparison. Choice **d** must match choice **c** in form. Choice **d** could be changed to *completing a triathlon.*

7. **e.** Because there are no grammatical, idiomatic, logical, or structural errors in this sentence, choice **e** is the best answer.

8. **a.** *Between* should be replaced with *among* because the sentence references three people. *Between* refers to an interval separating two things or people; *among* refers to being in the middle of several things or people.

9. **a.** *Principal* as a noun refers to the person in charge or a sum of interest-earning money. In this sentence the noun should be *principle*, meaning standard.

10. **a.** This sentence should use the subjunctive mood of the verb to express something that is imagined. The subjunctive form of *was* is *were.*

11. **c.** The comma in choice **c** should be placed before the quotation mark.

12. **d.** The second entity in a comparative sentence must match the form of the first entity. If we change choice **d** to *than making instant . . . ,* the two entities would match.

13. **d.** As punctuated now, this is a run-on sentence. However, if we change the comma in choice **d** to a colon or a semicolon, it is correct. We could also start a new sentence after *winter*.

14. **b.** This sentence contains a pronoun error. The noun *student* is singular, so the pronoun should be *his*. We know the student was a male because the sentence indicates that the mother was there to pick *him* up.

15. **d.** To take care of the error in parallel construction, we need to change choice **d** to something like *and to have his father come home. . . .*

16. **b.** *Good* should be replaced with *well* here because *well* is an adverb. Here, *well* describes how she *knew* (the verb).

17. **a.** The correct propositional idiom for choice **a** is *capable of.*

18. **a.** This sentence contains a word choice error. *Its* should be *it's*. *Its* shows possession; *it's* is a contraction for *it has*.

19. **e.** Because there are no grammatical, idiomatic, logical, or structural errors in this sentence, choice **e** is the best answer.

20. **e.** Because there are no grammatical, idiomatic, logical, or structural errors in this sentence, choice **e** is the best answer.

21. **d.** When a sentence compares two things, the form or part of speech of the two entities must match. In this sentence, *to be happy doing your job* must match the phrase after *than*. We could finish the sentence with *to be earning lots of money.*

Skills Test in Writing—Section 1, Part B

22. a. Compass directions, such as *north* and *east,* are not capitalized unless they refer to a specific geographic area. Choice **a** is the only choice in which both terms are lowercase.

23. b. This sentence contains double negatives: *no one* and *nowhere.* Choice **b** replaces *nowhere* with *anywhere* to correctly eliminate one of the negatives. Choices **a** and **e** are double negatives. Choices **c** and **d** do not make sense.

24. e. Choice **e** uses the correct past-tense verb form and the correct word choice for *their.* Choices **a, b,** and **c** incorrectly use *asking,* which doesn't match the parallel construction form of the other two entities in the list. Choice **d** uses *there,* which doesn't show ownership of the mail.

25. c. Choice **c** clarifies what the pronoun stands for, so the sentence makes sense. In choice **a,** it is unclear what the pronoun *it* represents. Choice **b** would be fine except that the verb is singular so we can't use a plural pronoun. Choices **d** and **e** indicate that Earth is destroying our resources, which doesn't make sense.

26. e. Choice **e** uses the correct possessive form of *men's,* uses the correct pronoun *his,* and uses the correct punctuation between two adjoining sentences (a semicolon). Choices **a, b, c,** and **d** are incorrect because the pronoun *their* does not agree with the noun it is replacing *(each). Each* is singular, so the pronoun must be *his* based on knowing that it is a men's team.

27. c. Choice **c** uses the correct adverb form *carefully* to describe how they were searching. It also uses the correct word choice for *through,* meaning in one side and out the other, and the correct spelling of *grains.*

28. a. Because *stimuli* is the plural form of *stimulus* and, therefore, requires plural verbs, choice **a** is the correct answer. Choices **b** and **c** do not use plural verbs consistently. Choices **d** and **e** change the plural *stimuli* to singular *stimulus* but then don't change the verbs to be consistently singular to agree with the subject *stimulus.*

29. b. Choices **a** and **d** create dangling modifiers because the introductory phrase does not match the noun that follows it. Choice **b** clarifies that *he* is repeating the experiment to improve his results. Choice **c** causes an incomplete sentence. Choice **d** changes the sentence's meaning.

30. e. To create parallel construction between the two parts of the sentence, choice **e** matches the verb *enraged* to the past-tense verb *cost.* Choices **a, b, c,** and **d** use *enraging,* which does not match the past-tense verb in the first part of the sentence.

31. b. Changing *spreading* to *spread* in choice **b** causes the sentence to become a command, which is a complete sentence. Choices **a, c, d,** and **e** create sentence fragments because they are subordinate clauses without a supporting independent clause.

32. a. *Vivid* is an adjective describing the description. Choice **a** uses the adjective form of *vivid* correctly and includes the apostrophe to show possession in *detectives'.* Choice **b** uses the adverb *vividly,* which is not correct in this sentence. Choices **c, d,** and **e** incorrectly create comparative forms of *vivid* by adding *more, most,* and various inaccurate endings.

33. b. To avoid double negatives, don't use more than one negative word in a sentence. In these choices, *neither, scarcely,* and *nobody* are negatives. All the choices except choice **b** use more than one negative, so they are all incorrect except for choice **b.**

34. e. Choice **e** makes the most sense. Because choices **a**, **b**, **c**, and **d** have misplaced modifiers, they are confusing. Choices **a**, **b**, and **d** sound like the dog has no shoes. Choice **c** is incomprehensible.

35. b. Only choices **b** and **d** use the correct adjective form of *delicious* to describe the noun *meal*. Choice **d** is incorrect because the meal is described as *who*, a pronoun used for living things, instead of *that*, a pronoun used for inanimate objects.

36. a. Choice **a** is correct because it uses the plural form *syllabi* instead of the singular form *syllabus* that choices **c**, **d**, and **e** incorrectly use. Also, choice **a** does not have a comma before *and*. A comma should not be used because *bought nine textbooks* is not an independent clause.

37. c. Choice **c** has an independent clause followed by a subordinate clause, so it is correct. Choices **a**, **b**, **d**, and **e** all have errors in subordination because they have two subordinate clauses with no independent clause.

38. c. Because all the countries in the world are being compared, we must use *most*, the superlative comparison term; so, choice **c** is correct. Choices **a**, **b**, and **e** are incorrect because they use *more*, which is used when comparing two items. Choice **d** is incorrect because *most population country* does not make sense.

The following is a chart of the different skills assessed by the questions in this practice PPST; you can use it to identify your strengths and weaknesses in this subject to better focus your study.

SKILLS TEST IN WRITING STUDY CHART FOR PRACTICE EXAM 4	
GRAMMATICAL RELATIONSHIP SKILLS	**QUESTIONS**
Identify Errors in Adjectives	27, 32, 35
Identify Errors in Adverbs	3, 16, 38
Identify Errors in Nouns	28, 36
Identify Errors in Pronouns	14, 25, 26
Identify Errors in Verbs	1, 10
STRUCTURAL RELATIONSHIP SKILLS	
Identify Errors in Comparison	6, 12, 21
Identify Errors in Coordination	34
Identify Errors in Correlation	17, 29, 31
Identify Errors in Negation	23, 33
Identify Errors in Parallelism	15, 24, 30
Identify Errors in Subordination	37
WORD CHOICE AND MECHANICS SKILLS	
Identify Errors in Word Choice	5, 8, 9, 18
Identify Errors in Mechanics	2, 11, 13, 22
Identify Sentences Free from Error	4, 7, 19, 20

Skills Test in Writing—Section 2, Essay Writing

Following are sample criteria for scoring a PPST essay.

A score "6" writer will:

- create an exceptional composition that appropriately addresses the audience and given task
- organize ideas effectively, include very strong supporting details, and use smooth transitions
- present a definitive, focused thesis and clearly support it throughout the composition
- include vivid details, clear examples, and strong supporting text to enhance the themes of the composition
- exhibit an exceptional level of skill in the usage of the English language and the capacity to employ an assortment of sentence structures
- build essentially error-free sentences that accurately convey intended meaning

A score "5" writer will:

- create a commendable composition that appropriately addresses the audience and given task
- organize ideas, include supporting details, and use smooth transitions
- present a thesis and support it throughout the composition
- include details, examples, and supporting text to enhance the themes of the composition
- generally exhibit a high level of skill in the usage of the English language and the capacity to employ an assortment of sentence structures
- build mostly error-free sentences that accurately convey intended meaning

A score "4" writer will:

- create a composition that satisfactorily addresses the audience and given task

- display satisfactory organization of ideas, include adequate supporting details, and generally use smooth transitions
- present a thesis and mostly support it throughout the composition
- include some details, examples, and supporting text that typically enhance most themes of the composition
- exhibit a competent level of skill in the usage of the English language and the general capacity to employ an assortment of sentence structures
- build sentences with several minor errors that generally do not confuse the intended meaning

A score "3" writer will:

- create an adequate composition that basically addresses the audience and given task
- display some organization of ideas, include some supporting details, and use mostly logical transitions
- present a somewhat underdeveloped thesis but attempt to support it throughout the composition
- display limited organization of ideas, have some inconsistent supporting details, and use few transitions
- exhibit an adequate level of skill in the usage of the English language and a basic capacity to employ an assortment of sentence structures
- build sentences with some minor and major errors that may obscure the intended meaning

A score "2" writer will:

- create a composition that restrictedly addresses the audience and given task
- display little organization of ideas, have inconsistent supporting details, and use very few transitions
- present an unclear or confusing thesis with little support throughout the composition

- include very few details, examples, and supporting text
- exhibit a less-than-adequate level of skill in the usage of the English language and a limited capacity to employ a basic assortment of sentence structures
- build sentences with a few major errors that may confuse the intended meaning

A score "1" writer will:

- create a composition that has a limited sense of the audience and given task
- display illogical organization of ideas, include confusing or no supporting details, and lack the ability to effectively use transitions
- present a minimal or unclear thesis
- include confusing or irrelevant details and examples, and little or no supporting text
- exhibit a limited level of skill in the usage of the English language and little or no capacity to employ basic sentence structure
- build sentences with many major errors that obscure or confuse the intended meaning

Sample 6 Essay

When the founding fathers of our Constitution included the Bill of Rights, they wanted to guarantee American citizens the right to free speech. Although freedom of speech is a valuable right of all American citizens, it has been abused by those who are manipulating the Constitution and its writers' intent so that they may gain fame, wealth, or attention. The only way to amend this problem is to impose censorship on these abusers. Unfortunately, the Internet has become a hotbed of abuse of free speech and needs to be censored, especially in our schools so that students are protected, education continues, and the authors of the offensive websites will eventually shut down their sites.

Use of the Internet in school has skyrocketed in past few years. It has opened a door to an aspect of education never dreamed of before. Students and teachers can use the Internet for research, demonstration, and to learn and practice new skills. However, these benefits can only occur when the Internet is used wisely. Of all the websites available through the World Wide Web, only a small percentage is really worthwhile. Many others simply use the Web to exercise their warped version of free speech. Students must be protected from this abuse. Some students who are curious purposely go to questionable websites. Once there they find it difficult to turn away. As humans, we have a natural inclination toward the bizarre and even salacious. That's why it's up to schools to protect their students from themselves—and their natural curiosity—by imposing restrictions on the Internet. Other students innocently type a word into a search engine and are directed to an offensive website. It is well known that certain violent and sexual images become imprinted on the brain and are nearly impossible to eradicate. Again, schools should protect their students from exposure to a potential long-lasting horror.

Another reason schools should have tight control over the Internet is to ensure that education continues uninterrupted. It's too easy to become sidetracked by intriguing, but unhealthy, websites and games. Yes, people should exercise some self-control, but if the school is in the business of education, it should make sure that all its accoutrements enhance education and do not distract from it. It's a waste of time and energy for school administrators to try to hunt down Internet abusers. That time and energy can be saved if the school has only an Intranet with preapproved sites. Schools should be educating students, not policing them.

Finally, if more schools make the decision to curb Internet access, maybe the people who create these offensive sites will be shut down. Most of these people make money off advertising on their Web sites. They promise advertisers that many people view their Web sites. If a large percentage of computer users were suddenly not included in that calculation, maybe these abusers would find better uses of their time and talents.

An Intranet is a great solution to the problem of Internet abuse. It allows students quick and easy access to preapproved, educational material. But it protects students from people who do not really understand the idea behind freedom of speech. "Censorship" is not a dirty word; it is a way to ensure that people do not abuse the right of free speech and make life more difficult for others.

Sample 4 Essay

Censorship is when anything that is considered offensive or harmful is limited so that people cannot have access to it. For some people that includes many things from realistic video games to certain types of music. I think censorship is not a good idea in America because that's part of what we fought for— freedom. Many people think the Internet should be under censorship, but I
don't agree.

Because it was invented, the Internet has been a great thing for many people. I enjoy doing research for school on it. There are many websites that have great information on them. I especially like to go on websites that deal with science and health. But some people think the Internet should be censored. They think students will go on Internet sites that are violent or have improper content on them. Its true that some students may go to these sites. But most students don't. Also, if you censor the Internet who will decide what gets censored and what doesn't. There are things on the Internet that are fine for older students but not for younger ones.

The problem with censorship is that it means different things to everybody. I don't think there should be pornography or super violent stuff on the Internet. But I do think some stuff is ok even if it may

have some questionable things on it. For example, a health website may have a picture or drawing of a naked person, but that's not pornography. Or a website about war may have violent images on it, but that's what war is about, and you can't really censor it or you don't have the truth.

I think that everyone needs to decide what is a problem for themselves and censor his own Internet instead of having the school do it. This will help teach students responsibility and make it so that all students don't have to pay for the actions of a few. Make students sign an agreement that they will not abuse the Internet at the school. A good compromise might be to block some obviously non-educational websites.

Sample 1 Essay

The school board is thinking about cutting off the Internet and going to an Intranet at the school. I think this is probably a good idea.

A lot of students waste time on the school computers. They say their doing research but their really just fooling around. They may not be playing games or anything, but they go to websites that have pretty much nothing to do with school or anything educational.

If we had an Intranet we could still use the computers for research and stuff but it would be for students who are serious about it, not students who just want to waste time. Anyone who wanted to do more research outside of school could do it at home or at the public library.

School is a place for learning and not fooling around on the Internet all day. The Intranet would avoid this problem and make it so that real students could do their work and the people who don't really want to use the computer seriously will think it's boring and not take up all the computers.

PRAXIS I: POWER PRACTICE EXAM 5

CHAPTER SUMMARY
Here is a full-length test based on the three elements of the Praxis I, the Pre-Professional Skills Tests (PPSTs) of Reading, Mathematics, and Writing.

The exam that follows is made up of three tests: a Reading test (multiple-choice questions), a Mathematics test (multiple-choice questions), and a Writing test (multiple-choice questions and one essay).

With this practice exam, you should simulate the actual test-taking experience as closely as you can. Find a quiet place to work where you won't be disturbed. Set a timer or stopwatch for each part of the exam to guide your pace.

When you have completed the exam, use the answer explanations to learn more about the questions you missed, and use the scoring guide in Chapter 8 to figure out how you did.

SKILLS TEST IN READING

1. (a) (b) (c) (d) (e)
2. (a) (b) (c) (d) (e)
3. (a) (b) (c) (d) (e)
4. (a) (b) (c) (d) (e)
5. (a) (b) (c) (d) (e)
6. (a) (b) (c) (d) (e)
7. (a) (b) (c) (d) (e)
8. (a) (b) (c) (d) (e)
9. (a) (b) (c) (d) (e)
10. (a) (b) (c) (d) (e)
11. (a) (b) (c) (d) (e)
12. (a) (b) (c) (d) (e)
13. (a) (b) (c) (d) (e)
14. (a) (b) (c) (d) (e)
15. (a) (b) (c) (d) (e)
16. (a) (b) (c) (d) (e)
17. (a) (b) (c) (d) (e)
18. (a) (b) (c) (d) (e)
19. (a) (b) (c) (d) (e)
20. (a) (b) (c) (d) (e)
21. (a) (b) (c) (d) (e)
22. (a) (b) (c) (d) (e)
23. (a) (b) (c) (d) (e)
24. (a) (b) (c) (d) (e)
25. (a) (b) (c) (d) (e)
26. (a) (b) (c) (d) (e)
27. (a) (b) (c) (d) (e)
28. (a) (b) (c) (d) (e)
29. (a) (b) (c) (d) (e)
30. (a) (b) (c) (d) (e)
31. (a) (b) (c) (d) (e)
32. (a) (b) (c) (d) (e)
33. (a) (b) (c) (d) (e)
34. (a) (b) (c) (d) (e)
35. (a) (b) (c) (d) (e)
36. (a) (b) (c) (d) (e)
37. (a) (b) (c) (d) (e)
38. (a) (b) (c) (d) (e)
39. (a) (b) (c) (d) (e)
40. (a) (b) (c) (d) (e)

SKILLS TEST IN MATHEMATICS

1. (a) (b) (c) (d) (e)
2. (a) (b) (c) (d) (e)
3. (a) (b) (c) (d) (e)
4. (a) (b) (c) (d) (e)
5. (a) (b) (c) (d) (e)
6. (a) (b) (c) (d) (e)
7. (a) (b) (c) (d) (e)
8. (a) (b) (c) (d) (e)
9. (a) (b) (c) (d) (e)
10. (a) (b) (c) (d) (e)
11. (a) (b) (c) (d) (e)
12. (a) (b) (c) (d) (e)
13. (a) (b) (c) (d) (e)
14. (a) (b) (c) (d) (e)
15. (a) (b) (c) (d) (e)
16. (a) (b) (c) (d) (e)
17. (a) (b) (c) (d) (e)
18. (a) (b) (c) (d) (e)
19. (a) (b) (c) (d) (e)
20. (a) (b) (c) (d) (e)
21. (a) (b) (c) (d) (e)
22. (a) (b) (c) (d) (e)
23. (a) (b) (c) (d) (e)
24. (a) (b) (c) (d) (e)
25. (a) (b) (c) (d) (e)
26. (a) (b) (c) (d) (e)
27. (a) (b) (c) (d) (e)
28. (a) (b) (c) (d) (e)
29. (a) (b) (c) (d) (e)
30. (a) (b) (c) (d) (e)
31. (a) (b) (c) (d) (e)
32. (a) (b) (c) (d) (e)
33. (a) (b) (c) (d) (e)
34. (a) (b) (c) (d) (e)
35. (a) (b) (c) (d) (e)
36. (a) (b) (c) (d) (e)
37. (a) (b) (c) (d) (e)
38. (a) (b) (c) (d) (e)
39. (a) (b) (c) (d) (e)
40. (a) (b) (c) (d) (e)

SKILLS TEST IN WRITING

1. (a) (b) (c) (d) (e)
2. (a) (b) (c) (d) (e)
3. (a) (b) (c) (d) (e)
4. (a) (b) (c) (d) (e)
5. (a) (b) (c) (d) (e)
6. (a) (b) (c) (d) (e)
7. (a) (b) (c) (d) (e)
8. (a) (b) (c) (d) (e)
9. (a) (b) (c) (d) (e)
10. (a) (b) (c) (d) (e)
11. (a) (b) (c) (d) (e)
12. (a) (b) (c) (d) (e)
13. (a) (b) (c) (d) (e)
14. (a) (b) (c) (d) (e)
15. (a) (b) (c) (d) (e)
16. (a) (b) (c) (d) (e)
17. (a) (b) (c) (d) (e)
18. (a) (b) (c) (d) (e)
19. (a) (b) (c) (d) (e)
20. (a) (b) (c) (d) (e)
21. (a) (b) (c) (d) (e)
22. (a) (b) (c) (d) (e)
23. (a) (b) (c) (d) (e)
24. (a) (b) (c) (d) (e)
25. (a) (b) (c) (d) (e)
26. (a) (b) (c) (d) (e)
27. (a) (b) (c) (d) (e)
28. (a) (b) (c) (d) (e)
29. (a) (b) (c) (d) (e)
30. (a) (b) (c) (d) (e)
31. (a) (b) (c) (d) (e)
32. (a) (b) (c) (d) (e)
33. (a) (b) (c) (d) (e)
34. (a) (b) (c) (d) (e)
35. (a) (b) (c) (d) (e)
36. (a) (b) (c) (d) (e)
37. (a) (b) (c) (d) (e)
38. (a) (b) (c) (d) (e)

Skills Test in Reading

Directions: Read the following passages and answer the questions that follow.

Use the following passage to answer questions 1–7.

1   Gray wolves once roamed the Yellowstone area
2   of the United States, but they were gradually
3   displaced by human development and hunted
4   by farmers and ranchers for preying on live-
5   stock. By the 1920s, wolves had practically dis-
6   appeared from the Yellowstone area. They
7   migrated north into the deep forests of Canada,
8   where there was less contact with humans.
9   The disappearance of the wolves had
10   many consequences. Deer and elk populations—
11   major food sources for the wolf—grew rapidly
12   without their usual predator. These animals
13   consumed large amounts of vegetation, which
14   reduced plant diversity in the park. In the
15   absence of wolves, coyote populations also grew
16   quickly. The coyotes killed a large percentage of
17   the park's red foxes and completely eliminated
18   the park's beavers.
19   By 1966, biologists asked the government
20   to consider reintroducing wolves to Yellowstone
21   Park. They hoped that wolves would be able to
22   control the population of the elk and coyote.
23   Many ranchers and farmers opposed the plan
24   because they feared that wolves would kill their
25   livestock or pets. Other people feared that the
26   wolves would not be well protected in Yellow-
27   stone anymore.
28   The government spent nearly 30 years
29   coming up with a plan to reintroduce the
30   wolves. Although the wolves are technically an
31   endangered species, Yellowstone's wolves were
32   classified as an "experimental" population. This
33   allowed the government more control over the
34   wolf packs. To counteract any potential resis-
35   tance, the government also pledged to pay

36   ranchers for livestock killed by wolves. Today,
37   the debate continues over how well the gray
38   wolf is fitting in at Yellowstone. Elk, deer, and
39   coyote populations are down, while beavers and
40   red foxes have made a comeback. The Yellow-
41   stone wolf project has been a valuable experi-
42   ment to help biologists decide whether to
43   reintroduce wolves to other parts of the coun-
44   try as well.

1. What is the main idea of the first paragraph of the passage?
   a. Gray wolves were unfairly treated by the ranchers and farmers.
   b. Canada provided a better habitat for gray wolves than Yellowstone.
   c. Gray wolves were displaced from their original homes by humans.
   d. Gray wolves were a threat to ranchers.
   e. It was important to reintroduce the gray wolves to Yellowstone.

2. According to the passage, why did biologists ask the government to reintroduce wolves in Yellowstone?
   a. to control the elk and coyote populations
   b. to restore the park's plant diversity
   c. to control the local livestock
   d. to protect the wolves from extinction
   e. to increase tourism revenue

3. In the sentence in lines 30–32, why does the writer include the word *technically*?
   a. to emphasize the legal definition of *endangered*
   b. to show that the government controls the wolves' status
   c. to explain why the wolves are endangered
   d. to highlight that the Yellowstone wolves are a special population
   e. to accentuate the scientific usage of the reintroduction

4. What is the most important organizing principle of the second paragraph of the passage?
 a. compare and contrast
 b. cause and effect
 c. chronological order
 d. order of importance
 e. classification

5. What is the implied main idea of the article?
 a. Yellowstone's wolf program was a mistake.
 b. The government is responsible for reintroducing wolves.
 c. Wolves are an important part of our national parks.
 d. Yellowstone's wolf program has been beneficial for the wolves and the park.
 e. It is important not to disrupt the delicate balance of life in nature.

6. Which statement, if it were true, would most significantly weaken the author's main argument?
 a. The government continues to monitor the populations of gray wolves, elks, and coyotes.
 b. The introduction of the gray wolf has increased the population diversity of the Yellowstone area.
 c. Yellowstone has been a protected area since its founding as a national park in 1872.
 d. The introduction of the gray wolf allowed scientists to consider reintroducing beavers to Yellowstone.
 e. The introduction of the gray wolf has resulted in the species suffering from a reduced genetic variability.

7. Which species endured the most similar experience to that of the gray wolves in Yellowstone?
 a. the polar bear, whose northern habitat is threatened by warming air temperatures and the resulting reduction of sea ice
 b. the possum, which was introduced in nonnative New Zealand in an effort to create a fur industry but ended up overpopulating the land
 c. the muskox, which was hunted to extinction in Alaska by about 1900 but brought back to repopulate the land in the 1930s
 d. the moa, a series of large New Zealand birds that were hunted to extinction by about A.D. 1400.
 e. the housecat, whose introduction to Australia has resulted in the extinction in dozens of other species

Use the following triple bar graph to answer question 8.

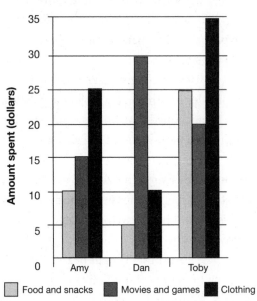

Purchases of Three Students in July

8. Which inference could be made from the information shown in the preceding graph?

    a. Toby will spend more on clothing in August than Amy or Dan.

    b. Dan is saving money to buy a large purchase at the end of the summer.

    c. Amy spent the same on clothing as she did on everything else in July.

    d. Dan's parents cook his meals and prepare snacks for him.

    e. Toby spent more on movies and games in July than either Amy or Dan.

Use the following passage to answer questions 9–15.

1   In July 1969, *Apollo 11* Commander Neil Arm-
2   strong became the first man to step foot on the
3   moon. Over the next several years, eleven more
4   men walked on Earth's satellite. However, after
5   geologist Harrison Schmitt left the moon in
6   December 1972, mankind has not returned.
7   The reasons why so much time has passed since
8   a manned landing on the moon are clear. The
9   financial costs of the trip are prohibitive, with
10 estimates of a return costing about $100 billion.
11 The moon's lack of atmosphere means that the
12 lunar surface has no protection from cosmic
13 rays' deadly radiation; astronauts put them-
14 selves in constant danger with any extended
15 trip to the moon. The dearth of other available
16 resources, such as water, means that astronauts
17 would have to carry their own resources
18 roughly 400,000 kilometers. In short, there is
19 little justifiable reason to take another jaunt to
20 the big rock in the sky. However, all this reason-
21 ing discounts the need for humans to continue
22 to explore their universe. If men will someday
23 step foot on Mars, they should first return to
24 the moon—if only to practice for the consider-
25 ably lengthier and significantly more difficult
26 trip to another planet.

9. In the context of the passage, *dearth* (line 15) can be replaced with which word to incur the smallest alteration in meaning?

    a. death

    b. scarcity

    c. importance

    d. abundance

    e. usefulness

10. According to the information in the reading selection, which inference can be made?

    a. A total of twelve men have walked on Earth's only natural satellite.

    b. The United States is planning a manned return to the moon.

    c. An astronaut cannot safely spend more than a week on the moon.

    d. There is no additional scientific knowledge to be gained from a return to the moon.

    e. A manned trip to Mars will be equally as hard as a manned trip to the moon.

11. Which sentence from the passage contains an opinion from the author?

    a. "In July 1969 . . . the moon."

    b. "Over the next . . . Earth's satellite."

    c. "However, after geologist . . . not returned."

    d. "The financial costs . . . $100 billion."

    e. "If men will . . . another planet."

12. Which statement, if it were true, would most significantly strengthen the author's main argument?

   a. The exploration of deeper space, including our outer solar system, is much more efficient if initiated from a space station instead of a satellite.

   b. The lack of an atmosphere on the moon means that astronauts would need to carry or manufacture their own oxygen.

   c. Since NASA sent its last astronaut to the moon in 1972, no other country has attempted a manned moon landing.

   d. Helium-3, an incredibly rare and valuable resource on Earth which can be used as a fuel, is found in high quantities on the moon.

   e. The government-run agency NASA retired its successful space shuttle program in 2011.

13. For which reason does the author most likely refer to the moon as a *big rock* (line 20)?

   a. to downplay the importance of returning to the moon

   b. to accentuate the massive size of Earth's only satellite

   c. to provide an additional incentive for man to return to the moon

   d. to describe the geological composition of the satellite

   e. to use a simile to describe the attributes of the moon

14. Which word best describes the author's attitude toward a potential manned mission to the moon?

   a. wasteful

   b. scientific

   c. dangerous

   d. essential

   e. timely

15. Which supporting detail best supports the author's main idea?

   a. After Neil Armstrong, only eleven more men walked on Earth's satellite.

   b. The financial costs of returning to the moon are excessive.

   c. The moon has no atmosphere with which to shield astronauts from radiation.

   d. Harrison Schmitt was the last man to walk on the moon in 1972.

   e. A return to the moon is vital if mankind is ever going to venture to Mars.

Use the following graph to answer question 16.

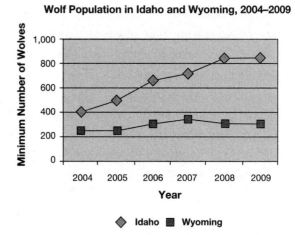

Wolf Population in Idaho and Wyoming, 2004–2009

16. Which inference can be supported by the information in the graph?

   a. The minimum wolf population in Idaho in 2002 was greater than 200.

   b. The combined wolf population in Idaho and Wyoming in 2007 was greater than 1,000.

   c. By 2010, there were more than 1,000 wolves in Idaho.

   d. The wolf population decline in Wyoming was a result of poor weather.

   e. In 2004 there were fewer than 500 wolves in Idaho and Wyoming combined.

Use the following passage to answer questions 17–19.

Arguably the most famous feature on the most famous mountain on Earth, the Hillary Step is a narrow, nearly vertical 40-foot rock wall near the peak of Mt. Everest. Covered in snow and ice at 28,750 feet, the Hillary Step presents the last great danger for climbers trying to reach the summit. Once conquered, it is only a few hundred feet of moderate climbing to the mountain's top at 29,028 feet—the planet's highest point. Named for Edmund Hillary, one of the two climbers to first ascend it, the step now features a fixed rope for modern-day climbers to use; such an advantage was unavailable during Hillary's initial 1953 ascent, making his achievement all the more venerable.

17. For which reason is the Hillary Step most likely the most famous feature on Mount Everest?
   a. The Hillary Step was named after the great climber Edmund Hillary.
   b. The Hillary Step acts as the final significant obstacle to the mountain's summit.
   c. The Hillary Step is one of the most difficult technical climbs in mountain climbing.
   d. Until 1953, the Hillary Step had not been successfully ascended.
   e. The highest point of the world is at the end of the Hillary Step.

18. In the passage, the word *venerable* most nearly means
   a. hazardous.
   b. technical.
   c. advantageous.
   d. victorious.
   e. admirable.

19. According to the information in the passage, it can be inferred that the Hillary Step
   a. is much easier to ascend now than it used to be.
   b. is responsible for countless casualties on the mountain.
   c. requires several hours of climbing to pass.
   d. is at the highest point on planet Earth.
   e. has only been ascended by two climbers in its history.

Use the following passage to answer questions 20–22.

1 In recent years, the local minor league baseball
2 team, the Dowshire Ducks, has become stan-
3 dard weekend entertainment for hundreds of
4 families. On summer afternoons, the bleachers
5 in Hulldown Stadium are teeming with cheer-
6 ing fans. But it wasn't always so. Even ten years
7 ago, ticket sales were limited, and the team was
8 largely ignored. The Ducks rarely won games or
9 placed well in regional tournaments. The
10 arrival of manager Duncan Brin in 2004, how-
11 ever, started a new era of success and fame for
12 the Ducks.

20. Which sentence best summarizes the main idea of the article?
   a. The Dowshire Ducks used to be an unsuccessful baseball team.
   b. Duncan Brin is the manager of the Dowshire Ducks.
   c. The Dowshire Ducks play in Hulldown Stadium.
   d. Manager Duncan Brin improved the status of the Dowshire Ducks.
   e. Going to see a Dowshire Ducks game is popular family entertainment.

21. Which organization best describes the structure of the passage?
  a. Details are provided through a series of contrasts, and then a main idea is provided.
  b. A main idea is provided, and then a series of supporting details is listed.
  c. A handful of comparisons are given, and then several dissimilarities are given.
  d. Definitions are given for several unknown terms, and then a main idea is given.
  e. A problem is posed, and then a series of potential solutions is discussed.

22. The word *teeming* in line 5 could be replaced with which of the following words to result in the least change in meaning of the sentence?
  a. crowded
  b. rooting
  c. energized
  d. vacant
  e. teaming

Use the following passage to answer questions 23–26.

1   A cursory glance at a globe will reveal a fasci-
2   nating observation: the continents of South
3   America and Africa, separated by thousands of
4   kilometers of open ocean, seem to fit together
5   like pieces of a jigsaw puzzle. The western edge
6   of central South America, part of modern-day
7   Brazil, juts out into the Atlantic Ocean at about
8   the same latitude where the coast of northern
9   Africa shrivels toward the east. The reason for
10   this geological phenomenon is not pure hap-
11   penstance. Both massive land masses were once
12   connected in a supercontinent called Gond-
13   wana, which also contained most of the land
14   found today in India, Australia, and Antarctica,
15   about 200 million years ago. The process
16   responsible for Gondwana splitting into
17   the two separate continents in their

18   current positions is called "continental drift."
19   The significant hypothesis, put forth by Ger-
20   man geologist Alfred Wegener in 1915, states
21   that parts of Earth's crust can shift over time
22   above the planet's liquid core. A later theory of
23   plate tectonics expanded on Wegener's discov-
24   ery, conjecturing that Earth's continental plates
25   move in different directions and therefore affect
26   the positions of the continents—including why
27   South America and Africa seem to fit despite
28   their locations on opposite ends of an ocean.

23. Which is the author's most likely purpose in describing the continents of South America and Africa as *pieces of a jigsaw puzzle* (line 5)?
  a. to contrast the significant difference between the land masses
  b. to describe the mystery of the continental shapes as a puzzle
  c. to minimize the geological importance of the continents
  d. to reinforce the corresponding physical relationship of the continents
  e. to illustrate the problems scientists faced in determining the causes of continental drift

24. The word *cursory* in line 1 could be replaced with which of the following words to result in the least change in meaning of the sentence?
  a. investigative
  b. superficial
  c. internal
  d. offensive
  e. cursive

25. Which statement, if it were true, would most significantly strengthen the author's main argument?

  a. Gondwana was once part of a much larger supercontinent called Pangaea.

  b. Fossils of the same type of plant have been found in parts of western Brazil and eastern Africa.

  c. The African island of Madagascar was once part of the supercontinent Gondwana.

  d. There are countless species of animals that exist in only South America or Africa but not in both continents.

  e. Ancient land bridges, now sunken, once connected the continents across the enormous oceans.

26. According to the passage, which inference can be made?

  a. Alfred Wegener developed the theory of plate tectonics.

  b. There was a time on planet Earth with no oceans.

  c. South America and Africa are roughly the same size.

  d. There is scant evidence that supports the "continental drift" theory.

  e. South America and Africa reside on different plates.

Use the following passage to answer question 27.

A sea spider, unlike the land animal that shares part of its name, does not spin a web to catch its food. Some sea spiders living thousands of feet underwater have developed an interesting technique to get their nourishment. Most sea spiders have eight legs—like land spiders— which they use to catch their food. The long legs have feathers that trap random pieces of food that fall down to the depths of the ocean. Then the sea spider runs its legs across its mouth for a tasty meal.

27. What is the primary purpose of the reading selection?

  a. to tell about the similarities between land spiders and sea spiders

  b. to describe the unique eating habits of a type of sea spider

  c. to warn people to stay away from dangerous sea spiders

  d. to explain how a land spider uses a web to catch its food

  e. to describe the appendages of the sea spider

Use the following passage to answer questions 28–32.

1 One of Benjamin Franklin's most useful and
2 important inventions was a stove called, appro-
3 priately, the Franklin stove. This invention
4 improved the lives of countless homeowners in
5 the eighteenth century and beyond. Compared
6 to the stoves that were used at the time of his
7 invention, Franklin's stove made keeping a fire
8 inside a home much less dangerous. His stove
9 could burn less wood and generate more heat
10 than previous designs. This feature saved its
11 users considerable amounts of money that
12 would have been needed to buy wood.
13   As its inventor, Benjamin Franklin was
14 offered the right to patent his stove. That would
15 have meant that only Franklin could have made
16 and sold the useful stoves, making Franklin one
17 of the richest men in the country. However,
18 Franklin turned down the opportunity for the
19 patent, believing instead that the stove should
20 be allowed to be used by anyone who wanted to
21 use the safer and more efficient technology. In
22 his autobiography, he wrote, "As we enjoy great
23 advantages from the inventions of others, we
24 should be glad of an opportunity to serve oth-
25 ers by any invention of ours; and this we should
26 do freely and generously."

28. The primary purpose of the first paragraph of the passage is to
  a. tell about one particularly useful invention of Benjamin Franklin.
  b. point out that Benjamin Franklin was responsible for many great inventions.
  c. explain the physical process of how a stove works.
  d. tell all the ways that Benjamin Franklin made money from his stoves.
  e. compare a variety of stoves from early American history.

29. Which function best describes the function of the word *however* as it appears in line 17?
  a. to provide important physical descriptions of a critical development
  b. to provide several additional benefits for a life-saving invention
  c. to contrast the advantages of an invention with its potential drawbacks
  d. to compare the apparent usefulness of an invention with its extreme costs
  e. to contrast an inventor's altruistic motives from the potential for great wealth

30. The meaning of the word *right* in line 14, in context of the passage, most likely means
  a. correct.
  b. good health.
  c. turn.
  d. legal claim.
  e. exact.

31. According to the passage, it can be concluded that Benjamin Franklin was
  a. afraid of making a fire inside his home.
  b. interested primarily in inventing things that would make him money.
  c. one of the richest people in America.
  d. less concerned with making money than with helping his fellow humans.
  e. a greater inventor than he was a politician or scientist.

32. It can be inferred from the passage that the Franklin stove was
  a. expensive.
  b. dangerous.
  c. efficient.
  d. small.
  e. stylish.

Use the following passage to answer questions 33–35.

Most species on the planet exist solely within a relatively specific temperate zone on the planet. Polar bears live only within the most northern latitudes; iguanas are found only in tropical locales; kangaroos are endemic only to the Australian continent. Human beings, known taxonomically as *Homo sapiens*, however, have been remarkably adept at populating the farthest corners of the planet—even those with extreme environments. Alert, a Canadian community home to several permanent residents, is only about 500 miles from the North Pole; the Ethiopian community of Dallol has an average temperature of 94°F; La Rinconada, a Peruvian city in the Andes Mountains, is nearly 17,000 feet above sea level. The ability of human beings to acclimate to their surroundings, no matter how unforgiving, is all the more impressive considering how few physical features of the species allow it such adaptability.

33. Which detail from the passage most directly supports the author's main argument?

   a. Polar bears live only within the most northern latitudes.

   b. Human beings are known taxonomically as *Homo sapiens.*

   c. Kangaroos are endemic to the Australian continent.

   d. A Canadian community is about 500 miles from the North Pole.

   e. Iguanas are found only in tropical locales.

34. Which fact would the author most likely use to further strengthen his or her main argument?

   a. The Mariana Trench, the deepest known point on Earth, lies more than 36,000 feet below the surface of the ocean.

   b. The port city of Arica, Chile, receives an average annual rainfall of 0.03 inches.

   c. Penguins are found throughout the southern hemisphere, from the equator to the pole.

   d. The surface temperature on Venus is believed to exceed 700°F.

   e. Only about 30 percent of Earth's surface is covered by land.

35. Which role does the habitat of the kangaroo most significantly play in the context of the reading selection?

   a. to contrast with the habitat of the polar bear

   b. to demonstrate humanity's encroachment on animal territory

   c. to supply an additional extreme environment

   d. to illustrate mankind's limited reach in Australia

   e. to provide a contrast to humanity's spread

Use the following passage to answer questions 36–38.

In the long history of soccer, no single player has changed the game as much as Pelé. Born Edison Arantes do Nascimento in Brazil in 1940, Pelé played professional soccer for 20 years, including in four World Cups for his native Brazil. Toward the end of his career, he also played for a North American soccer league. Though he was well past his prime, Pelé helped to significantly increase American interest in soccer. Counting his time in the American league, Pelé scored a total of 1,281 goals—the most goals scored by any professional soccer player. In fact, Pelé's athletic skills were so impressive that he was awarded the title "Athlete of the Century" by the International Olympic Committee. By the time he retired, no one had helped increase the popularity of soccer more.

36. Which sentence from the passage presents an example of an opinion rather than a fact?

   a. "In the long . . . as Pelé."

   b. "Born Edison Arantes . . . native Brazil."

   c. "Toward the end . . . soccer league."

   d. "Counting his time . . . soccer player."

   e. "In fact, Pele's . . . Olympic Committee."

37. Which detail from the passage supports the main idea the least?

   a. Pelé was born Edison Arantes do Nascimento in Brazil in 1940.

   b. Pelé played professional soccer for 20 years, including in four World Cups.

   c. Pelé helped significantly to increase American interest in soccer.

   d. Pelé scored a total of 1,281 goals.

   e. Pelé earned the title "Athlete of the Century."

38. Which athlete is most similar to Pelé, based on the given information about him in the passage?
   a. Cristiano Ronaldo, a Portuguese soccer player who is the highest-paid soccer player in history
   b. Dilma Rousseff, the 36th president of Brazil and the first woman to hold the country's highest office
   c. Babe Ruth, who helped make baseball the most popular sport in America by breaking home run records
   d. Charles Haley, who was a member of five Super Bowl–winning football teams from 1986 through 1999
   e. Landon Donovan, who scored multiple goals in the 2010 World Cup for the American soccer team

Use the following passage to answer questions 39 and 40.

It is a statistical anomaly that Barack Obama is generally recognized as the 44th president of the United States, yet only 42 different people held the presidency before him. This is due to the fact that Grover Cleveland served two non-consecutive terms in office, once from 1885 to 1889, and then again from 1893 to 1897. As the only president to serve non-consecutive terms, Cleveland is counted twice in the numbering of the presidents and is therefore considered both the 22nd and 24th President of the United States. Given the resulting disparity, it would be more rational to number the presidents based solely on their first term, ignoring any secondary tenures that could complicate the sequence.

39. Which best describes the author's attitude toward the current numbering system of the U.S. presidents?
   a. humorous
   b. illogical
   c. reverential
   d. presidential
   e. rational

40. Which word has the closest meaning to *anomaly* as it appears in the passage?
   a. data
   b. irregularity
   c. representation
   d. conclusion
   e. indiscretion

Skills Test in Mathematics

1. Boyd keeps track of the length of each fish that he catches. The following are the lengths in inches of the fish that he caught one day: 12, 13, 9, 14, 10, 8, 9, 17. What is the median fish length that Boyd caught that day?
   a. 8 inches
   b. 10 inches
   c. 11 inches
   d. 12 inches
   e. 9 inches

2. If w is divisible by both 24 and 6, which of the following statements is NOT true?
   a. w must be divisible by 12
   b. w must be divisible by 4
   c. w must be divisible by 3
   d. w must be divisible by 18
   e. w must be divisible by 8

3. Fact A: All dogs like to run.

Fact B: Some dogs like to swim.

Fact C: Some dogs look like their masters and like to swim.

If the previous three of the statements are facts, which of the following statements must also be a fact?

    I. All dogs who like to swim also look like their masters.

    II. All dogs who like to swim also like to run.

    III. Dogs who do not look like their masters do like to run.

  a. II only

  b. II and III only

  c. I, II, and III

  d. I and II only

  e. None of the statements is a known fact.

4. $\triangle JER$ has coordinates $J(1,-4)$; $E(8,-2)$; $R(4,2)$. What are the coordinates of point E after a reflection over the x-axis?

  a. $(2,8)$

  b. $(4,-2)$

  c. $(8,2)$

  d. $(-8,-2)$

  e. $(-8,2)$

5. When measuring the perimeter of a house, what unit would you use to report the results?

  a. centimeters

  b. inches

  c. millimeters

  d. kilometers

  e. meters

6. What is the product of $1\frac{1}{8}$ and $1\frac{3}{5}$?

  a. $1\frac{4}{13}$

  b. $1\frac{4}{5}$

  c. $1\frac{3}{40}$

  d. $1\frac{3}{15}$

  e. $\frac{109}{40}$

7. A merchant buys a product for $12.20 and then marks it up 30% to sell it. What is the selling price of the item?

  a. $3.66

  b. $36.60

  c. $15.86

  d. $12.50

  e. $16.72

8. "If you have your driver's license in New York, then you must either be over 18 *or* over 16 and have passed driver's education class." Considering the previous statement, which of the following is true?

  a. If you are over 18 in New York, then you have your driver's license.

  b. If you are under 18 in New York, then you cannot have your driver's license.

  c. Passing driver's education is necessary for having your driver's license in New York State.

  d. If you are 18 and have passed driver's education class then you have your driver's license.

  e. If you are 16 and have your New York driver's license, then you passed driver's education class.

9. Mario has a pocket full of coins. The table shows how many of each coin he has. What percent of the coins in his pocket are dimes?

COIN	NUMBER OF COINS
Penny	6
Nickel	2
Dime	8
Quarter	9

  a. 32%

  b. 68%

  c. 25%

  d. 8%

  e. 40%

10. Bren was hired to build out the interior for a new store, Beam & Anchor. Bren was paid $10,400 to do the job, which he completed in 13 days, working 8 hours a day. As part of his contract he needed to pay for the cost of the materials, which totaled $4,160. How much was Bren's hourly pay for the job?
  a. $100.00
  b. $60.00
  c. $40.00
  d. $80.00
  e. $50.00

11. A cardboard box measures $2\frac{1}{2}$ feet by 3 feet by 3 feet. Find the volume of the box.
  a. $18\frac{1}{2}$ ft^3
  b. 27 ft^3
  c. $20\frac{1}{2}$ ft^3
  d. $22\frac{1}{2}$ ft^3
  e. $23\frac{1}{2}$ ft^3

Use the following graph to answer questions 12–14.

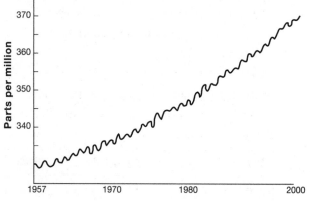

Charles Keeling measured the amount of carbon dioxide (CO_2) in the atmosphere from 1957 to 1997, and his results are shown in the preceding graph. The *x*-axis represents the year, and the *y*-axis represents the amount of carbon dioxide (in parts per million) that was measured.

12. If the trend in the graph continues, what is the best estimate for the amount of carbon dioxide that would be in the atmosphere in 2012?
  a. 360 parts per million
  b. 370 parts per million
  c. 380 parts per million
  d. 395 parts per million
  e. 410 parts per million

13. Which of the following numbers best represents the amount of carbon dioxide found in the atmosphere in 1990?
  a. $\frac{9}{25,000}$
  b. $\frac{333}{1,000,000}$
  c. $\frac{37}{100,000}$
  d. 36%
  e. 0.0036

14. Based on the information shown in the graph, which of the following statements might be accurate:

   a. The increasing popularity of alternative energy resources after the turn of the twenty-first century caused the increase of carbon dioxide found in the atmosphere to begin slowing.

   b. Since the data is a jagged curve of minor increases and decreases it cannot accurately be used to make generalizations about future levels of carbon dioxide in the atmosphere.

   c. The growth of the levels of carbon dioxide found in the atmosphere slowed significantly from 1970 to 1980.

   d. The increase of the human population has caused an increase in the burning of fossil fuels as well as an increase in deforestation, which has been the most likely cause of the increase of carbon dioxide found in the atmosphere.

   e. Since carbon monoxide only has *one* oxygen atom and carbon dioxide has *two* oxygen atoms, the levels of carbon monoxide found in the atmosphere are probably about half of the levels of carbon dioxide found in the atmosphere.

15. Tyson and Steve both collect skateboards. Tyson owns three less than seven times the number of skateboards Steve owns. If s represents the number of skateboards Steve owns, which of the following expressions represents the number of skateboards Tyson owns?

   a. $7s$

   b. $3 - 7s$

   c. $7s - 3$

   d. $(7s)(3)$

   e. $7s + 3$

16. If the number 4 is added to the data 5, 6, 7, 8, 8, 10, which of the following would stay the same?

   a. mean

   b. median

   c. mode

   d. range

   e. None of these would stay the same.

17. The perimeter of Kimberly's rectangular sunroom is 50 feet. Find the length of the sunroom if the width is 10 feet.

   a. 15 feet

   b. 40 feet

   c. 30 feet

   d. 25 feet

   e. 12.5 feet

18. There were 8.9 million bicycles in Beijing in 2001. Which number represents the number of bicycles in Beijing in 2001?

   a. 8.9,000,000

   b. 890,000

   c. 8,900,000

   d. 89,000,000

   e. 890,000,000

19. If $w@z$ is equivalent to $3w - z$, what is the value of $(w@z)@z$?

   a. $9w - 4z$

   b. $6w - 4z$

   c. $3w - 2z$

   d. $9w - 3z$

   e. $9w - 2z$

20. Examine (A), (B), and (C) and find the best answer.

   (A): $\frac{1}{3}$ of 12

   (B): 4% of 100

   (C): $\frac{1}{5}$ of 10

   a. (A) is less than (C).

   b. (A) and (B) are equal.

   c. (A) plus (B) is equal to (C).

   d. (B) minus (A) is greater than (C).

   e. (C) is greater than (B).

21. In Judy's math class, there are m men in a class of n students. Which expression gives the ratio of men to women in the class?

   a. $\frac{m}{n}$

   b. $\frac{n}{m}$

   c. $\frac{m}{m-n}$

   d. $\frac{n}{n-m}$

   e. $\frac{m}{n-m}$

22. Looking at the series: J14, L11, N8, P5, . . . determine what expression should come next?

   a. Q2

   b. Q3

   c. R2

   d. S2

   e. S3

23. If the radius of the following circle is 12 units, which sector has an approximate area of 43π square units?

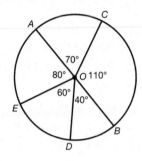

   a. sector *EOD*

   b. sector *EOA*

   c. sector *AOC*

   d. sector *COB*

   e. sector *DOB*

24. Molly owns a music store in Mar Vista. For Molly's first order, she purchased 800 CDs. After she sold these, she placed a second order for 1,200 more. After selling these as well, she ordered 2,100 more CDs. How much would Molly have saved if she had ordered all the CDs she purchased in one single order?

# OF CDS PURCHASED	PRICE PER CD
100–999	$1.50
1,000–1,999	$1.00
2,000–2,999	$.75
3,000+	$.50

   a. $1,200

   b. $1,575

   c. $1,925

   d. $2,050

   e. $3,975

25. $x^2 - 4x + 4x^3 \div x - 2 =$

   a. $5x^2 + 4x - 2$

   b. $x^2 - 4x^3 - 2$

   c. $-3x^2 - 4x - 2$

   d. $x^2 - x - 2$

   e. $5x^2 - 4x - 2$

26. On a random Tuesday, Huntington Floral has 40 red-veined plants and 24 flowering plants. Of these, 14 plants are both red-veined and flowering. There are also 10 plants that are neither flowering nor red-veined. Alexis runs into the shop that Tuesday and randomly purchases a plant. What is the probability that she purchased a red-veined plant without flowers?

   a. $\frac{13}{30}$

   b. $\frac{2}{5}$

   c. $\frac{1}{6}$

   d. $\frac{7}{30}$

   e. $\frac{3}{5}$

27. The varsity volleyball team still has 30 games to play before the season is over. So far, the team has played 65 games, and they have won 45 of them. Of the 30 games still left to play, how many must the team win in order for them to win a total of 60% of the total games played for the season?

   a. 12

   b. 18

   c. 30

   d. 45

   e. 57

28. If a is an odd number, b is even, and c is prime, which of the following equations could never be true?

   a. $a \times c = b$

   b. $a + b = c$

   c. $c \times b = a$

   d. $b \div a = c$

   e. $a + c = b$

29. Which of the following points is in the solution set of $4y + 6 > 3x + 15$?

   a. $(0,-4)$

   b. $(3,4)$

   c. $(4,3)$

   d. $(4,6)$

   e. $(5,6)$

30. Laura and Freddy want to put a fence around their rectangular vegetable garden. The garden measures 14 feet by 8 feet. If fencing is sold by the yard only, what is the smallest number of yards of fencing that Laura and Freddy will have to purchase?

   a. 44 yards

   b. 22 yards

   c. 14 yards

   d. 15 yards

   e. 38 yards

31. In the following diagram, what is the value of x?

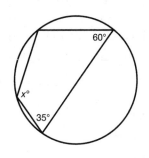

   a. 70°

   b. 60°

   c. 240°

   d. 120°

   e. cannot be determined

Use the following graph to answer questions 32 and 33.

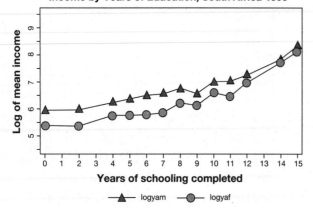

Income by Years of Education, South Africa 1993

Log of mean income

Years of schooling completed

△— logyam ⬤— logyaf

The preceding graph shows the relationship of how much income was earned in South Africa in 1993, by men and women, based on the number of years of education completed. The log of the mean income for men is represented with the line dotted with triangles and the log of the mean income for women is represented with the line dotted with circles (assume that the higher the log, the higher the salary).

32. Which five-year period of schooling had the largest influence on the salary that a South African woman made in 1993?
   a. 0 to 5 years
   b. 3 to 8 years
   c. 5 to 10 years
   d. 7 to 12 years
   e. 10 to 15 years

33. Which statement is NOT supported by the information in the graph?
   a. Women who completed nine years of schooling earned less than women who completed eight years of schooling.
   b. There is no difference in the mean incomes of males who completed zero years of education and males who completed two years of education.
   c. If the graph were to be extended to 17 years of schooling complete, women would be earning more than men.
   d. The greater the number of years of schooling, the less discrepancy there was between men's and women's incomes.
   e. In 1993, the log of the mean income for women with 12 years of schooling was less than the mean income for men with just 10 years of schooling.

34. Rounding 327.3785 to the nearest thousandth results in which of the following?
   a. 0
   b. 327.379
   c. 327.378
   d. 327.38
   e. 1,000

35. In the following diagram, if ∠1 is 30° and ∠2 is a right angle, what is the measure of ∠5?

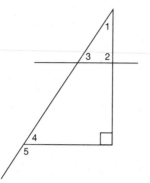

  a. 30°
  b. 60°
  c. 120°
  d. 150°
  e. There is not enough information to determine ∠5.

36. If the height of a triangle is 6 more than twice its base, b, which algebraic expression would represent the area of the triangle?
  a. $6 + 2b$
  b. $6b + 2b^2$
  c. $3b + b^2$
  d. $4b + (\frac{1}{2})b^2$
  e. $12 + 5b$

37. Which point on the number line best represents $\sqrt{11}$?

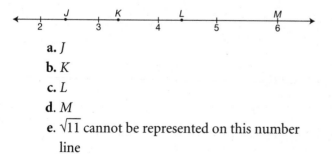

  a. J
  b. K
  c. L
  d. M
  e. $\sqrt{11}$ cannot be represented on this number line

38. Joan's average for her first three tests was 72. If she scored an 84 on the first test and a 68 on the second test, what was her score on the third test?
  a. 76
  b. 64
  c. 68
  d. 70
  e. 73

39. Based on the diagram, if lines L and M are parallel, which of the following equations is NOT necessarily true?

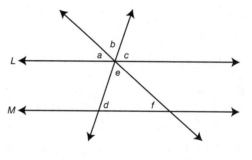

  a. $a + b + c = d + e + f$
  b. $a + c = 180 - e$
  c. $a + e + c = 180$
  d. $b + c = e + f$
  e. $a + b + c + d + e + f = 360$

40. If a drawer contains 7 knives, 4 spoons, and 9 forks, what is the probability that the first piece of silverware randomly drawn out of the drawer will NOT be a spoon?
  a. $\frac{1}{5}$
  b. $\frac{13}{20}$
  c. $\frac{7}{20}$
  d. $\frac{4}{5}$
  e. 16

Skills Test in Writing

Section 1, Part A

Directions: Choose the letter for the underlined portion that contains a grammatical error. If there is no error in the sentence, choose **e**.

1. Last summer when Kate <u>visited</u> Japan as part of her <u>master's degree</u> program, she <u>sees</u> many <u>Shinto</u>
            a   **b**   **c**   **d**

   temples. <u>No error</u>
         e

2. Gurney Williams offered this <u>advice</u> to <u>parents,</u> <u>"Teaching</u> creativity to your child isn't like teaching
                         a   **b**   **c**

   good manners. No one can paint a masterpiece by bowing to another person's precepts about elbows on

   the <u>table."</u> <u>No error</u>
       d   **e**

3. The <u>mother-to-be</u> decided she didn't want <u>to</u> take any anesthesia <u>during childbirth and labor;</u>
        a   **b**   **c**

   <u>naturally,</u> she wanted to give birth. <u>No error</u>
     d   **e**

4. Surrounding <u>oneself</u> with books and papers and <u>working extensively</u> to produce a coherent <u>analysis</u>
            a   **b**   **c**

   <u>and discussion</u> of a topic can be an exhausting process that many students <u>are required</u> to repeat again
       a   **d**

   and again. <u>No error</u>
            e

5. Many historians believe Adolf Hitler <u>prosecuted</u> the <u>Jews</u> because he viewed them as an inferior race
                              a   **b**

   and blamed them for Germany's defeat in <u>World War I.</u> <u>No error</u>
             c   **d**   **e**

6. <u>For me,</u> <u>going to school</u> <u>is harder</u> <u>than a job.</u> <u>No error</u>
     a   **b**   **c**   **d**   **e**

7. He <u>admitted</u> personal <u>guilt;</u> he <u>knew</u> what <u>he'd done.</u> <u>No error</u>
      a   **b**   **c**   **d**   **e**

8. <u>Irregardless</u> of the current trend of government <u>cutbacks,</u> experts <u>foresee</u> steady hiring in the
      a   **b**   **c**

   government's future. <u>No error</u>
       d   **e**

9. My <u>Yorkshire Terrier</u> Rocky is <u>extremely</u> afraid of <u>thunder;</u> <u>mainly,</u> when there's a storm I
           a   **b**   **c**   **d**

cover his ears. <u>No error</u>
           e

10. My sister <u>met</u> her husband in a <u>café;</u> he <u>was</u> very <u>tall.</u> <u>No error</u>
           a   **b**   **c**   **d**   **e**

11. Maco moved to <u>Greensboro, North Carolina,</u> with her family <u>in June 2004,</u> when her <u>mother</u> got a
                        a   **b**   **c**

job teaching at the <u>state university.</u> <u>No error</u>
               d   **e**

12. I <u>had never</u> felt more relaxed <u>then</u> when we moved out of the <u>busy, fast-paced city</u> into the quiet
     a   **b**   **c**

<u>countryside.</u> <u>No error</u>
   d   **e**

13. <u>Mens'</u> and <u>women's</u> gender <u>identities</u> <u>seem</u> to evolve as times change. <u>No error</u>
    a   **b**   **c**   **d**   **e**

14. The <u>customer</u> called the store <u>several times</u> <u>that</u> day, but <u>they</u> never answered. <u>No error</u>
       a   **b**   **c**   **d**   **e**

15. <u>During World War II,</u> the Allies <u>stormed</u> Italy and then <u>would launch</u> a <u>massive assault.</u> <u>No error</u>
          a   **b**   **c**   **d**   **e**

16. Although <u>Marco</u> is from Italy and <u>speaks Italian as his first language,</u> he <u>speaks</u> English <u>good.</u> <u>No error</u>
            a   **b**   **c**   **d**   **e**

17. Stunned by the <u>audacity</u> of the <u>man,</u> <u>it</u> was turning into a <u>volatile</u> relationship. <u>No error</u>
                a   **b** **c**   **d**   **e**

18. When it comes to selecting <u>accessories</u> to complete an outfit, many people are clueless as to how to
                                a

<u>compliment</u> their <u>wardrobe</u> with appropriate items that will best fit <u>an occasion.</u> <u>No error</u>
   b   **c**   **d**   **e**

19. Because <u>the city</u> <u>has</u> an inadequate transportation system, Clarissa <u>transfers</u> twice to get to work
              a   **b**   **c**

<u>each day.</u> <u>No error</u>
   d   **e**

20. Josh <u>surmised</u> his <u>father</u> was putting in <u>too</u> many hours at his job and <u>wasn't getting</u> enough rest. <u>No</u>
         a   b   c   d   e
<u>error</u>

21. <u>No matter what the teacher tried,</u> the <u>students</u> in her class <u>were not as engaged in this new unit in</u>
                  a   b   c
<u>economics</u> as much as <u>studying history.</u> <u>No error</u>
          d   e

Section 1, Part B

Directions: Choose the best replacement for the underlined portion of the sentence. If no revision is necessary, choose **a**, which always repeats the original phrasing.

22. I loved the book *The DaVinci code*, <u>and I enjoyed how Tom Hanks played the role</u> of symbologist Robert Langdon in the movie made from the book.
  a. *The DaVinci code*, and I enjoyed how Tom Hanks played the role
  b. *The DaVinci Code*, and I enjoyed how Tom Hanks played the role
  c. *The DaVinci code* and I enjoyed how Tom Hanks played the role
  d. *The DaVinci Code*, and I enjoyed how Tom Hanks played the roll
  e. *The davinci code*, and I enjoyed how Tom Hanks played the roll

23. The crowd was so thick, <u>no one couldn't go nowhere.</u>
  a. no one couldn't go nowhere.
  b. no one couldn't go anywhere.
  c. noone couldn't go anywhere.
  d. no one could go anywhere.
  e. no one could go nowhere.

24. The soldiers battled <u>in the streets, woods, and in the homes</u> of the citizens.
  a. in the streets, woods, and in the homes
  b. in the streets, the woods, and in the homes
  c. in streets, the woods, and the homes
  d. in the streets, in the woods, and in the homes
  e. in streets, woods, and the homes

25. If <u>the picnickers don't eat all the salads with mayonnaise in them within an hour, pack them away in the cooler.</u>
  a. If the picnickers don't eat all the salads with mayonnaise in them within an hour, pack them away in the cooler.
  b. Pack them away in the cooler, if the picnickers don't eat all the salads with mayonnaise in them within an hour.
  c. Pack away all the salads with mayonnaise in them if the picnickers don't eat them within an hour.
  d. If the picnickers don't pack them away in the cooler, eat all the salads with mayonnaise in them within an hour.
  e. If the picnickers pack them away in the cooler, don't eat all the salads with mayonnaise in them within an hour.

26. After storing the diamond in the secret compartment of the dresser for safekeeping, Alex absentmindedly sold it.

  a. After storing the diamond in the secret compartment of the dresser for safekeeping, Alex absentmindedly sold it.

  b. After storing the diamond in the secret compartment of the dresser for safekeeping, Alex absentmindedly sold the dresser.

  c. After storing it in the secret compartment of the dresser for safekeeping, Alex absentmindedly sold the dresser.

  d. After storing the diamond in it for safekeeping, Alex absentmindedly sold it.

  e. Alex absentmindedly sold it after storing the diamond in the secret compartment of the dresser for safekeeping.

27. There is a most unique flower in the garden.

  a. There is a most unique flower in the garden.

  b. There is a unique flower in the garden.

  c. There is a more unique flower in the garden.

  d. In the garden, there is a most unique flower.

  e. In the garden, there is a more unique flower.

28. Currently, estimated useful lives for equipments and furnitures range from between three and five years.

  a. equipments and furnitures range from between three and five years.

  b. equipment and furnitures range from between three and five years.

  c. equipment and furnitures range from between three to five years.

  d. equipment and furniture range from between three and five years.

  e. equipments and furnitures range from between three to five years.

29. Within the boundaries of the constellations Aquarius and Cancer are found?

  a. Within the boundaries of the constellations Aquarius and Cancer are found?

  b. What constellations are found within the boundaries of Aquarius and Cancer?

  c. Within the boundaries, of the constellations Aquarius and Cancer are found?

  d. Aquarius and Cancer are found with the boundaries of the constellations?

  e. Within the boundaries of Aquarius and Cancer of the constellations are found?

30. My idea of nirvana is a deliciously decadent chocolate cake and drinking cold milk.

  a. drinking

  b. a drink of

  c. drink

  d. drunken

  e. have drunken

31. Gulping down another few swallows of his orange juice, Mrs. Lewis grabbed her bag and escorted her son toward the door.

  a. Gulping down another few swallows of his orange juice, Mrs. Lewis grabbed her bag and escorted her son toward the door.

  b. Mrs. Lewis grabbed her bag and escorted her son toward the door as he gulped down another few swallows of his orange juice.

  c. Gulping down another few swallows of his orange juice; Mrs. Lewis grabbed her bag and escorted her son toward the door.

  d. Mrs. Lewis gulped down another few swallows of his orange juice and grabbed her bag and escorted her son toward the door.

  e. Gulping down another few swallows of his orange juice, Mrs. Lewis escorted her son toward the door and grabbed her bag.

32. My sister looked <u>angrily when I told her the</u> <u>jacket I had borrowed from her had been left at</u> <u>the beach.</u>

    a. angrily when I told her the jacket I had borrowed from her had been left at the beach.

    b. angrily when I told her I'd left the jacket I had borrowed from her at the beach.

    c. angry when I told her I'd left the jacket I had borrowed from her at the beach.

    d. angry when I told her the jacket I had borrowed from her had been left at the beach.

    e. angrily when I told her the jacket I had left at the beach had been borrowed.

33. When we left the concert, we <u>couldn't hardly</u> hear each other talking; the music had been so loud.

    a. couldn't hardly

    b. couldn't barely

    c. could hardly

    d. couldn't scarcely

    e. hardly couldn't

34. <u>The angry rooster chased the dog that was</u> <u>cackling loudly around the yard.</u>

    a. The angry rooster chased the dog that was cackling loudly around the yard.

    b. The angry rooster chased the dog loudly around the yard that was cackling.

    c. The dog that was cackling around the yard chased the angry rooster.

    d. The angry rooster that was cackling loudly chased the dog around the yard.

    e. The angry rooster around the yard chased the dog that was cackling.

35. Would it be <u>better or worse</u> for animals if everyone became vegetarian?

    a. better or worse

    b. best or worse

    c. best or worst

    d. better or worst

    e. better and worse

36. When the <u>Nambiar's flew to Jamaica, the airline</u> <u>lost their luggages.</u>

    a. Nambiar's flew to Jamaica, the airline lost their luggages.

    b. Nambiars flew to Jamaica the airline lost their luggages.

    c. Nambiar's flew to Jamaica, the airline lost their luggage.

    d. Nambiars flew to Jamaica, the airline lost their luggage.

    e. Nambiars flew to Jamaica, the airline lost his luggage.

37. <u>Since the Industrial Revolution, because people</u> have increased the concentration of carbon dioxide in the atmosphere by 30 percent by burning fossil fuels and cutting down forests.

    a. Since the Industrial Revolution, because people

    b. The Industrial Revolution because people

    c. Since the industrial revolution, because people

    d. Since, the Industrial Revolution because people

    e. Since the Industrial Revolution, people

38. <u>The Wheelers sold fortunately their home within 6 days of being on the market.</u>

   a. The Wheelers sold fortunately their home within 6 days of being on the market.
   b. The fortunately Wheelers sold their home within 6 days of being on the market.
   c. Fortunately, the Wheelers sold their home within 6 days of it being on the market.
   d. The Wheelers sold their home within 6 days fortunately of being on the market.
   e. The Wheeler's fortunately sold their home within 6 days of being on the market.

Section 2, Essay Writing

Carefully read the essay topic that follows. Plan and write an essay that addresses all points in the topic. Make sure your essay is well organized and that you support your central argument with concrete examples. Allow 30 minutes for your essay.

In an effort to combat obesity and increase healthfulness among students, the school board is considering changing the cafeteria menu to avoid all junk food and provide only low-fat meals and snacks. They are also considering eliminating soda machines. Supporters say this plan will help students slim down and have more energy for school. Opponents say this plan is unfair to students who will now have fewer choices in the cafeteria and will cost the school a great deal of money because the soda machines generate money for the school. In your opinion, do you think the schools should only offer low-fat meals and snacks?

In your essay, take a position on this question. You may write about either of the two points of view given, or you may present a different point of view on the topic. Use specific reasons and examples to support your position.

Answers

Skills Test in Reading

1. c. This paragraph explains that wolves used to live in the Yellowstone area until conflict with humans caused them to disappear. The wolves moved to Canada (choice **b**), and were a threat to ranchers (choice **d**), but these choices are too narrow and do not reflect the main idea of the paragraph. You can eliminate choices **a** and **e** because there is nothing in the paragraph to suggest that gray wolves were treated unfairly, or that it was important to reintroduce them to Yellowstone.

2. a. Biologists hoped that wolves would help balance the elk and coyote populations. Restoring the park's plant diversity (choice **b**) was a factor, but not the main motive. Ranchers and farmers objected to the wolves killing their livestock, so choice **c** can't be the reason for reintroduction. And although the wolves are technically endangered, the Yellowstone wolves are governed by special, looser rules, so choice **d** can be eliminated. There is no evidence to suggest that wolves were reintroduced to increase tourism, so choice **e** is not correct.

3. d. The phrase *although the wolves are technically an endangered species* suggests that the Yellowstone wolves are going to be an exception. More specifically, the word *technically* tells us that the exception will be to their endangered status. It only suggests the legal definition of *endangered* (choice **a**), but does not explain it. Choice **b**, that the government controls the wolves' status, is a true statement, but it is not the best answer to the question. The statement also does not explain why the wolves are endangered (choice **c**) or how science is utilized during the reintroduction (choice **e**).

4. b. Paragraph 2 describes the outcome of the wolf's disappearance. Although the events occur in chronological order (choice **c**), they are organized to show cause and effect. There is no compare/contrast in the paragraph, and the events are not given in order of importance, so choices **a** and **d** are incorrect. The paragraph is also not broken down by classification, meaning that choice **e** is not correct either.

5. d. The author concludes the article by listing some of the positive effects of the wolf's return: beaver and red fox populations are being restored, and elk and coyote populations are balancing to normal levels. Thus the author must not believe that the program was a mistake, choice **a**. Choice **b** is not broad enough to encompass the main idea of the whole passage. Choices **c** and **e**, on the other hand, are too general because the article only discusses Yellowstone Park and does not comment on the wolf's role in other national parks or about the disruption of life in general.

6. e. The author's argument is that the reintroduction of the gray wolf is beneficial. The only statement that provides a definitively negative result of the reintroduction would be the possibility of reduced genetic variability. The statements in choices **b** and **d** provide positive effects of the reintroduction, so they would strengthen the author's argument. The statements in choices **a** and **c** neither strengthen nor weaken the author's argument; because the information does not affect the argument, those choices cannot be correct.

7. c. Like the gray wolf, the muskox was driven to extinction within a particular geographic area, then it was reintroduced back to those lands at a later date. The polar bear is threatened, but it has not been reintroduced, so choice **a** is not correct. The possum was introduced to New Zealand, causing environmental havoc, but it was not reintroduced there, so choice **b** is not correct. The moa was hunted to extinction centuries ago and never reintroduced, and the housecat has not itself been in any danger of extinction, so choices **d** and **e** are not correct.

8. c. The only inference that can be supported from the graph is that Amy spent the same on clothing as she did on everything else in July: $50. The statements in choices **a**, **b**, and **d** are predictions based on the data that cannot be concluded. The statement in choice **e** is not true according to the information in the graph, since Dan spent more on movies and games in July than Toby did.

9. b. One of the reasons against another moon landing is the unavailability of important resources. The word *dearth* is used to describe this unavailability, or *scarcity*. The word *death* is similar to *dearth* in spelling but has a very different meaning, so choice **a** is incorrect. The opposite meaning of *dearth* is *abundance*, so choice **d** is incorrect. The resources may be important or useful, but the word *dearth* does not suggest those meanings, so choices **c** and **e** are incorrect.

10. a. The selection begins with the statement that Neil Armstrong was the first man on the moon and then mentions that eleven other men have also walked on the moon, ending with Harrison Schmitt in 1972. Therefore, it can be inferred that a total of twelve men have walked on the moon. The passage states that an extended stay on the moon can pose a danger to astronauts, but because it does not give any specific timeframe, choice **c** cannot be correct. There is no evidence in the passage to support the statements in choices **b** or **d**, so they are incorrect. Choice **e** is disproven with the final sentence; a trip to Mars will be *significantly more difficult*, not *equally as hard*.

11. e. The final sentence of the passage suggests that man *should* return to the moon. This is an opinion in contrast with the facts presented earlier in the selection. The first three sentences of the passage provide verifiable facts about the early manned trips to the moon, so choices **a**, **b**, and **c** must be incorrect. The financial costs of a trip to the moon, even if it's just an estimate, can be verified, so choice **d** is not correct.

12. d. The author's main argument is that mankind *should* return to the moon, despite all the reasons against it. If a rare and valuable resource were available on the moon, that would be another incentive to return—thus strengthening the argument. Choices **a** and **b** are incorrect: if space travel were easier from a space station instead of from the moon or if the moon has no oxygen, then there would be more reasons against a return—thus weakening the argument. The statements in choices **c** and **e** provide additional information about space travel but are not particularly related to the argument about a return to the moon; therefore, they are not correct.

13. a. In the midst of listing reasons not to return to the moon, the author describes the satellite as a *big rock*. This expression refers to the moon as something uninteresting or unimportant. Therefore, the purpose is to downplay the importance of returning, despite the fact that the author is merely making a counterargument. The author's purpose in using the expression is not to describe the physical characteristics of the moon, thus eliminating choices **b**, **d**, and **e**. Furthermore, it does not serve to describe a reason to return, making choice **c** incorrect.

14. d. Despite spending much of the passage listing reasons not to return, the author ends the passage by listing his or her support for a return to the moon. Therefore, the correct answer choice will contain a word that supports a return, such as *essential* (choice **d**). Choices **a** and **c** contain negative adjectives, so they do not match the author's attitude. While a return may be *scientific* or *timely*, the author does not focus on the scientific benefits or the timeliness of a return, making **b** and **e** less-than-ideal choices.

15. e. The author's main idea is that man should return to the moon, if only to practice for further expeditions into space. The details in choices **a** and **d** do not relate significantly to the main idea, so they are not correct. The statements in choices **b** and **c** contradict the author's main idea and therefore do not support it.

16. b. According to the graph, in 2007 there were more than 700 wolves in Idaho and more than 300 wolves in Wyoming; combined, the population of wolves in both states surpassed 1,000. The inferences in choices **a**, **c**, and **d** cannot be supported because that information is not given by the graph. The statement in choice **e** is not true according to the graph; the line graph shows a total of more than 500 wolves in the two states in 2004.

17. b. The passage states that once the difficult Hillary Step is conquered, it is only a few hundred feet of moderate climbing to the mountain's top. Therefore, the step is the final significant obstacle to the mountain's summit. Because there is still several hundred feet to ascend after the Hillary Step, however, choice **e** cannot be correct. The statements in choices **a** and **d** do not explain why the step is so well known but instead provide some history for a physical feature of the mountain. The statement in choice **c** is not supported by the passage; while the Hillary Step is surely difficult, it is extreme to suggest that it is one of the most difficult technical climbs in mountain climbing.

18. e. The end of the passage accentuates the difficulties that Edmund Hillary faced in his initial ascent of Mount Everest; therefore, his climb must be respected; the best synonym for *venerable* is therefore *admirable*. The climb itself may have been *hazardous* or *technical*, but *venerable* is describing the achievement and not the climb, so choices **a** and **b** are not correct. The rope is *advantageous*, and the resulting climb may be *victorious*, but neither word can be used to replace *venerable* in the passage, making choices **c** and **d** incorrect.

19. a. The passage mentions the advantage of the fixed ropes that adorn the Hillary Step, a climbing advantage that was not always available; therefore, though it may still be difficult to ascend, it is easier than it used to be. There is no mention in the passage that the step is responsible for many deaths or requires several hours to pass (choices **b** and **c**). The passage does state, however, that there are several hundred feet above the step, making choice **d** incorrect. Hillary and his Sherpa first ascended the step together in 1953, but the passage does not suggest that they have been the only ones to ever do so, thus making choice **e** incorrect.

20. d. The final sentence of the article states the main idea: Duncan Brin is responsible for the new success of the Dowshire Ducks baseball team. The sentences in choices **a**, **b**, **c**, and **e** only provide supporting details from the passage or other information that is not relevant to the main idea.

21. a. The beginning of the passage provides details about the Dowshire Ducks today, then contrasts those positive details with negative details with the team's past. The passage then concludes with the overall main idea. Because the passage does not begin with a main idea, a definition, or a problem, choices **b**, **d**, and **e** are not correct. While the passage provides a contrast between the past and present of the team, the organization is not entirely based on comparisons and contrasts, making choice **c** incorrect.

22. a. The word *teeming* is being used to describe the bleachers of a baseball stadium—specifically, how many cheering fans are in them. Therefore, the best word to replace *teeming* will likewise describe the size of the crowd. Although the word ends in –*ing*, *teeming* is an adjective; therefore, choices **b** and **e** do not contain proper words to use to replace *teeming* in the passage. The bleachers may be *energized* by the crowd, but the closest meaning of the word relates to the size of the crowd, not its energy, so choice **c** is not correct. *Vacant*, choice **d**, has the opposite meaning and is therefore incorrect as well.

23. d. The author follows the portrayal of the continents as puzzle pieces with a physical description of their shapes. Therefore, it is their physical relationship that he or she is most concerned with. The author's purpose is not to contrast the continents but rather to stress their connection, so choice **a** is incorrect. The purpose is also not to describe the mystery or minimize the importance of the continents, which means choices **b** and **c** are incorrect. There is nothing in the passage to suggest any problems scientists faced in determining the causes of continental drift, so choice **e** is also not correct.

24. b. The author uses the word *cursory* to suggest that it would not take much time to notice an obvious pattern in the globe's continental patterns. A replacement word, therefore, could be *brief*, *hurried*, or *superficial*. Choices **a** and **c** include words with an opposite meaning, so they cannot be correct. Choices **d** and **e** contain words that have little relation to the word *cursory* and are therefore incorrect as well.

25. b. The author makes the argument that the African and South American continents were once joined together. If the same plant was found to have lived on both continents, it would lend support to that argument. On the other hand, if species are unique to each continent alone, it would not strengthen the author's argument; therefore, choice **d** is not correct. The statements in choices **a** and **c** are largely irrelevant to the author's main idea, making those answer choices incorrect. The statement in choice **e** also does not reinforce the theory of continental drift, so it is not correct.

26. e. The final sentence of the passage states that different plates can move in different directions, resulting in the current positions of the continents. Therefore, it can be inferred that the African and South American continents exist on separate plates. Alfred Wegener developed the theory of "continental drift," but the theory of plate tectonics followed later; the passage does not suggest who proposed the theory of plate tectonics, but the statement in choice **a** cannot be inferred. Although there was no ocean between Africa and South America, that does not mean that Earth had no oceans; choice **b** is therefore incorrect. The passage does not compare the sizes of the continents, just their shapes, so choice **c** is incorrect. The passage also does not discuss the specific support for or against the continental drift theory, so choice **d** is not correct.

27. b. To find the primary purpose, you need to find the statement that best sums up what the entire passage is about. The best description of the passage's primary purpose is that it describes the unique eating habits of a type of sea spider (choice **b**). The passage mentions one similarity between land spiders and sea spiders—that both have eight legs—but this is not what the passage is mostly about, so choice **a** is not correct. The passage does not mention any warnings about sea spiders, so choice **c** is not correct. The statements in choices **d** and **e** are mentioned in the passage, but those statements are not the focus of the passage.

28. a. The first paragraph of this passage tells about one specific invention created by Benjamin Franklin: a stove called the Franklin stove. While Benjamin Franklin *was* responsible for many great inventions, the paragraph does not mention more of his inventions, so the statement in choice **b** is not the primary purpose. The paragraph does not tell much about how a stove works, so the statement in choice **c** is not the primary purpose either. The passage mentions that Franklin *could* have made a lot of money from his stoves (choice **d**), but he refused to patent it and so did not make money from the invention. The first paragraph compares stoves, but that is not the primary purpose of the paragraph, so choice **e** is not correct.

29. e. The word *however* separates the riches that Franklin could have received from his invention with his noble decision to share the stove's design. It is not being used to provide a physical description, provide additional benefits of the stove, contrast its advantages and drawbacks, or compare the apparent usefulness with its costs; therefore, choices **a**, **b**, **c**, and **d** are all incorrect.

30. d. Benjamin Franklin was the inventor of the Franklin stove. Therefore, according to the passage, he was offered *the right*, or permission, to patent his stove. Check the answer choices to see which word or phrase most closely fits the meaning of *right* in the given sentence. In fact, you can even replace the terms in the answer choices with the word *right* from the passage. Only *legal claim* (choice **d**) makes sense. While *right* may mean *correct*, *good health*, *turn*, or *exact* in other contexts, it refers to a legal claim in the context of the sentence. Therefore, choices **a**, **b**, **c**, and **e** are not correct.

31. d. Based on the fact that Franklin turned down the opportunity to patent his stove in the quote at the end of the passage, it can be inferred that Franklin was less concerned with making money than with helping his fellow humans (choice **d**). There is nothing in the passage to suggest that Benjamin Franklin was afraid of making a fire, so choice **a** is not correct. The passage mentions that Franklin *could* have become one of the richest people in America had he patented his stove, but because he did not he was neither extremely rich nor interested primarily in making money. Therefore, choices **b** and **c** are not correct either. While the passage describes Franklin as a great inventor, it does not describe his life as a scientist or a politician, so the statement in choice **e** cannot be inferred.

32. c. The passage mentions that the Franklin stove *burned less wood and generated more heat than previous designs*. This means it was very *efficient*, choice **c**. The price, size, or style of the stove was never mentioned in the passage, so it cannot be inferred that the Franklin stove was *expensive*, *small*, or *stylish*, choices **a**, **d**, or **e**. The Franklin stove was designed to be much safer than other stoves, so choice **b** is not true.

33. d. The author's main argument is that human beings are unique for their ability to live almost everywhere on the planet. The statement in choice **d** describes one human settlement near the North Pole, thus supporting the main idea. A statement about animals would not support the main argument as directly, so choices **a**, **c**, and **e** are not correct. Choice **b** is not correct because the taxonomy of the species is not directly related to the argument.

34. b. The author lists three human settlements with extreme conditions; a city that receives virtually no rainfall would also reinforce the argument that the human species has impressive adaptability skills. Facts about the Mariana Trench or Venus do not relate to places where human beings live, so choices **a** and **d** cannot be correct. Choice **c** is about penguins, so it cannot be correct either. Choice **e** would not reinforce the argument because it does not relate to the argument in any significant way.

35. e. The author lists three animals and their specific habitats. The author then contrasts those limited habitats to human beings' ability to live almost anywhere. Therefore, the role of mentioning the kangaroo's habitat is to contrast with humanity's spread. The role is not to contrast with the habitat of the polar bear; in fact, the habitat is similarly limited, so choice **a** is not correct. No mention is given of humanity's encroachment or limited reach, so choices **b** and **d** are not correct. The mention of the kangaroos in Australia does not provide an extreme environment, so choice **c** is not correct either.

36. a. It cannot be proven that one player changed the game of soccer more than any other player. The other four choices provide statements that *can* be verified, such as the year and place of his birth (choice **b**), a league he played in (choice **c**), the number of goals he scored (choice **d**), and the fact that he was given a title from a large institution (choice **e**).

37. a. The main idea of the passage is that Pelé was an amazing soccer player who helped transform the sport. His name, place of birth, and year of birth do nothing to support that main idea. The fact that he played for 20 years, helped increase interest in the sport, scored 1,281 goals, and was called the "Athlete of the Century" all help support the main idea, so choices **b**, **c**, **d**, and **e** are not correct.

38. c. The passage focuses on Pelé's talent and his impact on the game of soccer. Because he transformed his sport in a similar way, Babe Ruth is most similar to Pelé. Cristiano Ronaldo and Landon Donovan are great soccer players, but because they did not change the sport like Pelé did, choices **a** and **e** are not correct. Dilma Rousseff is from Brazil, but she did not influence a sport like Pelé did, so choice **b** is not correct. Charles Haley was a successful athlete, but he likewise did not have a lasting impact on his sport, so choice **d** is incorrect.

39. b. The author lists the numbering system for the U.S. presidents, then provides a *more rational* numbering system. Therefore, he or she most likely believes that the current system is *illogical*. That is the opposite of *rational*, so choice **e** is incorrect. There is no indication in the passage that he or she believes the numbering system to be *humorous*, *reverential*, or *presidential*, so choices **a**, **c**, and **d** are incorrect as well.

40. b. An *anomaly* is an abnormality or *irregularity*, which makes choice **b** the best option. The words in answer choices **a**, **c**, **d**, and **e** do not make sense in the context of the passage and do not share a close meaning to *anomaly*.

The following is a chart of the different skills assessed by the questions in this practice PPST; you can use it to identify your strengths and weaknesses in this subject to better focus your study.

READING SKILLS STUDY CHART FOR PRACTICE EXAM 5	
LITERAL COMPREHENSION SKILLS	QUESTIONS
Main Ideas	1, 5, 20, 27, 28
Supporting Ideas	2, 15, 33, 37
Organization	4, 21, 29
Vocabulary in Context	9, 18, 22, 24, 30, 40
CRITICAL AND INFERENTIAL COMPREHENSION SKILLS	
Evaluation	3, 6, 11, 12, 13, 23, 25, 34, 35, 36
Inferential Reasoning	8, 10, 14, 16, 19, 26, 31, 32, 39
Generalization	7, 17, 38

Skills Test in Mathematics

1. c. The median is the central number (or average of two central numbers) when the numbers are listed in increasing order (or least to greatest). In this case, the central two numbers are averaged to find the median: 8, 9, 9, <u>10</u>, <u>12</u>, 13, 14, 17. The average of 10 and 12 is 11, so Boyd's median fish was 11 inches. Choice **a** is the minimum. Choice **b** is the average, or arithmetic mean. Choice **d** is the mistaken median of the data when it is analyzed in the order presented, rather than in the order of least to greatest (10 and 14 are the center points in the given list, and the average of those is 12). Choice **e** is the mode, or the most frequently-occurring data point.

2. d. Since *w* is divisible by both 24 and 6, it must also be divisible by all the factors of 24 and 6. 18 is a *multiple* of 6, but not a *factor* of 24 or 6. For example, *w* could be 24, which is divisible by 12, 4, 3, and 8, but *not* divisible by 18.

3. b. First, evaluate each statement by focusing on the totality of each sentence—the word *all* is very strong and must have complete backing. Statement I does not have to be a fact, since facts A and C do not guarantee that *all* dogs who like to swim also look like their masters. We only know that *some* dogs who like to swim will also look like their masters. This eliminates choices **c** and **d**. Since *all* dogs like to run and *some* dogs like to swim, statement II does have to be a fact, since the subset of dogs who like to swim are contained in the larger set of all dogs who like to run. Similarly, statement III must be a fact because it has been established by fact A that *all* dogs like to run, so therefore, it does not matter if a dog looks like its master or not, it will like to run. Since statements II and III are correct, choice **b** is the answer.

4. c. When a point is reflected over the x-axis, its x-coordinate stays the same, and the sign of its y-coordinate changes. Therefore, when $(8,-2)$ is reflected over the x-axis the resulting point will be $(8,2)$. Choice **a** is the resulting coordinate when $(8,-2)$ is reflected around the $y = x$ line. Choice **b** is the resulting point when R is reflected over the x-axis. Choice **d** is the resulting coordinate pair when $(8,-2)$ is reflected over the y-axis. Choice **e** is the resulting coordinate pair when $(8,-2)$ is rotated 180 degrees.

5. e. The perimeter of a house is the distance around the outside of the base of the house. Centimeters, inches, and millimeters would be too small to measure a house and would be better to measure the distance around a coffee table. Kilometers would be appropriate to measure the distance around a large farm or industrial property. A meter is approximately three feet, and this would be the proper unit to measure the perimeter of a house.

6. b. The word *product* means multiply. To multiply mixed fractions, it is necessary to change each fraction into an improper fraction before multiplying straight across. Turn the mixed fractions into improper fractions by first multiplying each whole number by the denominator in its adjoining fraction. Then add that product to the numerator and put it over the original denominator:
$$1\tfrac{1}{8} = \frac{1 * 8 + 1}{8} = \frac{9}{8}$$
$$1\tfrac{3}{5} = \frac{1 * 5 + 3}{5} = \frac{8}{5}$$
Then to multiply fractions, multiply the numerators and denominators straight across and then reduce the fraction to its lowest terms:
$$\frac{9}{8} * \frac{8}{5} = \frac{72}{40} = \frac{9}{5}$$
Lastly, put $\frac{9}{5}$ back into a mixed fraction by dividing 9 by 5 (it goes in once) and putting the remainder of 4 over the denominator of 5: $\frac{9}{5} = 1\tfrac{4}{5}$. Choice **a** multiplies the two whole numbers and incorrectly adds the numerators and denominators of the fractions. Choice **c** multiplies the whole numbers and fractions independently, which is incorrect since each mixed fraction must be converted to an improper fraction first before multiplying. Choice **e** is the *sum* (addition) of the two fractions, not the product.

7. c. Multiply the price by the mark-up percentage to get the mark-up amount (but remember to turn the percentage into a decimal by moving its decimal two times to the left). $(\$12.20)(0.30) = \$3.66$ (incorrect answer **a**, since this is only the mark-up). Then add that to $12.20 to get the selling price of $15.86. Choice **b** is incorrect since it is $12.20 just multiplied by the incorrect conversion of 30% (3.0 and not 0.30). Choice **d** is just 30 cents added onto the original price, not 30 *percent*. Choice **e** is just an estimate, but it is not backed up by any correct math.

8. e. According to the statement given, if someone has his or her driver's license in New York, then it is certain that he or she is either over 18 years old, or is over 16 years old and has passed driver's education class. It does not guarantee the reverse—that if you are over 18 then you have your driver's license (this rules out choice **a**). Choice **b** is incorrect since you can have your license if you are under 18, as long as you have passed driver's education. Choice **c** is incorrect since you can have your license without having passed driver's education, as long as you are over 18. If you are over 18 and you have passed driver's education, it is *possible* to have your license, but these two things do not *guarantee* that you have your driver's license, which rules out choice **d**.

9. a. Percentage means "out of 100." If you do not have 100 items, then you can divide the "part" of something over the "whole" of something, and the resulting percent will be the number out to the *hundredths* place. Therefore, since there are a total of 25 coins in Mario's pocket, and 8 of them are dimes, the percentage of dimes in Mario's pocket is: $\frac{\text{\# of dimes}}{\text{total \# of coins}} = \frac{8}{25} = 0.32 = 32\%$. Choice **b** is the percentage of coins that are *not* dimes. Choice **c** is the number of coins in Mario's pocket, not the percentage of coins that are dimes. Choice **d** is the *number* of dimes in Mario's pocket, not the percentage of dimes. Choice **e** is the percentage of coins that are either nickels or dimes, since $\frac{10}{25} = 40\%$.

10. b. Since Bren worked 13 days at 8 hours each, he worked 104 hours. When the total amount of money paid ($10,400) is divided by 104, it comes out to $100 per hour (incorrect choice **a**), but this does not take into account the expenses Bren had for supplies. When those expenses are subtracted from $10,400, Bren's net income was $6,240. This divided by 104 hours yields $60 per hour. When Bren's expenses of $4,160 are divided by 104 hours, the answer is $40, but this is incorrect since it uses the expenses and not Bren's income, so choice **c** is not correct. Choice **d** is also not correct since it represents Bren's net income of $6,240 divided by 13 workdays of only 6 hours, and not 8 hours. Choice **e** is a good educated guess, but it is not based on any exact calculations.

11. d. To find the volume of a box, multiply the length, width, and height dimensions. First $3 \times 3 = 9$, then multiply 9 by $2\frac{1}{2}$. To do this, turn the $2\frac{1}{2}$ into the improper fraction, $\frac{5}{2}$, and multiply this by $\frac{9}{1}$: $\frac{5}{2} \times \frac{9}{1} = \frac{45}{2}$. This is equivalent to $22\frac{1}{2}$. Choice **e** is an incorrect conversion of $\frac{45}{2}$ into an improper fraction. Choice **a** multiplies 9 by $2\frac{1}{2}$ incorrectly (the $\frac{1}{2}$ is treated independently in this multiplication). Choice **b** is the volume of a box that measured 3 by 3 by 3, since $3 \times 3 \times 3 = 27$. Choice **c** is a good educated guess, but it is not based on any exact calculations using the dimensions given.

12. c. Looking at this graph, you can see that the approximate rate of growth of the amount of carbon dioxide found in the atmosphere has been about 10 parts per million each decade. In 1960, there were about 330 ppm, and approaching 2000, the approximation was close to 370 ppm. Therefore, the best estimate for 2012 would be 380 ppm. Choices **a** and **b** are incorrect since this would show a steady decline or leveling off of carbon dioxide, which is not the trend illustrated here. Choices **d** and **e** both estimate too high.

13. a. A good estimate for 1990 would be approximately 360 ppm. Written as a fraction this is $\frac{360}{1,000,000}$, which is reduced first by ten to $\frac{36}{100,000}$ and then by four to $\frac{9}{25,000}$. Choice **b** is a better estimate for a year before 1970, and choice **c** is a good estimate for the year 2000 $\left(\frac{370}{1,000,000} = \frac{37}{100,000}\right)$. Choice **d** would be 360 parts per 1,000, since $\frac{360}{1,000} = \frac{36}{100}$, which is equivalent to 36%. Choice **e** is one decimal point off, since $\frac{360}{1,000,000} = 0.00036$ and not 0.0036.

14. d. Choices **a** and **c** are not correct since the graph does not show a trend of slowing levels of carbon dioxide in the atmosphere in the twenty-first century *or* from 1970 to 1980. Choice **b** is not correct since although the graph does show a jagged curve, there is a clear trend of increasing levels of carbon dioxide in the atmosphere as time progresses. Choice **e** is not correct since no inferences on the levels of carbon monoxide in the atmosphere can be made based on the graph. It is likely that the expanding human population has lead to practices which have increased the levels of carbon dioxide found in the atmosphere, so choice **d** is an accurate statement.

15. c. *Seven times the number of skateboards Steve owns* should be expressed as "$7s$". Choice **a** is incorrect because it is just the expression for the 7 times the number of skateboards that Steve owns. Next, consider that "less than" means subtraction, but remember that the tricky thing when translating "less than" into an algebraic expression is that the order of the terms is flipped. This means that the "3" will come *after* the "$7s$" in the subtraction expression: $7s - 3$. Choice **b** is the expression for "$7s$ less than 3," while choice **e** is the expression for *three more than seven times the number of skateboards that Steve owns.* Choice **d** is *three times seven times the number of skateboards that Steve owns.*

16. c. The data set 5, 6, 7, 8, 8, 10 has the same mode as the data set 4, 5, 6, 7, 8, 8, 10, since 8 is the most commonly occurring number in both sets. The mean, or average, will become slightly lower since a new minimum has been added to the data set. The median, which is the middle number when the numbers are arranged from least to greatest, is 7.5 in the original set (the average of 7 and 8). In the new set the median is 7, so this has changed. Adding 4 to the data set changes the range from 5 to 6.

17. a. The formula for perimeter is $P = 2l + 2w$, and since you are given the perimeter and the width, substitute these values into the formula and solve for l:

$P = 2l + 2w$

$50 = 2l + 2(10)$

$50 = 2l + 20$

$30 = 2l$

$l = 15$ feet

Choice **b** is not correct since 40 feet is just the difference of the perimeter of 50 feet and *one* of the widths—it does not take into consideration that there are *two* widths and *two* lengths. Choice **c** considers the two widths of 10 feet and subtracts those from the perimeter, but then forgets to divide 30 feet by 2. Choice **d** just divides the perimeter by 2, which gives the length of 1 width plus 1 length, but then forgets to subtract the width of 10 from 25. Choice **e** incorrectly assumes that the rectangle is a square and divides the perimeter into 4 equal sides of 12.5 feet.

18. c. One million is written as 1,000,000, and eight million is 8,000,000. 8.9 million is eight million plus 900,000 which is 8,900,000 (choice **c**). Choice **a** is incorrect because it is never acceptable to put a decimal point in a number unless it is separating the whole numbers from the partial tenths, hundredths, thousandths, etc. Choice **b** is eight hundred ninety thousand, choice **d** is eighty-nine million, and choice **e** is eight hundred ninety million.

19. a. In this problem, the @ symbol is representing an operation where the first term is multiplied by 3 and the second term is subtracted from that product. Therefore $(w@z)@z$ will equal $(3w - z)@z$. This means that you will need to *re*-substitute $(3w - z)$ in for w in the expression $3w - z$: $3(3w - z) - z$. Next you must distribute the 3 to both terms within the parenthesis and then subtract the z: $9w - 3z - z = 9w - 4z$. Choice **d** is only the first step of distributing the 3 to $(3w - z)$, but it forgets about subtracting the second z. Choice **e** remembers to subtract the z but does this subtraction incorrectly to get $9w - 3z - z = 9w - 2z$. Choice **c** forgets to distribute the three and just does $3w - z - z = 3w - 2z$. Choice **b** incorrectly distributes the 3 to get $6w$ instead of $9w$.

20. b. First, evaluate (A), (B), and (C): (A): $\frac{1}{3}$ of 12 $= \frac{1}{3} \times 12 = 4$; (B): 4% of 100 = "4 out of 100" $= 4$; (C): $\frac{1}{5}$ of 10 $= \frac{1}{5} \times 10 = 2$. Choice **a** is not correct since 4 is not less than 2. Choices **c**, **d**, and **e** are also all incorrect statements.

21. e. Since there are m men in a class of n students, the number of women in the class must be $n - m$. So, the ratio of men to women in the class is therefore $\frac{m}{n-m}$. Choice **a** is the ratio of men to the entire class. Choice **b** is the ratio of the total number of students in the class to the number of men in the class. Choice **c** is the ratio of men to the negative of the number of women (since $m - n$ would give you a negative number). Choice **d** is the ratio of total number of students in the class to the number or women.

22. c. Each term is a combination of a letter and a number. The letter part of each pairing is skipping ahead by 1, and the number part of each pairing is decreasing by 3. Choices **a** and **b** fail to see that Q should be skipped over, and choices **d** and **e** go one letter too far. Choice **c** has the correct combination of 1 letter skipped and a number that is decreased by 3.

23. d. If the radius of the circle is 12 units, the area of the full circle is $A = \pi r^2 = \pi(12)^2 = 144\pi$. You are looking for the sector that has an approximate area of 43π, and since 43 is approximately one-third of 144, the correct answer will be the sector that contains about $\frac{1}{3}$ of the circle. Just by looking at the circle, it is obvious that sector COB is the closest to representing $\frac{1}{3}$ of the circle. Sector EOD only represents $\frac{1}{6}$ of the circle since $\frac{60°}{360°} = \frac{1}{6}$, so choice **a** is incorrect. Sector EOA only represents $\frac{2}{9}$ of the circle since $\frac{80°}{360°} = \frac{2}{9}$, so choice **b** is incorrect. Sector AOC represents $\frac{7}{36}$ of the circle since $\frac{70°}{360°} = \frac{7}{36}$, so choice **c** is incorrect. Sector DOB only represents $\frac{1}{9}$ of the circle since $\frac{40°}{360°} = \frac{1}{9}$, so choice **e** is incorrect.

24. c. Each of Molly's three orders uses a different price per CD. As the quantity goes up, the price per CD goes down. Her first order of 800 CDs cost her 800($1.50) = $1,200 (incomplete and incorrect answer choice **a**). Her second order of 1,200 CDs cost her 1,200($1.00) = $1,200. Her third order of 2,100 CDs cost her 2,100($0.75) = $1,575 (incomplete and incorrect answer choice **b**). Together these three orders cost Molly $3,975 (incomplete and incorrect answer choice **e**). In total she ordered 4,100 CDs. If she had bought all these at once, she would have paid 4,100($0.50) = $2,050 (incomplete and incorrect answer choice **d**). Her savings would have been $3,975 − $2,050 = $1,925 (choice **c**).

25. e. Using the order of operations stated in PEMDAS, first perform division: $4x^3 \div x = 4x^2$ (when dividing variables with different exponents, subtract their exponents). Then combine like terms by adding or subtracting only the coefficients of terms that have the exact same variables and exponents: $x^2 - 4x + 4x^2 - 2 = 5x^2 - 4x - 2$. Choice **a** accidentally makes the $4x$ term positive. Choice **b** accidentally adds the exponents when trying to incorrectly combine $4x^2 + 4x$. Choice **c** incorrectly combines $x^2 - 4x + 4x^2 - 2$ to get $-3x^2$ (by thinking that the minus sign after the x^2 came with the squared terms). Choice **d** makes several mistakes with combining exponents and only has the constant term, -2, correct.

26. a. Since 40 plants are red-veined, 24 plants are flowering, and 14 of those 64 plants are both, 14 needs to be subtracted from 64 so that those 14 red *and* flowering plants are not counted twice. Therefore the total number of red-veined and/or flowering plants in the shop is $40 + 24 - 14 = 50$. Since 14 of the 40 red-veined plants are also flowering, 26 of the red-veined plants are not flowering $(40 - 14 = 26)$. In addition to the 50 flowering and/or red-veined plants, there are also 10 plants that are not flowering or red-veined. This means that in total, there are 60 plants in the store. So the probably that Alexis bought a red-veined plant that is not flowering is $\frac{26}{60} = \frac{13}{30}$. Choice **b** is the probability that Alexis bought a flowering plant since $\frac{24}{60} = \frac{2}{5}$. Choice **c** is the probability that Alexis bought a plant that was neither flowering nor red-veined since $\frac{10}{60} = \frac{1}{6}$. Choice **d** is the probability that Alexis bought a flowering, red-veined plant since $\frac{14}{60} = \frac{7}{30}$. Choice **e** is the probability that one of the red-veined and/or flowering plants was *just* a red-veined plant and *not* flowering since $\frac{24}{40} = \frac{3}{5}$.

27. a. In total the team will play $65 + 30 = 95$ games. If the team wants to win 60% of their games, then find 60% of 95 by using multiplication: $0.60 \times 90 = 57$ games (incomplete and incorrect answer choice **e**). Since the team must win 57 games in total in order to have a record of 60% and they have already won 45 games, the team needs to win 12 more games. Choice **b** would give them 63 wins, which is over 66% when compared to a total of 95 games. 18 more wins would give a higher winning percentage than 60%, so 18 wins and anything above that is too many wins, making choices **c** and **d** incorrect.

28. c. The easiest way to approach this question is to substitute in real numbers that satisfy the requirements of each variable. Choice **a** could be true since 2 is a prime number and 2 times any odd number will give an even number. Choice **b** could be true since $1 + 2 = 3$, which is a prime number. Choice **c** could never be true since any number times any even number will always give an even number. Choice **d** could be true since 10 is an even number and dividing it by an odd number like 5 gives 2, which is prime. Choice **e** could be true, since 15 is an odd number, and 15 added to prime number 7 is 22, which is even.

29. d. Plug each answer choice into the inequality so that the first coordinate in the pair goes in for x and the second coordinate goes in for y. Identify the coordinate pair that results in a true statement. Using $(0,-4)$ gives $-10 > 15$, which is false, so choice **a** is incorrect. Using $(3,4)$ gives $22 > 24$, which is false, so choice **b** is incorrect. Using $(4,3)$ gives $18 > 27$, which is false, so choice **c** is incorrect. Using $(4,6)$ gives $30 > 27$, which is true, so choice **d** is correct. Using $(5,6)$ gives $30 > 30$, which is false, so choice **e** is incorrect.

30. d. The formula for the perimeter of Laura and Freddy's garden is $P = 2l + 2w$, and since you are given the dimensions for the length and the width, substitute these values into the formula and solve for the perimeter. $P = 2l + 2w$: $P = 2(14) + 2(8) = 44$ feet (incomplete and incorrect answer choice **a**). The next task is to turn this into yards. Do this by dividing by 3, since there are 3 feet in a yard: $44 \div 3 = 14\frac{2}{3}$ yards. 14 yards will not be enough fencing (incorrect answer choice **c**), so they will need to purchase 15 yards and have a little left over. Answer choice **b** incorrectly divides the 44 feet by 2 in order to convert it into yards. Answer choice **e** incorrectly finds the *area* of the garden by multiplying 14 by 8 to get 112 and then divides that by 3 to try to convert it into yards.

31. d. An inscribed angle is always half the measure of the arc it defines. The 60-degree angle defines an arc of 120 degrees. Notice that the x-degree angle defines the arc that makes up the remainder of the circle and that the circle contains a total of 360 degrees. Therefore, the arc that the x-degree angle makes must measure $360 - 120 = 240$ degrees (incorrect answer choice **c**). That 240-degree arc defines an angle that is half of its measure, which is 120 degrees. Answer choice **a** is the measure of the arc created by the 35-degree angle. Answer choice **b** is the measure of the angle opposite angle x.

32. e. In order to answer this question, look at the line that is dotted with circles, which shows how women's salaries changed as their years of completed schooling changed. The five-year period that has the steepest slope will be the period that had the largest influence on the salary that a South African woman made in 1993. This period was 10 to 15 years of schooling.

33. c. Choice **a** is supported by the graph since women who completed 9 years of schooling did indeed earn less than women who completed only 8 years of schooling. Choice **b** is also supported by the graph since males who completed 0 years of education had the same earnings as males who completed 2 years of education. The prediction in choice **c** that after 17 years of schooling the women's salaries would surpass the men's salaries is not supported. This is not likely since in all the other years the men are earning more than the women. Additionally, the women are not seeing any spike in earnings that is significantly greater than the increase in the men's earnings. Choice **d** is supported by the graph since the gap between men's and women's salaries lessens as the number of years of completed education increases. Lastly, choice **e** is supported by the graph since the mean income for women with 12 years of schooling completed was less than the mean income for men with just 10 years of schooling completed.

34. b. The thousandths place is three places to the *right* of the decimal point. In order to round a number to the nearest thousandth, you must look at the number that is *four* spaces to the right of the decimal point in order to determine if the thousandths number should be rounded up (if it is 5 or greater) or stay the same. In the case of 327.3785, the critical number to look at is the "5"—this indicates that the number in the thousandths place, the 8, must be rounded up to 9. This results in 327.379. Choice **a** mistakenly (but accurately) rounds 327.378 to the nearest *thousand* and not to the nearest *thousandth*. Choice **e** mistakenly and incorrectly rounds 327.378 *up* to 1,000 and not to the nearest *thousandth*. Choice **c** does not round the 8 in the thousandth place up but keeps it the same, and choice **d** rounds the given number to the nearest *hundredth* and not to the nearest *thousandth*.

35. c. Remember that the sum of the interior angles of a triangle is 180°. We know that since ∠1 is 30° and ∠2 is 90°, the measure of ∠3 must be is 60°. Since ∠2 is a right angle and is also a corresponding angle to the right angle at the base of the triangle, it can be deduced that the line segment is parallel to the base of the triangle. Therefore, ∠3 and ∠4 are also corresponding and congruent. This means that ∠4 is 60° (incorrect choice **b**). Since ∠4 and ∠5 make a straight angle, which has 180°, ∠5 must measure 120°. Choice **a** cannot be correct since 30° is an acute angle, and angle 5 is obviously an obtuse angle. Choice **d** would make a straight angle with ∠1 (since 150° + 30° = 180°), but angles 5 and 1 are not related.

36. c. If the height of a triangle is 6 more than twice its base, b, then the height should be represented as $6 + 2b$ (incorrect answer choice **a**). To write an algebraic expression representing the area of the triangle, use $6 + 2b$ for the height in $A = \frac{1}{2}(\text{base})(\text{height})$: $A = \frac{1}{2}(b)(6 + 2b)$. Next, distribute $\frac{1}{2}(b)$ to both terms in the parenthesis: $\frac{1}{2}(b)(6) + \frac{1}{2}(b)(2b)$. This simplifies to $3b + b^2$. Incorrect answer choice **b** forgot the $\frac{1}{2}$ in the area formula, so both terms are double what they should be. If the height of 6 more than twice its base is incorrectly represented as $h = (6 + 2 + b)$ then this would simplify to $(8 + b)$ and result in an area of $4b + (\frac{1}{2})b^2$, which is the incorrect answer given in choice **d**. Choice **e** gives the perimeter of an isosceles triangle with a base of b and a leg that is 6 more than twice its base: $(6 + 2b) + (6 + 2b) + (b) = 12 + 5b$.

37. b. Since 11 is not a number that has a whole square root, choose the closest two numbers above and below 11 that *do* have perfect square roots. Since 9 and 16 have perfect square roots, we know that $\sqrt{9} < \sqrt{11} < \sqrt{16}$. This means $\sqrt{11}$ must be between 3 and 4, since $\sqrt{9} = 3$ and $\sqrt{16} = 4$. Therefore, point K is the best estimate for $\sqrt{11}$. Using the same reasoning, since point J falls between 2 and 3, it must stand that J is between $\sqrt{4}$ and $\sqrt{9}$ since $\sqrt{4} < \sqrt{J} < \sqrt{9}$, so J cannot be equal to $\sqrt{11}$ and answer choice **a** is incorrect. The same reasoning rules out point L since that must be a number between $\sqrt{16}$ and $\sqrt{25}$. Lastly, M is not a possible answer since M is 6, and the $\sqrt{11}$ does not equal 6.

38. b. The average of three terms is the sum of those terms divided by 3. The sum of Joan's first 3 tests must be $72(3) = 216$ since conversely, $\frac{216}{3}$ will equal a 72 average. Since Joan's first two tests sum to 152 ($84 + 68 = 152$), the score of her third test must be $216 - 152 = 64$. Choice **a** is the average of Joan's first two tests, but that cannot be used because all three tests must be added together at the same time when calculating the average. Choice **c** is a mistake made when the average of the given scores is calculated first and then averaged with a final score. While it is true that the average of the first two scores is 76 and that a score of 68 would combine with a score of 76 to make an average of 72, this would be a weighted average, where the third score counts more than the first two scores. Choice **d** cannot work because 84, 68, and 70 have an average of 74 and not 72. Similarly, choice **e** is incorrect since a third test score of 73 results in an average of 75, not 72.

39. d. Angles b and e are equal since they are vertical angles. Therefore, if $b + c = e + f$ were true, this would mean that $\angle c$ would have to equal $\angle f$. Although angles c and f are part of the family of angles connected to parallel lines, these two angles are made with two different transversals, so there is no way to prove any congruence about these angles. This means that choice **d** is not necessarily true. Choice **a** is certainly true since straight angles $(a + b + c)$ have the same 180-degree measure that the sum of the interior angles of a triangle $(d + e + f)$ have. Choice **b** is true: since e and b are vertical angles, they are also congruent, and since $a + b + c = a + e + c = 180$, it follows that $a + c = 180 - e$. Choice **c** is true based on the previous statements that support choice **b**. Choice **e** is true since it has already been established previously that $a + b + c = 180$ and $d + e + f = 180$, so therefore, $a + b + c + d + e + f = 360$.

40. d. To find the probability of an event happening, the number of desired events must be put over the total number of events. In this case, there are 16 "desired events" $(7 + 9 = 16$ knives and forks) and 20 total events (total number of pieces of silverware). $\frac{16}{20}$ reduces to $\frac{4}{5}$. Choice **a** gives the probability that a piece of silverware *will* be a spoon since $\frac{4}{20} = \frac{1}{5}$. Choice **b** considers the probability that a randomly chosen piece of silverware will not be a knife since there are 13 spoons and forks. Choice **c** shows the probability of grabbing a knife. Choice **e** gives the number of non-spoons in the drawer, but doesn't relate this to a probability.

The following is a chart of the different skills assessed by the questions in this practice PPST; you can use it to identify your strengths and weaknesses in this subject to better focus your study.

MATH SKILLS STUDY CHART FOR PRACTICE EXAM 5	
NUMBER AND OPERATIONS SKILLS	**QUESTIONS**
Order	37
Equivalence	20
Numeration and Place Value	18, 34
Number Properties	2, 28
Operation Properties	25
Computation	6, 10, 24
Estimation	12
Ratio, Proportion, and Percent	7, 9, 27
Numerical Reasoning	3
ALGEBRA SKILLS	
Equations and Inequalities	29
Algorithmic Thinking	17
Patterns	22
Algebraic Representations	15, 19, 21
Algebraic Reasoning	8
GEOMETRY AND MEASUREMENT SKILLS	
Geometric Properties	23, 31, 39
The xy-Coordinate Plane	4
Geometric Reasoning	35, 36
Systems of Measurement	5
Measurement	11, 30
DATA ANALYSIS AND PROBABILITY SKILLS	
Data Interpretation	14, 32
Data Representation	13
Trends and Inferences	12, 33
Measures of Center and Spread	1, 16, 38
Probability	26, 40

Skills Test in Writing—Section 1, Part A

1. c. Verb tense should be consistent within a sentence. If choice **a** is past tense (*visited*), then choice **c** must be past tense (*saw*) also.

2. b. Choice **b** is incorrect because we must use a colon, not a comma, to introduce a formal quotation.

3. d. The adverb in choice **d** is misplaced. From the first part of the sentence we know the mother-to-be didn't want anesthesia, so that implies she wants to give birth naturally. That is different from the meaning taken from naturally in its current position. The sentence would be clear if we changed the second part to "she wanted to give birth naturally."

4. e. Because there are no grammatical, idiomatic, logical, or structural errors in this sentence, choice **e** is the best answer.

5. a. Choice **a** is an incorrect word choice. *Prosecuted* means to take legal action against. Hitler did not convict Jews through litigation—he *persecuted* (mistreated) them.

6. d. When comparing two entities, they must appear in the same form. In this sentence, if we replace *a job* with *holding a job*, both entities will match.

7. e. Because there are no grammatical, idiomatic, logical, or structural errors in this sentence, choice **e** is the best answer.

8. a. Choice **a** should be replaced with *regardless*. There is no such word as *irregardless*.

9. d. Choice **d** is a poor word choice. *So* or *consequently* would be better because they indicate a result.

10. c. It is incorrect to describe a present condition (he is very tall) in the past tense. So, choice **c** must be changed to *is* even though in the previous part of the sentence, we are talking about a past event (*met*).

11. b. Choice **b** is incorrect because dates that include just the month and year do not need commas.

12. b. *Than* must be used when referring to comparison, like this sentence is. *Then* refers to time or a sequence of events. Choice **b** must be changed to *than* because the sentence is comparing feeling relaxed before and after moving to the countryside.

13. a. When using an apostrophe to form a possessive form of a word, we add *'s* to plural words not ending in *-s*. Choice **a** is a plural noun that does not end in *-s,* so the plural form is *men's.*

14. d. The pronoun *they* does not have an antecedent. Therefore, we do not know who they are. We can fix this sentence by changing the pronoun into a noun. We might say, *but the customer service representative never answered.*

15. c. The verb forms in this sentence's compound predicate should be consistent in form. Choice **c** must be changed to *launched* to match the verb *stormed.*

16. d. In this sentence, *good* is used as an adverb to describe how Marco speaks. *Good* is an adjective; *well* is an adverb. Choice **d** must be changed to the adverb *well.*

17. c. The noun following a modifier must be the subject performing the action in the modifier. In this sentence we'd have to insert a noun that could be stunned (*Lucille realized this was turning into . . .*).

18. b. Choice **b** must be changed to *complement,* which means to match. *Compliment* refers to praise.

19. e. Because there are no grammatical, idiomatic, logical, or structural errors in this sentence, choice **e** is the best answer.

20. e. Because there are no grammatical, idiomatic, logical, or structural errors in this sentence, choice **e** is the best answer.

21. d. When comparing two entities, they both have to be in the same form. In this case we could finish the sentence with *as much as they had been engaged in studying history.*

Skills Test in Writing—Section 1, Part B

22. b. Choices **a**, **c**, and **e** are incorrect because they fail to capitalize the title of the book accurately. The first, last, and any other important words of a title must be capitalized. Choice **d** uses the wrong spelling for *role*. It uses *roll*, as in a portion of bread. Choice **b** correctly capitalizes the book title, includes a comma to separate the two independent clauses, and uses the correct spelling of *role* (as in a part played by a performer).

23. d. *No one, couldn't,* and *nowhere* are negatives. We can't use double negatives in the same sentence. Choices **a**, **b**, **c**, and **e** use double negatives. Choice **d** is correct because *no one* is the only negative used.

24. d. Choice **d** provides parallel construction; that is, each item in the list appears in a consistent form. These are all prepositional phrases. Choices **a**, **b**, **c**, and **e** do not provide parallel construction because they do not have consistent forms.

25. c. Choice **c** relays the clearest meaning here. We understand with no doubt that it's the salads that will be packed away. Choices **a** and **b** could be incorrectly interpreted that the picnickers will be packed away instead of the salads. Choices **d** and **e** change the meaning of the sentence.

26. b. The pronoun *it* at the end of the original sentence (choice **a**) has an unclear antecedent. We can't tell if the diamond was sold or if the dresser was sold. Choice **b** is the only sentence in which we know it was the dresser that was sold.

27. b. The adjective *unique* does not have a comparative or superlative form. We can't have degrees of uniqueness. A flower is unique (one of a kind), or it is not. Therefore, no matter what order you put the phrases in, choices **a**, **c**, **d**, and **e** are incorrect because they contain *most* or *more,* which are comparative terms.

28. d. Choice **d** is correct because the plural forms of *equipment* and *furniture* do not end in *-s.* Also, when using *between* to identify a range of years, we describe the range using *and* instead of *to.* Choices **a**, **b**, **c**, and **e** incorrectly include plural endings for *equipment* and *furniture* that end with *-s* and use *to* instead of *and* to state the range of years.

29. b. Choices **a**, **c**, and **e** represent errors in correlation; they are sentence (question) fragments. Choice **d** changes the meaning of the question. Choice **b** is correct because it adds the subject *what.*

30. b. Choice **b** contains correct parallelism because it matches the form of the noun *drink* to the noun *cake.* None of the other four choices match the form of the noun *cake.*

31. b. Choices **a** and **e** contain a dangling modifier because the person doing the action in the first part of the sentence doesn't match the noun following the clause. We know this because Mrs. Lewis does not match the pronoun *his.* Choice **b** is correct because it correctly identifies the son as the one gulping the orange juice. The sentence is clear and coherent. Choice **c** begins with a sentence fragment. Choice **d** sounds like Mrs. Lewis is drinking her son's juice.

32. d. Choice **d** correctly uses the adjective form of *angry* because—although it sounds strange—the sister didn't actively look with her eyes in a particular way. We are really describing her appearance, which takes an adjective. Also, the sequence of the phrases makes a difference in meaning. Choices **b** and **c** might be interpreted as saying the jacket had been borrowed from the sister while she was at the beach. Choices **a**, **b**, and **e** incorrectly use the adverb form of *angry*.

33. c. Two negatives do not result in a positive, as in mathematics. *Couldn't, barely,* and *hardly* are all negatives and must not be used together in the same sentence. Choices **a**, **b**, **d**, and **e** use double negatives; so they are incorrect. Choice **c** uses only one negative (*hardly*).

34. d. Choices **a**, **c**, and **e** are incorrect because they sound like the dog was cackling. Choice **b** is incorrect because it sounds like the yard is cackling. Choice **d** has all the modifiers placed correctly so that the meaning is clear.

35. a. Because we're comparing the condition of animals now and what the condition would be if everyone became vegetarian, we use the comparative forms for *good* and *bad.* The comparative forms are *better* and *worse.* The superlative forms are used in choice **c**, and choices **b** and **d** inaccurately mix comparative and superlative forms. Choice **e** changes *or* to *and,* which changes the meaning of the question.

36. d. There are several recurring errors in these choices: *Nambiars* should be plural, not possessive, so no apostrophe is needed; a comma should appear after *Jamaica* to offset the introductory clause; the pronoun identifying the luggage should be plural (*their* not *his*) because it replaces the *Nambiars*; and, *luggage* is plural without the *-s* ending.

37. e. Choices **a**, **c**, and **d** are incorrect—no matter where we put the comma—because both parts of the sentence are subordinate clauses and there is no independent clause. Choice **b** does not make sense. Choice **e**, in taking out the word *because,* changes the second part of the sentence to an independent clause and corrects the sentence.

38. c. The adverb *fortunately* must be placed in its correct position within the sentence to sound right. Choice **c** shows the best placement for this adverb—at the beginning of the sentence set off with a comma. Choices **a**, **b**, **d**, and **e** place the adverb inappropriately. Also, choice **c** includes the pronoun *it* to further clarify it is the home that was on the market, not the Wheelers.

The following is a chart of the different skills assessed by the questions in this practice PPST; you can use it to identify your strengths and weaknesses in this subject to better focus your study.

SKILLS TEST IN WRITING STUDY CHART FOR PRACTICE EXAM 5	
GRAMMATICAL RELATIONSHIP SKILLS	**QUESTIONS**
Identify Errors in Adjectives	27, 32, 35
Identify Errors in Adverbs	3, 16, 38
Identify Errors in Nouns	28, 36
Identify Errors in Pronouns	14, 25, 26
Identify Errors in Verbs	1, 10
STRUCTURAL RELATIONSHIP SKILLS	
Identify Errors in Comparison	6, 12, 21
Identify Errors in Coordination	34
Identify Errors in Correlation	17, 29, 31
Identify Errors in Negation	23, 33
Identify Errors in Parallelism	15, 24, 30
Identify Errors in Subordination	37
WORD CHOICE AND MECHANICS SKILLS	
Identify Errors in Word Choice	5, 8, 9, 18
Identify Errors in Mechanics	2, 11, 13, 22
Identify Sentences Free from Error	4, 7, 19, 20

Skills Test in Writing—Section 2, Essay Writing

Following are sample criteria for scoring a PPST essay.

A score "6" writer will:

- create an exceptional composition that appropriately addresses the audience and given task
- organize ideas effectively, include very strong supporting details, and use smooth transitions
- present a definitive, focused thesis and clearly support it throughout the composition
- include vivid details, clear examples, and strong supporting text to enhance the themes of the composition
- exhibit an exceptional level of skill in the usage of the English language and the capacity to employ an assortment of sentence structures

- build essentially error-free sentences that accurately convey intended meaning

A score "5" writer will:

- create a commendable composition that appropriately addresses the audience and given task
- organize ideas, include supporting details, and use smooth transitions
- present a thesis and support it throughout the composition
- include details, examples, and supporting text to enhance the themes of the composition
- generally exhibit a high level of skill in the usage of the English language and the capacity to employ an assortment of sentence structures
- build mostly error-free sentences that accurately convey intended meaning

A score "4" writer will:

- create a composition that satisfactorily addresses the audience and given task
- display satisfactory organization of ideas, include adequate supporting details, and generally use smooth transitions
- present a thesis and mostly support it throughout the composition
- include some details, examples, and supporting text that typically enhance most themes of the composition
- exhibit a competent level of skill in the usage of the English language and the general capacity to employ an assortment of sentence structures
- build sentences with several minor errors that generally do not confuse the intended meaning

A score "3" writer will:

- create an adequate composition that basically addresses the audience and given task
- display some organization of ideas, include some supporting details, and use mostly logical transitions
- present a somewhat underdeveloped thesis but attempt to support it throughout the composition
- display limited organization of ideas, have some inconsistent supporting details, and use few transitions
- exhibit an adequate level of skill in the usage of the English language and a basic capacity to employ an assortment of sentence structures
- build sentences with some minor and major errors that may obscure the intended meaning

A score "2" writer will:

- create a composition that restrictedly addresses the audience and given task

- display little organization of ideas, have inconsistent supporting details, and use very few transitions
- present an unclear or confusing thesis with little support throughout the composition
- include very few details, examples, and supporting text
- exhibit a less-than-adequate level of skill in the usage of the English language and a limited capacity to employ a basic assortment of sentence structures
- build sentences with a few major errors that may confuse the intended meaning

A score "1" writer will:

- create a composition that has a limited sense of the audience and given task
- display illogical organization of ideas, include confusing or no supporting details, and lack the ability to effectively use transitions
- present a minimal or unclear thesis
- include confusing or irrelevant details and examples, and little or no supporting text
- exhibit a limited level of skill in the usage of the English language and little or no capacity to employ basic sentence structure
- build sentences with many major errors that obscure or confuse the intended meaning

Sample 6 Essay

Obesity has become a major problem in the United States. This health problem leads to other serious issues such as heart disease and diabetes. The school board is considering a plan to help students fight this problem. The new lunch program based on nutritious food and the elimination of soda machines is necessary for students to obtain nutritious food, and the program will help students become healthier, more energetic, and even smarter.

Many students in our schools have a weight problem. More and more children and teenagers are battling obesity than ever before. Much of this is due to poor food choices. At home, many families have two parents who work or even just one parent who works two jobs. This leaves little time for shopping for and preparing nutritious meals. It's simply quicker and easier to go to a fast-food restaurant or throw some macaroni and cheese into the microwave than to prepare a well-balanced meal. That's where the school comes in. At least the school can provide students with a nutritious lunch. It may be the only really nutritious food the students get. While there might be some resistance at first, students will eventually begin to eat and enjoy the new food. If students become hungry enough, they'll try it and find that they actually like it.

They will begin to feel and look better. The soda machines do provide money for the school, but is the money worth the health of the students? Additionally, if we replace the soda vending machines with water vending machines, we will still make some money.

Eating healthy lunches will help students have more energy throughout the day. Students and teachers complain that many students tend to crash during the early afternoon classes. This is usually because students have eaten a lunch high in sugar and carbohydrates. This type of food gives a quick burst of energy, which the student typically uses up during the period itself, and then causes a rapid decline of energy, causing the student to feel sluggish and sleepy. Nutritious food would eliminate this problem. If students eat a meal of protein, whole grains, and vegetables, they will have a more steady supply of energy to keep them going throughout the day. Some opponents say that many students will boycott the new lunch program and not eat lunch at all, making them tired during the day. This may happen a few times, but most teenagers do not like the feeling of being hungry and tired. They will eventually begin to eat the food, even if it's just one part of the lunch that they like.

Finally, this new lunch program will actually help students increase their academic performance. Healthy food makes people feel better and perform with more energy and alertness. This means students will pay more attention in class, have more energy to do required work, and think more clearly and creatively. This can only lead to better grades and better test scores, something students and teachers alike are always pursuing.

The new lunch program may intimidate some students. People are creatures of habit and are initially resistant to change of any kind. But much of eating is an acquired taste for certain foods. While students may miss their tacos and chocolate chip cookies, they will eventually come to appreciate and hopefully prefer grilled chicken and a nice juicy apple.

Sample 4 Essay

School cafeterias are not well known for gourmet food, but over the years, they've gotten better at knowing what teenagers like to eat. Now the school wants to change all that by starting a new lunch program with nutritious food and eliminating the soda machines. Doing this will actually harm the students and waste a lot of money.

Lunch is one of the most important parts of a student's day at school. It's a time when students can relax and have fun. Part of that fun is enjoying the food. Students have their likes and dislikes, but usually there's something they will eat, even if it's just the packages of chocolate chip cookies that everyone likes so much. The point is to have something in the middle of the day that will give students some energy to make it through the rest of the day. It doesn't need to be a full meal of chicken, vegetables, and whole-grain rolls. Teenagers are picky about their food and they are also a little rebellious. If the school only offers food that many teens don't like, they just won't eat it. Then many students will be trying to make it through the day without lunch. Many students do not eat breakfast, so now they will have missed two meals. This could lead to students fainting or losing a lot of weight, which could also be dangerous. If the students do eat the full meals presented in the cafeteria, this could also be a problem. The lunches we have now are light food—sandwiches, tacos. If students eat a full meal and then go right out to play gym, they could get sick.

Having a program like this will also waste a lot of money. We all know that better food costs more money to buy and takes more skill to prepare. The school will have to increase its food budget and possibly hire different people to prepare the food. All this money will go to waste because most of the students won't eat the food. Burgers and tacos may not be the healthiest foods but they also don't cost very much and teenagers will actually eat it. Eliminating the soda machines will also cost the school a lot of money. The money from those machines goes toward school supplies that benefit the students. So once again, if we have this new lunch program students are being harmed. Yes, we could replace the soda machines with water machines, but they will definitely not generate as much income and students will have to sacrifice things such as sports equipment, uniforms, or art supplies.

People will say that the school has a responsibility to provide nutritious food for the students. First of all, burgers and tacos do have nutrition; it's not like students are eating nothing but candy for lunch. Secondly, we're only talking about one meal a day; many students get very nutritious food at home. One meal is not going to make that much difference.

This new lunch program could do more harm than good. I appreciate the school trying to make students healthier, but that really is a personal choice and the responsibility of students and their parents. The school should concentrate on educating students, not trying to change their diets.

Sample 1 Essay

The school board is considering changing the school lunch program so that all the food is low-fat. They are also interested in getting rid of all the soda machines. I think this is a terrible idea. No one likes low-fat food, especially teenagers. The teenagers of today like to eat junk food, they don't need healthy food pushed on them at school. Actually I don't even think the food that at the school I was student teaching at was that unhealthy. It's not like it is fast food or anything. OK, there's burgers, but their not all greasy or anything. If there is low fat food no one will eat it. No one wants to eat whole grain pitas with tuna in them. I've tried low-fat cookies and they were terrible. They tasted like cardboard.

As far as getting rid of the soda machines, that will cause a big problem. Teachers and students like to drink soda. It's refreshing and picks us all up in the afternoons. Also the soda machines make money for the school. Us teachers can get supplies and stuff from that money. I think the students will probably rebel if we get rid of the soda machines or you'll have a bunch of students cutting just to get to the store to buy some soda.

This program is a bad idea. I wouldn't put it in, but if you do watch out because the students and probably even some of us teachers are not going to like it.

8 ▶ SCORING YOUR PRAXIS I PRACTICE EXAMS

Your scores on the multiple-choice parts of the exam are based on the number of questions you answered correctly; there is no "guessing penalty" for incorrect answers and no penalty for unanswered questions.

The Educational Testing Service does not set passing scores for these tests, leaving this up to the institutions, state agencies, and associations that use the tests. Therefore, the interpretation of your score depends on the reason you are taking the test. For example, there will be a difference in the interpretation of your score if you are applying for a teacher-training program than if you are a candidate for educational credentials or for teacher selection. Whatever the case, though, it is necessary for you to do well on all three segments of the Praxis I—Reading, Mathematics, and Writing—so you must figure your score on each test separately.

The Reading test, the Mathematics test, and the multiple-choice section of the Writing test are scored the same way: First, find the number of questions you got right on each test. As noted earlier, questions you skipped or got wrong don't count; just add up how many questions you got right. Then, divide the number of questions you got right by the number of questions in the section to arrive at a percentage.

You can check your score against the passing scores in the state or organization that requires you to take the exam.

In addition to passing the multiple-choice questions, you must receive a passing score on the essay portion of the PPST Writing test. On this portion, the essay is read and scored by at least two writing experts, using a scale of 1 to 6, where 6 is the highest. The scores of the two experts are then combined. The scoring criteria are outlined in detail in the answer explanations. The best way to see how you did on the essay portion of the exam is to give your essay and the scoring criteria to a teacher or other reader whom you trust to see what scores he or she would assign.

What's much more important than your scores, for now, is how you did on each of the basic skills tested by the exam. You need to diagnose your strengths and weaknesses so that you can concentrate your efforts as you prepare for the exam.

Use your percentage scores and your performance in the individual skills found in the study skills charts in conjunction with the LearningExpress Test Preparation guide in Chapter 2 of this book to help you devise a study plan. You should plan to spend more time on the skills that correspond to the questions you found hardest and less time on the lessons that correspond to areas in which you did well.

ADDITIONAL ONLINE PRACTICE ▶

Whether you need help building basic skills or preparing for an exam, visit LearningExpress Practice Center! On this site, you can access additional practice materials. Using the code below, you'll be able to log in and take an additional full-length Praxis I practice exam. This online practice will also provide you with:

Immediate scoring
Detailed answer explanations
A customized diagnostic report that will assess your skills and focus your study

Log in to the LearningExpress Practice Center by using the URL: **www.learnatest.com/practice**

This is your Access Code: **8929**

Follow the steps online to redeem your access code. After you've used your access code to register with the site, you will be prompted to create a username and password. For easy reference, record them here:

Username: _____   **Password:** _____

If you have any questions or problems, please contact LearningExpress customer service at 1-800-295-9556 ext. 2, or e-mail us at **customerservice@learningexpressllc.com**

NOTES

NOTES